KT-371-441

THE ENCYCLOPEDIA OF
GHOSTS AND SPIRITS

Also by John Spencer

UFOs 1947–1987
Phenomenon
Perspectives
The UFO Encyclopedia*

* *Available from Headline*

THE ENCYCLOPEDIA OF GHOSTS AND SPIRITS

John and Anne Spencer

LONDON NEW YORK SYDNEY TORONTO

This edition published 1992 by
BCA
by arrangement with
HEADLINE BOOK PUBLISHING PLC

CN 9365

Copyright © 1992 John and Anne Spencer

The right of John and Anne Spencer to be identified as the authors of
the work has been asserted by them in accordance with the
Copyright, Designs and Patents Act 1988.

First published in 1992
by HEADLINE BOOK PUBLISHING PLC

10 9 8 7 6 5 4

All rights reserved. No part of this publication may be
reproduced, stored in a retrieval system, or transmitted,
in any form or by any means without the prior written
permission of the publisher, nor be otherwise circulated
in any form of binding or cover other than that in which
it is published and without a similar condition being
imposed on the subsequent purchaser.

Typeset by
Letterpart Limited, Reigate, Surrey

Printed and bound in Great Britain by
Mackays of Chatham PLC, Chatham, Kent

CONTENTS

ACKNOWLEDGEMENTS

As is appropriate for the compilation of an encyclopedia, and to avoid as much as possible the charge of bias, we have included only a small percentage of cases from our own files and taken the majority from a wide range of researchers in the subject. Permission has been sought for the inclusion of every case and in most instances has been willingly and helpfully given by the researcher whose name is credited in the 'source' line at the beginning of each case. However, despite our best efforts, in a small number of cases we have not been able to contact the researchers concerned and we trust that the inclusion of their work will not give offence; should it do so we hereby apologise. In every case the inclusion of a researcher's work in the encyclopedia has been because of the positive relevance we believe it holds to the subject of ghost research.

While thanking every contributor without exception for both their permissions and sometimes their active help, we would also particularly like to mention Andrew MacKenzie and Peter Underwood who have given such long and devoted service to the subject. Our interest in this subject was first kindled while we were still at school, inspired in the main by the writings of these two men.

We give special thanks to the Society for Psychical Research, and in particular to their secretary Miss Eleanor O'Keefe, for access to, and patient guidance around, their specialist library. Thanks also to the SPR for permission to quote from their journals, and to their director, Manfred Cassirer, for his advice and direction; if we have not always taken it, that is our fault.

We would like to thank Swedish researcher Bertil Kuhlemann for his assistance with the original manuscripts of 'What did

Harry Price want at Lund Hospital?' and Birgitta Lotay for her translation from the Swedish.

There are, of course, a great many prominent researchers who have added immeasurably to the field who are not represented in this encyclopedia; if we had had ten volumes to complete there would still have been difficulties of selection. The subject is so vast. The selection has been made on the basis of presenting the wide range of reported phenomena and inevitably this has meant excluding a great deal of what we would have liked to include. No slight is intended to those not represented here.

Our thanks to Peter Holding for his help and advice in the photography.

None of the above or any of the researchers mentioned in the encyclopedia are in any way responsible for the overall compilation, selection of cases or balance of subject matter.

PHOTO CREDITS
The authors and publishers are grateful to the following for permission to reproduce photographs:

The Aldus Archive: 4
The Cavendish Hotel, Harrogate: 6
William Corfield: 26; 27
Fortean Picture Library: 25; 28; 37
Maurice Grosse: 35
Peter Martin: 8
The Mansell Collection: 17; 33
Mary Evans Picture Library: 5; 32
Graham Morris: 34
National Maritime Museum: 12; 13
Paranormal Picture Library: 2; 9; 14; 18; 19; 24; 29; 30
Paranormal Picture Library/Peter Holding: 1; 3; 7; 10; 11; 15; 16; 21; 22; 23; 31; 36
Marie and Kevin Sutton: 20

INTRODUCTION
Ghostbusting:
The 'Science' of Investigating Ghosts

What is it like to hunt for ghosts?

What it is certainly not like is the brilliantly amusing but quite fictitious *Ghostbuster* films. There is a memorable scene in the first *Ghostbuster* movie where the team get their first assignment; their secretary announces to the client, 'Oh! They'll be totally discreet.' That scene is almost immediately followed by the ghostbusters' car screaming through the streets with a picture of a ghost emblazoned on it and lights flashing, and the ghostbusters move into the hotel, dressed like a cross between Flash Gordon and the SAS, carrying 'unlicensed nuclear accelerators' on their backs and devices to trap ghosts in their kit.

In relation to real-life 'ghostbusting', the only significant part would have been discretion. Ghost-hunters – and no one yet has really come up with an entirely satisfactory term for the job – have to be discreet. The emotions of people who witness ghosts, and particularly those involved in poltergeist cases, are often very mixed: anger, fear, embarrassment, even occasionally a feeling of guilt. At the outset, and often indefinitely, many people do not want their friends, relatives or neighbours to know what is happening to them.

From the ghost-hunter's point of view, ghost-hunting is very different from what many people imagine. Every ghost-hunt is different, and we will look at the main reasons for this shortly, but there are certain common features. One thing ghost-hunters come to terms with very early on is the knowledge that the vast majority of all vigils will be completely fruitless and without event. In the case of those that do produce events the 'excitement' is usually confined to one or two short bursts in an otherwise uneventful period. When one of the authors of this book (J.S.) was putting together a mass of electronic recording equipment for one specific vigil I was asked how I would have time to monitor all of the various instruments that I was taking. I imagine it sometimes looks quite impressive to have bags of (mostly borrowed) electronic equipment available for these special vigils but the reality is not one of frantic activity. The person I was speaking to seemed to have the impression that I would be running up and down between instrument readings, adjusting this instrument, monitoring that instrument and checking a third rather like the bridge crew of the *Starship Enterprise* during a pitched battle with the Klingons on *Star Trek*. The truth was that most of the equipment needed no attention whatsoever and the night passed with me dividing my time between watching nothing happening down one corridor, and watching nothing happening on the monitor of a fixed video camera pointing down another corridor. For real excitement try watching a completely unmoving television picture for ten hours!

When embarking on a ghost-hunt the first thing you must be aware of is the type of ghost you are looking for. Usually you will have been called in to respond to a particular sighting or other perception of a haunting by someone who will of course describe what they saw, heard or otherwise felt. The reason you must be aware at the outset of what you are looking for is because, in fact, ghosts are not one single phenomenon but rather form a range of phenomena, each requiring differing approaches. We will look at the main classifications shortly.

That said, it is equally important to be prepared for the unexpected; at the simplest level it would be embarrassing to be invited to investigate a report of a silent, gliding, visual apparition and consequently take with you only soundless video recording equipment, only to spend the night listening to psychic rapping noises with no way of recording them.

Another important point to be aware of is that knowledge of what you are expecting to see can actually influence the vigil; in the worst case it is possible for the ghost-hunter to 'hallucinate' precisely what he was expecting to see. For this reason it is, in my view, pretty pointless to ghost-hunt alone and I would recommend it always be done in pairs so that there is some independent corroboration of anything seen or heard. It is also wise if the second of the pair does *not* have the information about what is expected to be found or seen; this greatly improves the quality of perceived success if it is jointly agreed upon by someone who was expecting a particular event and someone who was not. I attended one vigil where I was the one kept 'in the dark' (literally for the most part) and when a particular clanging noise was heard (which was apparently what we had all been waiting for) I immediately started trying to pinpoint where it had come from and what it could possibly be. Having given me time for reflection my colleague asked for my opinion on the sound (actually with sufficient stress in his voice to give away the fact that this was the potential 'big moment'), and what I said rather put the brake on his enthusiasm. In fact my initial analysis turned out to be wrong but was pretty close – I thought it was a fridge turning off; it turned out to be next door's new central-heating boiler turning on. If we had both been sitting up through the night desperately concentrating on hearing that sound then I feel that the tension we would have created between us would probably have led us down a number of pointless blind alleys searching for all kinds of psychic manifestations when the sound did arise. Expectation, no matter how experienced you are, always distorts perception.

So a vast proportion of reports, possibly as many as 98%, can be solved by identifying the 'haunting' as something quite mundane. Of course, the other 2% can be absolutely fascinating. No one embarking on ghost-hunting in a serious way should imagine it to be full of thrills and spills, excitement and constant revelation; it's a good deal less like a rollercoaster ride and a good deal more like a slow walk down a long straight road with just an occasional sighting of a beautiful and brilliantly coloured butterfly to break the monotony.

The ghost phenomena in this book are classified according to 'type' (what happened, where it took place, and so on); the following classification is concerned with aspects of the actual investigation process:

'Recordings' of past events

Some people believe that certain events are in some way 'recorded' at the location where they happened and 'replayed' at certain other times. No real understanding exists of the mechanisms whereby this is possible, indeed it is very much theory rather than fact, but it may be, or at least it seems to be, that at certain times the conditions are right for an incident to be recorded: high emotion, fear, stress, or love, possibly in combination with certain atmospheric or geological conditions. It may be that certain types of rock formation containing particular minerals, or certain levels of humidity, or temperature, all combine to produce a 'recording' of an event. Take, for example, the case of the farmer's son ('The Student's Return', pp. 116–17) seen forever walking the pathways that used to exist on his farm just prior to his suicide. Perhaps the high stress that he was prey to at the time and which eventually caused his suicide, or some other aspect of his emotional make-up, possibly combined with other conditions, created a recording which has been replaying for some considerable time since the event.

What exactly triggers the replay is also uncertain; perhaps it is a recreation of the same atmospheric conditions or perhaps a quite different set of conditions need to exist. Perhaps percipients with one set of 'brain frequencies' can perceive what others cannot. These recording-type ghosts are often reported at the time of, or after, structural alterations to buildings and it's possible that changing the structure, perhaps changing the acoustic conditions or arrangements of metals and wood, in effect presses the 'playback' button.

The nature of this type of apparition often gives itself away, particularly after structural alteration, when the recording follows the structure or contours that existed at the time it originally took place. In other words, if the floor level has been raised then the recording will appear to walk along the old floor level and might be seen in the new room from just the knees up. If the floor level has been lowered, the apparition may seem to float a few feet above the new lower floor. If doors have been walled over in changing the arrangement of rooms then the apparition may seem to walk through a wall which was actually a door at the time when the 'recording' was being made.

Occasionally recording-type ghosts can be quite spectacular. There are even reports of whole armies at battle being seen as in the case of Edgehill. Recordings of things such as armies on the march or at war suggest that the initial process of recording is involuntary: heightened emotion may be part of the mechanism as such, but whereas it is possible to believe that in certain cases a person returns as a spirit to fulfil some mission in life it seems highly unlikely that every member of an army would seek to come back for the sole purpose of fighting a battle or war all over again. There would seem to be no emotional *need* at work but rather a simple 'playback' of what had gone before: the souls and spirits of the combatants do not form a part of the apparition.

Most of the famous and historical ghosts probably come into this category of 'recordings'; buildings like Hampton Court are reputedly haunted by several people. Catherine Howard, for example, made a bid to escape her captors and appeal to her husband King Henry VIII by running down a corridor towards the chapel he was in. Her ghost is reputedly seen running down that corridor periodically and this would seem to be a case of a 'recording' ghost caused by her extreme emotion at the time.

Recordings are not restricted to visual images. It seems that sounds can be recorded in much the same way as visions; indeed there are occasions when both are recorded and perhaps only one or the other is played back at any given time.

Recording-type ghosts tend to run down, rather like a battery after a period of time, and the frequency with which sightings, or whatever, are reported generally slows down until they have virtually stopped, presumably because the recording has been 'wiped out' by subsequent events in the area.

What chiefly characterises a recording-type ghost is that it does not interact with the people who see it; it may choose to walk clean through you if you happen to be standing in its way, or it may walk past you without any acknowledgement. If it speaks it will speak autonomously and will not respond to anything you say. It can best be likened to a holographic image, or a three-dimensional projection of a film. Imagine you are watching Charlton Heston as Ben Hur on your television. If you asked him, from your living room, 'Would you like a cup of tea?', you would hardly expect him to stop his chariot in the middle of the race, look out of the television and say, 'Why yes, thank you very much, Mrs Brown!'

If you are given a report of what seems to be a recording-type ghost then you will have certain advantages: you will probably have a good idea of exactly where the ghost walks or appears, as it will probably be in the same place every time and witnesses will record this for your investigation. Sound and vision recording should always be to hand; substances that can be spread on the floor where the ghost is reputed to walk are useful in case it leaves footprints. Obviously a recording should not do so but there are cases of what appear to be recording-type ghosts that also make stairs creak, suggesting mass (the alternative, of course, is that the stair creak is part of a recording of some earlier stair board). If the ghost is apparently keeping to the existing contours, moving through existing corridors and so on, then it may be useful to have something you can put in its way to see how it negotiates that; blocking a doorway with string attached to each corner is an option. For a list of items to have with you, see 'The Ghost-hunter's Toolbox' on pp. 369–74.

'Anniversary' Ghosts

Anniversary ghosts appear to be, by and large, recording-type ghosts, as detailed above. They are reputed to haunt on the anniversary of a particular incident – a person murdered on a particular day is often held to return to that spot on the anniversary of that day. This raises certain difficulties. For the sake of argument, let us suppose that a person was murdered on Sunday 28 February one year. Would the anniversary be every 28 February; would it fall on the last day of February (in which case it would have to take account of a February 29 once every four years)? Would it be the last Sunday of the month (in which case the precise date would vary considerably)? The point is just exactly what is the significance of the actual date? Given the adjustments in our calendar which we call leap years and which accommodate the fact that, in reality, each year contains 365 and a quarter days, then in fact our anniversary ghost should be getting fairly confused as to exactly *when* he should be making his return. The division of the year into 365 days with 366 every four years to 'catch up' is a very artificial concept. If the ghost is obliged to return at an exact moment after a fixed period of time has elapsed, then from *our* point of view that moment will seem to vary, because *we* are varying the length of our years.

In fact, what is far more likely is that the anniversary-type ghost will merely reappear at *about* the same time of year, on the basis that at any given point in a year the atmospheric conditions are likely to be similar from one year to the next. Therefore a ghost that reappears in winter will probably find its atmospheric conditions correct at *some* point during the winter months. November is particularly noted for fogs and if fog was part of the atmospheric 'requirement' then the ghost could be expected to 'walk' every November. That it should do so at 6.15 p.m. on 23 November *every* year would probably be a construct of the witness's imagination in hindsight. Those few cases where such precision is claimed have rarely proven to be of any use to investigators, the ghost simply not turning up when expected. On the few occasions where it is claimed that a ghost has turned up 'to order' there usually seems to be a sad lack of supporting evidence.

In conclusion, then, this type of ghost should be treated as a recording.

Presences

Many people do not report seeing a 'conventional' ghost or hearing the traditional footsteps walking down an empty hallway but rather report sensing a 'presence' which they find difficult to comprehend. It may be that in a particular room they feel they are always being watched; sometimes, even though nothing is seen or heard, the presence is even identified as a woman or a man or occasionally as a particular animal. Some people report a pleasant, benign presence while others sense a malevolent, evil, oppressive presence.

There is some evidence to suggest that such things are not imagined: many different people, some of whom have no knowledge of the opinions of others, will report exactly the same presence as people they have never met or spoken to. Sensitives (mediums) brought into the room without any prior knowledge of what they are going to encounter may indicate something which strongly supports the opinion given by the witness who has called in the investigators.

Nevertheless, in such circumstances the ghost-hunter must be prepared to be part-psychologist. Firstly, there is the question of the identification of a genuine presence by the witness. If the witness reports a benign friendly presence and then tells you that he believes it's his grandmother with whom he had a wonderful relationship when she was alive, the ghost-hunter might judge that the witness is quite correct: the presence might have given its identity away somehow. Alternatively, the ghost-hunter might consider that the witness *is* genuinely feeling a presence but is quite wrong in assuming that it can be identified as a loved one. Thirdly, the ghost-hunter might consider that the entire thing is a construct of the witness's imagination. Precisely how the ghost-hunter deals with this – and tact is always necessary no matter what the circumstances – will depend on the individual. This is as good a point as any to state a cardinal rule of ghost-hunting: *the witness is not a subject for scrutiny under a microscope but rather a joint partner with the investigator in the examination of a phenomenon*. The witness has the investigator's experience to draw on and is well advised to take the comments of the investigator very seriously, but in many ways we believe that the witness has the right to dictate the course of the investigation. Perhaps there is no better example of this than a situation we heard of where a ghost-hunter was called in to deal with a poltergeist. The ghost-hunter said that he would do everything in his power to examine the phenomenon as fully as possible. The witness was quite certain, however: 'I don't want you to examine it,' he said, 'I want you to get rid of the bloody thing!' If that can be a disappointment to the ghost-hunter, so be it; there'll be another one along in a while!

Presences are best dealt with along much the same lines as poltergeists. Indeed there is a close relationship between the two and this is examined shortly. In addition, there is a full chapter investigating poltergeists (see pp. 363–8) by one of the world's leading authorities on poltergeist phenomena, Maurice Grosse.

Poltergeists

As mentioned above, there is a specific section on poltergeists, by Maurice Grosse.

Poltergeists are very frequently reported ghost phenomena

though they are regarded by many ghost-hunters as not being ghosts at all. Where ghosts are understood as being apparitions in haunted places, poltergeists are usually thought of as haunted people. In other words, while many ghosts stay exactly where they are and can be seen by anybody who happens to be there at the right time in the right conditions, poltergeists move around with a particular person as their focus and are usually only experienced by that person or by the people around them. That said, their *manifestations* (moving furniture, things flying through the air, etc.) can be seen by anyone present at the time.

Poltergeist is a German word meaning 'noisy ghost', usually a very accurate description. Not only are poltergeists noisy in that they make crashing, banging noises – the sound of moving furniture when none is moved and even anomalous voices – poltergeists are also very physical in that they will lift, move and throw various objects, some of which it would be quite beyond the capacity of any normal person to move in the same way. Poltergeist phenomena encompass almost every other kind of paranormal event imaginable: electromagnetic interference with recording equipment, presences, apparitions – the list is virtually endless. As far as the preparations for dealing with a poltergeist are concerned there is virtually nothing that can be omitted from a ghost-hunter's toolbox.

Poltergeist activity tends to be reasonably short-lived, two months' duration being the average. That's the good news; the bad news is that when it's over the house is usually in need of some serious redecoration!

Interactive Ghosts

Quite different to recording-type ghosts, and not showing the violence or mischievousness of poltergeists, interactive ghosts are probably the principal evidence – or suggestion of evidence – that there can be survival of the spirit after death. Interactive ghosts correspond to what would happen if, in our earlier example, Charlton Heston actually *did* stop the chariot and agree to have a cup of tea while you were watching him on television.

The interactive ghost seems aware of your presence. It may address you, possibly by name, and respond to your questions and comments. If you move around, it may follow you and on occasions it will identify itself in some way.

Spiritualists believe such ghosts to be the proof of the survival of the spirit after death; there is undoubtedly some evidence to support this. The most unequivocal is where the ghost actively identifies itself, can be identified as someone who has died, and is able to give the witness information which only the dead person could have. Unfortunately, as with most spontaneous phenomena, such ghosts choose to appear either at random to people who are unable to prove their claim or to people who seem to have a vested interest in the survival of that spirit, such as the person's spouse, father, or child and so on. The degree to which wishful thinking and emotion are involved cannot always be accurately determined.

Hunting for such ghosts is never easy since they seem never to make appearances at convenient moments (but the same is true of virtually all paranormal activity). At best the ghost-hunter can hope to be invited by the witness to speak to the ghost and will usually spend a fruitless night sitting with the witness only to be 'stood up'. Obviously, all manner of visual and audio recording equipment should be on hand in case the spirit *should* put in an appearance.

Time Slips

What may seem to be an interactive ghost, as described above, may in fact be what is usually described as a 'time slip'. It is believed that certain ghost reports may in fact be 'time slips'; these are situations where it is possible that a 'window' opens up between two times, allowing people on either side of the window to see each other. In some cases it appears to allow for interaction. It cannot be determined with certainty whether or not one or both of the parties actually shifts in time or merely *perceives* another time. If there *is* a shift in time then it cannot be certain whether the past is drawn to the present or whether someone from the present is drawn to the past. The result is that the witness sees somebody who should not normally be there or perceives a shift in their surroundings, 'seeing' them as they would appear in a time other than the present. That said, one important difference between the two is that in a 'ghost' situation the ghost is an 'odd' element which intrudes on the everyday world, with time slips it is generally the witness who finds himself in the 'wrong' place.

As in all these cases we should emphasise that what we are discussing here are theories rather than facts; there is no hard proof that time slips are possible. That said, the evidence is there to be studied and should be given due consideration.

A good example of what seems to have been a time slip is the case of the skiers in Norway who encountered the angry woman in the 'skiing party' case (see pp. 244–6). She was clearly interactive, responding to them and they to her, and there was no evidence in anything she said that she was the spirit of someone who had died. In fact she was very adamant that she owned the land the skiers were on and that they were trespassing. The suggestion would seem to be that in fact from her point of view that was precisely what was happening; from the skiers' point of view they were on land they had a natural right to be on at that time of the year as confirmed later by the true owners.

If time slips do happen, if someone in, say, 1910 interacts directly with someone in, say, 1990 then of course the main question is precisely, who is out of time? Is the person in 1910 somehow transported to 1990 or is the person in 1990 somehow transported to 1910? In fact the most plausible suggestion (but it is no more than that) is that neither moves from his own time, but rather that some sort of 'doorway' opens up between the two where each can see the other in his own respective time. In other words, if the two tried to physically interact they would both seem like ghosts to the other.

Time slips cannot really be investigated at our present level of knowledge; they are reported after the event and no one has yet worked out exactly what conditions are required for the event to recur. When a person says, 'I went into a shop and clearly I was there in 1910, but this is 1990', if the investigator accompanies the witness back to that location, the shop is invariably the one in 1990 and no one has yet come up with a way of creating the conditions which will produce the 1910 shop to order. The only practical investigation in this sense is some book-worming in the local records to discover whether or not the description given accurately fits the shop that actually was there in 1910. In that case the investigator must decide whether something really happened or whether the witness is mistaken, perhaps as a result of remembering something which fascinated him as a child (or some such explanation). It may even, of course, be a deliberate hoax.

Ghosts of the Living
(Including Doubles, Doppelgängers, Vardogers, and Bi-locations)

The word 'ghost' is used to encompass a whole range of phenomena with broadly similar characteristics. In this instance we are referring to what are perceived to be ghosts but where the person seen as a ghost is in fact still alive. 'Doubles' occur when the same person is seen by different groups in different locations at the same time; none of the witnesses need be aware that they are dealing with anything paranormal and it only becomes apparent when the facts are put together at a later time. 'Doppelgängers' are a special form of double which usually appear near the 'true' person and are usually seen carrying out exactly the same acts as if they are in some way providing a simultaneous playback of what the person is doing. 'Vardogers' are forerunners in time: a person may go to a location for the first time and find that they are recognised by others who have been interacting with that person's vardoger which has preceded them. 'Bi-locations' are a special kind of 'doubling' where the person appears to divide himself into two (usually nearby) locations. A person might be seen doing two different things but each of the doubles may appear weaker than one whole person as if the effort of bi-location is somehow draining.

Occasionally a witness will report seeing something which has all the characteristics of a ghost, and will jump to the conclusion that he has seen a person who has died; the witness may then discover that the person is in fact still alive and well. Since there is no concrete definition of what a 'ghost' is that everyone can agree on, this sort of apparition counts as a 'ghost' along with all the others, but it clearly suggests that the idea that ghosts are the spirits of dead people – while not necessarily untrue – is certainly simplistic or only part of the answer.

Just as with time slips, ghosts of the living cannot really be subject to on-site investigation as no one has yet created the conditions which will produce them to order. They are reported after the event and the investigator is left with nothing to look at at the location. What can be done, of course, is to discuss the matter with the living person who was seen as the ghost. In some cases there is some evidence of that person having *caused* the event; we would then be looking at something like astral projection or an out-of-body experience. But on other occasions there is no suggestion that the person has any awareness at all of what the witness saw. In this case we might be looking at a construct of the witness's mind, albeit a genuine exteriorisation rather than just imagination. By 'genuine exteriorisation' we are referring to something constructed by the witness's own mind but not – as would be the case with fantasy – perceived only by that witness; something which, having been created, can then be perceived by other people.

Laboratory experimentation in cases such as that of 'Ruth' (see pp. 318–19) may offer some explanations of these types of ghosts, but such experiments are not 'ghost-hunting' in the strict sense.

Ghosts of the Dying (or Crisis Apparitions)

Ghosts of the dying (sometimes called crisis apparitions) bridge the gap between evidence for survival of the spirit and evidence for out-of-body experiences. Some crisis apparitions have successfully alerted people to dangerous situations as a result of which they have then been able to survive them, suggesting an ability to travel beyond the body in spirit form and interact with others to alert them.

There is also evidence that just after death, or on the point of death, people have appeared to their relatives or friends to explain what has just happened before those left behind could ever have had the information from any conventional source. Whether or not this represents an out-of-body experience prior to actual death is debatable (and there may be a time lapse after 'clinical' death before 'real' death, whatever that means, sets in). Alternatively the spirit may truly be freed from the body and, as is suggested by spiritualists, either passes on to another plane of existence or remains earthbound as a ghost.

Again, because of their nature, these types of reports cannot be investigated by the investigator being in the appropriate spot to witness the apparition again, but there is a certain amount of investigation that can be done to verify whether or not the person reporting the event could have received the information he claims he was told from some other source or whether the only explanation possible is the one he gave.

There seems little doubt that there is substantial evidence to support the idea of point of death or crisis apparition, but even then the precise nature of the mechanism must be subject to question and is perhaps outside the sphere of ghost phenomena altogether. It may be that, rather than a spirit physically leaving one location and visiting someone in another, a form of complex telepathy is taking place; again we have insufficient understanding of this mechanism to make this more than an interesting possibility.

Haunted Objects

Haunted objects are not really very much different from haunted places except that they are moveable. There are many reports of haunted skulls, cars, planes, and even one haunted, cottage-shaped biscuit container (see 'The Pottery Cottage', pp. 97–8). What is useful in these cases is that such objects will tend to change ownership over a period of time and if a series of subsequent owners all report the same sort of phenomenon then there is some evidence for an objective rather than subjective reality. The problem is always that it tends to be *one* investigator who puts together the pieces of the jigsaw puzzle and he may construct it according to his own predetermined wishes.

At least the investigator is dealing with a physical object that he can position according to his own plan or the witness's suggestions and can then conduct the usual types of investigations depending on what has been reported. If the object is credited with having caused a particular visual apparition then the investigator can set up his equipment accordingly. Obviously since it is possible, in these cases, to be present when the event actually occurs, then the usual recording equipment should be ready at all times.

Phantom Hitchhikers

The phantom hitchhiker is really no more than an interactive ghost as mentioned above. However, there are certain aspects of this particular type of report which suggest that it is also – more than any other type of ghost report – the product of folklore and mythology. This is not to suggest that there are no phantom hitchhikers but rather that the circumstances of the reports seem to be a very important factor in the types of stories received. The circumstances of the reports are often too 'pat' compared to other ghost reports; the hitchhiker can frequently be identified, and the way that the hitchhiker will have left the car, (for example, from the backseat between two witnesses) often seems to leave no room for ambiguity which is uncharacteristic of the general range of ghost reports. Investigation should therefore concentrate on why this particular sub-classification should have certain characteristics; preliminary work by folklorists suggests that stories of phantom hitchhikers obey the laws of folklore mutation far more than the broader range of ghost reports. Investigating phantom hitchhikers is no different from investigating interactive ghosts though you may need your driving licence and a vehicle!

Frauds

Apart from that very small percentage of reports which seem to indicate some truly paranormal experience, the vast majority of ghost reports tend to have a mundane explanation. That said, the reports are usually made in good faith. The banshee wail that is thought to precede the death of the eldest male of the family may in fact turn out to be some insignificant damage to the central-heating boiler flue which virtually turns it into a woodwind instrument when the wind is in the right direction. Nonetheless the sound is genuinely heard and the report genuinely given by the witness. Of course, some witnesses tend to make 'more' of a case than another percipient would do.

All that said, there are still reports that are deliberately fabricated for some particular purpose by witnesses who know full well that what they are telling the investigator is simply not the truth.

An investigator should not be suspicious of everyone who offers a report – most people genuinely believe what they are saying, but, significantly, are happy to accept an explanation in the cases of those reports that are solved. It is important that the investigator should work in a spirit of partnership with the witness and tact is always vital. Nonetheless, an investigator should always bear in mind the possibility that he may be being hoaxed. The person reporting the incident may have a particular reason for doing so – there are instances of council-house tenants reporting quite elaborate poltergeist phenomena simply because they want the council to rehouse them. Or it may be that the person reporting the incident is in turn being taken in by someone else in the household. I can think of no better example of this than one given by Peter Underwood, the President of the Ghost Club, who was called in by a father to investigate poltergeist activity apparently focused on his daughter.

A plant pot was by all accounts mysteriously appearing in various parts of the witness's house including the father's room into which his daughter was not supposed to venture. Suspicious of a human agent, Underwood 'doctored' the plant pot so that if moved it would leave a trail of fine sand. In addition substances were smeared around the young girl's bedroom door so that if she opened the door and left the room she would get them on her hands and feet. These included a purple dye and flour mixed with soot. When the plant was found in the locked room later that the night Underwood was able to trace a trail back to the girl's bedroom from where she had ingeniously transported the plant pot by climbing in and out of the windows, thus avoiding the locked doors. An examination of the girl revealed that her hands and feet were covered in traces of the 'marker'.

We cannot suggest any particular course of action to take in the case of suspected fraud other than to be alert at all times. The fraudster is one step ahead and will always be creating some new and innovative scam; all you can hope is that as an investigator you are alert enough to spot what might be happening and to create a test to discover the method being used by the fraudster who can then be revealed. Apart from being a detective the ghost investigator must be a psychologist and a tactician all at the same time. Creating a fraud is akin to a cry for attention. It may be very satisfying for the investigator to reveal the hoaxer but it will not help the hoaxer. If a fraud is discovered then, ideally together with some other more responsible member of the family, the investigator might suggest finding a reason for the cry for help before the hoaxer moves on to what may be more serious cries for help. How the investigator will handle this will depend very much on the circumstances of the case but if a cry for help is identified, then remember it is help that is required and not a crowing victory.

Somewhere between genuine reports and outright fraud are cases where there seem to be genuine phenomena, but where the witness fakes a 'display' for the investigator in order to convince him or her of the truth. This point is well covered in Maurice Grosse's chapter on how to investigate poltergeists (see pp. 363–8). As an investigator be wary of throwing the baby out with the bathwater; there may be a genuine case if you study it diligently. Only experience can bring skilled judgement.

ENCYCLOPEDIA OF GHOST REPORTS

NOTE: Headings in the Encyclopedia of Ghost Reports give information, where available, on the date and location of each event reported, followed by the principal source of each report. In some cases precise information is simply not available, or locations and other distinguishing features have been deliberately changed by the source in order to protect reporters' anonymity. Where possible, this is noted in the text.

Key to headings: D = date, L = location, S = source.

1
Ghosts and Visions
Associated with Particular Places

Probably the most common image of haunting is that of the haunted building, in other words a particular place with a reputation for 'being haunted'. This is far from the whole picture, as the collected cases in this encyclopedia will show, but certainly ghosts associated with one particular place are very commonly reported.

Asked what a 'typical' haunted building is like, most people would reply with a description of an ancient rambling mansion or something like the storm-lashed and lightning-illuminated castle in which Dr Frankenstein constructed his Creature in Mary Shelley's tale of 'a modern Prometheus'. No doubt such places have their ghosts, but as this section shows there seem to be no limitations to where you might meet a ghost. This chapter contains ghost reports from modern hotels, a public house, a hospital, a nursing home, suburban houses, a stone cottage in Zulu Africa and even the possibility that the ghost of a young boy may be scampering up and down the aisles of a modern supermarket.

Abbas Hall
D: Mid 20th century
L: Nr. Great Cornard, Suffolk
S: Philip Paul

Abbas Hall is located just a few miles from Borley Rectory. Events there were investigated by ghost-hunter Philip Paul who worked with the occupant, Yvonne Spalding. Her job was to look after the hall for the owner, a solicitor, in exchange for which she was allowed to live there rent free. She also tended a herd of Jersey cattle kept on the nearby estate of Lord Abinger.

Spalding reported hearing footsteps and heavy dragging noises in the bedrooms upstairs though she could find no explanation for these sounds. Lord Abinger apparently told her he had seen the face of an old woman looking in through the windows; when he and Yvonne Spalding went to investigate no one could be found outside.

On another occasion Yvonne was alone in the house in the evening, reading in the living room, when she heard the sound of the kitchen-door latch. Her dachshund dog and Siamese cat both stared at the door and, their heads moving in unison, appeared to be watching something moving across to the other door that opened on to the stairway. That latch then also clicked. Some seconds later she heard the heavy dragging footsteps in the bedroom above. Uncomfortable to say the least, she took the dog and cat and spent the night with a friend.

An African Pregnancy Test

D: 1952

L: Transkei, Zulu Africa

S: Andrew MacKenzie

Described by Andrew MacKenzie, a prominent researcher of ghost phenomena and author of several books on the subject, as 'one of the strangest accounts I have ever come across', this story of the haunting of a cottage in Zulu Africa in 1952 is highly intriguing.

It was related by Margaret Leigh and concerns her time in Africa when she was doing occupational therapy at a mission hospital in the Transkei, South Africa, where her husband was doing research work. They were living in a cottage 'which had a thatched circular living room with a small built-in cupboard on the thick rough-hewn stone wall'. The front door was heavy timber with no knocker. The cottage stood in a dry, empty, dusty landscape.

Later to have significance, a friend staying with the couple remarked, on seeing Margaret playing with her cat, Tivy, that she (Margaret) was acting 'as if [she] was broody'.

Shortly after this there was a knock at the door and Tivy leapt off the window sill on which he habitually sat sunning himself and went out of the room. On this first occasion they opened the door but could find no one there.

On subsequent occasions, after they had become used to the haunting, of which this was their first taste, they ceased bothering to open the door, often to the puzzlement of guests. If invited to open the door, the guests would also discover no one there.

As Margaret related, when the ghost entered they heard a shuffling limp, crossing from the door to the couch where he would sit down. Then he would get up and go to the cupboard in the wall; then back to the couch.

After talking to a local man Margaret's husband was able to determine that the apparition was that of 'Cousin John', the dead cousin of the widow's husband, who had once lived in the cottage. Of the actual movement of the apparition, the local man explained that Cousin John stored his drinks in the cupboard, and told his wife, who disapproved, never to go there as there was a bees' nest in it.

Perhaps significantly, John and his wife had been childless when the haunting first began. The knocking and presence of 'Cousin John' grew more frequent later that year when Margaret became pregnant. Several people who came to the cottage were unsettled or refused to remain there and even those who knew the story found it difficult to believe that the door could be banged on so loudly by 'nothing'.

It seems that after the birth of Margaret's child the haunting came to an end. Later they returned to England.

Some three years later Margaret and her husband revisited the mission and visited Tivy and the cottage. Without being prompted, the new owners asked if the couple had ever heard knocking at the front door and found no one there. Margaret made the connection immediately and declared, 'Your wife is pregnant.' The husband denied this, of course, not knowing at the time that his wife would give birth nine months later!

It appeared that Cousin John, for some reason never determined, liked to be around pregnant women.

Kay Anderson
D: 1973
L: Dattelen, Haard Kaserne, Germany
S: Andrew MacKenzie

In 1973 Mrs Kay Anderson and her four-year-old daughter were living in Germany where her husband was stationed in Dattelen at Haard Kaserne. In her correspondence with Andrew MacKenzie she described a periodic 'haunting'. A figure that Mrs Anderson thought might be a ghost would appear in her entrance hall where he could see into all of the rooms. Mrs Anderson described the figure as tired; he seemed to be waiting for something. He wore a long dark coat. Interestingly, Mrs Anderson said that she could only see the man out of the corner of her eye and not when looking at him directly, though she did get the impression that he smiled occasionally. She tried to speak with the figure in English, French and German but without success.

Even several years later Mrs Anderson believed that the figure might still be there watching or waiting as she had a feeling of sadness still around her.

Mrs Anderson had had other experiences. She had apparently had what she described as 'flashes' since she was a teenager and these seemed to increase after a minor head injury. She described them as being an impression rather than anything as definite as pictures or voices. She hoped that she would be able to develop the ability she seemed to be attaining.

Mrs Anderson's experience following a minor head injury is one that regularly occurs in psychic phenomena. For example, the Dutch psychic Peter Hurkos seems to have acquired extraordinary clairvoyant powers after a serious fall from a ladder and a period in a coma.

Acker Bilk

D: (No date)
L: Woburn Abbey, Bedfordshire
S: Ben Noakes

After being invited by the Duke of Bedford to judge a Dairy Queen competition at Woburn Abbey in Bedfordshire, the jazz musician Acker Bilk was invited to stay the night. Acker Bilk and the duke's son, the Marquis of Tavistock, sat up until around four in the morning talking about music before retiring. They walked together down the corridors to the Red Room, where Acker Bilk was to sleep, and stood outside finishing their conversation. As they were talking the outside doors of the double set of doors to the Red Room began to open on their own. Tavistock took no notice of this and eventually Acker Bilk had to point it out to him. Apparently Tavistock casually replied, 'Oh, don't bother about that. It's just a ghost. He often wanders around. I think we have seven in all at the Abbey.'

Borley Rectory

D: Early 20th century
L: Nr. Sudbury, Suffolk–Essex border
S: Various

Borley Rectory has the reputation of being the most haunted house in England. That may or may not be true; paranormal events being what they are, it may be fairer to say that Borley Rectory is the most *investigated* haunted house in England and perhaps even fairer to say the most *investigated, publicised* haunted house in England.

It was built in 1863 by Rev. Henry Dawson Ellis Bull who himself expanded the original building to accommodate a family that grew to include fourteen children.

The first reported paranormal incident occurred in the afternoon of 28 July 1900 when Ethel Bull, one of the Reverend's daughters, first saw a ghostly 'nun' when she was in the company of her sisters. Whether or not the apparition at Borley Rectory actually is a nun is uncertain; it seems to arise from the description of the apparition as a female figure dressed in dark clothes *like* a nun. In his book, *England's Ghostly Heritage*, Terence Whitaker offers as legend rather than certain fact that Borley Rectory was built on the site of a thirteenth-century monastery (fourteenth-century according to Christina Hole's book *Haunted England*). It was also suggested that the rectory was linked with a nearby convent at Bures. The rumour which linked these buildings was that a monk and a nun had fallen in love but had been killed before they had been able to elope. Their ghosts are said to have been reported frequently during the nineteenth century. While of dubious authenticity, this tale does at least tie in with the discovery of part of the walls of a former building dating from around that time (see below).

Ethel Bull was in the company of two of her sisters; they were returning from a party. All three entered the rectory garden and all saw the figure gliding near a stream that runs through the grounds. The figure was some way from them and no detailed features could be made out. The girls were frightened by the shape and general motion of the apparition but a fourth sister, called to the scene, apparently did not perceive the figure as strange and went to intercept it when it stopped; the figure then suddenly disappeared.

Various sisters saw the same apparition several times and on one occasion in November 1900 Ethel and the family cook witnessed the figure leaning over a gate.

Of apparitions inside the rectory, Ethel once woke to find a tall dark man wearing a tall hat near her bed who disappeared when she reacted to him; and on two other occasions she felt the presence of someone nearby though she could see nothing.

Ethel had a long life, dying at the age of 93 in 1961, almost 100 years after the building of the rectory, and to the end she maintained her story. As she herself said: 'What would be the use of an old lady like me, waiting to meet her Maker, telling a lot of fairy stories?'

The Rev. Canon W.J. Phythian-Adams, the Canon of Carlisle, read Harry Price's book and was fascinated by the case. He believed that the nun was not English but a French nun named Marie Larre who had eloped with her lover to England, been betrayed and murdered by him and buried in the cellar of a house that had formerly stood on the Borley site. This story has been connected to the finding of a female skull and jawbone there.

Between 1916 and 1920 a Mr and Mrs Cooper resided at the rectory, Mr Cooper being groom and gardener to the Bull family. They experienced considerable poltergeist activity including what sounded like the pattering of the feet of a large dog. They had seen the apparition of a dwarf-like figure in their bedroom which then disappeared, and on another occasion heard what sounded like the smashing of all the crockery in the kitchen although on inspection found none had even been disturbed. Cooper also saw out of his bedroom window the apparition of a black horse-drawn coach sweeping into the rectory courtyard where it promptly vanished. Like Ethel Bull, Cooper also saw the nun figure during daylight hours and watched it for several seconds before it apparently entered the house.

On 12 June 1929 the famous psychic investigator, Harry Price, visited Borley Rectory and began a long association with the building which lasted until his death at the age of 67 on 29 March 1948. During that time he was mostly associated with the then residents of the rectory, the Rev. Alfred Henning and his wife Eva. Indeed, for a year from May 1937 Price rented the rectory from Henning in order to undertake an extensive study of the phenomena occurring there, which he was to publish in his books *The Most Haunted House in England* and its sequel *The End of Borley Rectory*.

In July 1937 Henning, together with his wife and one of Price's investigating team, Mark Kerr-Pearse, were in the ground-floor library which overlooks the garden. Henning had personally ensured that all the doors and windows were locked, the only means of entry being the French window of the room they were in. Suddenly they could hear someone opening a door. All those gathered could then hear footsteps coming up the passageway leading from the kitchen and what seemed to be the swishing noise of long trailing clothing. To say that whatever it was had the full attention of those now watching the door to the room would be an understatement! They heard it come closer down the passage nearer to the study and then suddenly one of them moved forward and whipped open the door to confront whatever was outside. They could see nothing and at that moment the sounds ceased. (This is exactly the same effect noted in the case of the 'Oxford Hangings', pp. 106–7.)

In April 1942 Henning also reported paranormal activity in Borley church. During the Second World War blackouts a small lamp, which was usually left burning near the tabernacle, had to be extinguished at night; the church was locked during the period. Each morning those entering the church to re-light the lamp would discover that the wick had been removed. To prevent it happening heavy plates were placed over the lamp but these were found scattered on the floor each morning.

On another occasion a group of children waiting for their teacher inside the church heard footsteps on the porch and a key turning the lock from the outside. They were naturally alarmed at being locked in the building and when their teacher came some minutes later she was equally surprised to find the door locked from the outside. Henning commented, 'In view of all that has happened in the porch since then, I think the locking of the door was a paranormal experience.'

Henning and Price were apparently involved in a paranormal incident together one afternoon. They were standing in the chancel when they heard footsteps in the porch. Henning went to the door to see who it was but could see no one. He said, 'Anyone playing a trick would not have had time to disappear before I caught them.' The sound had been preceded by a screeching sound similar to birds and a few days later the same sequence of sounds was repeated and again nothing was seen.

Later that same year Henning was showing someone around the church when suddenly they heard the sound of the organ playing. As soon as Henning set foot on the porch the sound stopped. Inside they found the organ keyboard locked up. Henning believed that it was impossible for anyone to have escaped before being seen.

In August 1943 Henning and Price, together with their helpers, were exploring the site and discovered the remains of a female human skull and a jawbone (the rest of the body was never found) in the cellars of the old rectory. Whether or not this had anything to do with the hauntings has never been determined. Medical analysis of the jawbone showed a deep abscess which would almost certainly have been very painful for its owner. This has been connected to descriptions of the nun as 'miserable' or 'pale and drawn'. A ghost with toothache?

Because it was too big for them, the Rev. Henning had put the rectory up for sale, with the permission of the bishop, more or less from the day he moved in, preferring to live at the smaller Liston Rectory nearby. They had some trouble selling it but it was eventually purchased by James Turner, a writer who assisted Henning in typing up a manuscript of his account of the happenings, *Haunted Borley*. While Mr Turner was typing the manuscript for Henning a small lamp near him suddenly was apparently swept off the table as if by an invisible force.

The main rectory building was gutted by fire in 1939 and demolished in 1944. In August 1949 Dr Margaret Abernethy was driving towards the church to visit a patient at Borley Green when she saw a nun stooping in the weeds near the gateway to the rectory site. The nun smiled, looking directly at the doctor, and she was able to estimate her age as around 40 years old. Having driven a little way past the figure, she turned around to offer her a lift – as the nearest convent was some three miles away – but she was surprised to discover that the nun had vanished. She searched all around including the rectory garden but could see no one. Predicting the reaction of her colleagues, she said that they would dismiss the incident as a figment of the imagination. She was, however, certain that she saw what she claimed. Two weeks after the sighting a rosary was found in the area in which the nun had apparently been searching (which would surely strengthen the likelihood of its having been a real nun on this occasion as it seems most unlikely that a ghost nun would have been searching for the past 49 years for a rosary that happened to be found so easily at that time).

In 1951 James Turner sold the rectory cottage and the site to Mr and Mrs Robert Bacon who moved in together with their son and daughter and Mrs Bacon's parents, Mr and Mrs Williams. On one occasion, not long after they had moved in, Mr Williams was working behind the cottage when he heard footsteps following him. Believing it to be Mr Bacon he began to speak and, when he got no response, turned around. No one was there but he was quite certain he had heard loud and distinct footsteps. In August 1953 Mr Williams also saw, moving past the window, the head and shoulders of a black-clad figure wearing a cowl-like head-dress which would seem to be at least an echo of the 'nun' sightings. He could find no one when he searched the area outside. Mr Bacon's son, Terry, reported seeing a nun three times, noting that she was some three or four feet off the ground (was this the strange aspect of the figure which so puzzled Ethel Bull and her sisters?). This seemed to be an indication that perhaps the nun was a 'recording-type' ghost, 'playing back' events that had occurred many years before when perhaps the ground level was higher.

Mrs Bacon had several paranormal experiences, reporting household articles disappearing and re-appearing. Once Mrs Williams heard what seemed to be the panting of a dog behind her but could see nothing.

In the summer of 1954 Philip Paul, a prominent psychic investigator and former committee member of the Ghost Club, undertook a long-term excavation of the site which actually revealed very little but resulted in Borley obtaining massive media coverage. One important discovery made was of the remains of a wall suggesting that there had been an older building on the site. When fully researched this may reveal some details of the reasons for the hauntings at the rectory.

The Borley Rectory hauntings have certainly created controversy, mainly centred around the 'Harry Price years'. Price himself published *The Most Haunted House in England* and followed it up with *The End of Borley Rectory*. However, Eric Dingwall, Kathleen Goldney and Trevor Hall wrote *The Haunting of Borley Rectory* which basically accused Price of fraudulently creating many of the phenomena he had reported. They wrote, 'When analysed, the evidence for haunting and poltergeist activity for each and every period appears to diminish in force and finally to vanish away.' Two years later Dingwall and Hall published *Four Modern Ghosts* and still later Hall published *Search for Harry Price*. There were other publications a-plenty, including *The Ghosts of Borley: A Critical History* by Peter Underwood and Paul Tabori, which contains a well set-out and sober history of the research into the case. In addition virtually everyone involved in ghost research has commented on the rectory, whether or not they have had direct involvement.

Anyone seeking to understand this case should of course acquaint themselves with the publications already mentioned. Such a highly publicised case requires a somewhat enlarged entry in a work of this kind but clearly there is a limit to how much can be included here before the balance is lost, given the enormous amount of material available on this one case.

It is possible that Harry Price exaggerated or faked some of the claims he made but it seems certain that much of the activity at Borley Rectory was genuinely reported. In very recent years council houses have been built over the old rectory garden but there are still stories of the phantom nun occasionally being seen.

The Cavendish Hotel

D: 1988
L: Harrogate, North Yorkshire
S: Direct

The witnesses in this case have given the information directly to the authors but have both requested anonymity as neither of them wants any publicity or attention to result from their report. We have therefore been given exact dates and details of the people involved but these are withheld here at their request. They were recommended to speak to us by a mutual friend and they offered their stories because they hoped we might be able to throw some light on their experiences.

In November 1988 'Laura Collins' stayed at the Cavendish Hotel in Harrogate for one night. Together with a friend from work she had driven to the hotel, a journey of some one and a half hours from her work, to be ready for a typing exam the following morning. The two were not close colleagues but merely knew each other reasonably well through being employed at the same place. They arrived at the hotel around 7–7.30 in the evening, had dinner and retired to their respective rooms. Laura's room was described as modernised, containing a double bed, television and the usual ensuite toilet and bathroom.

After dinner, Laura watched some television and had a long and leisurely bath, mainly because there was very little else to do, and then went to bed, possibly watching some more television before going off to sleep. She was not sure of the time as the circumstances of the evening did not demand timekeeping.

At some point during the night Laura awoke and felt the bed 'dip' next to her. She described it as 'like someone had sat on it'. 'I didn't open my eyes, but I put my hand out and I felt the hollow.' Laura opened her eyes. She was startled to find a man sitting on the edge of the bed facing away from her as if he had just got up. He was bending forwards as if putting on shoes and socks. (Laura's description; in view of the fact that he was in pyjamas perhaps bedroom slippers might be more appropriate.)

Laura described him as wearing red-and-white-striped winceyette pyjamas. He was oldish looking, balding with a curtain of grey hair around his ears and the back of his head. He was fairly short in stature. She never saw his face, only his back, from where she was lying.

Laura was ready to scream but not sure whether to do it or not. Believing that the person was absolutely real, she found herself alone with a man in her bedroom and uncertain precisely what course of action would make matters worse or improve them. Before she had really had a chance to make up her mind the man stood up and walked towards the window. As he did so he disappeared.

We asked Laura whether that made her mind up about whether or not to scream and her only reply was, 'I didn't sleep for the rest of the night and I kept the light on.' It was fairly clear that it had become a situation where there were no rules to follow.

Laura did not discuss the incident with her friend because, as she explained, she herself did not understand it and felt unable to discuss it with others. She was also afraid that the story would be circulated around her workplace and to other people whom she might not want to be involved. (She did later tell her husband who took an open-minded and sympathetic attitude towards the story, and she told her boss, since the hotel was frequently used by the company. He seemed rather uninterested in the story.)

Laura sat her typing exam the following day; while she may have been somewhat on edge after her experience she was not in a state of extreme distress or agitation.

It was during the drive home when her colleague told her that she had not wanted to worry her but she knew that another friend of hers had had a nasty experience in the same room that Laura had been sleeping in. Laura had not told her anything about the events of the night before.

Laura was able to discover the name of the other person who had had the experience in room and put us in touch with her. We spoke to her the day after we had spoken to Laura. 'Anne Hughes' (pseudonym) had been in the same room in the same hotel approximately three weeks earlier for the same purpose; she also had had a typing exam the following day. She was also employed by the same company, in a different department. Her story was perhaps a little less dramatic from the paranormal point of view, although in fact it resulted in a hospital visit. It was interesting in view of Laura's account. Anne had been asleep and woke up hearing a bang. The bedside lamp was lying at the foot of the bed some considerable distance from where it had been positioned and she was quite certain that even if she had knocked it in her sleep she could never have knocked it anything like that far. As she woke up she sensed the presence of somebody sitting on the bed next to her. It must be stressed that, unlike Laura, Anne had no visual sighting of anyone.

The next morning she got up and found teethmarks on her thumb which she reported to the proprietors. They suggested that perhaps a cat had got in during the night. Anne felt this unlikely. When the incident had happened she had closely examined the whole room and was quite convinced that there was nothing untoward in it. Even so, she felt uneasy in view of what happened to the lamp.

Her thumb swelled up very badly and she ended up having to visit the local hospital where she got a tetanus injection. (She thought that the hospital would not be receptive to inquiries from us because the staff had indicated to her that they felt her visit to be somewhat unnecessary, to put it politely.) She certainly had no memory of being bitten, though the hospital agreed that it looked like bitemarks.

We asked both women whether or not they had ever had any other paranormal experiences. Anne could think of none but Laura had an interesting story to tell. She is one of twins; her sister, having lived some way away from her in England for a time, now lives in Australia. They have what she described as a 'strong telepathic link'. For example, Laura told us, she had sympathetic labour pains when her sister had a baby. Like many twins, they would both send identical presents to each other without having consulted each other on what the other wanted.

Laura told us that she had once been watching television with her husband, in England, feeling quite normal and unemotional when suddenly she had burst into tears. She could not give her husband any reason for it. They found out afterwards that her sister had just then had a miscarriage in Australia.

Laura told us that only a few weeks prior to our conversation she had had back pains which coincided with, as they later discovered, her sister's son's girlfriend giving birth to her sister's grandchild. Laura was not necessarily making a connection vis-à-vis every incident but explained that there had been so many during their lifetime that they felt sure there was a connection between them which manifested itself frequently.

We contacted the manageress of the Cavendish Hotel, Margaret Brown, to find out whether she would be prepared to discuss any other incidents that had occurred. We explained the details of the stories and were given permission to use the hotel's name. Ms Brown was most helpful and cooperative, but told us that there had been no other incidents and she was not aware of the two that we had heard of. However, she and the present owners have only been involved with the hotel for the past eighteen months or so and therefore would not have been there at the time when Laura or Anne had stayed.

Ms Brown told us that she had once lived in what was thought to be a haunted house in the West Country though she felt that she was not 'the psychic type'; almost everyone visiting the house had reported something but she had never seen or heard anything of an unusual nature. The hotel have agreed to let us know of any further incidents that may take place in the future.

A Childhood Companion

D: 1964
L: Twickenham, Surrey
S: Andrew MacKenzie

Amyand Park Road in Twickenham runs parallel to the main Richmond to Kingston train lines. In 1973 the houses there were demolished to make way for a supermarket and offices but prior to that the old Regency house that had stood at No. 10 had been the subject of a very gentle and seemingly pleasant haunting.

A Mrs Judy Miles reported to Andrew MacKenzie that in February 1964 she had been helping at a children's party at the house when she had seen a young child she did not recognise. Given the circumstances that was not particularly remarkable and she assumed that the boy belonged to one of the other adults there at the time.

The child was described as having light hair and a smiling face. He was dressed in a white pullover and trousers. The following day when Mrs Miles was with her own children in Richmond Park she asked her daughter if she knew who the boy was. Her daughter was unaware of the boy and could not fit anyone to the description her mother gave. At dinner that evening Mrs Miles asked the owners of the house about the boy; 'Mrs Buxton' (pseudonym) described him and was surprised when Mrs Miles confirmed the description. She had not expected Mrs Miles to have seen the child. Mrs Buxton then explained that she and other members of her family had seen the same child on many occasions, at first assuming him to be 'normal'. In her letter to MacKenzie Mrs Miles explained that Mrs Buxton had thought the child had run in from outside but then discovered that the door was locked. On searching, the child was not found. Although he never spoke she could hear his footsteps and other sounds of movement and noticed that he appeared when she was alone in the house or when her children were playing upstairs.

Mrs Buxton also heard her son talking to someone in his bedroom whom the child described as 'that little boy who comes to play'. Mrs Buxton knew that there were no other children in the house at the time.

On one occasion Mrs Buxton had been sitting reading a magazine when the child appeared and stood near her knees where she was sitting but did not touch her. He looked at a magazine she was reading and then up at her face. Mrs Buxton noticed his fine hair and a small brown mole on his chin. The boy ran out and Mrs Buxton tried to follow him but being heavily pregnant was slow to chase. On finding the road empty outside she assumed that he had returned to his parents and gone indoors somewhere.

At the time this account was first put down the young figure, whose clothes suggested he was fairly contemporary, had not been identified. The former owners of the house had been childless.

Whether or not the little boy still runs around the same area, this time perhaps in and out of the aisles of the supermarket, we may never know. Such a figure, even separated from parents, would be so commonplace in a supermarket that he could probably dart about it impishly for years without his 'identity' being realised.

The Combermere Ghost
   D: 20th century
   L: Combermere Abbey, nr. Whitchurch, Cheshire
   S: Various
Lord Combermere, having died, was being buried when a visitor

to his home, Combermere Abbey in Cheshire, took the opportunity to photograph the library which contained Lord Combermere's favourite carved oak chair. When the photograph was developed it showed the image of a bearded man, apparently Lord Combermere himself, sitting in the chair. The image is, however, a rather vague one.

A Cricketer at Home
D: 20th century
L: Bilborough Estate, Nottingham
S: Peter Underwood

A council house in Nottingham was the scene of several sightings of a cricketing ghost. Charles Hill was frightened away from the house by the ghost.

He had first woken in the middle of the night to see a young man dressed in traditional cricket garb with a handkerchief over the back of his neck but the apparition disappeared almost immediately. He assumed therefore that he had been dreaming.

Just a few nights later, while sitting up in bed watching television, he saw the figure again and was certain that he was not dreaming.

His daughter Sandra also saw the apparition and they decided to leave the house. An investigation was undertaken by the Ghost Club. During the investigation a sharp pistol shot was heard from somewhere in the room but not heard outside by other investigators.

During a seance the name of the ghost was given and the investigators were able to track down the probable ghost's mother who was still alive. Her son had been paralysed in an accident and had had to spend most of the rest of his life in the 'haunted' room. Being fond of cricket he often dressed in cricket clothes during the summer and to protect the back of his neck from sunlight (as he could not move into the shade) a handkerchief was often put over to protect it. After eighteen months of such confinement he shot himself with a revolver.

Drury Lane Theatre
D: 20th century
L: Catherine St, London
S: Peter Underwood

The actor Stanley Lupino had been in his dressing-room at the Drury Lane Theatre when he became certain that he was seeing the ghost of Dan Leno. It started with the feeling that he was not alone and then he saw the darkened shape of a man crossing the room and passing through a closed door. The theatre caretaker assured Lupino that there was no one else near his dressing-room or indeed in the theatre. Shortly afterwards Lupino was again resting in his dressing-room and when he looked in his make-up mirror he could see next to himself the whitened features of Dan Leno. Lupino was very scared by the apparition and left, not to return that night.

Lupino and his wife apparently saw Dan Leno yet again in the same dressing-room which they were later to discover was in fact the last one ever used by Leno.

This story was related by actor and comedian Arthur Askey in conversation with Peter Underwood. Askey was certain that Lupino had had the experiences he described.

Embalmed in Tar

D: 18th century
L: Hollinwood, Greater Manchester
S: Keith Poole

In the eighteenth century a certain Miss Beswick lived in the manor house at Birchen Bower, Hollinwood, now a part of Greater Manchester. At the time her house was surrounded by woods and fields and her estates included Rose Hill and Cheetwood. Most of the manor house was demolished after her death. She seems to have been a rather eccentric woman and farmed her own land until she became too old to do so.

When Miss Beswick received news of the Jacobite Rebellion of 1745 she believed that the Scottish Army, with Prince Charles at the head, would sweep through England claiming the fortunes of the landowners. Like so many wealthy landowners she hid as many of her own treasures as she could around her estates in locations known only to herself. And although the Jacobite Rebellion did not reach her lands she did not disturb her hidden treasures.

Later in life she was to receive a shock which profoundly affected her, or so it would seem from the provisions she made in her will. She believed that her brother had died; indeed so did the doctor who certified him dead. But as she looked into his coffin as the lid was being screwed down she suddenly saw that he was showing signs of life; the undertaker was stopped and her brother returned to his bed where he lay in a coma for some days until he recovered to live for many years. As Keith Poole relates in his book *Britain's Haunted Heritage*, Miss Beswick was clearly not very taken by the idea of being buried alive. She drew up a will leaving her estates to her family doctor, Dr White, and his descendants on the condition that after her death her body was always to be kept above ground. To add to the strangeness of her will, it also stipulated that every 21 years her body should be returned to Birchen Bower for a whole week.

When she died in around 1768, Dr White made the arrangements to have her body shrouded in bandages, leaving only the face exposed, and then embalmed in tar. The corpse was presented to the Natural History Museum and indeed was on the show in the Manchester Museum for a century. As reported in the *Manchester Guardian* on 22nd July 1868 they then apparently decided that enough was enough, the Commissioners of the Manchester Natural History Society 'deeming the specimen undesirable' and she was at last laid to rest in Harpurhey Cemetery.

According to local villagers, Miss Beswick's wish for her body to be returned to Birchen Bower every 21st year was also carried out; it had been there five times, and had always been placed in the granary of the old farmstead.

After Miss Beswick's death her ghost was seen by many villagers. While the manor house remained it was divided into separate dwellings and she was seen by people as they were having supper. Her appearance would be preceded be the rustling of her silk dress; she would then be seen in black gliding through the kitchen. In the kitchen the apparition disappeared, always at the same flagstone.

The apparition was seen as late as 1920, at that time next to a well near the stone cottage into which she had moved after she had become too infirm to live at the manor itself. A villager going to draw water saw a lady standing there and said she saw the apparition dressed in black silk and wearing the same white cap with frilled edge that she had worn while alive. She was apparently standing in a hostile, even threatening, attitude.

There were also reports that on many occasions the barn glowed as if there was a fire inside, light appearing through the cracks in its structure. It also gave off unearthly noises and few people would go near it. Whenever the barn was searched after such an occurrence there were no signs of charred wood anywhere. The story goes that the barn is the hiding place of the bulk of Miss Beswick's hidden treasure. Although one local man, Joe, did find a box of gold wedges which kept him in relative prosperity, it is believed that the bulk of the treasure has never been located.

Mrs Freeborn and the Ghost of Mrs Lyons
   D: 1981
   L: Bakersfield, California
   S: *Journal of the SPR*
In Andrew MacKenzie's book *The Seen and the Unseen* he refers to the case of Mrs Frances Freeborn who moved into a house in Bakersfield, California on 30 November 1981. The original report was presented to the *Journal of the Society for Psychical Research* by Dr L. Stafford Betty of the faculty of California State College, Bakersfield.

The first owner of the house had been a 'Mrs Lyons' (pseudonym) who died in 1976; the house was not then permanently lived in until Mrs Freeborn moved there.

Mrs Freeborn repaired and decorated the house which had been left in a state of disrepair since Mrs Lyons' death but she felt that something or someone *'disapproved of what I was doing'*. The spirit, whether it was Mrs Lyons' or not, seemed occasionally to disagree with the changes that were being made to the house though there was never any feeling at that time of hostility or danger.

One particular incident is of specific interest; Mrs Freeborn wished to hang a picture of three women dressed in early American outfits and attempted to hang it five times. On each occasion it seemed that the picture was taken down from the wall over night and left propped up beneath the spot where it had been hung. The nail would always still be in the wall and no explanation could be found for how the picture left the wall.

On one occasion Mrs Freeborn felt that she was directed by a presence to hang the picture in a particular place near the light switch on the bedroom wall. For Mrs Freeborn this was somewhat too a low position for her comfort. It may be relevant to consider that Mrs Lyons had been a very short woman who might well have appreciated the picture being at a lower eye level than usual.

On 25 January 1982 Mrs Freeborn experienced what she described as 'the most terrifying night of my life'. She was about to redecorate the main bedroom (which had, of course, also been Mrs Lyons' main bedroom) when she had a feeling of being watched. After she had gone to bed there was a noise in the kitchen as if the whole place was being torn up and she was driven out of the house by other disturbances. Trying to get out, she encountered an ominous sense of mass or pressure in the hallway. According to the report, she encountered three unspecified entities and fled the house in her nightclothes to spend the night at her ranch.

The hostile entities were exorcised from the house at a later time.

The Friendly Domestic Servant
D: 1982
L: West England
S: Andrew MacKenzie

A public servant, using the pseudonym 'Sir Robert Martin', reported to the Society for Psychical Research on an experience which took place at midday on Sunday, 26 September 1982.

Sir Robert, his wife and daughters (one using the pseudonym 'Julia') lived in a seventeenth-century farmhouse, which contained a workshop and storeroom, in a building originally a stable but used at one time as a chapel.

As Sir Robert and his daughter were returning home from church they drove into the courtyard and saw someone they believed to be Sir Robert's wife hurrying from the front door of the house, across the courtyard and entering the chapel (as that building was still known). When they went to the chapel door they found it was closed and chained; on opening it they discovered no one inside.

In fact Sir Robert's wife was in the kitchen and confirmed that she had not left it since her husband and daughter had left for the church earlier that day.

In his letter Sir Robert indicated that his wife and he had both been aware of a presence in the house for a long time, and the presence was also recognised by their three daughters though no one had ever had cause to be afraid of it. The assumption had been made that the presence was the ghost of a female domestic servant who had once worked at the house. The letter described fleeting glimpses of a form inside the house and an occasion when the presence seemed to help Sir Robert's wife on with her coat.

To add further to the mystery, the front door from which the figure had left the house had earlier been discovered to have been locked and in fact resisted attempts to open it. A locksmith was to be called the following morning while in the meantime the family used the garden door, as they did on returning from church, to get in and out. After this incident they tried the front door and it opened immediately. They believed that the ghost was friendly and had helped the family by fixing the lock.

Several options were considered including a doppelgänger of Sir Robert's wife but the best guess for an identity for the apparition would seem to be the apparition of a domestic who had attended mass when the chapel was in use around 1910. The question of why, or indeed how, an apparition can free a locked door is left unanswered.

A Ghostly Reader

D: 1940s
L: Nr. Lincoln, Lincolnshire
S: Peter Underwood

This case was discovered by accident by researcher John May and related by him to the President of the Ghost Club, Peter Underwood.

During the 1940s May had been asked to tidy up a garden for a person who had bought a house just outside the town of Lincoln. The new occupant had arranged for May to live in the house while the gardens were prepared and before he himself moved in.

On the day that May moved in, a Friday, he had worked all day in the garden, had a supper which he cooked himself in the kitchen and at approximately ten o'clock in the evening lit a candle, placing it in a candlestick holder so that he could read the paper. There was no electricity yet connected up.

At approximately ten-thirty he went around the ground-floor rooms securing the windows and doors before going upstairs to the room in which he had erected a camp bed to sleep the night.

In the drawing room, before locking the window, May placed the candle on the floor and looked out towards the road. He suddenly heard a noise behind him and he turned to see the drawing-room door key lying on the floor although it had previously been in the lock. The door itself slowly began to close. Not afraid, and with some knowledge of paranormal activity, May put the key back in the lock and opened the door. The door slammed shut again and the opened sash window also slammed downwards.

May was undeterred and locked up as best he could and then went up to bed. There were no further disturbances that night. However, on the second night, while he was sitting up in bed reading with a candle on a chair next to him, he noticed that the candle flame was getting dim and indeed that it appeared to be lighted over an inch above the wick itself. Suddenly the candle, still alight, lifted itself from the candlestick, dropped to the floor and rolled up against the skirting board. May recovered it to prevent it doing any damage.

With the candle back where it had been May got back into bed and started reading again. Shortly after he had laid the book down he noticed that the pages were beginning to turn, first slowly and then quite rapidly. Suddenly all of this ceased. It was the following morning when, from having made inquiries in the neighbourhood, May speculated that the spirit might be that of an elderly lady who had once lived in the house. She had been reclusive and May thought that she had perhaps become attached to the house and resented intrusions by others. May performed an exorcism and there were no further incidents. Indeed, the new occupant never realised how close he came to living in a haunted house.

Gill House
D: c. 1940
L: Nr. Broomfield, Cumberland
S: Peter Underwood

Gill House, near Bromfield in Cumberland, dates back, at least in part, to the early thirteenth century. During World War II it was used as a base for the Women's Land Army. From very early on many of the young women based there heard strange noises coming from one bedroom in one of the oldest parts of the house; rats were believed to be the cause but vermin inspectors found no trace of them. The noises became louder and occasionally footsteps could be made out. In the room from where those noises were emanating several girls reported a feeling of being choked and refused to stay there. Reports seemed to be focused on the period of three nights on the wane of the moon.

Miss Eouslby of the Women's Land Army sent a team to investigate the claims, including a Mrs Parkins, the vicar of Ainstable, Rev. N.C. Murray and his wife. They met with the warden at the house, Miss Mandale, who said that she had not herself experienced anything but was clearly concerned at the 'obvious horror and fear' felt by the girls.

Nothing much happened at first and Mrs Murray suggested tapping would '*often bring these things on*'. Accordingly Mrs Parkins gave a loud knock on the cupboard. She can hardly have known what she was about to unleash! Nothing much happened for a moment or two and then the knock seemed to be answered by a loud rustling sound. Suddenly a figure of a man appeared out of the cupboard making straight for Mrs Parkins and stopping close to her. A strange noise like the reeling in of a fishing-reel was heard by everyone and Mrs Parkins also reported a feeling of coldness while the form was near her. The figure then went towards Mr Murray and began tapping on the wall, making a metallic sound. Those present could smell a dreadful smell which, possibly by association, they likened to '*a leaking coffin*'. The figure walked about tapping for nearly three hours and then disappeared into a cupboard on the opposite side of the room from where it had appeared. All was then quiet and the team went downstairs.

The team told Miss Mandale that they thought the room was

haunted and that the girls should not be staying there, although they did not give her a full description of what had occurred.

Using a version of a ouija board, the Murrays (later together with Mrs Parkins) attempted to contact the spirits in Gill House and seemed to make some contact. The spirits were apparently Gerald Wreay and Lily, his servant. Gerald identified himself as a Jacobite in the reign of George I. It appears from the communication that Gerald was very wicked and had stolen sacred relics which he had hidden in Gill House. Asked if they could be located, the questioners were informed that the relics were now dust. At another seance the questioners were told that sometimes there were crowds of evil spirits at the house and they were advised to leave it alone.

A clairvoyant visiting the house shortly after these events felt two ghosts were present, 'a man wearing tight-fitting trousers and a girl'.

All 26 of the Women's Land Army girls stationed at the house apparently requested a local clergyman to exorcise the spirits from the house, alternatively they wanted the house closed down. To prove that there was nothing to be frightened of, Miss Mandale and Mrs How, the Cumberland County WLA organiser, declared that they would stay in the haunted room during the relevant period. They did not see the night out to the dawn. Before sunrise they left the room in a disturbed state. Mrs How apparently had three unpleasant experiences which reduced her to a state of panic; she recommended that the WLA remove the girls as it was not a suitable place for them. The hostel was then closed.

The house is now a private residence but the present occupier has not responded to questions about its state or about the possibilities of further investigation.

The Grenadier Public House
D: Various
L: Wilton Row, Knightsbridge, London
S: Direct (and various)

Some 170 years ago, 'The Guardsman' was an officers' mess and gambling room for the Duke of Wellington's regiment based in Knightsbridge, London. According to legend, a young officer, playing cards, was caught cheating and was attacked by his fellow officers. They stripped him and flogged the skin from his body, leaving him to die in the cellar.

'The Guardsman' is now the 'Grenadier' public house, where several landlords have reported a cyclical ghost whose appearances recur in September, around the anniversary of the young soldier's death. In some cases it is described simply as *'an indefinable but definite atmosphere'*; it has affected both people and animals and there have been sightings. One landlord's son saw a black shape outside his bedroom one September evening and his mother also saw a figure climbing the stairs who suddenly disappeared. A visitor to the public house saw a figure by the side of the bed in the middle of the night which then disappeared.

Another landlord, Geoffrey Bernard, reported poltergeist activity and shadows during the month of September.

John Spencer, one of the authors of this compilation, visited the public house in January 1991 and spoke to the present manager/licensee, Peter Martin, and two of his staff, Sara McCarthy and Kathy McVey.

Peter Martin told of one occasion when he was in the bar at around midnight with a Mr Edward Webber (a friend of the then landlord, Peter Martin being the relief manager at that time). They saw a bottle apparently lift from approximately one foot above floor height where the 'mixers' are stored to around head height in the middle of the bar area where it exploded.

Martin also told of several occasions when keys would go mysteriously missing and then turn up, equally mysteriously. On on occasion in 1988 or 1989 (Peter Martin could not be more specific) some electricians had arrived to do electrical repair work in the cellar. The keys to the cellar where the electricians were to work were found to be missing. They were usually kept under the mattress on Martin's bed but were not there when he looked for them. Eventually the keys were found but would not open the lock despite all the efforts made to open it, but a street cleaner who was a friend of the electricians assisted them and was apparently able to open the lock with no effort whatsoever. At the time of John Spencer's visit the street cleaner had apparently retired and his whereabouts were not known. (This 'interference' with keys is similar to a detail of the case 'The Friendly Domestic Servant', p. 40).

Peter Martin had come to the pub in January 1988 as the relief manager and took over as manager in February 1990; since that later date he has experienced no sightings.

He did make the point that ghost activity could easily be missed. Sometime between July and September of 1991 there was a break-in at the pub between four and seven o'clock in the morning. Despite the fact that several people where then sleeping in the building no one heard the break-in which was discovered by the cleaner when she started work.

John Spencer asked the staff for their opinions of ghosts in general and of the ghosts of the public house in particular; Peter Martin remained healthily sceptical and admitted that he was not inclined to such beliefs. Sara McCarthy had only been at the pub for approximately two weeks and had felt no presences or seen anything untoward. She also remained healthily sceptical. Kathy McVey had been at the pub for approximately four months and had also seen and felt nothing. With the most mischievous of pixie-like grins she explained, with commendable honesty, that she was prepared to believe in ghosts because she wanted to and felt that it was somehow exciting.

Holding Back with Prayers
D: 20th century
L: Wales
S: Rev. J. Aelwyn Roberts

The Rev. J. Aelwyn Roberts, in his book *The Holy Ghostbuster* (pub. Hale), describes an incident that happened to 'W.R.', a clerical colleague of his.

When W.R. moved into a run-down old priory and began to refurbish it he experienced a very unpleasant haunting. Having done a hard day's work renovating the Old Priory, W.R. was tired and fell asleep very quickly once in bed. It was a warm August night.

At about three in the morning W.R. woke up. On waking he realised that he was both cold and scared but could not determine exactly what it was that he was scared of. Suddenly he could hear a breathing and pulsating noise and saw a form in the old fireplace. Although the fireplace was black the form was blacker. It was apparently like a huge slimy octopus with white and watery eyes which W.R. thought the creature was using to try to kill him.

W.R. was riveted to the spot and unable to turn away. He recognised that the beast regarded him as its prey; despite fearing for himself and his family he just could not move. He made the sign of the cross and spent the rest of the night fighting the creature with prayers and reciting the psalms.

When morning came he suddenly felt his body becoming warm again; the devil beast had gone. W.R. knew then that he had won and that the beast would not return again to the priory.

The Home of Compassion

D: 1962, 1976

L: Thames Ditton, Surrey

S: Direct (and various)

One building with an interesting and up-to-date history of hauntings is in Thames Ditton in Surrey. Currently a nursing home for the elderly known as 'The Home of Compassion', it has a long and fascinating history in its own right. In earlier centuries it was Forde Farm and in 1782 was sold to Charlotte Boyle who renamed it Boyle Farm. It has been the home of Lord Henry FitzGerald and Lord St Leonards. In 1905 it was dedicated by the then Lord Bishop of Winchester under the charge of Mother Mary Margaret as the Home of Compassion. The home was run by the Sisters of Compassion, a nursing order of Benedictine nuns.

Local historian Tom Mercer published a history of Thames Ditton entitled *Tales and Scandals of Old Thames Ditton* and he refers to several of the apparitions seen at the home.

It seems that the white lady has been seen by many people including children visiting the home and members of the staff (one sister was working in the kitchens when she saw the ghost near her). It was also witnessed by a man attending to the boilers.

Tom Mercer records an incident in October 1962 when he went into the old (which I, J.S., have visited but which is now a fairly standard ward). There were some elaborate paintings on the walls which had been painted by one of the nuns, Sister Miriam. In the presence of and witnessed by three workmen who were working there at the time Mercer took a photograph of one the paintings; when developed it showed a strong line of wispy filament which seemed to be racing across the film. No one present saw anything while the picture was being taken and of course it could be no more than a film fault. It remains thought provoking, nonetheless.

We became interested in this particular case partly because of the frequency of reported sightings; we contacted the home and arranged for John Spencer to visit it in November 1991. I was met by the home's present Director, Don Walker, who proved to be most friendly and helpful. We spent some time discussing the history of the building and its somewhat eccentric internal architecture, which was clearly of great interest to Mr Walker. Properly conscious of his responsibilities, Mr Walker also confirmed with the Chairman of the Board of Trustees that I was permitted to interview people at the home and publish details of these interviews. I am grateful for that permission.

There have been many changes to the home, even in fairly recent years. The last nun to reside at the home died in 1976 and the home is now run by a Board of Trustees. Because of the changes some of Don Walker's stories were third and fourth hand by now but are nonetheless of interest. Don told me: 'People have reported hearing children and seeing dogs. Patients have seen them.' One patient apparently saw a dog on her bed and asked for it to be removed. No dog was there but the patient died soon afterwards. The dog is regarded as something of an omen of death; those who see it soon die. While these stories were well known there was nobody present at the home at the time when I was there who had had first-hand experience of them.

However, Don was able to introduce me to one of the present members of staff, Elizabeth Gadd, who herself had a most fascinating story to tell. Shortly after joining the staff in February 1990 Elizabeth Gadd had a disturbing experience in one of the lower corridors near the kitchens: 'It wasn't a figment of your imagination. I was going into the kitchen to get the supper things and this nun – I didn't see the face – but it had a white bit and a grey outfit like this.' (Elizabeth drew in the air the outline of a traditional nun's garb around her own body.) 'I saw the hands.' I asked why she didn't see the face, whether the apparition's head had been pointing down, but Elizabeth replied, 'No, just walking straight. I was too frightened. I just saw the nun's gown and her hands. I went into the kitchen to get the supper things and as I was coming out I turned around and looked and this nun was coming towards me. I put some of the stuff in my hands into the servery lift and I thought, "Oh, my God!" I never bothered to look the second time.' (Elizabeth showed us how she had hidden her eyes behind her hands as if with some fear.) 'When I had gone back into the kitchen and came out a second time it walked straight through me. Horrible sensation. Clammy. Panic.'

I asked Elizabeth if the outfit she was describing was what the nuns used to wear and she replied, 'I don't know what they used to wear, that's going back years ago.' (In fact there are virtually no pictures of the nuns and it is quite possible that Elizabeth would not know their outfit.)

I asked Elizabeth whether she had had any other paranormal experiences. 'Never. Never. I don't want another experience. I was in a terrible state.' But she did cheer up shortly afterwards and said with a smile, 'It's not the dead that do you any harm, it's the living.'

Another interesting though less recent story came from church warden Derek Potts. Don related the story to me: 'He was running some church affair here, and his wife suggested that he should go and look at the chapel because it was very interesting. He was at the bottom end of the cloisters, walked up, and as he got to the chapel the door opened, a nun came out of the chapel, waved to him to say, "No, don't come in"' and Don put a finger to his lips meaning silence. 'He didn't realise at the time there were no nuns here, he thought it was a nun. She had what he described as a white "shirt" on, he is not sure if she was in black or grey. This was in 1977 or 1978 at around eight p.m.' (the year after the last nun died). Don then told me, 'The cook said that the Mother Superior used to tell her she was very noisy and that she would make the same [finger to the lips] gesture.'

The House of Faces
D: 1970s
L: Andalusia, Spain
S: Andrew MacKenzie

Known locally as the House of the Faces, the small home in the mountain village of Bélmez de la Moraleda in Andalusia, Spain became internationally known in the 1970s for an extraordinary phenomenon. On 23 August 1971 farmer's wife Mrs Maria Pereira saw a mark on the floor of her kitchen which over a period of seven days turned into a face. Mrs Pereira was thought to be a medium, who might therefore be the 'cause' of this phenomenon.

The apparition scared both Mrs Pereira and her husband and one of her sons, Miguel, destroyed the image. However, another face began to form. The image was a very clear one and the local coucil cut out the portion of the stone floor containing the face and it was later exhibited on the wall. Analysis of the floor showed no reason for the apparition.

When the damaged floor was repaired a new face appeared and Miguel destroyed this also, sharing his parents' fears. After the floor had been repaired yet again another face appeared and over the year several different faces joined it. Some of the faces actually disappeared in December but new ones took their place. At one point crosses also appeared on the floor.

The house became something of a local tourist attraction, so much so that police had to control crowds that formed in the streets around it.

In April 1972 a Professor De Argumosa came from Madrid after hearing of the case. He declared that he had documents at the University of Salamanca which showed that a governor of Granada born in Bélmez in the seventeenth century had murdered five members of a local family, the murder having taken place somewhere near or even possibly in the haunted house itself. Since the house was close to a church it was also possible that the building was on the site of a former cemetery, and indeed when the floor was dug up human remains were found some eight to nine feet down. The cemetery theory was borne out by the fact that human remains were also found beneath neighbouring houses.

Professor De Argumosa also had recordings of sounds that had been heard in the house, including the voice of a child. The sounds resembled 'a mixture of hell and a brothel'. Maria Pereira, who, as mentioned, was widely reported to be the medium in the household, had not been present while the recordings were made.

On 6 June 1972 yet another face appeared on the floor, and at a later point it even seemed to change its expression. Other faces appeared around it later.

Experiments were conducted which involved covering the kitchen floor in foil (to reduce the opportunities for fraud and insulate the surface from the effects of the atmosphere), but the same apparitions formed under the foil, which had to be removed later because of the effects of humidity. In order to conduct as serious an investigation as possible Professor De Argumosa paid half of the cost of converting another room in the house to a kitchen to allow the old 'haunted' one to be left alone for study. Faces formed in the 'replacement' kitchen.

José Martinez Romero, an author-investigator, visited the Pereira home on 3 September 1981 and described an extraordinary incident. Romero reported he was able to witness with others small faces appearing and disappearing at random in the new kitchen. Romero considered that this may have been some form of hallucination since he had taken photographs, none of which showed the images. Romero later visited the house with Andrew MacKenzie in 1988. Of that visit Romero noted Mac-Kenzie's amazement but he felt more amazed himself that the faces had changed dramatically; the colours had become darker and with less definition in the outline. Romero had also indicated that he believed there was a connection between Maria's state of health and the images on the floor; when she was feeling ill the images would drain in colour. Romero believed that the images were disappearing and would 'die' when Maria did.

There has been speculation that Mrs Pereira was somehow projecting the image in a process similar to 'thoughtography', Ted Serios' claim that he could imprint a picture on to photographic film by the power of his mind. Perhaps Mrs Pereira could imprint pictures directly into the stonework of the kitchen floor. There has been a great deal of controversy about the House of the Faces, but, whether genuine or a hoax, there is no doubt that this is one of the most remarkable manifestations of recent times. There have, however, been many other incidences of images of faces appearing: in 1891 the face of a woman who had recently died was discovered etched in glass on a windowpane at her home in Indiana and though others tried to rub it off, it could only be removed by her son; in 1923, a face believed to be that of Dr Liddell, the Dean of Christchurch, Oxford, who had died in 1898, was reported to have appeared on a plaster wall of the cathedral.

We were interested in this particular case as one of the authors (J.S.) had recently been invited to examine a similar report about a location in the south of England. The images are not particularly clear but are definitely of interest and, given the nature of the 'development' of other similar phenomena, we shall watch to see whether the images become clearer over time. Unfortunately, at the time of writing, permission had not been given to disclose the whereabouts of these faces as the owners of the property were afraid of a 'tourist invasion'.

The House of the Faces has been the subject of much controversy and there are reports that a commission formed to investigate the claims determined that chemicals were used to create the faces which indicated fraud. They were said to be chemicals that could be purchased in drugstores, used for cleaning. The commission also stated, 'We could even determine the size of the brush hairs of the brush used to paint the faces.' However tempting it may be to write the case off, however, there are still the questions raised by the many witnesses who saw the faces forming or changing; studies of the paranormal are hardly ever clear cut or simple!

The Lady in the Guest House
D: 1973
L: Penzance, Cornwall
S: Andrew MacKenzie

John Jenson stayed at a guest house in Penzance, Cornwall on the night of 25 April 1973. The house had not yet been opened for the season but the owner agreed to give Mr Jenson and his wife two nights' accommodation.

After a meal in the town the couple retired to bed at around eleven o'clock in the evening, Mrs Jenson almost instantly falling asleep.

Mr Jenson became aware of a presence in the room which he believed to be female. Indeed Jenson described his feelings as identical to the feelings a man gets when he meets a woman and falls in love. Jenson reported that the presence closed in on him and surrounded him, leaving him with a feeling of ecstasy for an indeterminate period; he lost all sense of time. The presence apparently drifted away at last and faded completely.

On 18 October 1975, Mr Jenson stayed in the house again. He woke up in the early hours of the morning, had a glass of water to drink, and then saw the figure of a woman standing by the window. She was dressed in a white nightdress and was brushing her long grey-blonde hair. She looked pensive and sad. Having put her finger to her lips as if to silence him, she disappeared. She had the appearance of a youthful 65-year-old and Mr Jenson 'felt the same feelings as he had on the earlier occasion'.

Two nights later, Mrs Jenson woke up with a feeling as if her hand was being held by a pair of hands which she thought were 'the hands of an old woman'. Mrs Jenson found the experience frightening.

The owner of the guest house was aware of some strange matters relating to that room but for obvious reasons chose not to broadcast it.

The Large Fireplace
D: Late 19th or early 20th century
L: Buckinghamshire
S: Alice Pollock (*Portrait of My Victorian Youth*)

Having purchased a cottage in Buckinghamshire, Lady Thomson asked psychometrist Alice Pollock to use her psychic powers to discover whether the cottage would be lucky for her. Lady Thomson drew a plan of the cottage for Miss Pollock who was apparently at once drawn to a room to the right of the front door which she instantly described as 'a small room and there is a large old-fashioned fireplace where logs are burning'.

Lady Thomson was adamant that Miss Pollock was incorrect, believing it to be ordinary, and modern in style.

Miss Pollock was not put out; she maintained her concentration on that particular room and saw a young girl badly injured by fire being carried out of the room by grieving people to another room where she then died.

A week after this experience Lady Thomson visited the cottage and discovered that workmen renovating it had stripped away the modern fireplace and located an old open fireplace behind it, exactly as described by Miss Pollock. One villager was able to supply some details about the house to Lady Thomson, telling her, 'There was an old open fireplace there many years ago, but there was a dreadful accident when a little girl was left alone in the room. She fell into the fire and was badly burned, and she died after they had moved her into the room on the other side of the passage.'

London Bridge
D: 1971
L: Lake Havasu City, Arizona, USA
S: Legend

On 10 October 1971 the Lord Mayor of London, Sir Peter Studd, along with Jack Williams, the Governor of Arizona, officially dedicated London Bridge which had been re-positioned at Lake Havasu City in Arizona. The bridge had been dismantled stone by stone, shipped to America and rebuilt as a tourist attraction alongside the 'English Village' which consists of a 'typically American' view of England – double-decker bus, London taxi and so on.

Since that time there have been many reports of ghosts in Victorian dress strolling across London Bridge in the evenings, presumably recreating their walks of yesteryear. If the theory of recording-type ghosts is a valid one then certain conditions are required to recreate the recording; it certainly seems unlikely that conditions in Arizona would match anything in Victorian London!

To be frank, the tale sounds very much like an American version of an English ghost story and probably about as realistic as the English Village.

The Lonely Child
D: 1979
L: Grant, New England, USA
S: Andrew MacKenzie

In a case investigated by William Roll of the Psychical Research Foundation of North Carolina and reported by Andrew MacKenzie in his book *The Seen and the Unseen* there were repeated sightings of a small boy dressed in white. The sightings took place in a house in Grant, New England and the family concerned were given the pseudonym 'Berini'.

On 9 March 1981 Mrs Berini was at home with the two children from her previous marriage. Her husband was on night shift at a factory.

In the early hours of the morning she thought she saw her son outside her bedroom door but checked and found him asleep. The figure she had seen earlier then reappeared and she was able to see that it was much shorter than her fifteen-year-old son, more like a boy of about eight or nine years old, dressed in a white shirt, pants and shoes. She watched the apparition for something like two hours as it walked up and down in the hallway; she felt unafraid and peaceful.

At about the same time on 20 March the figure was seen again and this time Mrs Berini heard it speak. It must have been a sad experience for the child said, *'Where do all the lonely people go?'* and, *'Where do I belong?'*

On 23 March Mr Berini also saw the same form in the bedroom. It also spoke to him, telling him that a lie had been told and that the truth should be known. Mr Berini also saw the apparition for some time walking up and down the hallway until it disappeared.

On one occasion Mrs Berini's daughter Daisy, aged eleven, the child of a previous marriage, saw the figure in the hall and dived for cover under the bed sheets with her mother. The best guess as to the identity of the figure is that it might have been the apparition of her husband's uncle, who had died as a child of eight some fifty years before. Although Mr Berini's father could not remember how his brother had been dressed for burial a neighbour believed that the boy had been buried in the white suit he had worn to Communion. On one occasion the apparition knelt down in the hall in front of Mr Berini and apparently tried to pick up the hall rug. Mr Berini assumed it was looking for something and removed the rug and eventually the floorboard, finding a small metal medallion beneath the floor. However, since that had almost certainly been dropped there during the original laying of the floor (the boards were apparently firmly interlocked) and since the house was built when the deceased child had only just been born it seems unlikely that the medallion belonged to the child.

In the course of several statements made by the apparition it appeared that the lie it had referred to might relate to its twin brother who it blamed for 'taking something from the house'.

In a very interesting example of telephone interference – for which there are precedents in many paranormal subject areas – Mr Berini telephoned his father to tell him that his deceased younger brother was likely to call on him, as a result of something the apparition had said. Every time the young boy's name was mentioned the telephone went dead.

Some poltergeist activity was associated with the apparition; many times the telephone next to Mr Berini's bed would fly across the room and the bedroom closet door would repeatedly slam; Mrs Berini believed this might be the result of ignoring the figure. They had been ignoring the boy at the suggestion of the House Superior at the Catholic Community.

Although this would appear to be the most persistent haunting experienced by the family it was not the only one. In May 1979 Mrs Berini had heard crying in the house which sounded like, 'Mama, mama, it is Serena.' It occurred several times and was heard also by her husband. Her father-in-law remembered that he had had a sister called Serena who had died at the house at the age of five. (It should be noted that the voice, by contrast, had been attributed to a child of around the age of two.) The night after Mrs Berini heard 'Serena' in May 1979, one of her children from a former marriage nearly died as a result of an anaesthetic mistake during an operation. When the voice was heard in June 1979 it preceded a stroke which afflicted Mr Berini's grandmother and it was apparently also heard on the night before her death in November.

Another figure was seen in the Berini home by Mr Berini: a short, hunched, grotesque figure in black with very large feet that seemed quite demon-like and spoke of 'really disgusting things', principally sexual. There were several poltergeist-like attacks on Mrs Berini associated with the apparition and for a time they considered that the apparition might have represented Mr Berini's grandmother who had died two years earlier, as referred to above. She had apparently been angry with Mrs Berini and threatened to 'get even with her' as she blamed her for the death of one of her sons from a heart attack, allegedly brought on by the Berini's marriage.

Other poltergeist activity was reported: lights turning on and off, water turning off, disturbances in bedclothes and movements of religious articles.

After some six months the poltergeist activity ceased, possibly due to an exorcism performed in the house but also perhaps because poltergeist activity does tend to die away after a period of time, six months being quite an extended time for the average poltergeist.

Mrs Berini completed the Wilson and Barber Inventory of Childhood Memories and Imaginings, designed to measure a person's tendency to fantasise. Of 48 possibilities Mrs Berini only indicated two and Mr Berini only nineteen. Mr Berini had commented that he had no previous experiences of apparitions and did not actually believe in such things, presumably prior to his sightings.

William Roll was director of research at the Psychical Research Foundation. He investigated the claims and his analysis of the case indicated many possible explanations, including the possibility that, as a result of the stresses within it, the family might have 'constructed' the phenomena themselves.

Man in a Homburg Hat

D: 1950

L: Southsea, Portsmouth, Hampshire

S: Direct

Judy (who reported the incident of 'The Man in the Dressing-Gown', see pp. 234–5) told us a more menacing story from her childhood around 1950. Her father had died when she was young and she and her mother had moved in with her grandparents in Southsea in Hampshire.

The house was described by Judy as 'ordinary, turn-of-the-century Edwardian, detached, in a residential avenue in Southsea'.

Judy said, 'There was something very strange about that house that I was very aware of, my mother was aware of to a degree and my grandparents not at all. My mother always said that it was something that didn't like the young so the younger you were the more horrors it gave you.'

The report was less one of sightings and far more one of 'presence'. However, there was one sighting in the house not witnessed by Judy. She related the story of her grandmother and great-aunt who were alone in the house one afternoon. One of them went out of the room to go to the toilet and, glancing up, saw a man looking over the top of the stairwell a couple of flights above. There should not have been anybody in the house; the women thought it must be an intruder and – obviously not wilting wallflowers – they each grabbed a poker and set off in pursuit. They never found anybody or any sign of a break-in. Judy described the two women as not being prone to fantasy or flights of imagination.

Judy's one sighting in the house, was a vague impression consisting of a shadow which she was certain would not have formed given the light conditions and arrangement of objects in the hallway. She described it as 'a man in a Homburg hat'. To throw the shadow where it was Judy was sure that the figure would have to have been standing outside her grandfather's room just out of her sight from where she was.

What Judy described as 'the real thing' was her awareness of something she described as 'really awful'. It used to come into her room, she could hear footsteps across the floor. Even in the front room at night she could hear footsteps crossing the floor heading towards a basket chair which would then creak. She had considered, and was aware of, the possibility of 'recording-type' ghost sounds which might have accounted for that. Judy, however, could also hear breathing, which is also not impossible in a recording-type ghost, but perhaps was also responsible for her feeling it as an actual presence. Although her family tried to convince her of other explanations they simply did not seem to fit the bill and did not satisfy her; Judy remained unconvinced of anything other than that she had felt a real presence.

Judy says her family were very sympathetic to her fears, whilst believing them to be only imaginings. They moved her from the room she was in to another room; unfortunately, Judy now believes that 'the room they moved me into was the hub of whatever was wrong with the house'.

In that room Judy woke up one night and was convinced that in the corner there was 'something absolutely awful'. There was nothing to be seen but she could sense it 'pulsating'. Judy acknowledged that to claim the entity was pulsating when she could neither see nor hear it was 'a weird thing to say', but nonetheless she was certain of it. In fact, such a claim of certainty with no apparent reason is quite common in such reports.

With each pulse the thing was getting bigger and more powerful. Judy was convinced it was totally focused on her and she found it 'absolutely terrifying'. She wanted to put the light on but simply could not move. She was 'absolutely rigid in the bed', and pouring with sweat. Eventually she was able to free herself from the grip of terror and get the light on; 'it didn't make any difference at all'. She was convinced it was still there and growing but with nothing to be seen.

Judy managed to break free from the room eventually and ran shaking to her mother, jumping into her bed. She was shaking so much that the bed actually rattled. Her parents tried to convince her that she had had a nightmare but she was quite certain that was not the case.

At a much later time, following the death of both Judy's grandparents, her mother went back to clear out the house after it had been sold. Although it was the middle of summer Judy's mother remembered that although the house had only been empty for a couple of weeks 'she had never walked into such cold in her life'.

Maurice Maeterlinck's Discovery
 D: 1911
 L: St Wandrille Abbey, Rouen, Normandy, France
 S: Peter Underwood

Maurice Maeterlinck was a famous playwright who won the Nobel Prize for literature in 1911. The man who penned *Interior* and *The Bluebird* was fascinated by the paranormal and made several references to clairvoyants and the survival of the spirit in his works.

Maeterlinck and his wife lived in St Wandrille Abbey, a converted Norman abbey near Rouen in France, which was reputed to be haunted. One night in 1911 the Russian actor, Constantin Stanislavsky, stayed as a guest of the Maeterlincks. An American lady was also staying in another part of the house. In the middle of the night both Stanislavsky and the Maeterlincks were awakened by the screams of the American lady who claimed that she had seen the ghostly apparition of a deformed monk.

Maeterlinck was not one to ignore his own psychic abilities and although this was the first encounter with the paranormal in that house, that very night the various people there made an attempt to communicate with the spirits in the building. There was some limited success with table knocking and movement and a spirit made the claim that he was a monk named Bertrand. It was Stanislavsky who found a plaque in the old abbey on which he could decipher the words 'Bertrand: *pax vobiscum*: AD 1693'.

Maeterlinck believed that Bertrand might possibly have a connection with a secret room which was supposed to exist somewhere in the abbey. With Stanislavsky, he searched the house and particularly the panelling looking for secret compartments; eventually Maeterlinck found a hollow panel and pushed it open. Behind the panel they found the bones of a man who had been terribly deformed in life and who must have died walled up where he was discovered by the group.

The Church of Marton
D: c. 1970
L: Gainsborough, Lincolnshire
S: Andrew MacKenzie

Marton is a small hamlet at the fork of the A156 and the old Roman road, the A1500 in Lincolnshire. In 1891 the church there was restored and rebuilt.

Shortly after arriving in Marton to take over as vicar the Rev. Alan Taylor 'became aware of a curious circumstance at the parish communion'. Without actually seeing an apparition, the vicar 'formed a clear impression' of a bald-crowned elderly man with a mane of white hair flowing over his ears. Most significantly, he was thought to be wearing a dark-green cassock. Without experiencing anything more than a vague feeling, the vicar believed that the apparition was in some way connected with one of the servers at the church who was then thirteen. Two years after this event, when the reverend wrote to Andrew MacKenzie to report his experience, the boy was still serving at the church though the apparition had been felt less regularly.

Around a year after first sensing the presence, the vicar was talking to an old lady who had been in the parish for many years. She claimed that the description fitted a choir member who attended the church at the turn of the century. On being rebuilt in 1891 the church had adopted a colour scheme of green and red and the choir were given green cassocks, somewhat exceptionally, though they were replaced with the more traditional black just before World War I.

The Rev. Taylor may have had some of the qualities of a medium; he said that at funerals he often experienced emotional images which were not his own, yet he pointed out that at a funeral he would be the one person there *without* deep commitment to the deceased.

The Rev. Taylor obviously kept his feet very much on the ground in reporting his experiences; he did not put much stress on them as he could not identify the source or verify the feeling; in any case they were not very frequent, although they seemed very real to him. Rev. Taylor made the point that he believed the state of the emotion mattered more than the state of mind.

Minsden Chapel

D: 20th century
L: Nr. Hitchin, Hertfordshire
S: Peter Underwood

Minsden Chapel was built in the fourteenth century and in more recent years had been leased for life to author Reginald Hine.

Hine himself was something of a character; he was a respected solicitor and the author of the book *Confessions of an Un-common Attorney*, and a noted historian and bibliophile. To demonstrate his fairly uncommon character, he issued a warning in his writing that after his death his ashes would, he hoped, be scattered at Minsden Chapel and that, concerning trespassers and sacrilegious persons, he had pursued them with the law during life so he would pursue them as a ghost after his death.

Minsden Chapel was reputed to be haunted, the sounds of *'sweet and plaintive music'* had been heard and there were occasional sightings of a figure in white. Hine told Peter Underwood of the legends, which included a murdered nun, a phantom monk, the ringing of the lost bells of Minsden and the disappearance of the ghost monk to the sound of the music. With Hine's permission, Underwood decided to spend All Hallows' Eve at Minsden. (This was the night of the year when the ghost monk was reputed to walk.) He went with his brother, and another man, Tom Brown.

As soon as he arrived at the chapel, Underwood heard the sound of faint and distant music which he could not put down to any ordinary explanation as the ruins of the chapel were extremely isolated. The sound was heard also by Tom Brown but not by Underwood's brother who was only just behind him.

During the first All Hallows' Eve spent at Minsden with Tom Brown and another, Derek Clarke, all the witnesses saw what appeared to be a white cross glowing on the wall though all admitted it could have been a trick of the moonlight, though they felt it worthy of note.

The manner of Hine's death was rather extraordinary too. On retiring from the legal profession, he was talking one day to some friends on Hitchin railway station as the train approached. At one point he very casually said, '*Wait a minute*' and walked into the path of the train. He was killed instantly. He left a note addressed to the local coroner.

Old Doggett

D: 18th & 19th century
L: Eastbury House, nr. Tarrant Gunville, Dorset
S: Keith Poole

Eastbury House near the Dorset village of Tarrant Gunville, like many of Britain's stately homes, has a chequered and fascinating history. It was begun in 1717 for George Doddington who died in 1720 leaving his estate to his eccentric nephew George Budd Doddington.

The younger Doddington spent another fortune on the property and after his death it was sold to the Duke of Buckingham and partially demolished twenty years later. One wing only remains standing today.

In the forty years that Doddington occupied the property he lived lavishly; *so* lavishly that even he was unable to maintain the property. At one point he offered £200 per year and free accommodation to anyone who was prepared to run the place. No one took up the offer.

Much to the surprise of the locals, Doddington engaged a steward named William Doggett, known as 'Old Doggett', a man instantly recognisable by his breeches tied with yellow silk ribbons who was also known to steal from his employer, particularly when Doddington was absent and living in his London villa.

Doggett was trying to help his brother to avoid bankruptcy, principally by fraudulently selling the building materials left around the house, which belonged to his master. Since Doddington always announced when he would be returning to the house, Doggett had worked out that he could always repay the stolen money before he was caught out. Inevitably, on one occasion, Doddington returned without warning. Doggett realised that the game was up, went into his room and shot himself.

There were reports of Old Doggett being seen around the house and on the drive from the park gates, identifiable by the yellow ribbons on his breeches. In 1845, those who doubted that he was a ghost had their minds put at rest when workmen rebuilding the Church of St Mary in Tarrant Gunville exhumed the skeleton of a man with yellow silk ribbons around his legs.

Old Madame

D: 19th century

L: Lew House, Tavistock, Devon

S: The Rev. Sabine Baring-Gould (*Early Reminiscences*)

Old Madame is a classic White Lady ghost who haunts Lew House near Tavistock in Devon. Old Madame is thought to be the ghost of Margaret Belfield who married William Gould in 1740. Gould died in 1766, and Margaret followed him on 10 April 1795.

The White Lady is reputed to walk at night along a long upstairs corridor extending from the main staircase of the house to stairs at the other end of the building. The Rev. Sabine Baring-Gould who first reported this apparition, in 1923, told how his mother heard 'high heeled shoes, walking slowly along the corridor' but saw nothing despite adequate illumination into the corridor. Even when she followed the footsteps she saw no one.

On another occasion Baring-Gould's sister was sitting in her room writing a letter when she heard the footsteps; on opening the door she found no one. (Baring-Gould offered rats as an explanation for these footsteps.)

The reverend's daughter Barbara reported seeing a lady in blue who would come into her nursery and look at her, sometimes sitting by her bed. Another daughter, Diana, was in the care of a nurse who had fallen asleep. She was awoken by a tap on the door and a female voice that said, 'It is time for her to have her medicine.' When the nurse opened the door no one was there. (Although Baring-Gould's wife had not gone to warn the nurse he believed it was probably another servant who had spoken.) One night Baring-Gould was sleeping in the room in which Old Madame had died and his wife was caring for their daughter Beatrice (born 1874) who was ill. His wife had been trying to sleep in the room with Beatrice but woke her husband, telling him, 'I cannot sleep. I hear people tramping, carrying something down the stairs.' There was no apparent explanation for this and he argued that perhaps a windy night was causing noises. The following day, believing that Beatrice was not in a serious condition, they went to Launceston; later that day on their return Beatrice died in her mother's arms. Her coffin was carried down the staircase, making the same noise 'as my wife had heard on the night before her death'. Was premonition involved, or a ghostly warning?

In 1918 two nurses living with the family left because 'they had been frightened by seeing a female form at night walking in the nursery, and stooping over the beds of the children'.

On another occasion Alister Grant, who was smitten with the family's governess Miss Wilson, was walking along the road when he saw a figure he thought to be Miss Wilson walking along the avenue running parallel to it. He leaned over the wall to speak to her but as the figure disappeared behind trees he remembered that Miss Wilson was away on holiday and that the family was away in Bude. 'He became frightened and ran as fast as his legs would carry him.'

Local people often claimed that Madame Gould could be seen, dressed in white, scooping up handfuls of water from a nearby lake; in other accounts she is often seen 'sparkling as if covered with water drops'. The fact that many of these sightings were by people returning from the market or the local pubs may have played a hand, of course!

A Mr Symonds returning from America and unaware of Madame Gould's earlier death was riding a horse through Lew Valley when he saw the lady dressed in white satin sitting on a plough. He could see her face clearly in the moonlight as she was gazing up at the moon and he recognised her at once. He took off his hat and called out, 'I wish you a very good night, Madame'; she apparently bowed and waved in return. He thought at the time that she was looking very good for her age and only discovered later that she had been buried seven days previously.

Other people in the area saw the White Lady glide over the pond and there were many connections over the years between her apparition and water. Notably, when Baring-Gould and a solicitor friend, Mr Keeling, were in Lew House together in 1877, they heard a sound from the hall, a 'dragging sound as of a trailing silk or satin dress', but Baring-Gould considered that it sounded like a drift of rain that had swept the window and was surprised to find that it was perfectly dry outside. The implication would seem to be that Old Madame's dress may have sounded not just as if it was dragging but dragging heavily as if water laden.

One woman, Patience Kite, stealing apples from an orchard, was either struck by a severe guilty conscience or encountered Old Madame in guardian mood. Although this happened when Patience was a young girl she maintained the truth of the story throughout her life. Having filled her pockets with apples and holding one in her hand ready to eat, she suddenly encountered the apparition dressed in white standing in her way and pointing at the apple. She threw the apple away and ran across the orchard but encountered the White Lady again standing in front of her, pointing at her pockets. It was only when the girl had discarded all the stolen apples that the apparition vanished.

At Baring-Gould's daughter Margaret's 'coming out' ball many of the guests asked who was the 'strange lady in a dark dress with lace, and grey hair whom they had seen, who spoke to no one and was addressed by no one'. One report said that she had been seen standing under a portrait of Margaret Belfield and looked remarkably similar, though older than the portrait. Baring-Gould confirmed that there was no such guest at the ball.

Another friend reported to Baring-Gould that he had entered a room to find 'an old gentleman with either a white wig or with powdered hair, and opposite him an elderly lady in satin'. On inspecting the room Baring-Gould found no one but noticed that the seats the apparitions had occupied were those in which, on weekend evenings, parson Elford and Madame Gould had sat together.

Baring-Gould speculates that the White Lady may have been Susanna Gould, who died in her bridal clothes in 1729 and that the 'identity' of the White Lady was only 'granted' to Margaret Belfield by local superstition.

Phantom Smoke
   D: c. 1930
   L: Well Walk, Hampstead, London
   S: Peter Underwood

The actor Leslie Banks and his wife Gwendoline lived at a house in Well Walk, Hampstead until Banks' death in 1935. One of their daughters would frequently ask about the 'nice lady in a violet silk dress' that she and her sisters spoke to at the top of the stairs. She was never seen anywhere else and never when the parents were around. It appeared that the figure was seen by all three daughters but never by the adults.

On Leslie Banks' death the house was taken over by William and Patricia Johnson. About six months after moving in the couple were sitting quietly before dinner one evening, William reading the newspaper and his wife knitting. His wife noticed wisps of cigar smoke drifting in the air above his head, quite unsurprising were it not for the fact that William was not smoking a cigar! Together they watched the smoke apparently appear from nowhere, twist and curl in the air and then disappear.

Investigation failed to find the source of the smoke. Over a couple of years they witnessed the same event some four or five times.

When the Johnsons gave up the house during the Second World War several families lived in it as it had been requisitioned by the local council to house poorer people. Many of these people reported strange noises – sounds of objects moving, coughing and groaning – and at least two families refused to stay there because of those noises. It has been speculated that these arose due to the building work necessary to convert the house to its wartime use. Structural alterations in houses quite often bring about the onset of haunting phenomena (see the case of Royston Old Post Office, for example, on pp. 112–13).

After the war the Johnsons moved back to the house but did not report anything paranormal in the years that followed. The house had had an interesting history dating from around the beginning of the eighteenth century; it was occupied by, amongst others, a sea captain and his spinster sister, and John Keats and his brother (who died there). During excavation work, when the house was being fitted out during the war, a young woman's skeleton was found buried under the old kitchen.

Polstead Rectory

D: c. 1950
L: Nr. Hadleigh, Suffolk
S: Various

Shortly after having settled in at Polstead Rectory near Hadleigh, Suffolk in 1978, the Rev. Hayden Foster and his wife apparently asked a neighbour to help them as they could not spend another night on those premises. In the short time they had been there they had experienced strange noises and feelings. Mrs Margot Foster believed that some entity had attempted to strangle her.

The neighbours knew that the previous occupants had also experienced strange paranormal events during their stay at the rectory, returning to Ireland shortly afterwards. A friend reported at the time, that 'They had had a very bad time and had returned home to get over it. They were said to be rational people, making their comments all the more plausible. It seems that similar things had happened twenty-five years ago and there had been other claims in the subsequent years.'

However, the wife of a former rector stated that although she had heard sounds she had never felt any malevolence from any ghost's presence and didn't particularly think about it. Mrs Anne Simpson of the parochial church council said that she believed the place to be haunted and that there had been an exorcism some years ago.

Sir Ralph Richardson

D: 20th century
L: South of France
S: Peter Underwood

Sir Ralph Richardson and his wife took a holiday at a villa in the south of France. One night Sir Ralph was awoken by his wife telling him that someone was in the room. Sir Ralph could apparently see no one and said so to his wife who remained adamant that someone had been by the bed, 'looking at me'. Sir Ralph checked around the room and looked down the passageway outside but could find no sign of anyone. His wife gave a description of a brown figure; she had no other description except 'the impression of brownness'.

In a later conversation with a local lady who knew the history of the area they mentioned their villa and asked about its history. The villa turned out to be owned by the lady's own daughter who was at that time in England; it had fallen into disrepair and had been restored by an American lady who had lovingly attended personally to the details all around the building. Unfortunately she had had to return to America, was sad to leave and had never been able to return, having died suddenly. The woman was described as 'striking to look at': she was half Native American, and her nickname had been 'The Brown One'.

It was Lady Richardson's opinion that perhaps she had indeed now returned to her beloved house.

The Church of St Magnus the Martyr

D: Early 20th century
L: Lower Thames St, City of London
S: Philip Paul

The early eighteenth-century church of St Magnus the Martyr stands near the Monument to the Great Fire of London, in the City of London. According to three main accounts of sightings, the principal ghost of the church appeared to be a monk. The sightings took place before the Second World War and were outlined to investigator Philip Paul by the then rector, the Rev. H.J. Fynes-Clinton.

The first sighting occurred beneath a picture of Christ near the tabernacle in the church. It was seen by Mrs Gallaher, wife of one of the former rectors. She had seen a kneeling hooded figure, silent and motionless, from the side. Because of the angle and the hood she could not see a face. Within a few seconds of sighting the apparition it faded away.

The second sighting was reported by a church worker, Miss Few, who was apparently unaware of Mrs Gallaher's earlier experience. Miss Few saw the apparition in the vestry. She was sitting in the vestry doing some embroidery when she noticed, out of the corner of her eye, someone standing near her. Being somewhat deaf she was quite used to people being able to get near her without her hearing them and she paid little attention, believing that the rector had come into the room. The figure was wearing a straight cassock-like garment. Eventually she raised her head to look at the figure and was confronted by a very frightening sight: the figure was facing her and inside the dark cowl which should have surrounded a head there was nothing at all. She abandoned her work, and ran to find the Rev. Fynes-Clinton who calmed her down. When they returned to the vestry there was no figure to be seen.

The third witness was the verger who, again, was unaware of former experiences. He had apparently seen a monk-like figure gazing down at the tomb of Miles Coverdale, the former rector of St Magnus in the 16th century and the one person still buried in the church. By the time he found Fynes-Clinton and told him his story he was in a state of agitation and shock.

Fynes-Clinton had not experienced anything himself but was not sceptical of the claims and believed that the monk-like figure was probably that of Miles Coverdale himself.

A seance was conducted using a ouija board. Present were Daphne Lloyd-Evans, her husband David, Fynes-Clinton and Philip Paul. Also present was Gordon Banks, a press-photographer friend of Paul's. Daphne and David Lloyd-Evans were blindfolded during their trip to the church so they were unaware of precisely where they were when they were undertaking the seance.

David, a hypnotist, put Mrs Lloyd-Evans into a trance to enable her to receive the signals which she translated into automatic writing – her method of communication. The seance did not indicate Miles Coverdale as a source but 'located' one

'Elfreda' who appeared to date back to around the year 912 and a Walter De Courcy who was there around the year 1250. Nothing specific in the seance seemed to indicate the monk-like figure.

Just after the seance Fynes-Clinton confided that he himself had just had his own strange sighting, on the previous Friday. He had been standing near the door when he had seen a black-clad figure moving away from the altar to behind a pillar from which it did not reappear. Fynes-Clinton believed it was his verger but the verger in fact told Fynes-Clinton he too had heard strange footsteps in the church and they were certain that no one else had been there at the time.

The Salutation Hotel
D: 1975
L: Perth, Scotland
S: Peter Underwood

In mid-August 1975 Jack and Gwen Mott were staying in the Salutation Hotel in Perth, Scotland, during a touring holiday. The hotel has associations with Bonnie Prince Charlie (though frankly most older buildings in Scotland seem to). During the night they slept in single beds on either side of the bedroom door.

The night was very hot; suddenly Jack felt that his back was cold. He had been lying on his side with his back to the door. When he turned over he saw the figure of a Scottish soldier standing next to the door, unmoving but apparently quite solid. He was wearing green tartan and seemed not at all frightening. In fact Jack was able to turn over and go back to sleep without fear. At a later point Jack woke up again and turned back and the soldier was still there exactly as before. Gradually the soldier faded away.

Gwen was quite regretful that she had not been woken by her husband as she felt that she would have liked to have seen the ghost.

'Shoo!'
D: 1950
L: Anglesey, Wales
S: Rev. J. Aelwyn Roberts

In 1950 the Rev. J. Aelwyn Roberts, together with Elwyn Roberts, a member of the Psychic Research Society and an 'ultra-sensitive' (this clergyman often took such a researcher with him on his investigations as he regarded himself as virtually without any psychic abilities of his own), went to a house in Anglesey belonging to Peter and Bridget and their three-year-old son.

Evenings there had become something of a family ritual: Peter would arrive home around about six o'clock and play games with their son, Oliver, until around seven o'clock when the son would go off to bed.

At nine o'clock, just when Big Ben was striking for the news on television, according to the narrative, Oliver would come down the stairs as if sleepwalking. Each night Bridget would then take him back up to his cot. On the one night, when Peter went up to see what was happening just before nine o'clock, nothing at all happened and Peter heard Big Ben striking on the television while Oliver remained fast asleep. Whenever Peter did this Oliver would not move; whenever Peter stayed downstairs Oliver would turn up in the living room as if sleepwalking.

Eventually Peter asked his son why he left his bed in that way each night.

Oliver told his father that an old man had told him to get out of bed. He described him as an old man wearing a long nightdress and a 'Noddy' cap. The ghost apparently 'shooed' Oliver out of the room telling him to go to his parents. The 'sensitive', Elwyn Roberts, immediately felt a presence when he entered the house and paced around the child's room. Eventually he decided, that if the child's bed were moved, the haunting would stop. They did so, moving the bed with Oliver in it, and the group went back downstairs. Elwyn explained that there would be no further trouble and indeed when the vicar checked with the parents, Oliver's nine o'clock waking had come to an end on that night and had not recurred.

According to Elwyn, the bed was in the ghost's way, where it preferred to walk.

An 86-year-old neighbour living in the same area had a long memory of the previous owners of Peter and Bridget's house, recalling a sea captain named Lucas who had retired to the house together with his two daughters, Lucille and Victoria; he was assumed to be a widower as no wife was ever mentioned. Captain

Lucas was apparently very fond of whisky though he was never seen to be drunk. But in his last days he was said to have drunk two bottles a day and not even to have bothered to dress himself. He used to run around the house all day in a long nightshirt and a funny sleeping cap. Aelwyn was sure that it must have been bad-tempered Captain Lucas who was shooing Oliver back to his parents each night.

The Tape-Recorded Ghost

D: 20th century
L: Silverstone, Northamptonshire
S: Joan Forman

In her book, *The Mask of Time*, Joan Forman relates the story of an electrician who worked during the day in a Nissen hut on an old RAF airfield near Silverstone motor-racing circuit. He received complaints from a couple living nearby that they could not sleep because of the noise of his working during the night. The electrician did not work at night and knew that he was not responsible, but he assumed, reasonably, that someone was using his work-place and tools for an unauthorised purpose when he was not there.

To catch them out he left a tape recorder recording overnight in the building but when he played it back he found that it was still blank. On an impulse he sent the tape to a specialist and it was found that if the tape was played back at a different frequency all the sounds of a workshop – exactly those complained of by the couple nearby – could be heard.

Thwarted Mum-to-be

D: 1951
L: Tunbridge Wells, Kent
S: Andrew MacKenzie

In a cottage in Tunbridge Wells in 1951, Mr Robert Hughes was sleeping in a double bed with his young son Malcolm. In another room his wife was sleeping with Malcolm's older brother Anthony.

Mr Hughes woke to see the figure of a woman standing next to the bed leaning across him and 'staring intently at Malcolm'. Malcolm was sleeping soundly. The figure was fairly short, between 5 ft. 4 in. and 5 ft. 6 in. The woman, Hughes estimated, as being around 47 years old, her grey hair tied in a bun. Of her clothing Hughes described her dress as heavy, coloured green and brown and thickly pleated.

On being seen by Hughes the figure 'glided' away and went to the room in which Mrs Hughes and Anthony were sleeping. As the figure approached the side of their bed it slowly faded from sight.

When Mr Hughes described the apparition to his wife she said at once, that she thought it was Mrs Phillips. Mrs Ada Phillips had once lived in the cottage and had known Mrs Hughes. The Phillips were to adopt a baby but unfortunately Mrs Phillips had died suddenly the night before the adopted child was due to arrive. It was Mr Hughes' belief that Mrs Phillips was now visiting the house to see the children that were occupying it, having 'missed out' on children of her own.

Over the next twenty years Mr Hughes saw the apparition four times. The first time he saw her he tried to grab at her clothing but found it was 'insubstantial; like cigarette smoke'.

The Tulip Staircase
D: 1966
L: Queen's House, Greenwich
S: Various

This case rests entirely on a photograph taken at the Queen's House in Greenwich, on the Tulip Staircase. Apart from this, there is no known history of haunting in the building. A Canadian clergyman visiting England took photographs of the staircase while on an archetypal tourist tour; when it was developed there appeared to be two outlines of figures climbing the staircase. Photographic analysis indicated no double exposure which might have suggested that there was somebody on the staircase at the time. This is thought to be unlikely and the photographer believed no one was on the staircase when he took the picture, hence the ghost theory.

Brian Tremain, the museum's own photographer, took his own photograph in an attempt to determine if the 'ghost' photograph could have been a fake. This experiment has itself created some controversy, some believing it to be a poor comparison.

Wildenstein Castle
D: 1953 (& earlier)
L: Nr. Heilbronn, Germany
S: Andrew MacKenzie

Adolf Hermann Erwin was born in Berlin on 7 August 1884 and died of diphtheria at Wildenstein Castle on 18 May 1890 at the age of five. Wildenstein Castle is no stranger to sightings; there have been several reports of goblins, for example, seen in the castle.

On 1 March 1953 the future Baroness von Lobenstein reported seeing a boy in a sailor's suit in the kitchen of the castle, looking at her with a friendly disposition. He suddenly disappeared.

The baron – at this time her fiancé – was in hospital and she wrote to him about the incident. He believed that she had seen the ghost of Adolf Erwin. He told her that Adolf's photograph was kept in the storeroom and when the baroness saw it she agreed it was 'quite similar' to the apparition she had seen. She admitted that she could not be sure she had not been told about the child before.

Of several tales of hauntings in Wildenstein Castle, perhaps the most dramatic is that concerning an American officer billeted in the castle in 1945. What seemed to be a young woman dressed in white walked into his bathroom while he was having a bath and stared at him, making him feel uncomfortable. Eventually he left the bath to push her out of the door and on trying to do so pushed his hand straight through the figure which then disappeared. Somewhat disorientated by events he ran stark naked into the castle kitchen and a gathering of village boys.

A further series of events were reported which included poltergeist-like activity: the baron was pouring a glass of wine when the glass rose off the table, strange sounds, sightings of monks and phantom music.

Wycombe General Hospital
D: 1986
L: High Wycombe, Buckinghamshire
S: Direct

'Claire' reported this story directly to us; it relates her own experience in Wycombe General Hospital in early July 1986. She was in the maternity unit having her second son. On the night in question she was awake in the middle of the night:

The alarm bell was going off behind the nurses' station. They were ignoring it. It must have gone off about five or six times; in the end they called up a janitor who went along to the room which was then the patients' dining room. It was quite a long way from the nurses' station down the corridor. He went along to this room which was empty and came back saying he could not find anything wrong. The following morning I asked the nurse on duty why didn't they answer the alarm? What was going on? She said that the room used to be the children's nursery room where they kept the babies and the alarm kept going off in the middle of the night in that room while the children were there. They had everything checked out, all the wiring, and they couldn't find any reason for it. In the end the young nurses refused to go along to that room in the middle of the night so they decided to move the nursery. She said that was why they ignored the alarm.

2
Ghosts of
the Famous

Many famous people in history are alleged to have come back to us from beyond their graves. Henry VIII's wives in particular must be amongst the most frequently reported famous ghosts, at least in England. Does this indicate that there is some special quality which makes these famous people come back when many less famous seem not to? Probably not, although there might even be an argument in support of that suggestion: famous people usually become so because of some single-minded sense of purpose which drives them forward where lesser people would sit back and rest on their laurels. Perhaps that determination lets certain spirits rest less easily.

More probably, however, the high frequency of reports of famous people is attributable to the viewpoint of the witness reporting the sighting. If a ghostly figure in a long flowing dress is seen walking through the corridors of Hampton Court Palace it is far more exciting to believe you have seen the ghost of Jane Seymour than merely one of her ladies-in-waiting or indeed a servant girl or other 'ordinary' person. Even amongst the famous there seem to be certain ghosts more well known than others; no doubt many of Henry VIII's wives are reported because those particular queens of England are very well known whereas there would be a great many figures from history that the average person would be hard pressed to put a name to, even if he saw them.

That said, certain reports do seem too precise to be mistaken – the imposing figure of Abraham Lincoln in the White House, a Finnish painter recognised from her portrait and (on the face of it more straightforward) the ghost of Harry Price who actually identified himself to the witness.

Anne Boleyn

D: Many, including 1985
L: Blickling Hall, Tower of London and Hampton Court
S: Joan Forman

Anne Boleyn was the second wife of King Henry VIII. Their marriage changed the course of English history: Henry was already married to Catherine of Aragon and could not obtain a divorce from the Roman Catholic Church. In order to obtain his divorce he therefore created a reformed version of the church, putting himself at the head – a direct challenge to the authority of the Pope.

Having obtained his divorce and married Anne, the king's most driving need was a son. His previous queen had only given him a female heir (Princess Mary). On 7 September 1533 Anne Boleyn gave birth to a girl, Elizabeth (who was to become Queen Elizabeth I). The relationship between the king and Anne Boleyn deteriorated; he began to court a new queen in Jane Seymour. However, Anne became pregnant again and there was a brief reconciliation, but the child was stillborn. Henry determined to be rid of Anne and trumped up a charge of treason, arresting her and confining her to the Tower of London. Her execution had been scheduled for 18 May 1536 but in fact took place the following day as there had been a delay while a skilled executioner was brought in from Calais.

Anne Boleyn's ghost is a prolific one and there are many reports of her appearances. Undoubtedly many reports arise because ghosts seen will be attributable to the most famous 'possible' source when that may be inappropriate; however, some have the suggestion of a little more substance.

Among the more hysterical there are the stories of headless horses galloping to Blickling Hall in Norfolk, her family home, ridden by a headless horseman and of course the headless young woman herself. Traditionally the apparition appears on the anniversary of her death. Further elaborations of the tale include a severed head in her lap.

Anne's ghost has been seen by several people in the corridors of Blickling Hall although the present building dates from virtually one hundred years after her death. Nonetheless, it *is* on the same site as the original building and there are many accounts of ghosts which do seem attracted to particular locations.

The administrator of the building, Mr Steve Ingram, had an experience of a more specific nature in 1985. Mr Ingram and his wife share a flat in Blickling Hall. One night he was awakened at 1.30 a.m. by the sound of footsteps in the passageway outside the bedroom. The sound was of light female footsteps on rush matting, changing briefly to someone stepping on a thinner material and then on to thick carpet. Mr Ingram worked out the path of the footsteps: down the rush matting in the corridor outside, across the thin mat by the doorway and across the carpet of the bedroom. Evidently the person causing the footsteps was now standing at the foot of the bed and Mr Ingram assumed it was therefore his wife returning from the bathroom.

When he switched on the bedroom light he discovered his wife asleep next to him and the bedroom door shut; no one else could be seen in the room. It was the following morning when someone pointed out that this incident had occurred on the anniversary of Anne Boleyn's execution.

The National Trust took over Blickling Hall in 1946; one of its administrators was Mr Sidney Hancock. On one occasion Mr Hancock looked out of the kitchen window of the hall towards the lake and saw a woman walking down towards the lakeside. She was wearing a long grey gown with a white lace collar and a white cap. Hancock was concerned that she was either lost or trespassing and went out to ask if he could help or if she was looking for someone. The lady apparently replied, '*That for which I seek has long since gone.*' Hancock briefly turned away and on looking back discovered there was no one there and nowhere she could have gone to. Although the description of the clothes worn by the figure did not match those which Anne wore to her execution, they could well have been the sort of clothes she might have been wearing in the days leading up to it.

Anne Boleyn is also reputed to haunt Hampton Court – along with most of Henry VIII's wives in fact – though there she apparently wears the blue dress in which she appears in a portrait in that building. Predictably, she is also said to haunt the Tower of London where she was executed. She has been traditionally seen, again predictably, as a headless female figure identified by her clothing; she generally appears near the Queen's House in which she was confined prior to the execution.

Michael Faraday

D: 1962

L: Royal Institution, London

S: Andrew MacKenzie

Michael Faraday was the nineteenth-century scientist whose work forms the basis of the understanding of electricity and its modern-day uses. He was a laboratory assistant to Sir Humphrey Davy in 1813 at the Royal Institution in London and succeeded him as Professor of Chemistry in 1833. He worked for most of his life at the Royal Institution.

His ghost is believed to haunt (benevolently) the Royal Institution and has been reported by many people. One report was from Professor Dr Eric Laithwaite, Professor of Heavy Electrical Engineering at Imperial College, London. He was giving a lecture at the Royal Institution in 1962 and felt a presence near him, which he believed to be Faraday, saying, '*Now it's all right, lad. You are doing fine.*' He identified the spot where he thought the voice was coming from – the same spot on which many had indicated they had also felt a similar presence.

Dr Laithwaite gave the Christmas lecture for children at the Royal Institution in 1964, one of a series of lectures which were started by Faraday himself. That a practical scientist, grounded in conventional science, should report such a story is in itself important. Dr Laithwaite was conducting a live experiment in front of his audience using two coils of wire; if all went perfectly, a ball would leap out of a dish when an electrical current was applied. However, if he did not pick precisely the right moment to turn on the current then the ball would rather impotently rattle about but not make the dramatic leap. The first two times that he turned on the current nothing significant happened, which was not surprising. The odds on the leap occurring first time were estimated by Dr Laithwaite to be 696 to 1 against. As he was about to turn the current on for the third time he heard a man's voice tell him that it *would* work when he tried the third time; indeed the voice indicated to him that he ought to announce the success of the experiment to the children in the audience even before he did it. This Laithwaite did and sure enough the experiment worked perfectly.

Apart from coincidence or the possibility of psychic interference, the question, of course, is whether or not Professor Laithwaite was assisted in his experiment by an entity or whether or not something caused Professor Laithwaite to use what we would have to describe as psycho-kinesis to make his experiment work to the greatest effect. Almost certainly Professor Laithwaite is no more able to answer that dilemma than anyone else.

What was important about the case was that it took place in front of a mass of witnesses.

Andrew MacKenzie, in his book *The Seen and the Unseen*, says of Faraday that he was sceptical of the spirit world. Brian Inglis in *Natural and Supernatural* describes Faraday as 'a deeply religious man to whom the idea of communicating with the spirits might have been expected to appeal, but from his private correspondence it was clear that he embarked on the investigation of table-turning because he detested what he regarded as a revival of superstition'.

Perhaps Faraday remains to this day as surprised as anyone by his present form!

Professor Laithwaite summed up the experience with ideas that should be taken to heart by every scientist. He indicated that the problem with science was that everything had to be labelled and pigeon-holed but that the fact that some things didn't fit into the appropriate labels did not mean that they weren't real.

Meri Genetz and Karl Wargh

D: 1977

L: Helsinki, Finland

S: Andrew MacKenzie

At a party in Meritullinkatu, Helsinki in Finland on 12 February 1977 the hostess, Mrs Pia Virtakallio, met one guest whom she did not know. She was a woman of medium build, with strange dark eyes and wearing somewhat old-fashioned clothing. Since the woman had arrived with Professor Erik Stenius, Mrs Virtakallio assumed that she was his wife. Despite a temperature of –30°C outside, the woman had apparently arrived without a coat.

Professor Stenius did not introduce the lady and Mrs Virtakallio simply led her to an empty chair and carried on chatting to other guests. At one point the unknown lady offered to help in the kitchen but Mrs Virtakallio declined the offer and did not see the lady again, nor did she see her leave.

When Mrs Virtakallio asked a friend, Dr Kivenen, why Professor Stenius had not introduced his wife, Dr Kivinen replied that Mrs Stenius had not been at the party. As it turned out, no one had seen the lady except Mrs Virtakallio. On examining the guest book Mrs Virtakallio found she recognised all the signatures; there was no one she could not account for.

Three years later Mrs Virtakallio was reading a magazine article about the painter Meri Genetz (who died 3 April 1943). She had once lived, with her husband Karl Wargh, in the same apartment. From her picture, Mrs Virtakallio became quite adamant that Meri Genetz had been the mysterious guest at the reception; she also realised that the 'presence' she had sensed in the kitchen on several occasions was probably that of Karl Wargh who, of the pair, was the one interested in cooking.

It may be relevant that Karl Wargh died early, at the age of 42, and that Meri Genetz was killed suddenly during an air raid, aged 58. Both may have felt that there were many things left undone in their lives.

King George II
D: Since 1760

L: Kensington Palace, London

S: Joan Forman

The last days of King George II's life passed in Kensington Palace near Hyde Park, where he was confined because of illness. Although he longed to return to Hanover he was forced by his health to remain in England. He had come to the throne in 1727, and throughout his reign, until 1760, England was caught up in many conflicts: in Europe, where the king at the age of 60 became the last British monarch to lead his men into battle at Dettingham in 1743. In America there was the fight for independence from England; in addition Britain was in bitter conflict with France over possession of Canada.

In October 1760 the king was awaiting news from Hanover but

fierce gales were keeping ships in their continental ports and preventing them sailing to England. Even during the worst parts of his illness the king would apparently look out of the palace windows at the weathervane to see if the wind had changed and he often asked in a heavy accent, 'Why don't they come?' The king died on 25 October without ever receiving the news he awaited.

Since that time there have been reports of the monarch's face looking out of the window towards the weathervane and one or two people claim to have heard the heavy accent asking, 'Why don't they come?'

Lady Jane Grey
D: Many, including 1957
L: Beauchamp Tower, Tower of London
S: Joan Forman

Lady Jane Grey was the granddaughter of Mary Rose, Henry VIII's youngest sister. On the death of Edward VI in 1553 she was therefore one of those in line for the throne although the next heir should have been Henry VIII's daughter Mary, his child by Catherine of Aragon. Jane was proclaimed queen but after ten days was arrested and Mary assumed the crown. On 12 February 1554 her husband, Guilford Dudley, went to his death; his ghost has been seen in the Beauchamp Tower of the Tower of London, quietly crying, perhaps in anticipation of the execution. Lady Jane was executed the same afternoon and has reappeared many times since.

On 12 February 1957, 403 years to the day after Lady Jane Grey's death, a guardsman named Johns in the Tower of London saw a likeness of her on the battlements above him. He alerted a second guardsman who confirmed the sighting.

Catherine Howard
D: Since 1542
L: Hampton Court Palace, nr. Kingston
S: Terence Whitaker

In 1541, towards the end of his life Henry VIII married the young Catherine Howard. She failed to curb her sexual indulgences with younger men and was eventually arrested and confined in Hampton Court.

Knowing that she would lose her life, and also knowing that there were many who wanted to see her family's dominance over the throne broken, she realised that if she was to live it would only be by appealing directly to the king. She devised a plan to escape from her guards and reach the king when he would be praying in the Chapel Royal which was at the other end of a gallery that ran from her own rooms.

She made her attempt and reached the door of the Chapel Royal but could not get through before the guards caught her. She hammered on the door, screamed to her husband and was dragged back down the gallery screaming and crying.

Since her execution on 13 February 1542 there have been many reports of Catherine re-enacting this bid for freedom down the gallery and many have heard her frantic screams. There have also been reports of a figure in white moving along the gallery.

John Keats
D: 1976 (before 1977)
L: Keats House, Keats Grove, Hampstead, London
S: Peter Underwood

London taxi driver Gerry Sherrick, with one of his sons, was outside the Hampstead home that had once belonged to the poet Keats. Sherrick was a poet too and a lover of the classics and wished to see the house where John Keats had lived. As he approached he saw a man sitting outside the house reading a book, dressed in nineteenth-century clothes; he believed it must be a publicity gimmick.

The next day Sherrick took his wife and family to Keats' house but was told that the house was closed to the public due to repairs. Sherrick then described the man outside whom he had believed to be a publicity gimmick attracting people to the house though this obviously could not now be the case. The official took them into the house, apparently in tears, and showed them a picture hanging on the wall; it was the poet John Keats sitting outside the house in exactly the pose that Sherrick had described.

Abraham Lincoln
D: After 1865
L: White House, Washington
S: Daniel Cohen

Of the paranormal events reported in the White House in Washington, probably the highest number relate to President Abraham Lincoln, the first president of America to be assassinated. As far as can be determined the first report of Lincoln's ghost was made by Grace Coolidge, the wife of the 30th president, Calvin Coolidge. She apparently saw Lincoln staring out of the Oval Office window.

Queen Wilhelmina of the Netherlands, staying at the White House during the term of office of President Franklin D. Roosevelt, opened a door in response to a knock and found herself standing in front of Lincoln who was wearing a top hat and traditional garb. When she told President Roosevelt of the encounter he merely replied that the bedroom that the queen was staying in was also known as the Lincoln Room and that there had been many other reports of his ghost at that place.

Lincoln was also seen in that same room sitting on a bed, putting on his boots, by one of Roosevelt's secretaries. Even Roosevelt's terrier dog was credited with reacting to Lincoln's ghost when others couldn't see it.

After his death in 1865 Lincoln's body was transported back to Illinois for burial on a special funeral train. It was an extraordinary form of mobile lying-in-state with thousands of people lining up to see the train pass along the route. A great many legends have grown up around the train and there is the story of a ghost train manned by skeletons following the route each year. As described by the *Albany Times*, 'It passes noiselessly. If it is moonlight, clouds cover over the moon as the phantom train goes by. After the pilot engine passes, the funeral train itself with flags and streamers rushes past. The track seems covered with black carpet and the coffin is seen in the centre of the car, while all about it in the air and on the train behind are vast numbers of blue-coated men, some with coffins on their backs, others leaning upon them.'

Harry Price
D: 1948
L: Malmö and Lund, Sweden
S: Dr John Björkhem (*Det Ockulta Problemet*/The Occult Problem)

Founder of the National Laboratory of Psychical Research at the University of London, Harry Price was a prominent ghost-hunter of the first half of this century. Although there have been some questions regarding his analysis of the Borley Rectory sightings and indeed accusations of his having deliberately manufactured phenomena there, his reputation nonetheless spread far and wide. He died in March 1948.

At about the same time, a Swedish man known by the pseudonym 'Erson' saw a figure appear beside his bed speaking English, which Erson could not understand. The figure appeared regularly, so much so that Erson was able to learn some English and hold some conversations with the ghostly apparition. On one occasion Erson tried to photograph the figure, which appeared fairly solid, but the photographs apparently showed nothing.

At a hospital where Erson was undergoing treatment, he discussed the ghost with one of the doctors who – by a fortunate coincidence – happened to be interested in psychical research. From Erson's description the doctor was able to identify the ghost as Harry Price.

There has never been any explanation as to why the ghost-hunter should have appeared in a foreign country to someone who knew nothing of him, could not converse with him and was apparently uninterested in the field of work he had undertaken throughout most of his life.

Sir Walter Raleigh

D: 1983
L: Byward Tower, Tower of London
S: Joan Forman

Sir Walter Raleigh was imprisoned at the Tower of London for extensive periods from 1603 until his execution in 1618. One yeoman on guard in the Byward Tower on a February night in 1983 was in the guardroom in the early hours of the morning when the handle of the door rattled. He believed it was due to the fierce wind but when he looked at the door he could see through its glass, on the far side, looking into the room from the doorway, Sir Walter Raleigh, exactly as the portrait in the Bloody Tower shows him. Apparently Sir Walter was very solid looking, remained for a short while and then vanished.

Approximately a year and a half later, another yeoman saw the same vision in the same place.

Sir Walter, who was executed in October 1618, is another very persistent ghost reported at the Tower of London. It has been speculated that because he had considerable freedom during his internment and was able to walk around the Tower seeing many friends and acquaintances and presumably striking up something of a relationship with his jailers, his ghost may still walk cheerfully around the corridors looking in on their descendants.

Sir Walter's ghost is also reported to haunt Sherborne Castle, in Dorset, his former home.

Jane Seymour
D: Many
L: Hampton Court Palace, nr. Kingston
S: Joan Forman

Of Henry VIII's six wives Jane Seymour was one of the luckier, not ending up with her head on the block and indeed finding herself still firmly in the heart of the king when she died. She was only queen for around a year and gave birth on 12 October 1537 to the king's much desired son, Edward (who would become Edward VI). She died just twelve days after his birth on 24 October at Hampton Court, leaving Henry with much sorrow at her passing.

Jane's ghost has been seen at Hampton Court around her former apartments usually walking along the corridors and down the stairs. She appears dressed in white holding a lighted candle with a steady unwavering flame. It's a rather 'spooky' appearance for a queen held to have been fun-loving in her young life and no one has offered a reasonable explanation as to why she should appear in so sombre a state.

Dylan Thomas
D: 1973
L: Cwmdonkin Park, Wales
S: Peter Underwood

In conversation with Peter Underwood, the president of the prestigious Ghost Club, Dylan Thomas declared that he had seen the ghost of his father several times after his death and had felt his presence on many occasions. He believed that those who in life fought off death – as had his father – perhaps lingered on more so than those who willingly passed away.

Interestingly, Dylan Thomas's own ghost is held to haunt the Old Boat House at Laugharne in Dyfed where Dylan Thomas worked. Margaret Hopkins met Dylan Thomas on one occasion in 1939 when she was with a friend who knew him well. On a later occasion in 1973 she was in Cwmdonkin Park (where Dylan Thomas had spent time as a youth), sitting on a seat reading a paper. Apparently she was assailed by a shower of stones, turf and twigs that came down the slope behind her but she could see no one in sight. The gardener nearby had heard nothing. Apparently Margaret suddenly got the impression that perhaps Dylan Thomas was playing a joke with her. He had written a poem about a hunchback at whom stones had been pelted in that very park, possibly on the very spot where she was now sitting. She thought it quite typical of Dylan Thomas's sense of humour though she was open to an alternative and more prosaic explanation.

On another occasion, Constantine FitzGibbon had just finished his biography of Dylan Thomas, called *Life of Dylan Thomas*, and was reading Thomas Hardy's poem 'To Lizbie Browne'. Dylan Thomas himself had once read that same poem to FitzGibbon. As he read it in the dark in his study he was suddenly quite convinced that someone was standing just behind him looking over his shoulder reading the poem. He saw no one when he turned round but wondered whether Dylan Thomas or perhaps Hardy or Lizbie Browne herself was looking on.

3
Haunted Objects

There are occasions when ghosts seem to attach themselves not to particular places but rather to particular objects and will follow those objects even if they are moved considerable distances. This section includes a haunted oil painting, a skull surrounded by paranormal phenomena wherever it was sited, a haunted wardrobe mirror that affected different generations of a family and even a small pottery cottage that transported its attendant ghost from Manchester, England to Las Vegas, USA.

Antoine's Oil Painting
D: 1960
L: Putney, South London
S: Philip Paul

Mrs Dorothy Jenkins of Clarendon Drive, Putney, South London purchased an oil painting in a Fulham junk shop to which she had been attracted. It was a picture of a young woman in a red velvet gown, and it was about four feet square and showed some signs of scorching. The painting was signed 'Antoine'.

The picture brought with it a great many problems although Mrs Jenkins had been advised not to get rid of it as that might increase the intensity of the unpleasantness towards her.

Both Mrs Jenkins and her son, in turn, suffered nervous breakdowns in the period following the purchase of the picture, which hung in both of their bedrooms at different times.

Investigator Philip Paul arranged for a medium, Ena Twigg, to assist in the investigation. He did not give her full information about the matter being investigated but merely asked if she would 'psychometrise' objects somewhere in London; she accepted. (Psychometry is the method used by some mediums to gain impressions of people and events by touching objects they have owned.) At the time of the investigation Mrs Jenkins had her friend, Mrs Violet Smith, with her and Paul arrived with Ena Twigg, Leslie Howard, the assistant editor of *Psychic News* and Ena's husband, three newspaper reporters and a photographer, all of whom had expressed interest in the case.

Attempting to double-bluff the medium, Paul led her straight to the picture on the grounds that she would probably expect to be taken to a 'neutral' object first. Apparently Ena Twigg felt immediate horror and distress. She spoke almost incoherently of various feelings and events including hearing music, seeing blood and what seemed to be descriptions of confinements; use of truth drugs, preventing shaving and discussing what may have been electric shock therapy.

Many of these comments related to the difficulties being experienced by Mrs Jenkins' son who was not present that evening. Indeed of several other objects psychometrised by Ena Twigg only a photograph of Mrs Jenkins' son produced anything by way of results.

During the test the paintings had been arranged in the room in a particular order and before Ena Twigg, now without her blindfold, was brought back into the room after the test had ended the paintings were put back in their proper places. On entering the room Ena Twigg claims to have seen a bright flash of light moving from one point to another. The point at which it started was the painting by Antoine and the place where the light apparently went to was the spot where it had been during the experiment.

Philip Paul does not recall any derogatory comments on the part of the reporters but in Ena Twigg's biography, *Ena Twigg, Medium*, she wrote, 'The reporters were not at all impressed with the accuracy of my performance . . . For the most part they believed and said that "somebody must have tipped her off in advance". With some people it wouldn't matter if you brought the sun, moon and stars down and put them in their proper rotation. They would still be doubters.'

Dickie's Skull
  D: 18th century
  L: Tunstead, Milton, Derbyshire
  S: Keith Poole

Properly known as Tunstead Farm, this farmhouse near Chapel-en-le-Frith in Derbyshire has for many centuries also been known as 'Dickie's Farm'. Dickie is a skull which, until recently at least, has been resting in the farmhouse since the early eighteenth century. There are several legends (which are impossible to verify) as to whose skull 'Dickie' is or even whether it is a male or female skull, but there have been several ghost hauntings in the farmhouse which are associated with the remains.

Dickie apparently maintained a certain hold over the farmhouse in a number of ways:

If any strangers were on the land Dickie would alert the owners of the farm with a series of furious knockings on the walls, seemingly more efficient than any guard dog.

Dickie's 'security alarm' was apparently a little inconvenient at certain times such as when farm labourers had to be recruited for peak-time activity. Two farm labourers assigned to sleep in the outbuildings left very quickly, unable to sleep with the bizarre noises they could hear. Similarly, three labourers trying to sleep after working all day were continuously disturbed by the noise of people throwing the farm implements around in the hayloft above them; when they inspected the hayloft it was tidy and undisturbed in appearance. They too left very quickly.

To an apparently astonishing degree of accuracy, Dickie's knocks also acted as a warning of a death in the family or as a warning that farm animals needed care or assistance.

Dickie had powers of self-protection too. One day when the noises were extremely loud and frantic, the farmer discovered that Dickie had been stolen. When the skull was traced to a house in Cheshire the villains were *very* glad to get rid of it, having been plagued by disturbing noises since taking home their booty.

Perhaps less certainly, but nonetheless attributed to Dickie's powers by the locals, was the inability of the London and Northwestern Railway to construct a bridge across fields and farmlands near Tunstead Farm. Apparently the various efforts of the engineers to erect a bridge failed and eventually the construction engineers moved to another site, though that site too was plagued with difficulties for which Dickie was credited.

Having become something of a local character the suggestion

by one tenant that Dickie be buried in consecrated ground was resisted locally and he was returned from the burial site to the farm.

On one occasion the skull was thrown into a reservoir but had to be retrieved and returned home after all the fish were poisoned.

Rather irreverently, Dickie's skull was turfed out of the farmhouse during refurbishments and thrown into a heap of manure. The workmen could not succeed in any of their work and were assailed by strange and oppressive noises which they eventually retraced to the manure heap. They were able to restore their work to peace and sanity only when they took the skull back to the house.

Unfortunately, in 1988, as related by Keith Poole in his book *Britain's Haunted Heritage*, it was reported that Dickie had been lost. However, no doubt when some local changes come to Dickie's unfavourable attentions he will – literally – be heard from again.

The Grandfather Clock
D: 20th century
L: Winnipeg, Manitoba, Canada
S: Prof. Colin Gardner

So frequent are cases of timepieces that seem to have a special significance with respect to the deaths of their owners that they are often known as 'stopping-clock' hauntings. And so it is appropriate to include at least one in this collection. However, this particular case is a little different since it involves not just a 'stopping' but also a 'starting' clock.

Stephen lived in Winnipeg, Manitoba in Canada and for as long as anyone could remember had made a special effort to maintain the grandfather clock in the house. Every Saturday afternoon he would clean and lubricate the mechanism of the clock and ensure that it was properly wound every evening, claiming that such loving care would maintain its accuracy. Stephen died at the age of 72 and the grandfather clock stopped at exactly the same moment; the hands were fixed at the time of his death and refused to move.

The family decided that it would be somehow inappropriate to have the clock fixed and they left it as it was as a tribute to Stephen.

Stephen left no son and there were no grandsons either which was unfortunate since traditionally the male line would have inherited the clock. Stephen's wife Molly decided to keep the clock since there was no obvious person to pass it on to and, in any case, it gave her a feeling of her husband's presence around her which she did not want to change.

Approximately a year after Stephen's death Molly was shocked to discover that the grandfather clock was now ticking; it appears that it had started when the house was empty and indeed on inspection the hands had moved just ten minutes from the position that they had been fixed in for so many months.

Molly and her neighbour Frank sat down to discuss the mystery of the starting clock. The telephone rang and the husband of Molly's youngest daughter, Lori, told them that Lori had given birth to a son just fifteen minutes previously. Molly and Frank both checked the clock and discovered that since it had started fifteen minutes had elapsed. It appeared that the clock had started working by itself at the exact moment of the first male heir's birth.

Perhaps those investigators with an inclination towards a belief in reincarnation will be keeping a close eye on the characteristics of Stephen's grandson as he grows older.

The Hexham Heads

D: 1971

L: Hexham, Northumberland

S: Various

Two stone heads were found in the garden of a house in Hexham in 1971 and appeared to attract hauntings wherever they were located. The house in the garden of which they had been found became haunted by a shape 'half-human, half-sheep-like' and the children there had to be comforted from their frights. The family moved out.

The heads were sent for examination to Dr Anne Ross at a museum in Newcastle; she immediately felt a presence associated with them though she herself was no stranger to examining such artefacts.

The heads were in her home and one night she became aware

of a fierce coldness and saw a black shape some six feet high, half-man and half-wolf, in the doorway. It left the room and she followed it down the stairs; halfway down it leapt over the banister and dropped into the downstairs hall and ran to the back of the house.

Shortly after that Dr Ross and her husband returned from a trip to London to find their children in a state of great anxiety. They too had seen the same shape and again it had started on the stairs and then dropped into the hallway and run to the back of the house. Other members of the household and even the family cat seemed to be reacting to something; poltergeist activity began with doors slamming on their own.

Dr Ross decided to get rid of the heads but one colleague who usually assisted her refused to have anything to do with them after seeing them. Chemist Dr Don Robins eventually took them and found them to have a high percentage of quartz. He was interested in the possibility that crystal structures store energy.

The heads were buried but this resulted in disturbances in the area of the burial; more recently they have disappeared without trace.

Mirror, Mirror
D: 20th century
L: Nr. Philadelphia, Pennsylvania, USA
S: Prof. Colin Gardner

Americans Tim and Judy Corvina inherited a wardrobe from Tim's grandmother. The origin of the large wardrobe was unknown but it was thought to be early nineteenth century and to have been a wedding present to the grandmother many decades before. It was placed in the second bedroom of Tim and Judy's house, which for a time doubled as the nursery for the couple's newborn son.

Once or twice, while attending to her son, Judy noticed an odd shimmering light coming from the wardrobe's mirrored door and on the second occasion she saw the image of an old woman peering out. The woman wore a high-necked dress and a white hat and as the woman's eyes turned to look at Judy so Judy fled the room in fear.

Judy told her husband but *he* was unable to see anything in the mirror other than his own reflection. They spoke to Tim's parents about the apparition one evening. Tim's mother recalled that when she was very young she had once noticed a strange shimmering light from the mirror and had seen a vision inside it though not of the woman whom Judy had seen. She had in fact forgotten about this story until her memory had been jogged by the couple relating their own story. The scene that Tim's mother had seen had been of herself walking down her own street and talking to her neighbour as if watching a television replay. Tim's mother recalled several other visions in the mirror and on discussing it with her brother, Wayne, found that he too had seen strange images. As her memory unlocked she recalled an extraordinary vision she had had decades before; it is almost unbelievable that she could have forgotten it unless it was suppressed because it was so traumatic. In the mirror she had seen American troops fighting, dressed in an identical uniform to that worn by her brother, Wayne, after he joined the American Army. Watching in the mirror she saw the death of her own brother though it was two months later when the family was notified that he had been killed in action. After that she never went near the wardrobe again.

A Mummified Foot

D: (No date)
L: Lamport Rectory, nr. Northampton
S: Peter Underwood

Writer Denys Watkins–Pitchford recalled experiences at Lamport Rectory near Northampton where for 30 years his father had been the rector. One rather minor incident consisted of a very loud sound similar to tons of coal being emptied down the stairs; this alarmed everybody at a dinner party though nothing could ever be found.

However, the main story related to his grandfather (who was also a parson) taking home a mummified foot purchased in an antique shop. That night the foot was put in a locked room at the top of the house. During the night a young relative, Amy Watkins-Pitchford, dreamed of a horrific ceremony where priests amputated a girl's foot. Amy got out of bed to go to see her mother and opening her bedroom door saw the box, which earlier had been locked up at the top of the stairs, with the foot protruding from it.

The foot was buried in consecrated ground following this disturbing event.

Nautical Woodwork
D: 1935
L: Nr. Reigate, Surrey
S: Peter Underwood

Sax Rohmer, creator of the character Fu Manchu, built Little Gatton between Reigate and Redhill in Surrey. Ornamental oak panels, furnishings and other woodwork were installed in the house from the *Mauretania* which was Rohmer's favourite ship. In conversation with Peter Underwood, Rohmer explained that in bad weather the woodwork would creak and groan exactly as if it were an old ship in heavy seas. Even frequent visitors found it somewhat disturbing.

The house had a sad and doom-laden quality about it. Sax's wife, Elizabeth, recalled that a maidservant (who had in fact commented on first coming to the house that the garden reminded her of a cemetery) had been killed by a lorry outside the gates. In the same lane two other boys had been killed, fire had killed a young girl, a man had committed suicide in the neighbouring house and a gardener had hanged himself in the garden.

The property was sold to speed-ace Sir Malcolm Campbell who once remarked to Elizabeth that the windows had been blown out and that he would not buy the house now if he could change matters.

The Peach Trees
D: 1971
L: El Paso, Texas, USA
S: Prof. Colin Gardner

Lila Rosario had two dwarf peach trees in tubs on her patio, on either side of the door. A local ten-year-old boy, Larry, played a mischievous game with Lila (who was nearly 60) attempting to pick the unripe peaches; this would result in a chase through the streets which both seemed to find pleasantly satisfying.

In early 1971 Lila informed Larry and his parents that she was going to Salt Lake City in Utah for her father's funeral and asked Larry if he would take the peach trees to his house and look after them. She made him promise not to pick the fruit until it was ripe, and indeed to care for the peach trees sensibly.

This seemed a rather strange request since Lila was only going to be gone for two weeks and instructions which included the winter months should have been most unnecessary.

It was over a month later when Lila's son visited Larry's family and informed them that Lila had died two weeks after arriving in Salt Lake City.

From that time on, whenever Larry attempted to pick an unripe peach Lila's ghost would tell him off and shout at him in the playful manner that Lila had done in life. This continued for five years until the haunting stopped.

Larry has never picked an unripe peach since.

A Pottery Cottage
D: 1982
L: Greater Manchester and Las Vegas, USA
S: Prof. Colin Gardner

Haunted cottages might seem to belong in the section on haunted buildings, but in this case the cottage in question is in fact a small pottery container which might be used to hold biscuits or other small objects. The story starts in Bolton, Greater Manchester, when Mrs Hilary Spence was visiting her Aunt Jean on a trip from the USA. Hilary caught sight of the small cottage and commented on it favourably to which her aunt Jean virtually demanded that she take it as she was most welcome to it. It was very clear that Aunt Jean was glad to be rid of it. The precise way in which it had come into the family and the precise time were not known.

Mrs Spence put her ornament on display in her bungalow in Las Vegas and used it for storing household items such as stamps, pens, shopping lists and so on. Very soon Mrs Spence noticed a strange shadow lurking on the bathroom door which was near one corner of the living room. Then, once or twice, she saw the ghost of a man walking through her house and she focused on the pottery cottage as the source of the haunting.

When Hilary's daughter, Billie, visited she often said how much she liked the cottage; but on one occasion when she was talking to her mother she suddenly felt tremendously cold although it was an extremely warm day. In addition she felt the materialisation of a ghostly figure standing beside her. But Billie was more fascinated than actually afraid and her mother told her, '*He won't harm you.*'

On a later visit, when Billie had again commented on how much she liked the cottage, her mother told her she could have it.

Very soon after getting the pottery cottage home Billie began seeing the anomalous shadows and the ghostly figure in *her* home; she too connected them with the cottage. She tried to eliminate the hauntings by putting a variety of different objects into the cottage but none worked until she decided to empty it completely. From that point on she experienced no further hauntings, the implication seeming to be that the figure 'living' in the cottage now had enough room in the empty container and had no need to wander about outside.

The Skull of Theophilus Broome
D: After 1670
L: Higher Chilton Farm, nr. Yeovil, Somerset
S: Various

There is many a supernatural tale of skulls and other dismembered parts of the body haunting people with a view to being reunited with the remainder of the corpse. The skull of Theophilus Broome offers precisely the opposite scenario.

Theophilus Broome (spelt Brome in some accounts), was a Royalist during the English Civil War but he defected to the Roundheads in horror at the inhuman acts Royalist troops carried out in the name of their king. In particular he despised the Royalist habit of severing the heads of victims and spiking them on rails as trophies. On his deathbed he made a plea to his sister that his head should be separated from his body so that even if his body were exhumed no head could be discovered which could then be impaled as a trophy. His plea to his sister was that his skull should never leave his farmhouse.

Theophilus Broome died aged 69 on 18 August 1670.

Over the years since that time several tenants of the farmhouse at Chilton Cantelo, near Yeovil, Somerset, have attempted to remove the skull, only to be plagued by horrid screaming noises until it was replaced. One tenant went as far as trying to have the skull reunited with the body in Broome's grave and even secured permission for this. During the attempt to exhume the body the sexton's spade broke in half, convincing all concerned that this was not in accord with the wishes of the subject of the exercise. The skull was again returned to its home.

Broome's skull still resides at the farmhouse and has been credited with good actions towards those who treat it properly. During an early visit to the farmhouse, prior to their marriage, the now Mrs Kerton was about to walk across a black shadow on the ground when Mr Kerton called out to her, alerting her attention, that she had dropped her coat. It turned out that the shadow was not a coat but the top of an uncovered well which she would otherwise have fallen into; the couple attributed their good fortune to the skull to whom they had shown respect.

In the mid 1970s TV celebrity Dave Allen visited the farmhouse to record a programme. He apparently became scared by something that happened while driving home and told Mr Kerton that he never wanted to visit the house again.

When a well in the garden suddenly opened up during another TV film crew's visit to the farmhouse Mr Kerton claimed that *'Broome was trying to tell them something.'*

4
Recordings and Replays

The popular and simplistic interpretation of ghosts is that they are the spirits of the dead for some reason bound to the earth, or choosing to remain so in order to complete a task, stay with a loved one. Possibly some ghosts are this but there are a great many cases where such an explanation is simply not adequate. Certain ghosts appear totally to ignore the surroundings they are seen in, walking through walls, sitting on seats that are not there and seeming oblivious of the witness who may be in very close proximity to them. Such reports have given rise to an explanation that these hauntings may be some form of replay of a former emotive event. Perhaps a combination of certain conditions at some time in history found a way to 'record' a particular set of actions at a particular location where on later occasions, if the right conditions apply, the recording then replays in front of whoever happens to be there. Such an explanation suggests that no actual spirit or presence is involved and would suggest that at least these particular hauntings were a curious but quite natural phenomenon.

This section contains accounts of what may be the emotional traces of suicides, murders, fatal accidents but also, by contrast, the story of a happy and chuckling man reading his newspaper in a rocking chair. This last case is suggestive of something slightly more complex since the sounds he was making had all the characteristics of a replay but the witnesses were able to see the present-day rocking chair moving backwards and forwards.

The Antique Shop
D: 20th century
L: Petworth, Sussex
S: Peter Underwood

Before opening an antique shop of her own, Joyce Underwood, wife of Peter Underwood of the Ghost Club, had a section of the Petworth Antique Centre. Alone in the shop one day, Joyce saw an old lady dressed in black near the open door; she came in and walked up a step into another part of the shop. Wishing to offer assistance, Joyce searched for her but could not find her. Furthermore, she was certain that there was no way that the old lady could have left the premises without being seen.

After the proprietor of the centre returned from lunch Joyce described the lady and was told that it was a ghost she had seen, one that had often been reported.

According to the description, this would seem to be a 'recording' type of ghost: the lady was apparently walking around what had once been an open courtyard and stepping up into what had once been perhaps her own cottage facing the courtyard.

A Baby's Death, A Father's Remorse

D: 20th century
L: Northern England
S: Prof. Colin Gardner

'Sally Rawlinson' had been seven months in her new house and was extremely pleased that she had completed its much needed refurbishment following a period of some decay. Even at the time of purchasing it she had been surprised at its low price and the length of time that it had been on the market. One night she had been sleeping in her newly decorated bedroom when she awoke with, at first, no particular cause apparent. She lay in bed listening and could hear voices; she became concerned as she realised they were coming from very close to where she was lying, though she could see no one. The voices sounded like a conversation between a couple. Furthermore Sally could hear the footsteps of a man and creaking floorboards despite the fact that the whole house was now thickly carpeted.

Sally was able to listen to them disappearing across the bedroom and on to the landing and she could hear what seemed to be a man bringing a baby into the bedroom in which she was lying. Suddenly she heard what sounded like someone falling down the stairs, and the screaming cries of the child. Then silence.

Afraid, Sally ran from her bed to the kitchen and sat there drinking tea to calm herself down. Unable to return to her bedroom she spent the rest of the night in the lounge on the couch.

The next night she forced herself to stay in her bedroom and slept soundly, without interruption. Although she was beginning to convince herself it was only a dream it took a couple of weeks before she was comfortable about sleeping in the bedroom. It was some time later, after a night out with some friends, that she returned home exhausted, and fell instantly asleep in her bed. Just a few hours later she woke up and listened to the replay of the whole dreadful incident that she had heard before: the voices of the man and the woman, the argument, the heavy footsteps and the creaking floorboards, the thumping and the crashing, the screeching of the tiny baby and then the silence.

Once again Sally was back in her kitchen drinking tea and feeling terrified. One interesting point occurred to her: on both occasions the noises had troubled her on a Thursday night.

Sally asked the local priest to bless the house, hoping that it would allay the haunting. While willing to do so, the priest was not particularly optimistic about the outcome. Both he and his predecessor had apparently attempted to allay this haunting in the same house several times over the years and had never succeeded. On one visit he had gone through the ceremony while listening to the screaming child and had realised that the ceremony was not working. Nonetheless the priest performed an exorcism for Sally and for a month afterwards there was peace.

On the night when it recurred, this time a Friday night in August, Sally had a guest staying with her, a friend named Carol. Sally woke in the early hours and listened to the blood-chilling replay of the sounds and the screaming and, as often before, she ran from the bedroom and sought refuge in the kitchen. It was Carol who came out screaming, '*My God! Whatever was that?*' Sally was relieved that Carol had heard it too, reinforcing her belief in its reality and she explained as much as she could to her.

Research by the Institute for Psychical Research examined the previous twenty years of the house's history, involving some fourteen previous owners. This alone indicates the short period of time that some of the owners had stayed there. Eventually, the research led to a woman (referred to by the Institute for Psychical Research only as 'Mrs T.') who had a sad explanation to offer.

Some twenty years earlier Mrs T., her second husband and her two children had been living in the house. At the time when they had moved in Mrs T. was eight months pregnant. Shortly afterwards their son was born and turned out to be a baby whose nights were frequently very disturbed.

Brian became stressed, as a result of often being late for work after having to get up six or seven times during the night. The child was extremely demanding, requiring attention every couple of hours. Mrs T. had had to introduce bottle-feeding as well as breast-feeding so that her husband could assist and also in order to supply the baby with the necessary nutrients.

One night, when the baby was ten weeks old, both Brian and Mrs T. awoke for about the third time that night and Brian volunteered to make another bottle of feed so that Mrs T. could get some extra sleep.

Brian apparently fed the baby but the child threw back the feed, and then needed cleaning and changing. Brian carried the baby to the top of the stairs in order to take him down to clean and change him, but in his tiredness slipped and crashed down the stairs. Brian had to tell his wife that although he had called for an ambulance their son was already dead.

Perhaps even more sadly, Brian was never able to cure his own remorse over what had happened and something like a year later took his own life. In order to put the memories behind her Mrs T. and her family moved away.

This case is strongly suggestive of the 'recording' theory as it appears that Sally heard the conversation between Mrs T. and Brian; Mrs T. was still alive at the time.

Christopher's Big Feet

D: 1960s or 1970s
L: England
S: Peter Underwood

Shortly after moving into a new house dog breeder and editor Barbara McKenzie began hearing strange noises. At first she believed it to be the central-heating system but eventually she came to the tentative conclusion that the house was haunted.

The noises were like footsteps coming down the stairs and were usually heard during the day. It was her eldest daughter, however, who realised that the footsteps were coming from where there was no staircase. The next time Barbara heard them she listened carefully and agreed with her daughter that the footsteps sounded as if they were coming down stairs but not the stairs that were presently in the house.

An examination of records of the farmhouse that had previously occupied the site indicated that the footsteps were coming from the position of the original staircase, destroyed when the farmhouse was demolished. One of the older people in the village was able to tell Barbara that a young man called Christopher had, she thought, taken his own life in the farmhouse in the 1920s.

The noises got more intrusive; in addition to the footsteps they could hear pacing upstairs and the sound of gunshots. They had heard the shots before but had believed them to be made by people shooting rabbits. They realised that the shots were always linked with the footsteps and were heard soon after them. Eventually Barbara met an older woman from the village and confessed to her that she had been hearing what she assumed was a ghost. The woman's reply was quite enlightening. She indicated that she thought the ghost belonged to Chris, who lived in a house which had formerly stood on the site of the present house. The woman admitted that Chris's death was on her conscience as she had been one of a group of youngsters from the local school who had taunted Chris during his life. The woman indicated that she believed Chris would never hurt anybody, in his life or his death.

Barbara asked the lady why Chris had taken his own life: it was apparently because he had enormous feet and had been ribbed about it throughout his life by the other youngsters in the village. In 1912, when Chris was eighteen years old, he had shot himself.

Barbara visited Chris's grave and felt somehow personally involved. She arranged for the house to be exorcised after which the sounds ceased.

The College Hangings

D: 1950s
L: Oxford
S: Rev. J. Aelwyn Roberts

Peter Edwards, a friend of ghost investigator the Rev. J. Aelwyn Roberts, went up to Oxford University in 1950 aged eighteen. During the early part of his first night Edwards found it strange that despite the fact that there were 300 students or so in the building the whole college seemed to be extraordinarily quiet; he was perhaps a little disappointed at this. He fell asleep and was awoken during the night by excited voices shouting and screaming from the quadrangle underneath his window, on which he could see the reflections of torches from below.

Edwards lay in his bed listening to the loud pounding of feet thumping their way up the stone staircase outside his room. He could hear frantic shouting and screaming outside his adjacent living-room; he even heard the sound of someone smashing down the living room door. He was becoming unnerved by the noises. He could hear voices quite distinctly, one of them shouting, apparently in the living room, calling to 'cut down' somebody.

Edwards believed that he was probably the victim of a practical joke, some sort of typical student 'initiation' ceremony. He went to the bedroom door to confront the people and see what it was they wanted. When he opened the door the room in front of him was completely quiet and still; the door to the main stairway and landing was undamaged and closed. Edwards opened it and stepped on to the landing; he could see and hear nothing other than the faint sound of what was probably the night-porter's radio in the distance.

The following morning one of the dons, probably quite innocently, asked him whether he had slept well and Edwards felt unable to prevent himself from blurting out the whole story. Almost without expression, it seems, the don explained the story quite simply.

He told Mr Edwards that there had been two suicides in room 16, one he believed in the 1850s and the other around 1908. The don apparently believed that Edwards had heard a replay of one of those previous events.

Edwards seems to have been hearing a repeat of one of the

hangings. If that is the case, then there are a number of questions to be answered. Why, when he opened the bedroom door, did the sounds stop? If in fact this is evidence of the 'recording' theory of ghosts, then presumably by opening his bedroom door and appearing in the room he somehow changed the conditions for the 'playback'; the only other explanation that would fit that particular situation is if there was a specific reaction to his presence by the ghosts. Assuming that Edwards was hearing a replay of one of the hangings then the question was, which one was it? While it might be possible for the ghost of the poor victim to return, it seems certain that some of the voices he was hearing were clearly those of people who had not died in the room. More extraordinarily, if one of the incidents took place in 1908, then some of the people that he was listening to might well still have been alive at the time he was listening to them replaying their scene.

If it was a 'replay', then clearly some of the emotional content of the event could have imprinted itself on that room and be capable of replay without the assistance of the (possibly still living) originators.

On the other hand, as is considered in J. Aelwyn Roberts' book *The Holy Ghostbuster*, there is also the question of whether or not the people that were present in the room during that earlier event – those still living at the time Edwards was listening to their voices – were in fact assisting in the re-enactment in some way; and the book speculates on whether or not, perhaps in other parts of the world, those people, now 42 years older, were perhaps apologising to friends or colleagues around them for their momentary lapse of attention or for unexpectedly 'dozing off' for a moment.

The Commissioner's Suicide
D: 1871
L: Hoshiarpur, Punjab, India
S: Lord Halifax

In his *Ghost Book*, Lord Halifax relates a story told by his nephew, Charles Dundas. It is the story of a friend of Dundas named Troward, who was travelling across India in 1871 to take up an appointment at Hoshiarpur in the Punjab. Together with his wife and servants they arrived at their destination in the evening and made ready for bed. Because the usual accommodation was not available the party was offered an alternative bungalow. They made ready their camp beds, had some food and were about to go to bed when the servants began to claim that they did not like the bungalow and were unwilling to spend the night there. They also suggested that Mr and Mrs Troward should not do so either.

However, it was late, the Trowards were tired and they told their servants they could not make alternative arrangements at that time; they went to bed. In the middle of the night Mr Troward was awakened by a loud noise and the subsequent crying and screaming of his wife. She claimed that a man in a grey suit had come up to the side of the bed, leant over and said, *'Lie still, I shall not hurt you.'* He had then fired a gun across her.

It was the following morning when the Trowards discovered that the former commissioner at Hoshiarpur, Mr DeCourcy, had shot himself in the bungalow in the middle of the night, having just told his wife, *'I shall not hurt you.'*

The Ferryboat Inn

D: (No date – centuries old)
L: Holywell, St Ives, Huntingdonshire
S: Peter Underwood

Legend has it that hundreds of years ago Juliet Tousely hanged herself when her love for woodcutter Tom Zoul was unrequited. She was buried near the Great Ouse river at Holywell and her grave marked by a plain stone. Legend also has it that the ghost of Juliet, a classic 'lady in white', walks the river on the anniversary of her suicide, reputed to be 17 March.

In more recent years The Ferryboat Inn was built on the site of the event and the gravestone incorporated into its floor. Modern legend has it that Juliet's ghost can be seen in the inn on the anniversary, near her gravestone.

There have been teams of investigators examining the claims but the ghost has not been so cooperative as to turn up when recording equipment was present. However, the stories continue with claims of doors that open by themselves, unexplained chilliness in the bar, the reaction of animals to the gravestone and, if nothing else, an admission by the landlord that people avoid the inn on 17 March (ghost researchers excepted, presumably!).

Happily Reading in a Rocking Chair
  D: 1947
  L: Perranporth, Cornwall
  S: Terence Whitaker

Two middle-aged ladies were holidaying in Perranporth in Cornwall in 1947. They were staying in a holiday village and had been allocated an old dilapidated chalet which annoyed them intensely as many far better locations were apparently unoccupied. Nevertheless they settled down for their first evening in the bedroom of the chalet.

At around eleven thirty in the evening they heard the sound of footsteps padding around outside and heard a dog growling at the door. Although they looked out of the windows they could not see anything; since it was night this is perhaps no indication of anything extraordinary. There may well have been a dog or, given later events, perhaps the dog was a visitor from the past.

After a short while they heard their chalet door open and then close. The women were well aware that they had bolted and locked the door and this gave them some cause for concern. They could hear footsteps padding in the living room. Then there was silence and shortly after that the rustling of what sounded like someone turning the pages of a newspaper. They could hear a chuckling laugh, apparently a very pleasant one with no hint of evil or malice. It was exactly as if a person had come into the living room and was having a pleasant time reading the newspaper. They could hear a creaking noise accompanying the sound.

The women got out of bed, took up what small objects they found close by as weapons and threw open the door to the living room, ready to confront whoever was there.

In fact no one was there and there was nowhere where anyone could have hidden. Suddenly they saw that the wicker rocking-chair was rocking backwards and forwards with regularity. Terence Whitaker, in his book *England's Ghostly Heritage*, stresses that the movement of the chair was not the dying motion of previous rockings but rather the deliberate steady rocking of a chair occupied by someone.

The picture therefore seemed very clear. The ladies were hearing someone who had come into the room (after having settled his dog down?), picked up his newspaper and was enjoying reading it, sitting in the wicker chair and chuckling at whatever humorous passages were in it. At one point they did think they heard the sound of an invisible dog which corroborated their earlier speculation.

Although there was no obvious sign of malice from the sounds, the women's nerve could not take what they were experiencing and they hid in the bedroom until daylight when they demanded to be moved to another site. On hearing their demand, the owner of the holiday village admitted that there had been similar reports previously.

No explanation for this case was ever found, the chalet has long since been demolished and the identity of the newspaper reader never discovered. Whether or not it constitutes a haunting in the accepted sense of the word is debatable; it appears that the person in the chair was acting quite normally within his own context, and there seems more evidence for the women having heard him going about his everyday business during his day-to-day, life than any suggestion of a visitation as a result of, for example, death or stress. As in all these cases, the reader must decide on the appropriate classification for him or herself.

The Landings at Dieppe

D: 1951
L: Puys, nr. Dieppe, France
S: Various

On 19 August 1942, in the midst of the Second World War, a massive raid took place at Dieppe.

During early August 1951 Mrs Dorothy Naughton and her sister-in-law, Agnes, were staying near Dieppe at Puys. At around four o'clock in the morning Mrs Naughton awoke hearing sounds coming from the beach; her sister-in-law awoke some twenty minutes later. Going out on to their balcony, they could hear the sounds of men crying, gunfire, dive bombers, and landing craft. The noises continued for some three hours.

Mrs Naughton had also reported much fainter versions of the same noises the previous Monday but had not thought it worth pursuing.

Investigation indicated that the noises were similar to those which would have been heard almost a decade previously.

The New Year's Eve's Nun

D: 1939

L: Cheltenham, Gloucestershire

S: Peter Underwood

A case which repeats itself with regularity is obviously a boon to any researcher as it provides the opportunity for prediction and therefore the collection of information. The case known as the 'New Year's Eve Nun' would seem to be just such a case, although unfortunately the apparition has not appeared in recent years and may have faded away as these events sometimes do.

At the time when the building in question was a girls' school a nurse there, Margo Vincent Smith first reported seeing the form of the nun at six-fifteen in the evening on New Year's Eve 1939. In fact it was the headmaster who pointed out the figure sitting at the edge of the playground. Together the headmaster and Miss Vincent Smith watched the nun apparently sit down although there was no chair on which she could sit. Perhaps in some former time a white-habit-clad nun had sat on a chair that had existed there. Perhaps she had been thinking through a problem, and her emotional intensity had left its imprint.

The couple watched the figure from the window but when the headmaster attempted to see if he could get closer it disappeared.

Margo Vincent Smith also saw the same apparition the following New Year's Eve at seven-fifteen in the evening. (It has been suggested that the difference may have been due to changes in Greenwich Mean Time and British Summer Time.) This time the headmaster got to the edge of the playground and saw that the figure was apparently three-dimensional, well-formed and well-defined.

An interesting facet of the case (suggestive of the electrical interference more commonly reported in 'technological' cases such as UFO reports) was that when the headmaster shone a torch at the apparition, it went out and thereafter the torch could not be made to work again. Margo Vincent Smith did not feel comfortable in the presence of the unmoving form and no communication was attempted by either her or the headmaster.

The building is now a private residence and the present owners have not encouraged psychic researchers.

The Old Post Office
D: 1892

L: Royston, Hertfordshire

S: Peter Underwood

From 1892 until well into the twentieth century, a number of paranormal sounds were reported at Royston Old Post Office. Commonest of all was a sound resembling wood being chopped which was reported by many different members of staff at different times. After hearing the sound of the 'wood chopper' during the night many workers refused to do night duty.

Another sound was that of breaking glass. The last postmaster, John Freeman, was in the building at three o'clock in the morning when he heard what sounded like the crash of breaking glass. He checked the whole building but could find none broken. Shortly afterwards he mentioned the sound to the night-delivery man. The delivery man seemed to believe that Freeman was imagining things when suddenly they both heard the sound of glass being smashed in the next room. They searched that room but could find no broken glass anywhere there or indeed anywhere else in the building. The following morning Freeman also checked neighbouring houses and found that no one had suffered a broken window during that night.

Freeman also heard another series of sounds. They sounded like a door banging but immediate investigation produced no explanation. On one occasion Freeman himself examined all the doors after hearing the sound and found them all standing wide open. As he was conducting his examination he began to realise that what seemed to be an echo of his own footsteps was in fact a separate set of footsteps walking behind him, though no one could be seen. Freeman also said that on one occasion he had watched a key turn in a door by itself.

One possible explanation for the anomalous noises, and particularly for the wood-chopping sound, was that they might be the echo of horses on the stable floors at the manor house across the road. However, this theory was dismissed when the sounds were heard when no horses were present.

Another suggestion was that they were an echo from Royston Cave which was right next to the Old Post Office. This cave is bell-shaped and some 26 feet high, and 17 feet across. The cave contains carvings and paintings of images that are believed to date from the time of Richard the Lionheart and the Crusades. No elaboration on that theory was forthcoming.

Exactly the same sounds and noises were reported consistently from 1892 until 1936 when the new Post Office was opened. They were also heard many years later when the old building was being converted into a community centre and indeed they were investigated at that time by Peter Underwood and Tom Brown. What was clear then was that the workmen, who had no knowledge of the history of the building, were reporting exactly the same noises during their conversion work as had been heard years before. Underwood points out that during the Second World War the building was used as a servicemen's club and the floor level of the building was altered. No paranormal sounds were heard during that period, but they began again when the floors were returned to their original level.

The Phantom Violinist

D: 1956

L: Stainland, nr. Halifax, Yorkshire

S: Terence Whitaker

Mr Albert Paradise first moved to his cottage in about 1920, when he was still a child. The cottage is in Stainland near Halifax, Yorkshire. Because Mr Paradise's father had a fear of gas and electricity, the house did not have anything other than a coal fire and oil lamps or candles until his death in the 1950s.

On New Year's Eve 1956 Mr Paradise was in bed listening to the radio; he had not been drinking despite the festive season. Mr Paradise had left the bedroom curtains open and was lying in bed listening to music. In the room was a fireplace with a Victorian print above it. Mr Paradise apparently saw a face appear in the frame where the picture was, and then watched – in terror – as a figure appeared to walk out of the fireplace and towards the bed. Mr Paradise described the apparition as having a white face, sunken eyes and long flowing white hair.

Even more extraordinary, the figure was apparently playing a violin. Mr Paradise left the bedroom at fairly high speed, and in terror.

A few nights later he got the feeling that someone was behind him when he was in the kitchen and was too afraid to turn around; he remained rigid in the kitchen, afraid to go to bed. Terence Whitaker wrote up the house in his book *England's Ghostly Heritage*. He indicated that no further reports were received of the apparition after the fireplace had been bricked up and the house fitted with electricity.

Sax Rohmer's Sighting
D: (No date)
L: Haiti, West Indies
S: Peter Underwood

Sax Rohmer, creator of fictional detective Fu Manchu, and his wife Elizabeth were together on the terrace of a hotel they were staying in in Haiti when they saw a native girl approaching, carrying a fan. She sat in a cane chair fanning herself and staring at the Rohmers rather boldly. Before they could speak to her she got up and walked into the hotel. Rohmer followed her.

Inside the hotel he could see no one and the desk clerk denied that anyone had just walked in. The mystery was never solved.

Rushbrooke Hall
D: Since 1579
L: Nr. Bury St Edmunds, Suffolk
S: Peter Underwood

In 1578 Queen Elizabeth I visited Rushbrooke Hall in Suffolk. During that time an unknown lady was murdered and thrown through a window into the moat. It was reputed that on each anniversary of the Queen's visit the whole episode was re-enacted.

On the anniversary of the Queen's visit in 1942 Peter Underwood and three friends arranged to stay the night in the appropriate room.

Just before two o'clock in the morning the window slammed back against the wall, violently and apparently of its own accord. (Underwood concedes that it may simply have been insecurely fastened but points out that it had been securely closed for at least three hours previously.) The group looked out of the window and as they were looking down into the moat they felt an icy draft passing over their heads. From the moat below came a dull 'plop' as something apparently hit and disturbed the surface of the water.

St Dunstan's Church
D: 1930
L: East Acton, London
S: Peter Underwood

During the 1930s there were well-documented sightings of a procession of hooded monks in St Dunstan's Church, East Acton. They were originally reported by the Rev. Philip Bousted and confirmed by the Rev. Hugh Anton-Stevens. Anton-Stevens was adamant that up to a dozen monks could be seen walking up the central aisle of the church on occasion. He described them as wearing gold and brown hooded habits. In addition he described a violet hooded monk that he had been able to have conversations with on a number of occasions. He also stated that three other people had seen the monk.

The procession was apparently best seen out of the corner of the eye and seemed to disappear when looked at directly. This may at first seem rather a suspicious characteristic but may in fact be the result of a characteristic of whatever frequency waves were transmitting the image; once understood, it may be no more 'paranormal' than any other energy pattern.

One newspaper man, former naval officer Kenneth Mason, saw the procession of monks coming up the aisle and courageously decided to bar their way. Rather alarmingly, they apparently walked right through him.

After publishing an article in which he described talking to one of the ghostly monks, and indeed claimed that the article had been dictated to him by the monk, Hugh Anton-Stevens became rather distressed by the type of publicity he attracted. From that point on he did not encourage investigation.

Noel Streatfeild
D: (No date)
L: Sussex
S: Peter Underwood

When Noel Streatfeild was a child in Sussex, where her father was a curate, she and her brother and sisters often saw the ghost of a young girl in a crinoline. Sometimes the girl was accompanied by an adult. Visitors to the house often told of seeing the apparitions and many refused to stay as guests there again.

After the Streatfeilds had left and a new vicar took over the house, his wife saw, through the dining-room window, exactly the same apparition standing on the lawn. In their time in the house the vicar and his wife saw the young girl many times.

After a period there they decided to modernise the house and during repairs to the staircase the skeletons of a young child and a woman were discovered. They were given proper burial and the ghosts appeared no more.

A Student's Return

D: 20th century

L: Nr. Preston, Lancashire

S: Prof. Colin Gardner

The emotional content of some hauntings is highlighted by those ghosts that appear around the time of particular anniversaries. Some people believe that 'anniversary' ghosts are further confirmation of the 'recording' theory and that they appear around event-anniversaries because at those times the weather and other conditions happen to be about the same each year. The following episode concerns a possible anniversary ghost connected by emotion to a particular place and time.

'Bob and Kathy' moved into a new semi-detached bungalow in a small village in Lancashire. Neither of them had any interest or previous experience of anything paranormal and they were therefore all the more surprised to find themselves inheriting the ghost with their bungalow.

Their later investigation was to prove that very few owners of the bungalow had lived in it for long: the longest time an occupant had lived there was just over three and a half years and many had stayed for a considerably shorter period of time. Indeed, Bob and Kathy themselves would shortly leave their bungalow, adding to the list of short-term residents.

Shortly after moving into the bungalow Kathy was in the kitchen washing up when she saw a shadow cross the kitchen window and looked up. She could see the apparently solid form of a young man in old brown corduroy trousers, a dirty grey jacket and muddy heavy shoes. The clothes were generally contemporary and indeed the figure could have passed for a youth from a local farm. Kathy watched the man walk through the garden towards a hawthorn hedge; she rushed out to find out why he was wandering around in her garden. She could find no sign of him.

In subsequent weeks this sequence repeated itself many times. The figure would always walk with its head down looking at the ground; he would walk to the back door of the bungalow but instead of knocking on it, which it seemed he was going to do, he would then turn and walk to the bottom of the garden. Kathy was able to watch him walk through the thick hawthorn hedge into the middle of an adjoining field where he would vanish. He would sometimes appear faintly at some random point on his regular route; sometimes he would appear faint and perhaps a little translucent; at other times very solid and 'real' looking. He was always dressed the same way, he always had the same expression and always kept to the same route (this suggests the 'recording' theory with the difference between translucence or solidity perhaps being dependent on climatic conditions and so on).

Kathy did not tell her children as she did not want to alarm them. Although her husband was understanding he never managed to see the figure and he remained sceptical.

During a Sunday afternoon visit, as Kathy's parents got out of their car and approached the house they saw the figure of the young man walking towards the bungalow. They followed him towards the back of the house and on reaching it found the back door, which opened into the dining room, ajar. Not wishing to interrupt what they thought was their daughter's other visitor, they cautiously approached. The ghost was no longer visible to them, and no one inside saw him. Inside, Bob, Kathy and the children were having coffee and finishing off lunch when the parents knocked on the door. Kathy's mother asked who the other visitor was and was told that there was no other visitor. Kathy's mother and father both confirmed having followed the young man along the drive, and they described him. Kathy knew immediately that it was the description of the same person she had been seeing and took comfort in the fact that it was clearly not just her imagination (though perhaps a little less comfort in the now more certain knowledge that he was a ghost).

Months passed and the man appeared no more; Kathy began to push him into her past. Suddenly, a year later, Kathy was at the rear kitchen window looking at the flowers when she suddenly saw the figure walking past. Three days later Kathy and her parents were sitting on the patio at the rear of the bungalow when the young man suddenly walked in from the driveway and proceeded to walk around the garden in front of everyone. Kathy's mother shouted at him but received no response. Both Kathy and her mother followed the figure (though afterwards they wondered what they would have done if they had caught up with him!) and watched him disappear as always. In fact, no attempt by Kathy to attract the attention of the apparition ever elicited any sort of response; the figure simply continued to trace and retrace an identical path. The only conclusion that they were able to come to about the figure was that it only appeared in October.

Now concerned for his wife, Bob was able to request help from the Institute for Psychical Research, whose Professor Colin Gardner later published an account of the events in his book *Ghost Watch*. He was able to undertake an investigation.

Before the bungalow had been built the land had been part of a farm which still included the fields at the rear of the house. A path had once existed, cutting across the land where the bungalow and its garden now stood, which corresponded exactly to the route taken by the figure.

It seems that the couple at the farm had tried to encourage their son to study hard at school rather than work the land and he had done so and had gained a place at university. However, he had become troubled and would often walk the path around the fields with his head down, trying to arrive at some decision in his mind. As is often the case with young men, the parents were unable to break into his isolation and assist him; they could only hope that he would work out the problem for himself. Unfortunately he did not and one afternoon in October their son threw himself into a pond and drowned.

Jeremy Thorpe

D: 20th century

L: Old Priory, Trethevy, North Cornwall

S: Ben Noakes

The one-time leader of the Liberal Party, Jeremy Thorpe, was on holiday at Trethevy in North Cornwall, during his university days.

At a dinner party at the Old Priory, Mr Thorpe went to the bathroom, noticing a particularly strange stone slab that broke up the otherwise ordinary room.

As he came out of the bathroom and was walking back along the passage to go back downstairs he noticed a monk in a brown habit going into the bathroom. The monk ignored Mr Thorpe's 'Good evening'.

On asking the host and hostess who the monk was he was told that it was the prior and that he had 'lived' at the priory for several hundred years. He had apparently been murdered there and laid out on the slab that was now part of the bathroom; although he was seen frequently he had never been in any way unpleasant to guests.

5
Fights
and Battles

In the previous section we looked at replays and recordings of ghostly phenomena. If at least one of the factors governing the embedding of the replay into the environment in the first place is the emotion of the moment then it is hardly surprising that fierce and passionate battles should leave their impression through time. This section looks at a variety of battles apparently being replayed across England, Scotland and as far afield as India and Croatia.

Apparition of Spirits
D: (No date)

L: Ancient Campania, Italy

S: Legend

In *The City of God* St Augustine reported the case of witnesses who heard and saw a spectral battle between evil spirits taking place on a plain in Campania in Southern Italy, and found afterwards that the footprints of the men and the horses could be seen on the ground. No battle had in fact taken place but shortly afterwards one did, on exactly the same site. This report from the Roman Civil Wars is too old for investigation and remains purely anecdotal, but if it has any substance it suggests that the 'recording' theory of ghosts would have to encompass the possibility that the recordings can be 'replayed' before the actual event itself has happened; it would therefore be transcending the natural laws governing the passage of time as we understand them. Perhaps such an event is more easily – but no less controversially – explainable in terms of premonition.

The Battle of Edgehill

D: 1642
L: Nr. Kineton, Warwickshire
S: Various

The battle of Edgehill in Warwickshire was the first major battle of the English Civil War in 1642, involving 14,000 men in combat. Shortly after it took place, on four successive weekend nights, many visitors to the battlefield were able to see the event 'replay' itself. As described in a pamphlet published at the time, 'A great wonder in heaven shewing the late apparitions and prodigious noyse of war and battels, seen on Edge-Hill, neere Keinton, in Northamptonshire 1642.' The king, Charles I, sent out some notables to witness this event and they swore statements that they had done so.

The Flaming Sword

D: 1888
L: Verasdin, Croatia
S: R.J.M. Rickard and J. Michell (*Phenomena*)

In August 1888 several witnesses at Varasdin in Croatia saw the extraordinary spectacle of infantry divisions marching through the skies led by a captain with a flaming sword. The apparitions occurred over three days, each time lasting for several hours. Investigations failed to discover any real soldiers that could have accounted for the apparition, by way of mirage, or any other explanation for this repeated yet highly localised phenomenon.

Highlanders on Skye

D: 1956
L: Cuillin Hills, Skye
S: R.J.M. Rickard and J. Michell (*Phenomena*)

In November 1956 Oxford geology student Peter Zinovieff and his half-brother Patrick Skipwitch were camping in the south of the island of Skye, in the Cuillin Hills. At approximately three o'clock in the morning Peter heard some strange noises and saw, outside the tent, many kilted Highlanders charging across the stony ground. He woke Patrick who confirmed the sighting; both of them were frightened. The following night they were camping a little higher in the hills and deliberately staying awake to see whether or not the spectral army would return. It did not and they fell asleep. However, at 4 a.m. they were awakened by the same noises and saw the Highlanders stumbling across the boulders, perhaps in retreat, and looking half dead. The following morning they told their story to a Mr Ian Campbell at Sligachan Hotel, on the coast near Loch Sligachan; he told them that he had heard of such reports before and believed the soldiers to be ghosts from either the thirteenth century or 'the 1745 Jacobite rebellion'. The Jacobite Rebellion was led by 'Bonnie Prince Charlie' to restore the Stuarts to the Scottish throne, though it failed, leaving Charles running 'over the sea to Skye'.

An Indian Mutiny
D: Late 19th or early 20th century
L: India
S: John Masters (*Bugles and a Tiger*)

John Masters, who served in the Indian Army in the 1930s prior to Indian independence, wrote of several ghost sightings in his book *Bugles and a Tiger*, published in 1956.

A friend of his who was serving in the Indian Cavalry was living in the old sturdily built bungalows that had been erected before the Mutiny of 1857. Many such bungalows still existed in places such as Meerut, Delhi and Bareilly.

One June night the friend awoke, finding his room hot and airless; outside it was silent. On the wall above his bed he could see a flickering light which suggested a bonfire burning on the lawn outside; when he got up to look he could see no fire. Despite this he could still see the reflected flames flickering on the wall before they died away.

This occurred for four nights running, getting stronger and brighter each time. On the fourth night he left his bungalow and went out on to the veranda. On the lawn he could see two 'strangely dressed figures' moving around; he thought they were armed and decided to approach them, but as he did so he discovered there was nothing there.

A historical check of the area found that another bungalow had once stood near his, in the same grounds. On a June night in 1857 two soldiers from the Bengal Native Cavalry had murdered their adjutant and destroyed the other bungalow, burning the bodies of the adjutant, his wife and children. This act had triggered the Mutiny in the area. It appears that the flames he saw reflected on his wall were ghosts of the destruction of the neighbouring bungalow.

Otterburn

D: 1960

L: Otterburn, Northumberland

S: *Weekend* magazine

Otterburn in Northumberland is the site of a battle fought in 1388 when the Scots, led by Douglas, defeated the English.

In November 1960 a Mrs Dorothy Strong was in a taxi when she suddenly witnessed the phantom army that had been reported by others in the area. Her story is extraordinary in that it seems to also indicate some parallels between this rather ancient phenomenon of battle 'replays' and the more modern one of UFO sightings, particularly that of vehicle interference: 'Suddenly the engine died, the fare-meter went haywire and the taxi was as if it was being forced against an invisible wall. The soldiers seemed to close in on us and then fade into thin air.'

Did the presence of a spectral army affect the taxi's electrical circuits; did some mechanism of the taxi's electrical circuits cause the 'replay' of the spectral army to appear; or did some quite unconnected force manage both to interfere with the circuits of the taxi and at the same time trigger the replay?

Souter Fell

D: 1735

L: Cumbria

S: Various

Anniversary ghosts, those ghosts seen on specific anniversary dates, always hint at some sort of emotional content. However, we have also suggested that anniversary ghosts are effectively 'recordings' of events which 'replay', given the correct atmospheric and other conditions. The point about them is that they often retrace specific steps that the original being traced out in some earlier time.

The ghost army first seen on Souter Fell in the English Lake District in 1735 is a variation that needs to be considered – it appeared where no army could be, given the terrain, suggesting that if it *was* a replay it had somehow moved its location.

In this instance the army was seen on the mountainsides and since they are not likely to have significantly changed form in recent history, the replay seems to have shifted from its former location. Any other explanation for this particular anniversary haunting must take account of what would seem to be quite probable formation of troops in a quite improbable location.

It was Midsummer Eve 1735. A farmhand from a farm owned by a Mr Lancaster looked up from the fields to Souter Fell. Souter Fell is on the northern side of what is now the Keswick to Penrith A66 road above the village of Scales and near the peak known as Blencathra. Souter Fell, as the farmhand knew, is some 900 feet high and its sides are precipices, quite inaccessible for an army. Yet he saw a huge army marching east to west until it disappeared in a cleft in the mountainside. The farmhand told Mr Lancaster what he had seen but his claims were rejected with scorn and when the story got out to the local villagers they joined in the debunking.

Exactly two years later, on Midsummer Eve, Mr Lancaster was forced to eat his words! Looking up, at the same place, Mr Lancaster first saw a number of men leaving their horses and instantly rejected his initial impression that there might be a hunt taking place; no hunt could possibly operate at such a height. Some ten minutes or so later they were followed by what seemed to be a regiment of the cavalry, behind which came the infantry. Behind them were some stragglers running to catch up with the army. Again, the whole lot disappeared into the mountainside.

Mr Lancaster and his family, all of whom had witnessed the event, went home and told their story to the villagers. Given what had happened two years before he might have been wise to have been more cautious for he too fell prey to their scorn and ridicule.

On Midsummer Eve 1745 Mr Lancaster was prepared for the replay of the sighting he had had eight years earlier, and ten years to the day of the original sighting by his farmhand. This time he had with him twenty-six other people to verify what he hoped they might see.

Apparently they all saw the incredible army moving over the summit of Souter Fell. Even carriages were seen, which had not been reported before, and the procession went on for some considerable time, much to the incredulous amazement of the watching group. So convinced were they that the following day many of them climbed Souter Fell to inspect the hoof marks of the horses and the wheel tracks of the carriages, yet they found nothing to suggest that such a procession had ever passed, although it had been less than 24 hours before. Their statements were sworn before a magistrate.

The inevitable also happened: people who had seen similar apparitions but had had the caution to keep quiet about them for fear of ridicule now came forward. As is also usually the case, those who came forward had slightly different stories to tell: that of Mr Wren suggests that it was the actual location which was prone to recordings rather than the spectres. Mr Wren of Wilton Hall stated that on a summer's evening in 1743 he had seen a man and a dog chasing some wild horses at a most precarious part of Souter Fell. He had been with his farmhand who had confirmed the sighting. Presumably he had not believed it likely that they had been there in body, but rather only in spirit, given the terrain. Although there were suggestions offered to explain the ghost army – mirages, visions and so on – the Lancaster family stuck to their belief that what they had seen was real.

6
The Wicked
and the Cruel

Whatever the explanation for ghosts and hauntings, the likelihood that they can be created by wicked and cruel acts seems distinctly high. Almost any explanation for ghosts can accommodate this factor; for those who believe that ghosts are the spirits of the dead, the victims of cruelty may well return to seek revenge or to give their side of the story. For those who believe ghosts to be recordings then the emotions and passions may well be one of the factors which imprints the recording in the first place. The stories in this section include the spirit of a man in prison in an iron cage, the ghost of a wild and wicked man put to death for the murder of his children and other ghostly victims of man's inhumanity to man.

Calverley Hall
   D: 17th century
   L: Yorkshire
   S: Keith Poole

This case was reported by Keith B. Poole in his book *Britain's Haunted Heritage*.

At the turn of the sixteenth century Walter Calverley was the occupant of Calverley Hall which dated back through his family to 1135. Although a country squire by virtue of circumstance, Calverley spent a good deal of time in London leading the hedonistic life of a playboy and rake, drinking, gambling and womanising. Such a lifestyle leading to an almost inevitable conclusion, Calverley became virtually bankrupt, mortgaged the Hall, failed to meet his debts and ended up getting his brother imprisoned for non-payment as he had stood guarantor.

On a visit to his country home, in a fit of drunkenness, he

accused his wife of unfaithfulness and on 23 April 1604, he dashed into the Hall, speared his four-year-old son's head with a dagger and carried the bleeding child into his wife's bedroom. In the room a nurse was sitting with the second child in her arms when Walter ran in holding the dagger, the corpse of his now-dead son under one arm, and drove the dagger into the second child's body, killing him also. He went on to assault the nurse and then stabbed his wife, leaving her for dead.

Not yet content, he rode off on horseback towards the village of Norton to murder his third son who was in the village with his nurse. He was arrested before reaching him, and sent to Wakefield jail.

At York Assizes he was tried for murder and found guilty. Had he pleaded guilty his property would have passed to the Crown and he therefore refused to do so; having been found guilty, the penalty passed on him was to suffer death by *peine forte et dure*. This is a particularly unpleasant form of execution where the victim is tied to a stone floor and heavy weights placed on the stomach, gradually increasing the pressure, until the victim is slowly crushed to death. Sentence was carried out in York Castle and Walter was buried at St Mary's Church in Castlegate. It seems that his body was later removed to Calverley Churchyard to lie amongst his ancestors. Hauntings are reported at the churchyard and not St Mary's Church.

In the 1600s an insubstantial form displaying an angry face and mad eyes – and holding a blood-stained dagger was seen; most commonly it was reported as gliding along the lane from the hall to Calverley Church. Less likely, and certainly more hysterical, were the reports of Calverley and his drunken colleagues riding around in the woods on headless horses; there were even reports of headless horses galloping around inside the hall, up the stairs and into the bedroom where the murders took place. Reports of the ghosts of the two murdered children crying out for their mother were also made.

These reports from the 1600s ceased for a time but recurred in the late eighteenth century as witnessed by a report from a Mr Burdsall, a Wesleyan preacher who had been at the hall one night.

Mr Burdsall woke up shortly after falling asleep feeling pressing on his chest. The bed moved and Mr Burdsall was thrown out. This happened three times until finally at one o'clock he gave up and got dressed, not returning to the bed.

On 5 January 1884 Calverley Church bell rang at one o'clock in the morning but ceased as soon as the villagers put the key in the door to investigate the noise. No investigation was in fact undertaken, possibly due to fear, but Walter Calverley's ghost was unanimously elected chief suspect.

Shortly after this, some local boys conducted a seance to see if they could raise Calverley's ghost. They frightened themselves sufficiently to end up running away in all directions, having seen a mysterious 'something'.

Since that time there have been no further reports.

Marie LeMoyne
D: 1948
L: Barnwell Castle, Northamptonshire
S: Joan Forman

Described by Joan Forman in her book *Haunted Royal Homes*, the story of the haunting of Barnwell Castle by Marie LeMoyne is indeed atmospheric.

During 1948, Northamptonshire local historian Tom Lichfield and a friend who exhibited psychic abilities undertook a series of seances in order to investigate apparent hauntings and rumours surrounding Barnwell Castle in Northamptonshire. Three such seances were held, two at Lichfield's house and a third within the castle ruins themselves. The first seance took place on 20 September 1948 during which a spirit claiming to be a former abbot of nearby Ramsey Abbey was apparently contacted. The abbot informed those gathered at the seance that the castle had been used as a court of justice and execution in the fourteenth century, a fact which was later verified by records of the abbey.

Another spirit came through at this seance, identifying herself as Marie LeMoyne. The castle had been completed in 1266 by a Berengarius LeMoyne. Marie referred to horror and an untimely death and said that she herself had died while the castle was still being built and that her secret lay in a chest in the dungeon. She had apparently been imprisoned in the castle but did not reveal who had imprisoned her.

Tom Lichfield's researches uncovered three pieces of information to substantiate Marie's story: one of the owners of the castle named LeMoyne had had a wife named Marie, whilst another local legend told that Berengarius LeMoyne had walled up a woman alive in the still uncompleted structure. Further records indicated that a Marie LeMoyne had indeed died during the building of the castle.

Ten days later, on 30 September 1948, the second seance was held and Berengarius LeMoyne himself 'came through'. Berengarius LeMoyne blamed his excesses on his mind having become unhinged due to the pressure put on him by Abbot William of nearby Godmanchester, who was apparently trying to claim the castle and the lands for the church.

On 9 November 1948 the third seance was held in the northeast tower of Barnwell Castle itself. According to Joan Forman, the seance was brief, but with frightening results. The seance contacted Berengarius LeMoyne and asked him what he wanted to say. He apparently replied: '*I* will fire to warn you.' Suddenly above the heads of both Lichfield and his colleague there was a sharp crack and when the two men turned they found themselves looking at the upper body of a monk poised in the doorway. The two were terrified and left immediately. It was some time later that Tom Lichfield found the insignia of the LeMoyne family in another local church; it was the upper torso of a monk carrying a folded whip in his hand.

Angharad Llewelyn
D: 1969
L: Wales
S: Andrew MacKenzie

Detective Inspector D. Elvet Price, of the Metropolitan Police Force, stayed the night in a Welsh hotel in June 1969. Just before he settled down for the night a minor incident occurred which may have had a bearing on what was to follow. As he was going to the bathroom he saw a woman walking towards him dressed in long old-fashioned clothes. Although he greeted her she walked past him like a zombie and as if he did not exist.

Once in his bedroom Detective Inspector Price put out the light and fell asleep. It was approximately one-thirty in the morning when he awoke, hearing banging, choking and gasping noises in his room; they seemed to be at floor level. He felt a tremendous coldness engulfing him and he switched on the lights. The noises stopped and, having confirmed that no one else was in the room, Detective Inspector Price put out the light and went back to sleep. At three o'clock in the morning exactly the same noises and cold recurred and gave Price some cause for concern. Still he managed to get back to sleep.

At four-fifteen in the morning the same thing happened yet again and this time Price was too scared to ignore it, but he left the light on and with no further manifestation was able to sleep soundly for the rest of the night.

Talking to a local policeman, Price discovered that the pub he had been staying in was reputed to be haunted. The conversation led to Price discovering the history of an event that had taken place in 1920 in the same pub/hotel.

On 30 August 1920 Angharad Llewelyn, the wife of the landlord, Guto Llewelyn, died a violent death in an upstairs room in the building. It seems that she had been roughly beaten, so severely throttled that her windpipe was broken, and she had been bruised and beaten around the abdomen and thighs. Her husband was charged with her murder, initially alongside a lodger at the hotel, Dai Richards, but the case against the latter was later dropped.

At the trial witnesses said that, although Angharad Llewelyn was *a good and dutiful wife*, her husband was hot-tempered and prone to violence. On the night of her death Angharad Llewelyn had stormed upstairs and refused to come down after an argument when her husband had become angry because neither Angharad nor his servant had used a new milk separator that he had purchased.

Dai Richards went upstairs shortly afterwards and discovered that there seemed to be something wrong with Mrs Llewelyn. He called down to her husband, but fell asleep on the end of the bed while waiting for him; at the trial he claimed his beer had been drugged.

Llewelyn said that he had awoken in the early hours of the morning and had gone upstairs to find his wife dead and Richards lying on the end of the bed, though in fact he never accused Richards of her death.

The judge stated that he believed the prosecution's case that

Llewelyn had killed his wife in a 'crime of passion' and that Llewelyn himself had been shocked to discover that she had not recovered from her injuries, which he had not intended to be fatal. Llewelyn was sentenced to five years' imprisonment.

This case has the emotional content of so many ghost reports but also perhaps suggests a 'recording'. It is possible that conditions in the room were appropriate for a recording to 'replay'.

Whether or not the woman seen by Detective Inspector Price when he was going to the bathroom was really in the hotel at that time or whether that itself was also a recording from an earlier time is open to question. The following morning Detective Inspector Price was able to confirm that in fact he was the only guest at the hotel that night.

The Man in the Iron Cage
D: c. 1786
L: Lille, France
S: Lord Halifax

Lord Halifax's rather dubious collection of ghost stories, first published in 1936, contains the story of 'The Man in the Iron Cage'. In 1865 a family staying in a house in the Place du Lion d'Or in Lille, France were disturbed during the night by the sound of footsteps in the room above which turned out to be an unoccupied, empty room. (This same story is attributed to 1785, or 1786, in other account). During their visit to town the family were told about the ghost in the house but asked the locals not to spread the stories around as it would frighten their servants.

After hearing the footsteps again, the mother of the family asked her maid who was sleeping in the room above, but once again was told that the room was empty. Within a week most of the French servants had experienced the ghost and were determined to leave the house.

During this time the story came out that in the room where the steps had been heard there had been an iron cage in which someone had once been imprisoned and whose ghost was presumed to be haunting the building.

The English maids also saw an apparition going through their room and were extremely frightened.

A tall thin figure was seen by members of the family, who

believed it to be one of their own number playing a practical joke, but it was very quickly discovered that the suspect was asleep and had been for over an hour. The maid confirmed that that was precisely the figure that they had earlier seen.

Two people living locally, Mr and Mrs Atkyns, visited the family shortly before they were due to leave the house and laughed at their stories of ghosts. Mrs Atkyns, with her terrier dog, determined to sleep in the house but apparently the next morning awoke frightened and disturbed, having seen an intruder which the dog refused to go near.

In response to this story's publication in *Cornhill* magazine, in the 1890s its author, the Rev. Sabine Baring-Gould, forwarded a letter to Halifax which had been sent to him and which appeared to corroborate the story. The writer of the letter had stayed at the Hôtel du Lion d'Or at Lille with two friends in 1887. They believed this might have been the same building, now converted. They had heard sounds very similar to those reported by the previous family during some of the sightings: slow dragging footsteps; and when they read the account in the magazine had been struck by the comparison and believed that perhaps they had experienced something similar. The man in the iron cage was held to be the heir to the house who had disappeared mysteriously. Legend has it that he was imprisoned in the iron cage by his uncle and later murdered by him.

Anne Palmer

D: 18th or 19th century
L: Rose Hall, Montego Bay, Jamaica
S: Peter Underwood

During the eighteenth century the island of Jamaica was dominated by sugar-cane plantations and the plantation landowners were the lords of the island. Most of the great mansions on the island belonged to them, and the highest social status was accorded to them.

From the 1750s onwards John and Rosa Palmer lived at Rose Hall in Montego Bay until Mrs Palmer's death on 1 May 1790. Theirs had been a relatively happy and decently run plantation with servants and slaves regarded and treated as if they were part of the family.

Late in life, at the age of 72, John Palmer met and married a 28-year-old girl from Tahiti called Anne, who became the second mistress of Rose Hall. Anne's history was already rather chequered before her marriage to John Palmer. She had had three husbands, all of whom had died under mysterious circumstances, with each death adding to her wealth and social standing. Rumour had it that Anne had murdered one husband with the help of the *obeahman*, a sort of voodoo witch doctor.

Anne's reign at Rose Hall was one of cruelty and scandal. The list of her sexual conquests even included her stepson as well as many of the slaves on the plantation. It was rumoured that she would periodically select a particular slave for her favourite and he would be given great personal attention until she tired of him, after which he would suddenly and mysteriously disappear.

John Palmer's son, Anne Palmer's stepson, with whom she was having a sexual relationship, was also having a relationship of his own with one of the slave girls. For reasons of his own, one of the plantation overseers reported the relationship to Anne Palmer, who had the young girl painfully put to death while she watched. Her stepson left Jamaica never to return, driven away from her by her cruel excesses. Gradually the Palmers became ostracised by those who had been their friends and Anne reputedly worked out her frustrations by torturing the plantation slaves, whose screams and cries were heard by many.

The inevitable happened; one night Anne Palmer was murdered in her bed by the slaves she tortured. The story has it that she was not buried but that her bones were thrown under the shade of a tree on the estate, preventing her spirit from resting.

Even after the death of John Palmer and the gradual decay of the now-abandoned estate, it was rumoured that screams and cries of terror could be heard echoing from the empty rooms.

One of the last caretakers of the estate broke his neck when he fell down the stone steps into the cellar and legend has it that he was pushed by the ghost of Anne Palmer.

Kittie Rankie
D: 19th century
L: Abergeldie Castle, Aberdeenshire
S: Joan Forman

Abergeldie Castle in Aberdeenshire is reputed to hold the ghost of Kittie Rankie who was burned as a witch on a hill overlooking the castle, after having been imprisoned in its cellars. In the mid-nineteenth century the daughter of a local doctor, Patricia Lindsay, was happy to play in the castle cellars during the day but would never do so after dark. Then she feared hearing the terrifying noises and ringing of bells that were said to haunt the cellars and which were ill omens for the clan Gordon who had originally lived in the castle and for whom it had been built.

Rosehall

D: 20th century
L: Nr. Rickmansworth, Hertfordshire
S: Peter Underwood

In his autobiography, *No Common Task*, the president of the Ghost Club, Peter Underwood, relates a story of a ghost of a beheaded person at a farmhouse in Hertfordshire, near Rickmansworth, called Rosehall.

Rosehall was a seventeenth-century farmhouse with nineteenth-century additions and was occupied for a time by Peter Underwood's maternal grandparents. The story is of a traveller who spent the night at Rosehall having been taken in by the occupants, presumably as a humanitarian gesture, given the terrible weather that night. He slept in one of the bedrooms in the farmhouse and during the night awoke to see the apparition of a man dressed in brown and green with golden buttons. The witness could not see the man's head, though this was apparently due to the fact that he was bending down in such a way that his head was hidden by the curtains of the four-poster bed he was in.

The next morning the visitor related his story to his hosts who admitted that the room was reputedly haunted by a headless ghost and they apologised for putting him in that room but it was the only one that had been available. They added that they themselves had not seen the apparition.

Later, the traveller started to tell his story to some people and was interrupted by two ladies who had also stayed at the farmhouse and had had an identical experience; they believed they had identified the apparition as that of a man who had been murdered in the room some years before, and who had had his head cut off.

Peter Underwood contacted the Hertfordshire county archivist and discovered that there had been a prayer meeting at the house at some point in the past in an attempt to 'lay' the ghost when it had been particularly active; it seemed that only strangers to the farmhouse had seen the apparition and never the owners. The people who owned Rosehall at the time of Underwood's inquiries thought *the story was nonsense*. However, when Underwood took some Ghost Club members to the house, three of them independently asked whether one particular bedroom was the one in the story and all 'guessed' correctly.

Sellis, Valet to the Duke of Cumberland

D: After 1810

L: St James's Palace

S: Joan Forman

Ernest Augustus, Duke of Cumberland, born on 6 June 1771 the son of King George III, became deeply unpopular. Although brave and intelligent, he combined these admirable qualities with viciousness and cruelty. He enjoyed his royal position hugely and showed almighty arrogance towards 'the common people'. One particular misdeed has been documented.

On 31 May 1810 Sellis, Cumberland's valet, was found dead in St James's Palace in London. He was found in bed with his throat cut from ear to ear; nearby was a bloody razor. At the inquest, no doubt in deference to the duke's position, the jury brought in a verdict of suicide. However, there may have been more to the story. It was believed that the duke might have seduced Sellis's daughter or wife, and that Sellis had tried to murder the duke. Then he had committed suicide or possibly the duke had killed him.

According to the testimony given at the inquest, the duke awoke during the night to find he was being attacked with blows from a sabre. As he struggled out of bed he was struck on the thigh: he called to his second valet, Neale, who ran in to attend the duke's injuries. Sellis was also called but was found lying dead in his bed.

And yet, if the duke really had been asleep a sabre attack would most likely have killed him. Furthermore it was rumoured that the razor with which Sellis had 'committed suicide' had been found several yards from the bed. The duke himself complained that he had suffered severe injuries which were hardly likely to have been self-inflicted just to elaborate the story, but the precise degree of the injuries is uncertain and may well have been quite light.

The public certainly seems to have favoured the murder theory and the duke was extremely unpopular in the years following the incident, being derided whenever he made public appearances.

There were many accounts of Sellis's ghost haunting St James's Palace in the years afterwards. The apparitions included Sellis with his throat cut and blood pouring out. Other reports included the sounds of struggling and shouting. It would appear that this particular apparition has faded away with time and there have been no recent reports.

Dick Turpin
D: 20th Century
L: Apsley Guise
S: Peter Underwood

This story relates to a house called Woodfield in Apsley Guise near Milton Keynes, Bedfordshire. It apparently came to light because the present owner was attempting to get a rates reduction on the grounds that the house was haunted! Peter Underwood heard of this and was able to make inquiries. The first part of the story concerns an earlier house on the same site, occupied some 200 years ago by a girl and her father. Whenever the father was away the girl would invite her lover to come and join her; the two were caught when the father returned unexpectedly one night. According to the legend, the lovers heard the father returning and hid themselves in a large cupboard in the pantry. They thought they were safe but the father had seen them getting into the cupboard and pushed heavy furniture up against the cupboard door, imprisoning them there where they died together.

The second part of the story concerns the highwayman Dick Turpin who is held to have discovered the bodies of the girl and her lover and used his discovery to blackmail the father into providing him with an occasional hide-out during his nocturnal activities.

Stories of ghosts around the house include the ghosts of the lovers, the hoof-beats of Dick Turpin's steed and the apparition of Dick Turpin himself.

According to the story, the bodies of the lovers were removed from their cupboard and buried beneath the floor of one particular room. During the last war Doreen Price, a fifteen-year-old girl evacuated to the house, claimed that she saw the girl's apparition reaching towards her in that room.

The elderly tenant of the house, Mrs Amy Dickinson, reported having heard strange sounds inside the house. A seance held at the house in which Peter Underwood participated revealed some information, some of it somewhat contradictory. Although there seemed to be evidence of a distressed woman and distressed lovers, the stories did not coincide with the legends. It appeared from the seance that one set of occupants of Woodfield may have been shot; there may have been an incident where a girl was raped and shot in front of her lover who was then shot. Of course there is the possibility of more than one tragedy having taken place either in the house or in the building that previously stood on the same site. During a subsequent seance Underwood saw what appeared to be the form of a face near the shoulder of medium George Kenneth though, as is typical of Underwood's meticulousness, he reserves the strong possibility that it was merely a trick of light or had some other logical explanation. He was unable to attract the attention of other people at the seance, who might otherwise have been able to corroborate his story, to the apparition. There was some corroboration, however, as Underwood's attention had originally been attracted by Peter Craven, who pointed out the form to him; Peter Craven was the medium's assistant.

Struggle at a Window
   D: (No date)
   L: Nr. Hitchin, Hertfordshire
   S: Peter Underwood

This story, related by the president of the Ghost Club, Peter Underwood, is important if only because he says it was the inspiration for him to set out on a lifetime's ghost-hunting.

While walking in the countryside with his uncle, Underwood had got into conversation with an elderly man living near a reputedly haunted mill near Hitchin in Hertfordshire.

According to the story, the mill had last been owned by an arrogant landowner who had made himself very unpopular by his meanness and wickedness, and his penchant for defiling young girls. There were many tales of girls who had been tricked into visiting the mill and subsequently raped; some had never been seen again. The most disturbing episode concerned a widow and her five daughters who had been threatened with eviction from one of the mill-owner's cottages following the death of her husband. On the day before the threatened eviction one of the daughters, a young and attractive girl of seventeen, went to the mill to appeal to the owner to extend their time of stay.

Concerned for her daughter, who had not returned, the widow gathered together a troop of neighbours and together they went to the mill where they heard the sounds of screaming coming from a room high up in the building. The mill-owner and the girl were evidently locked in a struggle when suddenly the mill burst into flames. The bodies of the owner and the girl were found together the next morning.

Underwood was told that the screaming could still be heard on September nights and there were those who believed they had seen the struggling figures of the man and the girl in the window even though that room now had no floor.

7
Ghosts with
a Message

Some hauntings may be random or at least *appear* to be pointless, but there are certainly many cases where the ghost appears to have a specific message to deliver and there are occasions when the accuracy of the message can be verified. This section contains such variety as murder victims returning to pinpoint their killers, a great grandmother protecting the newest born of the family by alerting her daughter, a message from Sir Malcolm Campbell to his speed-ace son and the crew of a crashed airliner protecting those they left behind.

Lady Beresford and the Black Velvet Ribbon
    D: 18th century
    L: Not given
    S: Lord Halifax

Brother and sister Lord Tyrone and Lady Beresford were orphaned as infants and placed under the guardianship of a couple with unorthodox religious beliefs. Those viewpoints were adopted by the children and drew them together in later life. Even in later life, when they were both married, they continued to be very close.

One morning Lady Beresford appeared at breakfast looking ill at ease, very pale and wearing a black ribbon around her wrist which she refused to speak about. She said to her husband, 'Let me beg you, Sir, never to ask about this ribbon again. From this day forward you will not see me without it. If it concerned you as a husband, I would tell you at once. I have never denied you any request, but about this ribbon I can say nothing and I beg you never to bring up the subject again.' She was agitated throughout breakfast and concerned that the post had not arrived. Her husband asked her if she was expecting a letter and what was causing her anxiety about the arrival of the post. Lady Beresford replied, 'I expect to hear that Lord Tyrone is dead, that he died last Tuesday at four o'clock.' Her husband was taken aback by this statement since he had never known his wife to be superstitious or to harbour thoughts of death. When the post did arrive a servant handed Lady Beresford a sealed letter which confirmed exactly the event she had described.

Lady Beresford further stunned her husband that breakfast by telling him, 'I can assure you without the possibility of doubt that I am now with child and the child will be a son.' Seven months later she gave birth to a son.

Her husband died a few years later and Lady Beresford moved to a smaller house. She lived in the company of a clergyman, his wife and young son but later caused a degree of scandal by marrying the young son despite the great difference in their age and social standing. There were great difficulties in the marriage, and a period of separation followed, but suddenly Lady Beresford reconciled herself with her husband and nine months later gave birth to their son.

Some weeks after the birth Lady Beresford was speaking to the clergyman, who had known her family for many years, and told him that she was in particularly good spirits because she was 48 that day. Thinking that it would please her to discover she was wrong, he told her that when he had looked up her date of birth in the parish register he had discovered that in fact she was only 47 that day. Lady Beresford was horrified and cried, 'You have signed my death warrant!'

Withdrawing to her room, she called together her eldest son, now twelve years old, and her friend Lady Cobb to confide her story to them. She told them of the circumstances surrounding the time she first wore the black velvet ribbon. It appears that her brother, Lord Tyrone, had, as they had agreed in life, appeared at her bed during the night after his death to discuss the validity of their religion from '*the other side of the bed*'. He told her then that he had died on the previous Tuesday at four o'clock. He also told her that she was pregnant and would have a son and gave her other details of her future, all of which apparently turned out to be accurate. He had foretold of her then husband's death and her second marriage and even the details of the unhappiness the second marriage would bring. Lord Tyrone's apparition had then informed her, 'You will die in the forty-seventh year of your age.'

When Lady Beresford asked the apparition if there was any way that her death could be prevented Lord Tyrone told her that if she did not accept the temptation of a second marriage she would cheat death.

It was only when Lady Beresford believed she had passed her 48th birthday that she felt she had beaten the warning and on realising that in fact she had only just entered that fateful year it became clear that she had not done so. Before midnight Lady Beresford was dead.

The black velvet ribbon is probably the least believable element of the story: if it is not a complete fiction then it is probably simply a detail from Lady Beresford's life which has become associated with the ghost phenomenon. According to Lady Beresford, she demanded proof of Lord Tyrone's authenticity as a ghost and he had touched her wrist at her behest, permanently withering the nerves and muscles beneath his touch. Lord Tyrone had then insisted that she bind her wrist and never let anyone see it, hence the black ribbon. When Lady Beresford died, Lady Cobb sent the servants from the room and unbound the wrist, which was indeed withered.

Buried Alive

D: Unknown
L: Italy
S: Philip Paul

This horrific story lacks sufficient detail to bear subsequent investigation, but it is included in Philip Paul's book *Some Unseen Power*.

It took place in an Italian village where a woman in her early forties died, causing great distress to her close relatives. The relatives sought to communicate with the dead woman and were apparently successful.

The woman, now deceased and speaking from 'the other side', indicated that she had been mistakenly taken for dead whilst in a coma and had been buried alive. Inside her coffin after burial she had come to and found herself hopelessly trapped. Shock and suffocation had eventually resulted in her death.

Her relatives were now more distressed than ever and had to admit to their priest that they had held the seance. Concerned at their hysteria, the priest managed to persuade the authorities to exhume the body.

When the coffin was opened the corpse was lying twisted, knees, hips and forehead bruised by repeated blows against the interior of the coffin and fingernails torn from clawing at the underside of the lid.

Sir Malcolm Campbell

D: 1964

L: Lake Eyre, Australia

S: John Pearson (*Bluebird and the Dead Lake*)

In 1935 speed ace Sir Malcolm Campbell came close to death in a serious crash at Utah when the wheel of one of his Bluebird cars caught fire. His son Donald often wondered how he had felt that day.

In 1964 Donald Campbell was driving his new Bluebird car on Lake Eyre, a dry salt lake in Australia during what was eventually to be a successful bid for the land-speed record. On the first of the two runs through the measured mile he ran into serious difficulties. At the end of the run, Campbell was sitting in the cockpit while the wheels were changed when Ken Norris, a member of the Bluebird team (indeed, one of the designers of the vehicle), noticed that Campbell was 'suddenly staring up at the perspex canopy in front of him. All the tension and strain seemed to have gone from his face. His eyes were open wide. Then he suddenly took a deep breath, shut his eyes and seemed to relax.' Campbell made the second run successfully, achieving the world land-speed record, though at great risk. The salt-lake track had disintegrated, the wheels had cut into the surface and rubber had torn from the tyres.

After the run Norris asked Campbell about that moment in the car when he was staring at the cockpit canopy:

'Don, what happened this morning . . . when you were sitting there in the cockpit waiting for the start, something happened to you, didn't it?'

Campbell described what happened: 'It was the most incredible thing I've ever experienced. You know what happened on that first run? I nearly killed myself. I was so near going out of control that it wasn't funny, and when I was sitting in the cockpit at the end of the run I really thought I had had it. For I knew the second run would be worse, I saw no hope at all. It was then that it was so extraordinary. You know how the canopy lifts up with the windscreen in front of the cockpit? Well, I suddenly looked up into it and there was my father reflected in the windscreen as clearly as you are sitting there now. I even recognised the white shirt and flannels he used to wear. For a few seconds he just looked at me, smiling. Then he said, "Well boy, now you know how I felt that time at Utah when the wheel caught fire in 1935. But don't worry, it will be all right, boy." Then he faded away.'

And it had indeed been all right!

Charles Dickens' Fictional Ghost
D: 1861

L: England

S: Charles Dickens

In 1861 Charles Dickens published *All The Year Round*, a collection of fictional ghost stories. It included the story of an artist travelling by train from London up to the country on 13 September who met a young lady who made him a strange request – that he should take a very close and careful look at her because one day he would be asked to paint her portrait from memory.

At the country house to which the artist had been travelling, he met the lady once again, sat next to her at dinner and engaged her in conversation as he would any other member of the dinner party. It was only afterwards that he discovered he was the only one who had seen the lady and he concluded that she was therefore a ghost.

Two years later the lady's father met the artist and asked him whether or not he could paint a portrait of his daughter who had died two years ago on 13 September; the father would give him a verbal description of her. Of course the artist realised exactly what had happened and was able to draw the lady he had met on the train, and at dinner, to the astonishment of her father.

This was a fictional tale and not a report of an encounter. The twist was yet to come . . . Dickens received a letter from an artist who not only claimed that the story was true but that it had happened to him on 13 September. Dickens apparently investigated the artist's claim and was so impressed that he published an account of it. As to how Dickens had fictionally picked up on to the truth. . .?

An Early Morning Alarm Call
    D: (No date)
    L: South Alberta, Canada
    S: Prof. Colin Gardner

According to the book *Ghost Watch* by Professor Colin Gardner of the Institute for Psychical Research, Sonya Fourche and her parents were staying at a hotel in Southern Alberta, Canada while touring the Canadian national parks. Sonya was a diabetic and required an insulin injection each morning, making her very dependent on alarm calls.

The hotel was duly asked to make an alarm call at precisely eight o'clock each morning; breakfast was to be left outside the door at the same time.

At precisely eight o'clock on the first morning the telephone in Sonya's room rang and a voice told her that it was eight o'clock, and that her breakfast would be outside the door in five minutes. Sonya gave herself the necessary injection of insulin and collected her breakfast and coffee. The following morning the telephone rang and the voice repeated the message of the previous morning. Sonya got up, gave herself her injection insulin, opened her door and found no breakfast whatsoever.

While waiting for them to deliver it she took a quick shower and, by now dressed, opened the door again – still no breakfast. Considering that it was now time her parents were up, she went down to their room but found them both asleep.

They were not amused to be woken up at something just after five o'clock in the morning. Sonya protested that she had had her eight o'clock alarm call but sure enough it was just after five o'clock. Sonya, checking her own watch back in her room, confirmed the time.

The family complained to the desk staff at the first opportunity; they were certain that no one would have come on to the desk until eight o'clock and that there would have been no one to make the call at five o'clock. Indeed, they pointed out that the telephones were switched off until eight. Suddenly the desk clerk realised that Sonya had been in Room No. 6 and explained, in a rather offhand way, that she had been woken up by the ghost of a desk clerk who, some years earlier had died in the hotel but seemed not yet to have given up work. Sonya was offered a book in which to write down her experience and which already contained the experiences of many previous victims of years gone by.

Professor Gardner's book does not indicate precisely which hotel was concerned, perhaps for obvious reasons, but according to Gardner, the hotel allowed the researcher to contact previous residents and from that the Institute of Psychical Research believed the evidence for the haunting was considerable.

Kevin Firmin

D: 1968
L: Yorkshire
S: Prof. Colin Gardner

Mary and Kevin Firmin had been married for sixteen years until 1955 when Kevin tragically died of throat cancer. He had suffered for several months with Mary nursing him at home; he died at three o'clock in the afternoon on Christmas Eve.

In the thirteen years after that date Mary spent Christmas Eve at her house in a kind of homage to her lost husband. However, that thirteenth year she agreed to spend the day with her sister Joan who lived nearby. Like Mary, Joan was also a widow and like Mary had brought up a (now-adult) son, Gordon. Unlike Mary's married son, Michael, Gordon was a confirmed bachelor and still lived at home with his mother; therefore he would be sharing Christmas Eve with them. After lunch on the day when Mary and Joan had been planning their Christmas Eve together, they were walking back to the village shops when suddenly Mary saw a frightening apparition. It was proceeded by a buzzing in her ears (interestingly a common report of UFO witnesses prior to their encounters); looking across to the church and the graveyard where Kevin was buried, Mary suddenly saw the apparition of her dead husband. He was dressed exactly as she remembered him, indeed in a sweater that she had knitted for him. Then he gestured towards the figure next to him. Mary found herself looking at Gordon, Joan's son with whom she had spent the morning and who was alive and well. Mary gasped and was so stunned she could say nothing; they staggered to a nearby cafe to sit down. Joan was alarmed at her sister's condition but Mary was able to tell her nothing about what she was seeing.

Mary had always wanted to see her dead husband and never had; now his reappearance was something she wished had not happened.

On Christmas Eve Gordon arrived, as promised, to collect Mary in his van and take her to lunch. Later in the evening Gordon left to go out with friends while Mary and Joan listened to the radio. Later Joan suggested they go to the local pub for a drink. When they arrived Joan spotted Gordon's van outside and said that they would probably see him in the pub. They were unaware that there was already a commotion inside the pub where an ambulance was being called.

In the pub they found Gordon's friend Terry and asked if Gordon was with him. Terry was taken aback and with obvious concern took the ladies outside. Sitting against the brick wall of the pub Gordon was seemingly unconscious, his head lolling on to his chest. The ambulance could be heard approaching through the night. When Joan knelt beside her son and lifted his head she discovered he was dead.

Mary virtually passed out that evening, so powerful were the emotions running through her: her horror at the death of her nephew and her pain for her sister, especially on Christmas Eve; also because of that frightening apparition that had now become a horrific reality.

Flight 401

D: After 1972
L: America
S: John Fuller

Late in the evening of 29 December 1972 a Lockheed L-1011 wide-body aircraft crashed in the Florida Everglades with considerable loss of life amongst both the crew and passengers. It marked the start of one of the most extraordinary tales of ghostly protection of modern times.

Even before the crash there had been a remarkable example of precognition concerning one of the airline's stewardesses, some two weeks before the flight. She described to her colleagues that she had had a premonition, and had seen an L-1011 coming in over the Everglades on a flight approach to Miami International late at night; she had seen the left wing crumble and the fuselage smashing into the ground; she also heard the cries of the injured. Asked when it was going to happen, she said, 'Around the holidays, closer to New Year.' Her colleagues asked her if they were going to be the crew and the stewardess replied, 'No, but it's going to be real close.' It was only a last-minute change of flight assignment which prevented that stewardess and her colleagues being the crew of Flight 401 which was to fulfil her premonition.

However, it was after the crash and the death of the crew that the 'protective' ghosts came into the story. Following the incident, the ghosts of Captain Bob Loft and the flight engineer, Second Officer Don Repo, appeared in several instances on identical aircraft, usually ones which had requisitioned recycled parts from the crashed L-1011.

The following is a selection of the apparitions as noted in John G. Fuller's book *The Ghost of Flight 401*:

At John F. Kennedy Airport where an L-1011 was being turned around for a flight to Miami it was reported that a vice-president of Eastern Airlines who had boarded the plane ahead of the regular passengers spoke to an Eastern Airlines captain in uniform who was sitting in the First Class section. During the conversation the vice-president suddenly realised he was talking to Bob Loft, who had died in the earlier crash. At that point Loft simply vanished and disappeared. A search of the plane was made and no sign of the captain found. The vice-president would not reveal his name.

At John F. Kennedy Airport again it was Captain Bob Loft who was seen by a captain and his two flight attendants. They apparently talked to him before he disappeared, causing the flight to be cancelled. The captain also declined to give his name.

An unnamed flight attendant opened one of the overhead compartments during a check of the First Class cabin and came eyeball to eyeball with Bob Loft's face. Another flight attendant at Miami opened a door in the galley oven compartment and saw the face of Second Officer Don Repo looking out at her.

While caterers were loading plane 318 (the most haunted of the L-1011s following the crash) there was a commotion when the catering crew left the plane saying they wouldn't go back. Apparently they had seen the flight engineer standing in the galley and he had disappeared in front of their eyes, leaving them 'very excitable'.

During a flight of plane 318 a male voice came over the PA system announcing the seat-belt and no-smoking precautions, yet no one on the crew had made the announcement and the PA system had not been in use.

During another flight of plane 318, from Atlanta to Miami, the crew heard a knocking coming from the 'hellhole' below the cockpit (which had been heavily implicated in the original crash of Flight 401). The engineer went down into the cramped workspace and saw the face of Second Officer Don Repo looking at him.

A flight engineer doing the pre-flight inspection of an L-1011 saw a man in an Eastern Airlines second officer's uniform sitting in his seat at the engineering panel. The engineer recognised Don Repo and the apparition said to him, 'You don't need to worry about the pre-flight, I've already done it.' The apparition then vanished in front of the engineer.

A stewardess in the lower galley of an L-1011 found that one oven indicated an overloaded circuit and a man in an engineer's uniform appeared to fix it. Another flight engineer appeared later and insisted he was the only one on the plane. The flight attendant, looking at Don Repo's photograph, identified him as the man who had first fixed the oven.

One captain from the flight of an L-1011 spoke to Repo, who commented, 'There will never be another crash of an L-1011 . . . We will not let it happen.'

A female passenger in the First Class section of plane 318, which was still sitting on the runway, found herself sitting next to an Eastern Airlines flight officer in uniform. The required head count of passengers had not yet taken place. The engineer apparently looked sick and pale and the passenger tried to speak to him but he would not respond. The passenger called the stewardess who agreed that the flight officer seemed ill. Then, in front of several other passengers as well as these two, the flight engineer simply disappeared leaving the woman completely hysterical. Shown photographs of Eastern Flight engineers, she picked out Don Repo.

The incidents which qualify the case for entry in this section include:

Aircraft 318, assigned designation Flight 903 from New York to Mexico City, was involved in another incident when a stewardess looking at the oven window saw the face of Don Repo looking back. The stewardess called another and together they went back to the galley and also called an engineer from the flight deck. In the galley all three heard Repo speak to them, saying, 'Watch out for fire on this airplane.' Then he disappeared. Although the plane reached Mexico City successfully it was on the next leg of its flight when one of the engines on the starboard wing would not start. Although the plane was safely cleared for take-off, at an altitude of 50 feet one engine stalled and backfired several times, needing to be shut off immediately. The plane was brought back to the runway and taken out of service. The disassembly of the engine showed no reason whatsoever for its malfunction.

Following this incident, when the plane was overhauled its cockpit voice-recorder was removed. In his book, John Fuller asked why that should have been done since it could have nothing to do with the faulty engine. He speculates that it may have had to do with rumours that parts were being removed from plane 318 because they were connected with the apparitions.

John Fuller undertook a ouija board experiment to contact the apparitions, with apparent success, and received two interesting messages from the ghost of Don Repo. One was the question, *'Did mice leave that family closet?'* and the other, *'To go into waste basket pennies sit there boys room.'* Fuller contacted Don Repo's daughter, Donna, and his wife, Alice, and the two apparently bizarre phrases were shown to have meaning. It seems that some mice had nested in the attic above the room they referred to as 'the family room' and despite Alice's son John setting traps they were hard to get rid of. The reference to the closet was resolved because access to the room was through the family room closet. Of the pennies Alice pointed out that Don Repo had collected Indian head pennies in a barrel which were in their son's room.

Grandpa Bull

D: 1932
L: Wiltshire
S: *Journal of the SPR* (1932)

One evening in February 1932 a Mrs Edwards and her eldest daughter, Mary, watched Samuel Bull, Mrs Edwards' father, walk to her bedridden mother's bedside and place his hand on her forehead. Samuel Bull had died eight months previously.

The sightings of Samuel Bull were confirmed by his wife, Mrs Jane Bull; Mrs Edwards's husband, James Bull; a grandson of the deceased along with other members of the family including a five-year-old child who recognised the figure as 'Grandpa Bull'. On one occasion the apparition was continuously visible for half an hour. He appeared quite normally solid to anyone who saw him.

The family lived in squalor in a house where certain rooms had been condemned as unsafe; now living and sleeping conditions were becoming even more strained by three of the children having to move downstairs since they refused to sleep upstairs where the apparition of their grandfather was walking.

An investigation by the Society for Psychical Research was undertaken and the Rev. George Hackett compiled a report. He believed that the members of the family gave acceptable, clear and definite answers to questions raised during the investigation, and a local resident Admiral Hyde Parker believed that the family were being truthful. Suggestions that the family might have been concocting the story to draw attention to their living conditions in the hope of acquiring better accommodation were considered but disregarded in view of the good faith of the witnesses.

Perhaps more importantly, it is worth noting that there are many reports of hauntings from people living in poor conditions and many of the classic poltergeist cases (such as the Enfield poltergeist or the Runcorn poltergeist, among others) have occurred in deprived circumstances. Rather than the simplistic suggestion that people concoct stories to acquire better council accommodation, it seems at least equally possible that squalid conditions create the stress necessary for the poltergeist to 'focus'. In this case we are not dealing with a poltergeist but

1. Abbas Hall, nr. Great Cornard, Suffolk: Lord Abinger and Yvonne Spalding both reported visions and sounds here

2. Woburn Abbey, Bedfordshire, has a number of ghosts, according to the Marquis of Tavistock

3

4

Borley Church and
churchyard (3) which,
along with the now-
demolished Rectory
(4), was a much-
haunted site. Harry
Price, the famous
psychic investigator,
(5) studied Borley over
a period of almost
twenty years

5

6. The Cavendish Hotel,
Harrogate: two independent
reports of similar hauntings here
were made to the authors
of this encyclopedia

7. The Theatre Royal,
Drury Lane: haunted by
the ghost of Dan Leno

8. The Grenadier Public House, Knightsbridge, London: various landlords have reported a ghost here, said to be that of a young soldier flogged to death for cheating at cards

9. The Home of Compassion, Thames Ditton, Surrey: haunted by its former nuns?

15. Kensington Palace: King George II has been heard and seen here, apparently still awaiting news from Europe

16. Keats' House, Hampstead: the poet's ghost was once seen outside this, his former home

17. President Abraham Lincoln haunts the White House in Washington and has been seen many times since President Calvin Coolidge's wife first saw him staring out of the Oval Office window

18. The Byward Tower in the Tower of London is said to be haunted by Sir Walter Raleigh

19. The Castle Inn, Edgehill, Warwickshire, is built on the site where King Charles I raised his standard for the famous battle of Edgehill

20. The Cuillin Hills, Isle of Skye: Highland soldiers from an earlier time have been seen here

perhaps similar forces were at work to create or allow for the appearance of 'Grandpa Bull'; until the mechanisms are understood these must be considered valid alternatives.

Great Grandmother's Warning

D: 20th century
L: Not given
S: Prof. Colin Gardner

On a fiercely cold day in February Edith Clegg was travelling by bus to visit her sister, Vera. She had left her two daughters, Alma and Hilda, in the house. Although Hilda actually lived nearby, since her husband was serving with the army in Germany and she was seven months pregnant she was staying with her mother at the time. Edith intended to return to the house at around ten o'clock that evening.

After a cold and unpleasant journey Edith arrived at Vera's house and was walking towards the front door when she suddenly saw the image of her dead mother standing in front of the door dressed in the clothes she always wore; then the apparition disappeared.

While Vera was making a cup of tea to warm Edith up and Edith was taking off her winter coat, the apparition of her mother reappeared. Her mother said nothing but her expression was worried and she pointed to the door twice, giving Edith a clear message that she should leave immediately. Then suddenly she disappeared again.

Despite the cold and the obvious attractions of a warm cup of tea, Edith realised that she simply had to return to her house, which she did. She was only just in time. Hilda's baby was arriving very prematurely and the ambulance was not going to get there on time. Alma cried with relief at her mother's return. Edith helped to deliver the baby, aided, she believed, by the presence of her dead mother. The baby weighed no more than a kilogram and was lucky to have been born alive, let alone to continue living. Edith warmed the infant in a drawer from a dressing table with blankets and a hot-water bottle until the ambulance came. It was generally accepted that she had saved the infant's life. Edith in turn gave thanks to the help her own dead mother had given her.

The Guilt of an Unmarried Mother

D: 1983

L: North Wales

S: Rev. J. Aelwyn Roberts

The Rev. J. Aelwyn Roberts was visited at his vicarage by an elderly couple who were concerned about their house becoming cold and depressed. They were not reporting specific noises or sightings but simply a feeling that the house was not a happy one. They had isolated an area at the top of the stairs near their bedroom door as the centre of this sensation but the vicar simply suggested at the time that a crucifix or cross on the wall and a few prayers would cure the problem.

A month later this remedy had not worked and the couple now slept downstairs, unable to face going upstairs where they regarded the ghost as having taken over. The Rev. Aelwyn Roberts now agreed to try and help and, together with Elwyn Roberts, a 'sensitive' with whom he often worked, visited the house. Elwyn Roberts agreed that the landing was the place to be as that was the area of strongest 'feeling' about the case.

Eventually Elwyn announced that the ghost was approaching and that he could feel her shyness. The ghost was crying and wanted to inform them that she had not killed her baby.

The full story gradually came out. The ghost was an unmarried mother named Margaret Ellis. They received the impression of a figure 73 and a date 1836, information relating to an Ernest Johnson and a house concerned with the mining of copper.

Margaret apparently gave birth to an illegitimate child, presumably by Ernest, but the father hired two vagabonds to kill the child; these two threw the baby down the stairs, resulting in its death. Local gossip suggested that the vagabond story was untrue and that Margaret Ellis had killed her own baby.

Aelwyn Roberts wrote to the rector of the parish and received a reply confirming that there was a Margaret Ellis who had been buried on 27 March 1873 (the 73 of the information?) At the time she was 76 years old. No other confirmation of information from the medium was possible.

During the seance the couple told Margaret that they did believe she had not killed her child and from that time on the house seemed to be warm and healthy and at peace. Elwyn said that the ghost left the landing with a lovely smile on her face, whilst the Rev. Roberts commented that Margaret was the most 'human' of the ghosts he had encountered.

Capt. W.G.R. Hinchcliffe
D: 1928
L: Surrey
S: John Fuller

Captain W.G.R. Hinchcliffe, together with Elsie Mackay, daughter of Lord Inchcape of the P & O shipping empire, set out on 13 March 1928 to fly across the Atlantic to make the first east to west transatlantic flight. They were lost during the flight, presumed to have crashed somewhere near the Azores.

Emilie Hinchcliffe, the captain's wife, was at home with her children in mid-July 1928 when she was awakened one night by the sound of heavy footsteps moving along the hall outside her bedroom door. She assumed it was some member of the Sinclair family who were staying with her at the time but in the morning it was they who asked if she had been walking around the house during the night. Emilie visited medium Eileen Garrett who claimed to pass on messages from her now dead husband. During one conversation Emilie asked, through the medium, whether or not Hinchcliffe had been in the house. Hinchcliffe confirmed that he had been in the house and had nearly touched a red travelling clock by his wife's bed but had been afraid of frightening her. Emilie asked Eileen about the morning when she had heard the footfalls. Eileen confirmed that it had been at four o'clock in the morning and that Emilie's husband had wanted to go through the motions of how he had prepared for a morning flight as he used to do in the summer, to give her the impression of his being there in a familiar way.

Bethan and Brian James
D: 1960s or 1970s
L: Nr. Llangefni, Anglesey, Wales
S: Rev. J. Aelwyn Roberts

Bethan met Brian when she was 22, at a discotheque in Beaumaris on the island of Anglesey, Wales. By the end of the year they had become engaged and married shortly afterwards when

Brian inherited his smallholding of 30 acres along with the family business following his father's death at the age of 57.

Six months later Beth was pregnant, which put some strain on the family income. Their child, Aled, was followed a year later by Bryn and, what with one problem and another, Brian decided to give up the business and work in a factory in Llangefni.

When Bethan and the children got out of bed one Saturday morning they found a note from Brian saying that he had left for Builth and would return that evening.

At seven he returnèd home looking very upset. He had been asked to take some cows to Builth Wells and had done it in order to earn some extra money for the family. Bethan asked Brian why he was so upset and he explained that on the way back he had been stopped by the police who would now probably prosecute him because the tax on his van had expired and he had cancelled the insurance. He was likely to face a serious fine which the family could ill afford.

Bethan lost her temper and called her husband a fool. He was stupid and slow-witted and she would probably have been better off marrying the village idiot, she raged. Then she went to her bedroom and slammed the door. Ten minutes later she heard the report of a shotgun and when she found Brian lying by the paddock stile he was already dead.

At the coroner's inquest a verdict of accidental death was given, the possibility of suicide being mainly ruled out by the coroner on the grounds that people who commit suicide generally choose the place where they do it fairly carefully. No one he had ever heard of had committed suicide whilst standing on the top rung of a stile. The coroner believed that the gun had had a faulty trigger which might have gone off as Brian was climbing over the stile.

Bethan was pleased with the verdict but in her heart thought that it was probably not correct; subsequent events were to confirm this. It was five months after the funeral that Brian's ghost returned to her. In the past, whenever he had come home with something on his conscience, perhaps when he had been out late drinking with his friends or some other such misdemeanour, he would whistle between his teeth and Bethan would know he had something on his mind. On this night five months after the funeral Bethan heard that same whistling between the teeth in her bedroom and she could hear the rap, rap, rap, of what sounded like his fingernails on the chest of drawers, another habit that he had had in life.

After that Brian visited Bethan two or three nights a week and it disturbed her very much. Although she had loved him his returning made her unhappy. Despite her love and the fact that his death had caused great pain and tears she had recognised that now she had to continue her life without him. She wanted her husband to stay away and leave her to get on with her life.

At her parents' suggestion Bethan and the children moved from the farmhouse to a little cottage in the village nearby.

In this case it appears that the emotional intensity of the situation, for either Brian or Bethan, or both, was too high because Brian moved to the new location and continued to visit Bethan. It was some three months after she had moved into the cottage when she heard the rapping on the chest of drawers and the whistling sound.

Bethan contacted the Rev. J. Aelwyn Roberts and asked him to help her. In his book *The Holy Ghostbuster*, Aelwyn Roberts tells how he asked if his friend, Elwyn Roberts, might assist in the work and Bethan agreed. Elwyn Roberts was a research scientist credited by the Rev. Roberts as being a powerful 'sensitive'.

While Mr Roberts, Elwyn and Bethan were in the cottage one night discussing the situation, Bethan said, 'He is here now,' and Elwyn immediately confirmed this, saying that Brian was standing in the hall. The Rev. Roberts could see nothing but that was not unusual. Elwyn allowed Bethan to become totally relaxed, though not hypnotised, and was thus able to communicate with her former husband.

In the communication Brian confirmed that he had indeed committed suicide (which Bethan had always in her heart believed to be the case) but he also said that he had instantly regretted what he had done, it had been a spontaneous act of foolishness. It was the feeling that he had to explain this to Bethan which drove him to keep returning, to say sorry for what he had done. In the nights when he had come to her bedroom he had been trying to shout to her that he was sorry but she had never heard him.

Bethan was satisfied that, having got his message across, Brian would now be released, leaving her and her children to live in peace.

The Rev. Roberts seemed satisfied with the case, and with both Elwyn's professionalism and Bethan's sensible attitude. He believed the case had been fully resolved and that there was no further need for work on it.

Mrs Leaky

D: After 1636
L: (Not given)
S: (Not given)

Mrs Leaky was the unfortunately named mother of a prominent British ship-owner in the seventeenth century. She died in 1636 after rather curiously warning her friends that if they met her after her death they would wish they hadn't.

Shortly after her funeral her ghost appeared near her son's home. A doctor reported that he had helped a lady across the street; her touch was very cold, she talked without moving her lips and she returned his kindness by kicking him in the backside.

Mrs Leaky took to haunting her son's ships, making a number of dramatic gestures such as sitting on top of the mast and whistling in a bloodchilling fashion. Although her son never apparently saw his mother's ghost, his wife, Mrs Leaky's daughter-in-law, reported seeing her several times. Then there is the astonishing story that their five-year-old daughter screamed from her bedroom, 'Help, help, Father, Father, Grandmother is choking me,' but was found dead when her parents reached her.

Shortly after the child's funeral the ghost appeared to the daughter-in-law, the dead girl's mother, who confronted the entity and asked her why she was haunting the family. Mrs Leaky's ghost apparently told her to visit the Lord Bishop of Waterford who was her uncle, and tell him that he must repent of his sins or be hanged. The ghost informed the lady that the sin he was to repent of was that he had once married Mrs Leaky's sister and had given her a child which she had killed and secretly buried. According to the story, the bishop confessed that all this was true and Mrs Leaky, now at peace, was not seen again.

Richard Morris and the Ghost of Richard Tarwell

D: 1730s
L: Devon
S: Daniel Cohen

This case concerns events on the Devon estate of George Harris in 1730. Harris was the head of a wealthy Devon family and held an important position in the court of King George II. George Harris was in London when he received a message from home asking him to return, which he did.

His butler, Richard Morris, then told him what had happened in his absence. Morris had been awakened by noises during the night and, without thought of his own safety, had burst into the butler's pantry to encounter the intruders. He had believed they were probably members of the household staff as he was sure that no one could have got into the house without making too much noise. However, when he burst in he came face to face with two rough-looking robbers and a fourteen-year-old boy called Richard Tarwell who had been taken in to the household staff just weeks previously as a kitchen help. Morris apparently indicated he believed that it was Tarwell who had let the robbers into the house.

The following morning the other servants found Morris; he had been tied up but not particularly injured. After this he had sent for his employer.

Investigation found neither the silver, the robbers nor Richard Tarwell and although Tarwell's father believed his son to be innocent he was presumed guilty as he had apparently absconded along with the other criminals.

George Harris was asleep in bed one night when he suddenly found himself fully awake and could see, by the dim light of a lamp, a young boy standing at the end of the bed. He knew that it was Richard Tarwell. Harris had earlier gone around with his butler locking up the house and had been impressed by the painstaking way in which Morris had ensured the whole house was secure. He was therefore surprised to see Tarwell in the house and assumed he must have been hiding there for some months. The boy said nothing but beckoned him and Harris felt compelled to follow. It was as he was crossing the room that he realised Tarwell was moving without making a sound and realised that in fact he was seeing an apparition. Despite this he felt no fear and followed Tarwell's ghost down the stairs to a side door. The door was open despite being one that he had specifically watched Morris lock that same evening. (It is interesting to consider that although Tarwell may have been able to move through matter in the classic ghostly manner, he had apparently made provision for Harris's need for a more conventional exit.)

Harris and the apparition walked approximately 100 yards away from the house to the shadow of a large oak tree. The ghost then pointed to the ground, walked around the tree and disappeared.

The next morning Harris gave two footmen spades and asked them to dig at the point indicated by the apparition. Sure enough the decomposing body of Richard Tarwell was unearthed.

Harris reasoned that Morris's description of the original crime had not been entirely accurate. For Richard Tarwell to have let in the criminals he would have needed the keys that Richard Morris had used when locking up the house and which he very ostentatiously kept with him. Clearly, now, the butler was involved. He guessed that Richard Tarwell had become innocently caught up in the butler's plot with the two robbers. The police were called and Morris confronted. He broke down and confessed. The villains were indeed his accomplices; he had let them in but while they were stealing the silver Richard Tarwell had woken and surprised them by walking in on their crime. One of the robbers had killed him and buried the body. They had then tied Morris up to shift the blame to the boy.

Thanks to the ghost of Richard Tarwell, Richard Morris hanged for the crime.

Laura and Sid Perelman
D: 1979
L: French Alps
S: Ben Noakes

Laura and Sid Perelman were both friends of the illustrator Ronald Searle. Laura died in April 1970 at the age of 58.

Ronald Searle was drifting into sleep during a stay in the French Alps on the night of 17/18 October 1979 when suddenly an apparition of Laura appeared before him. She was acting just as she had in life, tapping ash from her ashless cigarette as she always used to do. She told Ronald Searle that Sid was dead.

The next morning Searle's sister-in-law called from London to tell him that she had just heard on the radio that Sid Perelman had been found dead in his hotel room in New York having died sometime during the previous night.

A Scientist's Report
D: 1974
L: Nr. Middlesbrough, Cleveland
S: Andrew MacKenzie

On the evening of 7 May 1974 Mr Clive Stirland, a metallurgist employed by British Steel's Middlesbrough Research Centre, was alone in his sitting room. He suddenly felt an almost physical jolt. Mr Stirland swiftly considered all manner of explanation: time-slips, an atomic bomb exploding some miles off, cars crashing outside. As Mr Stirland moved towards the window he suddenly saw a vision of his father who had died over twenty years before. The apparition was insubstantial and misty but nonetheless clear in detail. It had natural colour and stature; Mr Stirland commented that it was like looking at something through the rotating blades in the electric fan. The figure of his father was surrounded by auras of gold, silver and blue; Mr Stirland felt that a feeling of intense love was radiating from the apparition. He became emotionally overwhelmed, astonished and bewildered.

The apparition remained visible even when Mr Stirland went into the kitchen, but disappeared when he made the conscious decision to write the letter that he had been about to write when he had been 'interrupted'.

It appears that the decision to carry out some particular act, therefore changing the state of his conscious mind, destroyed the circumstances that had brought about the apparition in the first place.

The whole incident lasted just over a minute.

Lt. James Sutton
D: 1907
L: Portland, Oregon, USA
S: Daniel Cohen

On 12 October 1907 Lt. James Sutton died from a bullet wound to the head at Annapolis, Maryland. An official investigation followed which concluded that Lt. Sutton had become drunk at a navy dance and had got into a fight with his colleagues on the drive back to their camp. On arriving at the camp he is alleged to have taken two pistols, and was arrested carrying them. He apparently began to fire them, got into another fight and then deliberately put one of the pistols to his head and pulled the trigger.

Lt. Sutton's mother lived in Portland, Oregon and had previously already reported several psychic experiences. Before hearing of the death she already knew that something terrible had happened to her son. She was then informed that he had taken his own life. Suddenly she had a vision of her son in front of her saying, 'Momma, I never killed myself. My hands are as free from blood as when I was five years old.' The apparition went on to tell Mrs Sutton that he had been shot by others and then the scene dressed up to make it look like suicide. Mrs Sutton was able to give details of the fight and her son's wounds long before she should have known about them through 'conventional' channels. She contacted the Society for Psychical Research in America and their investigator concluded that she had indeed come up with some information in an unusual fashion.

James Sutton was buried in the Arlington National Cemetery, America's chief military cemetery, and in 1909 the body was exhumed. Medical examination located several of the wounds that the apparition had indicated but which were not mentioned in the navy medical report on the death. Although there was no final resolution to the case, and in particular no murder inquiry, Professor James Hislop of the American Society for Psychical Research found that the navy's own inquiry had been somewhat incomplete; it had not laid down the reason for the initial fight, nor had it put forward any reason why the lieutenant should have killed himself. Further, the professor found that the testimonies of the witnesses were not at all consistent.

After the exhumation, the appearances of Lt. Sutton's ghost tapered off and eventually stopped.

The Three Drovers
D: Early 19th century
L: Nr. Crowland, Lincolnshire
S: Peter Underwood

Amongst the papers of the Huddleston family of Cambridgeshire was the story of an extraordinary encounter with three ghosts by one 'Isaac Kirton', in fact identified as A. Huddleston. It seems to date from the early part of the eighteenth century.

Overtaken on his journey by a fierce storm, 'Kirton' stayed at a travellers' inn for the night. Apparently the landlady had tried to dissuade him but on his insistence had given him a room which 'was never used' but which was the only one available.

During the night his sleep was disturbed by a knock on the door which came repeatedly; eventually he unlocked it and peered into the passage which was empty. After he had closed the door the knockings were repeated, the passage was again empty and yet after the door was closed again there came knocking. Kirton called out, for the originator of the sounds to identify himself. By way of answer three apparitions glided into the room.

The apparitions told Kirton that they were drovers who had been on their way home from a fair and who had stopped at the inn. They had made it plain that they had plenty of money with them and the landlord of the inn had murdered them in order to rob them and had buried their bodies in the backyard. Kirton followed the three apparitions into the backyard where they pointed to a particular spot. Kirton placed his whip there and then returned to his room.

Understandably he did not sleep for the rest of that night. Kirton, who was well known in the area, elicited the help of a nearby cottage-owner and paid him to dig on the spot indicated. They disinterred the bodies of three men 'in an advanced state of decomposition'. The constable was called, and the landlord arrested. He was so shocked at how his crime had been discovered that he confessed. After his trial he was executed.

8
Omens
of Death

Ghosts and hauntings are frequently associated with ghostly forewarnings of death to follow. Such phenomena include ghostlights (which are particularly famous in the Celtic and Gaelic countries), the corpse candle (which reportedly precedes deaths and funeral processions), and even so specific a case as a pilot seen in death by his friend and who later died when his plane ditched.

The Corpse Candle
D: Various
L: Wales and London
S: W. Sikes, P. Matthews, M. Griffiths

An extraordinary phenomenon and one of the most frequent omens of death reported in Wales is the Canwyll Corph, or Corpse Candle. We have taken our account from *British Goblins* by Wirt Sikes, published in 1880.

Possibly having similar origins to spooklights and other forms of earthlights, the Corpse Candle has nonetheless become a part of folklore and ghost legend. According to legend, the size of the candle seen indicates the age of the person about to die; the larger it is, the older they will be. If two candles are seen, one large, one small, it represents a mother and a child. If the flame is white a woman will die, if red a man.

One story reported to the author of *British Goblins* by a Welshwoman was as follows: 'One night her sister was lying very ill at the [Welsh woman's] house, and [the sister] was alone with her children, her husband being in the lunatic asylum at Cardiff. She had just put the children to bed and had set the candle on the floor preparatory to going to bed herself when there came a 'swish' along the floor like the rustling of grave clothes [shrouds], and the candle was blown out. The room, however, to her surprise remained glowing with a feeble light as from a very small taper, and looking behind her she beheld 'old John Richards' who had been dead ten years. He held a Corpse Candle in his hand, and he looked at her in a chill and steadfast manner which caused blood to run cold in her veins. She turned and woke her eldest boy, and said to him, "Don't you see old John Richards?" The boy asked, "Where?", rubbing his eyes. She pointed out the ghost, and the boy was so frightened at the sight of it that he cried out, "Oh, wi! Oh, dduw! I wish I may die!" The ghost then disappeared, the Corpse Candle in its hand; the candle on the floor burned again with a clear light and the next day the sick sister died.'

A story told by Thomas Matthews was more gruesome, and included the Corpse Candle, coming out of his father's mouth, going down to his feet, and disappearing back into his mouth shortly before he died. When Thomas Matthews was asked whether the candle was of real wax he was of the opinion that it was made of the 'spirit of wax'.

A phenomenon similar to this was reported in a London hospital when nurses observed a pale blue flame burning in a man's mouth shortly before he died. It was suggested that this might be ignited hydrogen resulting from decomposition inside the body.

Another story of the Corpse Candle came from Maurice Griffiths, once schoolmaster of Pontfaen in Pembrokeshire and subsequently a baptist preacher.

Griffiths was coming from Tre-Davydd and from the top of a hill saw a light in the valley below. This puzzled him. He considered that it might be the type of light reported before a funeral though, in fact, he did not believe in those stories. He noticed that the red light remained motionless for approximately fifteen minutes on the route to Llanferch-Llawddog Church. Griffiths watched the light eventually go into the churchyard and then into the church itself. When it came out it returned to the churchyard before disappearing.

Some days later the young son of Mr Higgon of Pontfaen died; the funeral procession remained for approximately fifteen minutes at the spot where the light had been (the reason being that they had to cross water and waited for some people with boots to help them over). Furthermore the child was buried in the same spot where the light had hovered after coming out of the church.

The Ghost Light of Caithness
D: Late 19th century, early 20th
L: Latheronwheel, Scottish Highlands
S: Alasdair McGregor

As a young man at the turn of the century Mr Arnold Millar often visited relatives in the village of Latheronwheel on the east coast of Caithness. One New Year's Night, and for three or four successive nights, many of the local people saw a light on the highest point of the road which they thought might be the lamp of a coach or vehicle. However, no vehicle ever reached the village or was actually seen. The day after the light was last seen a storm at sea sank a number of vessels from the fishing fleet out of nearby Lybster, killing the crews of two of the boats. Once the storm had cleared search parties climbed the cliffs, peering down in the hope of locating the corpses that might have been washed ashore. One body was found at a point said to be exactly where the light had been seen; it was brought up the cliffs and laid by the side of the road, by chance on the precise spot where the light had been.

Thereafter the light was thought to be an omen of disaster and stories began to circulate of earlier sightings and earlier disasters, now coloured more by legend than reality.

The Lights of Stornoway
D: Early 20th century
L: Isle of Lewis
S: Alasdair McGregor

Light phenomena have been reported on the east coast of the island of Lewis in the Outer Hebrides, near the main town of Stornoway.

One such report came from a local man, Kenneth MacDonald, who at the age of twelve had been playing with four friends when they saw a huge light flare in the ground near them. All the boys saw the light and it terrified them enough to make them run for home. The old folks of the nearby village of Sandwick declared that somebody would be found dead on that spot. Later, in 1935, a young man, worse for wear from drink, was lost and was later discovered at the spot, having died from exposure.

Another case from the same area related to a man named Morrison, also a local. He was returning from a night out in Stornoway in the company of a farmer's son. They were both heading towards Stoneyfield in the farmer's trap when they reached the point where the road branches off to Holm. Morrison got off and walked along it on foot to his home there. As he looked back at the trap, now heading off towards Stoneyfield, he could see a strange light travelling in front of it and no great distance from it.

The next day Morrison spoke to the farmer's son, whom he had been with the previous night to ask if he too had seen the light. 'I certainly saw it, and I whipped the pony as hard as I could in an effort to overtake it. But I could not gain an inch on it,' he said. 'Instead of turning in at Stoneyfield, I drove straight ahead, following it down as far as Holm Farm. I lost sight of it in turning the corner at the byre there.'

A day or two later the old farmer, whose son had seen the light that night, was drowned in Stornoway harbour and his body carried to Holm Farm in the Stoneyfield farmer's trap.

The White Lady

D: 1619 + others

L: Prussia

S: Daniel Cohen

White ladies are not particularly rare in ghost reports but the White Lady of Prussia was particularly associated with the foretelling of death. She apparently appeared to members of the ruling family of Prussia, the Hohenzollerns, shortly before they were to die or some tremendous disaster befall the family.

In one of the white lady tales, the ghost of Frederick the Great appeared to his nephew, Frederick William, telling him not to invade France and threatening that unless he called off the invasion the White Lady would visit Frederick William and, as the ghost of Frederick the Great said, 'I'm sure you know what happens to those who see her.'

There is a report that the White Lady appeared in 1619 to the then ruler John Sigismund, who died the day after; that she was seen at the Old Palace in 1806 shortly before Prince Louis of Prussia was killed; and she was apparently seen in June 1914 during the reign of Kaiser Wilhelm II. Although Kaiser Wilhelm did not die, his relative, the Archduke Ferdinand, was assassinated in that month, sparking the Great War.

The Wing Commander
D: WW II
L: RAF base, Egypt
S: Daniel Cohen

There are many tales of crisis apparitions during war; this particular case seems to be something of a cross between a message and a premonition.

Commander George Potter and Flying Officer Reg Lamb spent an evening drinking in the officers' mess (it was during World War II, at an RAF bomber base in Egypt from where planes were flying out to the Mediterranean to prevent sea-borne supplies reaching General Rommel). Also in the mess at the time were others, including a wing commander referred to as 'Roy'.

Laughter from Roy and the group of people with him caused Potter to look over towards him at which moment he had a frightening vision of death. He saw what appeared to be the head and shoulders of the wing commander slowly moving in a background of blue blackness. His eyes were missing, his lips drawn back from his teeth and his flesh blotched in greenish purple and partly peeling off. Potter himself broke out into a sweat and started trembling at the vision.

Potter stared at the vision for an unknown length of time until he became aware that Reg Lamb was pulling his arm and saying, *'What the hell's the matter? You've gone white as a sheet. As if you've seen a ghost.'* Potter described the apparition to Lamb who looked across to where Roy was sitting but could see nothing.

They both knew that Roy was flying the following night but decided that they could do nothing to prevent that as no reasonable grounds could be offered. The next night Potter heard that Roy and his aircraft had been shot down and had ditched in the Mediterranean. There was a report that the crew had managed to climb into a life raft and Potter believed for a time that his vision had been incorrect. Sadly it turned out not to be for Roy had perished. Potter realised that he had been seeing the image of the wing commander in the blue blackness of the Mediterranean at night, floating in death. His head and shoulders must have been held up by a life jacket.

9
Ghosts at Time of Death

It is very commonly reported that those who die are seen by others as ghosts at the time of their death. Usually the appearance is to a close friend or relative, though this particular fact may be a statistical flaw: in order to be certain that the ghost has been seen at the time of death it is obviously necessary to be able to determine what that time was and while it is often possible to do so when the figure is *known* to the witness, a ghost appearing to a stranger and unidentified by him or her obviously could not be identified as an apparition at time of death, simply because the facts could not be checked out.

Nevertheless, there does seem to be a high percentage of reports which can be accurately attributed to the moment when a person dies, often without the witness knowing about the death until much later. This section includes a wide variety of such claims – a telephone call that turned out not to have been real; the appearance of a man to his brother who was instantly certain that it was the result of a death even though he had no information at that time to confirm his feelings; the appearance of a father to his son in the middle of a busy day at the office; and the charming story of a dying wife comforted by her husband while her family tried to keep the news of his death from her to save her distress.

The Bedroom Visitor
D: (No date)
L: (Not given)
S: Prof. Colin Gardner

Harry and Elizabeth were a close couple. Nearly 80 years old, Elizabeth was in hospital suffering from terminal cancer and convinced that she would die on her birthday, which was Christmas Day. She had always said that this would be the case.

Sadly, three weeks before Christmas Harry also became ill and had to be admitted to another hospital nearby. When Elizabeth's family visited her they decided not to tell her about her husband's illness as it would only distress her further. Elizabeth knew that in any case Harry could not visit her at the hospital as he was too weak, even before his illness; there was no point in adding to her distress. But it made it all the harder that Elizabeth always asked about her husband.

While visiting Harry at his hospital the family also agreed not to tell him how ill his wife was and not to tell him that she would not be coming home. He would often ask how she was doing and when she would be returning home.

A week before Christmas Harry died and the family kept this from Elizabeth also. They were certain that it would be unkind to tell her. But from that time on the family were surprised to discover that Elizabeth never asked about her husband, in spite of always having done so before, and the thought crossed their minds that perhaps, at some level, Elizabeth knew that her husband had died.

On Christmas Day the family visited Elizabeth and had to follow through their lies about her husband; indeed they said that they would be going to see him shortly after they left her (which was only partly a lie as they would be visiting his grave). Elizabeth said nothing though smiled weakly before falling asleep.

Later that day the news reached the family that Elizabeth had died in her sleep, exactly as she had always predicted, on her birthday.

When the family returned to the hospital to make the funeral arrangements they spoke to the ward sister with whom they had become very close over the weeks. Elizabeth's daughter told her that she bitterly regretted the fact that Elizabeth's husband had not been able to visit her at the hospital to comfort her. However, the ward sister assured them that Elizabeth's husband Harry had indeed visited her shortly before she died; the family thought this a lie in the worst possible taste. The sister only then learned of Harry's death, but she was certain that he had come in every day of the past week to see his wife. She could not be mistaken as Elizabeth proudly showed everyone Harry's photograph which was by her bedside all the time. Not only did the sister see Harry but several of the other nurses did too. Even the ward doctor had put off his examination of Elizabeth until Harry had gone, recognising that she was with her husband.

Mrs Herbert Davy
D: End of 19th century
L: Newcastle-upon-Tyne
S: Mrs Herbert Davy (*Phantasms of the Living*)

In her book *Phantasms of the Living* Mrs Herbert Davy of Newcastle-upon-Tyne referred to an episode which took place at the end of the last century. Mrs Davy had gone to a nursery to purchase flowers for the garden, her husband was at the moors. Mrs Davy waited outside while her groom went in for the purchases. Suddenly she had a feeling of unaccountable sorrow and she immediately felt that an accident must have befallen her husband. In fact nothing had happened to her husband, but her feeling was not entirely unfounded: a child who had lived with them almost as their own and was then living in Kent had died that day.

Death of a Gardener
D: 20th century
L: San Diego, California, USA
S: Prof. Colin Gardner

When Neil Rogers (a pseudonym given by investigator Colin Gardner to protect the witness's identity) arrived home one evening he discovered that his father, Alan, and mother, Annie, were not at home as they usually were. Exceptionally, the house was empty. The young man sat down and watched television, waiting for them to arrive, and some 30 minutes later a car pulled up and his mother got out. Neil's father had had a heart attack that afternoon and had been rushed into hospital; Annie assured her son that it was not serious and that he would be home in a few days.

Talking to his father in hospital the next day, Neil was surprised and perhaps even angry with himself that he had not sensed his father's anguish in any way. It seemed strange to him that he had felt nothing as he felt very close to his father. His father calmed his fears and told him that there was no need for him to worry, Annie had dealt with everything perfectly well. Neil's father even joked that when the time came for him to die he would make sure he said a last goodbye to his son; in any case he did not plan to die yet as he wanted to see his grandchildren. At this time Neil was not yet married but a wedding was planned.

In the years that followed Neil and his wife had a daughter, Katie, who was the apple of her grandfather's eye. They enjoyed spending time together in the garden. When Katie was six years old Neil's wife announced another pregnancy. Alan was apparently very pleased but also rather distracted by the news that the child would be born that October. Later that day Alan took Katie into the garden where she had a small plot in which she was allowed to plant whatever she wanted to. Neil watched from a distance, not wanting to intrude, while Alan set out a similar plot of land which was to be for his new grandchild. Alan asked Katie to make sure that she looked after it for her brother so that he could enjoy it for himself when he was old enough, and he told her to help her brother choose the right plants and so on. Neil therefore believed that for some reason his father did not expect to be alive when the baby was born in October; he was also surprised at his certainty that the child would be a boy.

That summer Neil was in his office with his partner when he suddenly heard his father say, 'Well, I guess that's it, son. Kiss Katie for me, and you take good care now, goodbye.' Neil turned and saw his father standing in the office dressed in old trousers and a short-sleeved checked shirt. He was holding a garden trowel in one hand and a bunch of marigolds in the other. It was very obvious that Neil's partner had seen and heard nothing; without a word Neil rushed home.

On arriving home he ran straight into the garden. There he saw his father lying dead on the lawn, dressed exactly as he had seen him and holding a garden trowel in one hand and a bunch of marigolds in the other.

On 3 October Katie's brother arrived. When Neil took Katie to the hospital to see her mother and new brother, Neil commented that he wished his father could see the new baby. Apparently

Alan had more than kept his promise to say goodbye to his son, for Katie laughed and said, 'But Daddy, Grandpa *is* here, standing beside Mummy. Can't you see him?'

Daniel Dunglas Home
D: 1846
L: America
S: Lynn Picknett

A celebrated Victorian medium, Daniel Dunglas Home, believed he had paranormal gifts from an early age. When Home was thirteen, his friend Edwin died some distance away from where Home was. Home had a vision of Edwin making three gestures in the air which he believed meant that his friend had been dead for three days. This was precisely correct. (Home also saw the apparition of his mother prior to receiving news of her death.)

Harry Evans
D: 1967
L: Dulwich, London
S: Andrew MacKenzie

In January 1967 Mrs Cynthia Aspinall of Dulwich saw her friend, Harry Evans, standing in his garden without a coat. She was a little surprised as Harry was in his mid-seventies, and it was a very, very cold day. Evans lived with his sister, Kitty; they had been together since their parents died 50 years ago.

Mrs Aspinall was pleased to see her friend as she had been away for a month but she was sad to see him looking so pale and drawn. Harry was just two feet away when Mrs Aspinall spoke to him but she got no response at all; he *stared straight through [her]*. Not having elicited even a simple response, Mrs Aspinall parted with a warning to Harry not to be out in cold weather without an overcoat or he might catch a chill.

At home later Mrs Aspinall told her husband that she was wondering what she had done to offend her friend. Because he had not spoken to her she thought he must be ill.

Some days later Mrs Aspinall was having coffee with friends who included Harry's sister, Kitty. Mrs Aspinall mentioned to Kitty that she knew of a place in Scotland that would suit both Harry and Kitty very much for a holiday; suddenly Kitty burst into tears. A friend broke the embarrassment by telling Mrs Aspinall, '*Harry died a month ago.*'

Of course Mrs Aspinall was terribly shocked: she told those there that she had been speaking to him just days ago, and indeed had been near enough to touch him. Kitty was in such distress that Mrs Aspinall tried to retract her statement, saying she had got the dates wrong and so on, but she knew she had not.

Mr Aspinall confirmed to investigator Andrew MacKenzie that his wife had mentioned seeing Mr Evans and not receiving a response. One of the other women at the coffee meeting confirmed that something similar to Mrs Aspinall's recollection had taken place. She recalled Kitty saying how much she missed her brother and that they had been close. She confirmed that Cynthia had then arrived and started questioning Kitty about Harry, commenting that she had spoken to him the day before. The woman recalled Kitty being upset by Cynthia's inquiries.

Harry Evans had in fact died of leukaemia at the age of 75 at Dulwich Hospital in mid-December 1966.

Mrs Aspinall offered an interesting theory to explain the apparition; perhaps it was not 'inspired' by Harry Evans but rather by his sister who may have been inside the house, thinking of her brother, and possibly projected the image which Mrs Aspinall saw. Mrs Aspinall was no stranger to the paranormal, as she came from a family of psychics and had previously reported other cases of precognition.

The Figure in White

D: 1837
L: Blandford, Dorset
S: Lord Halifax

In July 1837 three-year-old Polly Allen was playing in the garden of her house near Blandford when she saw, and asked her mother to come out and see 'The tall woman in white who is coming down the hill opposite.' She described the figure as coming down through 'the Bache Gate' and down the hill. Her mother told her that she was talking nonsense as nobody would be dressed in white in that area on a working day, but Polly and her sisters went to see if anyone was there. They could see no one.

At the time when Polly saw the apparition, her father, along with two other men, had been drowned while cutting weeds on the River Stour. It was after Polly had told her mother about the apparition that the local minister visited as it was his duty to tell Mrs Allen of her husband's death.

Although the child's reported seeing a tall woman when it was her father who had died, he himself was very tall, and it may have been the gliding motion that gave the impression of female grace.

Lord Halifax concludes his story with a point that he says may or may not be relevant: 'Some six or seven months before he was drowned, John Allen came home one night from Blandford in exceedingly low spirit. As soon as he got into the house he sat down and cried bitterly for more than an hour. When his wife asked him what was the matter he replied that he had seen that which told him he should not be long here. He never would describe to his wife what it was he had seen, but after that evening he suffered periodically from low spirits.'

Baroness Josef von Franckenstein
D: Early 20th century
L: America
S: Ben Noakes

During the early days of Baroness Josef von Franckenstein's childhood in the early years of this century, the impressionist painter, Morten Schamberg, and the photographer, Charles Sheeler were frequent visitors to her family in the various parts of America that they lived. When the family moved to Cincinnati, however, they were unable to visit because of the distance and the cost of travelling.

In 1918, during a worldwide influenza epidemic, the baroness and her sister were ill in bed with high fevers. One morning the baroness awoke and saw a figure in the doorway dressed in a long white robe. The figure approached the baroness, sat on her bed, took her hand and told her not to speak. He further told her that she would recover from her illness. It was Morten Schamberg. The baroness noted that her sister was still asleep and she herself fell asleep peacefully holding Morten's hand.

The family later learned from Charles Sheeler that Morten Schamberg had died that morning in New York from the same influenza epidemic.

Professor Sir Charles Frank
D: (No date)
L: (Not given)
S: Ben Noakes

A Professor of Physics at the University of Bristol, Sir Charles Frank, might not be thought of as a typical reporter of the paranormal. However, in a short report to editor Ben Noakes he related the story of his wife's Finnish grandmother waking in the morning to see her half-brother standing by her bed and telling her that he had come to say goodbye.

The grandmother immediately told her husband what had happened; later she received a letter telling her that her half-brother had committed suicide at the same time that she had seen his apparition.

The Friends of the City Churches
D: Early 20th century
L: London
S: Philip Paul

The Rev. H.J. Fynes-Clinton, Rector of St Magnus the Martyr Church in the City of London (see pp. 68–70 for the church's own history of hauntings), was a leading light in a society set up to promote public awareness of churches, called the Friends of the City Churches.

While addressing a meeting of the society, he saw a parishioner named Newman join the audience in front of him. He was quite surprised as Newman had been seriously ill. When the address was over the rector went to the place where he had seen Newman standing, in order to speak to him, but he was nowhere to be found.

It was the following day when he learned that Newman had died 48 hours previously.

Johann Hofer and the Grey Audi
D: 1980
L: Val d'Adige, South Tyrol, N. Italy
S: Andrew MacKenzie

Johann Hofer (pseudonymous, as are all references given in this case) had been visiting his fiancée in a small village in the Val d'Adige in the Southern Tyrol when, at eleven o'clock in the evening of 4 May 1980 he set out to return to his home at Val di Pennes about an hour away. Hilda Saxer and her sister Christine, Johann's fiancée, had asked him to stay for a while after their pizzeria had closed so that they could share a meal together but Johann had insisted he had to leave. Christine watched him drive off; it was 11.05 p.m.

Johann's journey home took him through a series of tunnels through the mountains. The fourteenth tunnel was a short false tunnel designed to protect the road from falling rocks and snow; it was in this tunnel that the tragedy happened. A huge piece of rock, from high up the mountain, crashed through the roof of the tunnel destroying it completely and crushing Johann in his car. Johann must have died instantly at 11.30 that evening. But Johann's drive home was not yet finished!

The investigator of this case, Graziella Piccinini, located another driver on the road who had been just ahead of Johann's car. He had driven through the fourteenth tunnel and heard the rock fall, indeed the back of his own car was slightly damaged, but by accelerating he managed to drive out of the tunnel without injury. The driver slowed down and looked behind and saw that a car was trapped under the rocks; since no other motorist was reported missing and no other car located in the rubble, this must have been Johann's car. The driver confirmed that the accident had happened at around 11.30. Miss Piccinini also pinpointed the driver who first encountered the landslide after it had happened and he confirmed that this was at approximately 11.40, just ten minutes later. All of this confirms the time of the accident and Johann's death with reasonable certainty.

However, at the same time, eleven-thirty in the evening, Hilda Saxer saw Johann in his distinctive grey metallic Audi (the car in which he had died) driving past as she stood at the door of her pizzeria; seemingly seeing her, Johann slowed down, waved and smiled. Hilda waved back and watched the car drive round the bend in the road. She was of course surprised to see him still in the village since he had said he had to leave half an hour before.

Although not married, Johann and Christine had a child and on the night in question the child was sleeping at her aunt's house with Christine's mother, Maria. Suddenly Maria woke up feeling that somebody had come into the room; for several minutes she felt and heard the footsteps of someone walking up and down. Maria became afraid, mainly because she had experienced things like this before, and she immediately became concerned that there might have been a tragedy in the family. She wanted to get to the pizzeria to see her daughters but was too terrified to move. Even after the footsteps ceased Maria stayed awake until the girls came home after midnight. Maria estimated the footsteps to have been around eleven-thirty in the evening, although this might have been with the benefit of hindsight. At the time Maria thought the footsteps might signify the death of her elderly sister who was ill.

Johann's father, Josef, woke up at his home, certain that he heard his son's car returning. Apparently the car made a very distinctive noise and there was a particular manoeuvre which his son always made to get into their yard where he parked the car; Josef heard this very clearly. Acknowledging that his son was now home, Josef went back to sleep. It was not until the next morning that he found the car was *not* parked where it should be. After a few telephone calls, it became clear that Johann could not be found.

As soon as Josef heard about the landslide he became convinced that his son was buried in it, knowing the time that he would have been travelling and having discovered the time when the accident happened. Curiously, as soon as Josef saw the debris he knew exactly which part of the tunnel that the car must be buried in. Although the tunnel and the debris covered eighty metres of road, it turned out that he was accurate to within a metre. Because of the danger to workmen, the authorities were reluctant to remove the rubble and of course were not convinced that there was someone in there at all. Eventually Josef secured permission for just a few metres of excavation – which he knew would be all that was needed as he knew exactly where the car was, though for no reason that he could give. The car and Johann's body were recovered.

In all Miss Piccinini interviewed three direct witnesses and nine people involved with the case in the three to five weeks immediately following the event which makes the investigation quite thorough and immediate. Many aspects were covered and carefully tied up. In particular, Hilda confirmed that she had no doubt she had seen Johann, for three reasons: she recognised him at very close range and knew him well; he had waved to her indicating his recognition of her; and his car was very noticeable, particularly the coloured stripes on the back window which made it very distinctive and which she saw as the car drove away. The investigation also determined that there was sufficient lighting at the spot Hilda had said she was when she saw the car for her to have been able to make the identification.

Knowing precisely when Johann had left the pizzeria, and calculating the driving time up to the scene of the accident (indeed Miss Piccinini retraced the route), she was certain that Johann could not have turned around and come back into the village and then still managed to be at the scene of the accident at the relevant time.

In addition to Josef's extraordinarily accurate knowledge of where his son's car was buried is the fact that the normally light-hearted Josef had become very depressed over the weekend and had told his wife, 'I feel something awful is going to happen.'

The case is an extraordinary one: not only did Johann apparently manifest after or at death in three locations – to his father, near his child, and to his fiancée's sister – but he also apparently manifested in an Audi car which was smashed to pieces under tons of rubble at the time. This is not unique and there have been many cases of ghosts riding coaches and horses and, of course, cases of ghost locomotives, but this is probably the most contemporary sighting of this particular phenomenon yet recorded.

Douglas Jardine
  D: 1958
  L: Lord's cricket ground, London
  S: Ben Noakes

On 19 June 1958 Col. D. Pritchard was in the pavilion bar at Lords before the start of the England–New Zealand test match. Standing alone at the end of the bar, just a few yards from Pritchard, was Douglas Jardine (probably most famous for the 'body line' cricket tour). The two were well acquainted and Jardine was, in Pritchard's words distinctive and impossible to mistake. The two apparently caught each other's eye and raised glasses to each other over the distance.

Shortly after, Pritchard finished the conversation he was having and went over to speak to Jardine but could not find him. Just before the start of play that day the loudspeaker announced that Jardine had died the previous day in Switzerland.

The Lady in the Chair
D: 1960
L: Reynoldston, nr. Swansea, Wales
S: *Journal of the SPR* (June 1963)

As reported in the *Journal of the Society for Psychical Research* of June 1963, in June 1960 'Mr and Mrs P.' were staying with Mrs P.'s mother at Reynoldston near Swansea. Mr P. had a curious and continuous feeling that there was a woman sitting in a chair in the kitchen during mealtimes. The chair was quite clearly empty and it was very much a mental impression of her rather than his seeing any visual apparition. It was so strong that on several occasions he looked up to address the person, and so strong was the feeling that his surprise at seeing no one in the chair far outweighed his surprise at the feeling itself. It was as if he simply could not believe there was no one there.

Not having a visual image of the person, or even a sense of *knowing* the female presence that he was detecting, Mr P was unable to do much to identify the woman. However, one night during this time he had a curious dream in which he found a strange symbolism that led him to believe he had identified the woman. He dreamt of a stuffed crocodile which he discovered was an old sign representing the apothecary or doctor.

Mrs P. had been trying to identify the female Mr P. had been sensing, and it seems that she had settled on a retired woman doctor who lived in Runfold in Surrey. The two had met twelve years ago and had kept in contact, notably because they were both interested in the paranormal. Indeed, in the previous month, on 14 May, Mrs P. had written a letter to the doctor but had received no reply, which she found surprising as her replies were always very prompt.

Knowing that the doctor had been rather ill and not having had a reply to the letter, and now listening to her husband's sensing of a female presence, Mrs P. began to feel that the doctor might be dead and that she had used this method of drawing her attention to that fact. As to why the approach had been made through her husband, Mrs P. believed it might be because he was scientific and lacked imagination when it came to mysteries.

On 21 June Mrs P. telephoned her doctor friend but learned from her housekeeper that she had died on 1 June.

This is a particularly interesting case. Mr P. had never met the doctor and yet it was he who detected her presence; indeed the spirit seems to have directed herself specifically at him.

Thomas, Lord Lyttelton of Frankley
D: 1779
L: Mayfair, London and Dartford, Kent
S: Keith Poole

This case was described by Keith B. Poole in his book *Britain's Haunted Heritage*. Poole noted that Dr Samuel Johnson commented that it was one of the most extraordinary reports he had heard of.

On Thursday 24 November 1779, Lord Lyttelton, 35, was staying in his Mayfair house having just returned from Ireland. Guests staying with him included Lord Fortescue, Lady Flood, two daughters of Mrs Amphlett, both of whom he was having an affair with, and Baron Westcote, his uncle.

That night Lord Lyttelton was woken by what sounded like the fluttering of dove's wings. He drew back the curtains of the four-poster bed he was sleeping in to be confronted by an astonishing sight: a tall figure in white pointing a finger at him and telling him to be ready to die in three days.

According to Baron Westcote, from whose diary of events the case is extracted, Lord Lyttelton was so concerned that he called for a servant from a nearby room; the servant found him sweating and agitated.

At breakfast the next day Lord Lyttelton was pressed for the reason why he seemed so quiet and disturbed and he told his breakfast guests all that had happened that night. Lord Lyttelton spent the day in Westminster in the House of Lords and returned home that night in a better state of mind. By the following morning he tried to comfort his anxious-looking guests by telling them they were foolish to be thinking of the ghost. He decided that they should all spend the weekend at Pitt Place in Surrey, his country home.

By this time his usual joie de vivre had returned and he was joking about beating the ghost and seeing no reason why he shouldn't live past the threat. At breakfast the next morning, Sunday, he had obviously slept well and was in a fine mood: 'If I live over tonight I shall have jockeyed the ghost for this is the third day.'

That night Lord Lyttelton retired to bed at an uncertain time. He believed it to be eleven o'clock but the clock had been advanced; there were rumours that either he had put the clock forward in order to deceive himself or that his guests had done so in order to deceive him. (Presumably they believed that if he did die it would be as a result of anxiety and that by removing the anxiety they would release the tension and save his life.)

However, in the minutes that were to follow Lord Lyttelton had a fit (this was not quite exceptional – he had had several which were blamed on the excesses of his rather dissolute lifestyle); a servant then ran for help. On his return his lordship was dead. The prophecy had apparently been fulfilled, but the world had not heard the last of Lord Lyttelton.

One of his lifelong friends, Miles Andrews, the MP for Bewdley, was having a party at his house in Dartford in Kent to which Lyttelton had been invited but which he did not attend. Andrews went to bed early, leaving his guests to enjoy the party, as he was not feeling well.

Suddenly the curtains on Andrews' four-poster bed were pulled aside and Andrews stared at the figure of Lord Lyttelton in front of him. Lyttelton was dressed in the nightclothes that Andrews retained at his house for Lord Lyttelton's frequent visits. Andrews assumed that Lord Lyttelton had accepted the invitation to the party and had turned up late, but Lyttelton said nothing to him. Believing it to be one of Lyttelton's jokes to turn up dressed in his nightclothes, Andrews threatened to throw something at him and picked up a slipper, at which the form finally said, 'It's all over with me, Andrews,' in a rather depressed voice and walked out of the door into an adjoining closet. Andrews went to the door, opened it and found the closet empty; the nightclothes that he kept for Lyttelton were hanging on the peg behind the door. It was eleven o'clock, the time of Lyttelton's death at his home in Surrey.

Andrews was frightened by what had happened and summoned his servants, telling them not to allow Lyttelton into the house if he should arrive; he still harboured the suspicion that this was some kind of joke and he went back to bed.

The following morning when he heard of Lyttelton's death in Surrey, Andrews is said to have fainted. 'The event affected him for three years.'

A Message from the South Atlantic

D: 1840
L: Bratton Clovelly, Devon
S: Rev. Sabine Baring-Gould

Sabine Baring-Gould, in his book *Early Reminiscences* recalls an example of apparition at death from the last century. On 3 January 1840 his mother had been reading the Bible in their dining room at Bratton Clovelly when she saw on the other side of the table an apparition of her brother, Henry.

Henry was serving in the navy in the South Atlantic at the time and could not have been there in person; Sabine Baring-Gould's mother immediately recognised that this was a death apparition and made an entry in her Bible indicating that she had seen his form at that time.

Over a month later the news reached the family that Henry had indeed died on that date near Ascension Island.

Wilfred Owen

D: 1918
L: Nr. Victoria, West Africa
S: Harold Owen (*Journey from Obscurity*)

On 11 November 1918, Armistice Day, the cruiser *HMS Astraea* was anchored in Table Bay near Cape Town, South Africa and the captain was throwing a party to mark the end of the war. Harold Owen did not feel festive, but rather 'flat'. He was apprehensive about the safety of his brother, the poet Wilfred Owen, who was serving on the Western Front in the army. He contemplated sending a cable inquiring about his health but did not do so, yet he was certain that something was wrong. After this the cruiser sailed for the Cameroons.

Throughout this period Harold remained in low spirits and was unwell. The cruiser was lying off Victoria and Harold had gone to his cabin when suddenly he saw Wilfrid sitting in his chair, dressed in a khaki uniform. He knew that there was no possibility that Wilfred could really be there, and with the blood draining from his face asked him, 'Wilfred, how did you get here?'

Although Wilfred did not move or speak, his eyes pleaded with Harold, trying to make him understand; then, suddenly, Wilfred broke into a beaming smile. Harold found nothing odd in his brother's silence and was comforted simply by the smile and the presence of the man. The meeting seemed quite normal and without strangeness. When Harold looked away briefly and then back again, Wilfrid was gone.

Harold was uncertain whether or not he had seen his brother or whether it was his imagination. One thing was certain, he knew that his brother was dead. He described it as an absolute knowledge with no doubt whatoever; the fact that he had not heard that Wilfred was dead made no difference whatsoever to his conviction. Despite this Harold recognised that he could not explain why he had the strength of conviction that he did. He simply accepted that his brother was dead and held no hope for an alternative, as he wrote in his autobiography, *Journey from Obscurity*.

Wilfred Owen had been killed on 4 November 1918 and his family received the news on Armistice Day. Although Harold's vision of his brother was sometime after that, it is important to note that it was from that date he had become depressed and anxious for his brother, although he had been occupied by other matters. It was when he was first alone and able to give himself time to think that the apparition of his brother 'came through'.

Philip Paul
D: 1938
L: Stoke Newington
S: Philip Paul

Philip Paul is an experienced 'ghost-hunter' and a one-time member of the Ghost Club committee. In his autobiography, *Some Unseen Power*, he relates a story concerning his sister and a possible time-of-death apparition.

It was February 1938 when, as a young boy, Paul saw his brother Ralf carrying the body of his sister Doris out of the bathroom, dangling limbs dripping with water. Attempts to resuscitate Doris by this elder brother failed and the family had to accept that she had died. Paul relates the terrible effect that the death had on his family, his mother requiring sedation and his father never recovering from the shock of hearing about his daughter's death when he arrived home from a late shift at his job as a station master.

Doris had apparently died of a hemorrhage of a duodenal ulcer. She had been suffering from internal pains for some time but had refused examination by the family doctor on the grounds that he was a man and she was unusually modest. This point was to have significance later.

Some six miles away, at Stoke Newington Doris' closest friend, Violet, had had an extraordinary experience which she later related to the family. She was alone in her flat, her two sisters having gone out. She was quietly reading a book after her meal. Suddenly she heard three knocks on the window and she looked outside. She could see nothing but was able to eliminate the possibility that a tree branch or some other object had been striking the pane. She closed the window and went back to reading, but the knocks were repeated. For no obvious reason, given the circumstances, she became afraid and, rather than go back to the window, she locked herself in her bedroom until her sisters returned.

The following day, talking to Paul's family, Violet recalled that the knocks had occurred at about 11 p.m., around the same time – and possibly at exactly the same time – that Doris had died in the bath.

Paul speculates that his sister's spirit sought out her closest friend for several reasons; there had been the usual differences between the young girl and her mother, perhaps eliminating her from Doris' immediate thoughts for contact at the point of death. Paul also eliminates himself on the grounds that his sister's extreme modesty would have prevented her coming to his room, even in spirit form, as she would presumably have appeared naked from the bath. Perhaps then, he speculates, she appeared to her closest friend, or tried to, attracting her attention by knocking on the window. If Violet had not been so frightened perhaps she might have been able to receive some message from Doris or even have seen her. She might even have been able to save her. Interestingly, this case is similar to 'The Telephone Call That Wasn't' (see below), where the person concerned did succeed in getting a message through.

The Telephone Call that Wasn't

D: c. 1919
L: Montpelier Square, London
S: Lord Halifax

This account was given to Lord Halifax by a priest in March or April 1919.

The priest had been asked to visit a patient living in Montpelier Square, not to give the last rites but merely to cheer the patient up as it was felt she could yet recover. The priest was somewhat concerned when he saw the patient – he felt that the last rites would be more appropriate – but he kept to his promise and said afterwards that he would go back the next day to give the last sacrament. On leaving the house he gave the nurse the telephone number of the oratory where he could be contacted should the lady's condition deteriorate.

During the night the priest was awoken by a figure he took to be the father on telephone duty that evening; he was saying something about a sick call. The father told the priest, 'There is no time to lose. There is a telephone message.' The priest did not ask where the telephone message had come from but immediately linked it to his visit of that day; he dressed and left to visit the woman again. It was a quarter to four in the morning and as the priest went out he noticed that the father who had spoken to him had left his light on in his room.

When the priest arrived at the house he found it dark and closed. He rang the doorbell several times, banged on the door but could awaken no one although there must have been several nurses in attendance in the house. It was some twenty minutes after his arrival before the door was opened; the priest went straight to the lady's room where he could hear her saying: 'I do wish Father would come.' For some half an hour before his arrival she had been asking to see him. The priest administered the last rites.

As he was leaving the nurse mentioned to him that his arrival had quite startled her; nonetheless the priest thanked her for telephoning. 'But I did not telephone', she replied. They assumed that somebody else had.

Back at the oratory the priest spoke to the father on telephone duty that night, apologising for his rather vague conversation after having been woken up. The father denied that he had woken him up and was adamant that he had had no telephone calls that night. He said that he had been unable to sleep and had therefore left his light on in his room – a fact which the priest had himself noticed on leaving.

The priest even checked at the telephone exchange but was told that there had been no calls to the oratory on the night in question.

Tommy

D: 1940s

L: Talysarn, Wales

S: Rev. J. Aelwyn Roberts

Tommy was the son of Mrs Annie Jones, a widow in her eighties, living in Talysarn. She was enormously proud of her son who was in the Middle East fighting with the army and they were in regular correspondence; Mrs Jones would share Tommy's letters with many local people including the Rev. J. Aelwyn Roberts, who noted this case in his book, *The Holy Ghostbuster*.

When she got a letter to say that he was returning to England and would soon be back with his mother she was enormously proud and excited. But before she was able to see him she received a telegram saying that he had been killed on active service.

Rev. Roberts described her as being very distraught. She apparently took to her bed. A doctor was called but could find nothing physically wrong, yet three weeks later her condition deteriorated further. The reverend was sitting with Mrs Jones when suddenly, at one point, the old lady sat up in bed with the ease of a much younger woman and took on the countenance of a young girl's smiling face. She apparently reached out, calling for her son by name. Mrs Jones even held the reverend's hand up to where she could apparently see her son standing. The reverend felt that he had been introduced to her son. He believed that Tommy had been present in the room with them and that, as she died, she and her son had gone off together.

Uncle Reggie
D: 20th century
L: New Zealand
S: Ngaio Marsh

When novelist Ngaio Marsh and her family were living in New Zealand, and Ms Marsh was a young girl, they had a visit from Uncle Reggie, her father's 'wild' brother. Afterwards he returned to England, and some time later Ngaio's mother, who appears to have had many instances of second sight or prescience, woke during the night, telling her husband, '*Reggie is about and I think he wants us.*' Convinced that this was important, her mother made a note of the incident, including the time and date and put it in a safe place.

It was some weeks later before they received a letter from England saying that Uncle Reggie had died in his garden chair during the heat of the day at exactly the same moment that Ngaio's mother had woken and made the note on the other side of the world.

Peter Underwood: The Gamekeeper Turns Poacher
D: 1960s or 1970s
L: Hampshire
S: Peter Underwood

For more than half of his long life Peter Underwood, President of the Ghost Club, has probably had more experience of ghost phenomena than anyone else. As well as dealing with those who have witnessed paranormal events, Underwood has one or two stories to tell of his own experiences of presences and so on during his investigations. However, he has one particularly striking story of a ghost experience of his own, which he has recorded in his autobiography, *No Common Task*.

Shortly after moving to his cottage in Hampshire, Underwood was travelling daily to and from London. He became quite friendly with a railway employee at the village station, 'a middle-aged, pleasant individual of distinctive appearance'.

One evening Underwood noticed that neither his friend nor anyone else was on duty but thought nothing more of it as it was quite late. Not being able to telephone his wife as the local telephone box had been vandalised, Underwood decided to walk the three miles from the station to his home. Some few hundred yards from the station Underwood saw a tall house on the left of the road; he could see his friend working up on the roof and waved to him. He resolved to ask him whether or not he did odd jobs which might be something Underwood could make use of in the future.

In fact, Underwood did not see his friend the next day, so in the evening he asked the man who took the tickets for news of him. He told him, sadly, that his friend had been on duty, had fallen ill in the booking office, and had died of a heart attack only the day before.

Underwood protested that he had seen him on top of the house nearby but was told that his friend in fact lived on the other side of the village nowhere near where Underwood had suggested. In fact no one could think which tall house Underwood could be referring to. When he investigated the walk himself Underwood could find no tall house where he had believed he had seen it previously. Underwood was quite certain that he saw the man after he was dead though could not think why that should be. He was apparently advised by a spiritualist colleague that their friendship might have brought about the reunion.

10
Ghosts Associated with Transport

One aspect of ghosts and hauntings which confirms, for those who need confirmation, that ghosts are not solely the inhabitants of stately homes and ancient castles are the frequent reports of ghosts associated with various forms of transport. This section contains reports of a haunted submarine, a haunted train, haunted cars, airfields and aircraft and such legends as the Flying Dutchman, a ghostly ship reputed to forewarn those who see it of impending disaster.

A Figure on Horseback
D: 1967
L: Denton, Lincolnshire
S: Andrew MacKenzie

John Watson, his mother, and a navigator were driving in a car rally on the night of 28/29 January 1967. They had passed Belvoir Castle and were on a road just south of Denton when, as the car rounded a bend, John Watson suddenly saw a dark, figure on horseback about to cross his path; he jammed on his brakes to avoid a collision. The figure was dressed in the traditional highwayman garb of tricorn hat and cloak. Neither the navigator nor Mr Watson's mother saw anything.

In September 1968 Mr Watson organised another rally in the same area and a companion, Pete Shenton, came up and said that he too had seen the same figure and was able to point to the exact same point. Like Watson, Shenton had been in his car with a navigator and rear seat passenger but only he had seen the apparition. In both cases the figure had simply disappeared immediately the car had braked. In fact in both cars the other passengers were amazed that the car should suddenly have thrown its brakes on although in both cases the passengers were also impressed by the drivers' apparent sincerity.

There have been reports of a similar highwayman figure from other people in the area although they are less well corroborated. There has been some speculation as to why only the drivers should see the figure and not the passengers and it has been suggested that it is the degree of concentration on the road which creates a minor 'altered state of consciousness' in the driver whilst the other passengers remain marginally more relaxed. To explain away one such apparition as 'highway hypnosis' is in fact popular with sceptics whereas this case of two different reports of a very similar figure at the same location would seem to suggest more than that.

Rather than the apparition being a product of highway hypnosis, perhaps highway hypnosis itself creates a state where a genuine external event can be perceived as a result of the altered state of consciousness.

Interestingly, the vast majority of lonely-road-at-night UFO sightings also tend to occur *just after the car has turned a bend*, as was the case in these highwaymen reports. Why these types of events should be so frequently perceived 'from the corner of the eye' by so wide a variety of people throws up important questions about their objective reality. Were it possible to put it to the test, it would be interesting to discover the predispositions of these witnesses, and whether they are genuinely seeing a highwayman in some cases and a UFO in others, or whether all the witnesses are seeing 'something' which, though genuinely external to the percipient, is nonetheless interpreted differently according to the set of the percipient's own mind.

The Flying Dutchman
D: Since 1820
L: South Atlantic
S: Legend

More of a legend than a true ghost report, the Flying Dutchman is probably the most famous of the ghosts of transport. It seems to stem from the early 1800s when stories in various British publications formed the basis of a play and eventually Wagner's 1843 opera, its most famous presentation to the public.

The legend tells of a sailing ship rounding the Cape of Good Hope during a fierce storm, but the captain refuses to put into safe harbour despite the pleas of the frightened crew. A glowing form, sometimes suggested to be that of Christ, appears on the deck to the relief of the sailors but then, to their horror, their captain challenges the apparition, threatens it and claims that even God could not sink his ship (a horrific and legendary forerunner of a claim actually made for the *RMS Titanic*!). The spirit apparently takes up the challenge, places a curse on the captain and dooms him to sail the seas forever, tormenting sailors by bringing misfortune on all who set eyes on him and his ghostly vessel.

If the Flying Dutchman has any origin in real life it is probably with seventeenth-century sea captain Bernard Fokke. Fokke was apparently so successful in the face of danger and difficulty that it was believed he was aided by supernatural powers, a belief that was strengthened when his ship disappeared without trace; it was presumed to return as the ghostly Flying Dutchman.

In the early morning of 11 July 1881 King George V, then a young naval officer, reported sighting the Flying Dutchman in the South Atlantic.

Sightings of the Flying Dutchman are held by more superstitious sailors to be omens of tragedy or death.

The Ford Anglia
D: 1970s or 1980s
L: Not given (England?)
S: Prof. Colin Gardner

At sixteen years old, Martin bought a dilapidated 1963 Ford Anglia and installed it in his parents' garage where he intended to restore it ready for his seventeenth birthday.

Not having been used for five years, the car was in very poor condition: flat tyres, rusted metalwork, stiff hinges, damaged chrome, torn upholstery and fabric lining, seized brakes – and all this before even looking in the engine compartment which was in no better condition.

After ten months Martin had virtually transformed the car. He had worked on it most evenings and weekends, had spent a good deal of money buying replacement parts and now, only two months from his seventeenth birthday, the only area still needing real attention was the electrical system.

Martin had a close friend, Stephen, and they would go out together on Stephen's motorbike. This was of great concern to Martin's parents who had in fact been very relieved that Martin had chosen a car rather than a motorbike for himself. However, it seemed apparent that Martin's real attention was focused on the car which he would soon be able to drive and so they allowed Martin his days out as a reward for the hard work he was putting in.

Tragically, one Saturday afternoon the couple were informed by the police of a disastrous road accident in which Stephen had been critically injured and Martin killed.For several weeks Martin's parents were in a state of numb shock. They were shortly due to fly to Spain for a previously booked holiday, and they were debating whether or not to go and also what they were going to do about Martin's car. Martin's mother was adamant that it should not be sold as it represented something of their lost son.

As the holiday approached they became aware that for the past three nights they had been hearing vague sounds of banging and shuffling from inside the garage – of course it could not be Martin who was dead. When they really focused their attention on the sounds they would stop. On one night when they heard the sounds Martin's mother was so distraught that his father ran to the garage to see what was happening. As he opened the garage door he heard what he was certain was the sound of a spanner being dropped on the concrete. It was dark inside the garage and he turned on the light. He searched thoroughly but there was no one there, and no spanner or other tool on the floor. One mystery was that the car's engine compartment was open, though Martin's father was sure Martin would have closed it as he always did when he had been working on the car. Martin's father closed the car bonnet and left the garage.

For several evenings between six-thirty and nine o'clock they continued to hear the sounds of work inside the garage but whenever they investigated there was nothing to see. Sleepless and distraught, they decided that they *would* take their holiday in Spain and they returned feeling more refreshed.

On their return the next-door neighbours told them that they had been concerned about the loud and almost feverish sound of car repairs coming from the garage in their absence. Lights had been on in both the garage and the house. The neighbour had believed that perhaps the family had cancelled the holiday in order to finish the car in time for their son's birthday, possibly as some kind of tribute, but when they realised that that was not the case they had called out the police three times to check for intruders though none were ever found. The last time the police had arrived the garage light had been on and the car could be seen through the small garage window with its engine compartment open.

Martin's father had no doubt in his mind whatsoever that the engine compartment had been closed when he left for Spain. Martin's toolboxes, which had been stored under the workbench, were now sitting together on top of the workbench.

On Martin's birthday the couple were understandably upset. In the early afternoon, suddenly, they heard the sound of a car engine starting up in the garage and when they rushed out to see what was going on, the Ford Anglia was sitting there with its engine purring. When Martin's father reached in to turn off the ignition he discovered the keys were not in the lock, they were hanging on a hook on the workbench. Confused and unable to understand what was happening, Martin's father telephoned the local garage asking for someone to come and inspect the vehicle.

For approximately a quarter of an hour the Anglia's engine continued to run then suddenly it faltered and stopped. At this point the already very distraught mother thought she saw Martin at the back of the garage and heard him say, 'Look Mum, I've done it!' She accepted that this could have been a trick of her imagination, upset as she was.

The mechanic from the garage arrived and explained that the car must have started by a short circuit in the ignition wires, but he could not understand why it should stop since there was adequate fuel for it to keep running. However, some of the ignition wires were not even connected and the choke cable was hanging on the workbench.

The haunting of the garage stopped after that day. Some time later the car was sold to one of Martin's friends who discovered that he only needed to connect up the ignition wires and choke cable in order to start the car which then ran perfectly.

Martin's parents now accept that the car was started by their son's ghost and indeed have since recognised the significance of it starting up at five past two in the afternoon on Martin's birthday, this being the exact time of his birth. According to Professor Colin Gardner of the Institute for Psychical Research – who investigated the case and wrote it up in the book *Ghost Watch* – the Institute had been alerted to this story by a neighbour from across the road who had watched a ghost leave the front door of Martin's house and pass through the closed garage door.

One popular theory of ghosts first suggested by Sir Oliver Lodge in *Man and the Universe* at the beginning of the century, is that ghosts are like a tape-recording replaying some event in the person's life which is witnessed by others in another time. However, this case would seem to indicate a development from what had happened during Martin's life involving Martin's active participation. Since the recording theory has much to be said for it (many ghosts *do* appear to different witnesses doing exactly the same thing over and over) this story at least suggests that explanations of hauntings may be a little more varied.

Peter Gammon
D: (No date)
L: Brands Hatch and Snetterton
S: Peter Underwood

Specialist writer of motor-racing journalism and books Doug Nye obtained details of this story from Peter Gammon, a successful racing driver during the 1950s. It was passed on to Peter Underwood.

Gammon had been driving at Brands Hatch when he apparently lost control coming out of Druid's Hairpin. Somehow the car did not spin and control was regained, preventing a very nasty pile-up. Gammon was a spiritualist meeting some weeks later when the medium discovered that the late racing driver, Mike Hawthorn, had 'taken over' Gammon's body and controlled the car through the incident. Hawthorn wanted to apologise for hurting Gammon's arm during the incident; Gammon did indeed remember that while trying to recover the car his arm had hurt quite badly and he had had to flex his fingers to ease the pain. According to the medium, Hawthorn had put Gammon in a trance and used his own skills to take over the car, but he had injured Gammon's arm because he had not been used to the muscles in Gammon's body.

On a later occasion, this time at Snetterton, it appears that Hawthorn repeated his protective driving for Gammon. The sports car span off after racing down the main straight and suddenly Gammon found himself sitting stationary on the grass. The master switch was turned off, the gear lever was in neutral and the fuel pumps were switched off. This is exactly what should be done to avoid a fire after an incident but Gammon could remember doing none of this. He himself was lying in the passenger seat. A medium told Gammon that Mike Hawthorn had placed Gammon in the passenger seat and had neutralised the car for safety's sake. Hawthorn apparently also warned Gammon to give up racing before he got killed.

The Griffin
D: 1679
L: The Great Lakes, North America
S: Legend

Built in Niagara, the *Griffin*, a sailing ship owned by explorer Robert Cavelier de Lesalle, first set sail on 7 August 1679 on the Great Lakes of North America. On 18 September 1679 it sailed through Green Bay back towards Niagara but was never seen again. Since then, there have been several reports of the ghostly *Griffin* sailing the Great Lakes over the centuries.

The Impossible Flight
D: 1947
L: Corinth Canal, Southern Greece
S: Direct

In late July 1941 Bill Corfield was seventeen years old; his brother Jimmy was home on leave from the RAF. Jimmy was 24 years old and, like many older brothers at the time, a father figure to his younger brother. Being a pilot officer in the RAF, Jimmy was also Bill's hero figure.

Bill's ambitions were very clear. He said to Jimmy, 'I want to be a pilot like you.' Perhaps he was a little disappointed at his brother's reply: 'No, you haven't got the temperament. You stay on the ground and get a ground job in the RAF.' It was only later that Bill realised Jimmy was all too well aware of the horrific loss of life of RAF air crews and was trying to put his younger brother off so dangerous a career.

On 12 August 1941, the day before his 25th birthday, Jimmy flew with some 44 Blenheims on a low-level raid across the North Sea, across Holland and into Germany where the aim was to bomb two factories just outside Cologne. This was to be a big daylight surprise attack, encouraged by Stalin who had asked Churchill for a dramatic gesture designed to halt the confidence of Hitler's march into Russia. Jimmy had with him an observer and a wireless operator/air gunner, both named Williams though not related to each other.

All wartime military operations were of course dangerous and daylight raids often more so than most; on the way back the Blenheims were attacked both by ack-ack from the ground and by German air fighters. Twelve Blenheims were lost, including Jimmy Corfield's plane.

It was some two weeks later that a German patrol found the bodies of Jimmy and his crew washed up at the northern end of Texel Island, just off the Dutch coast. Many bodies lost in the North Sea were washed up there; it was something of a 'focus point' of tides in the area.

Bill was shattered but if he thought that his relationship with his older brother was over he was mistaken. One decision, however, was taken there and then with finality and determination: Bill *would* be a pilot.Bill was posted to No. 28 Elementary Flight Training School (EFTS), at Wolverhampton. This was the only EFTS in England at the time since most airfields were 'operational'. Bill went on to Service Flying Training School at Cranwell where he got his 'wings'. He was then posted to an Operational Training Unit on Wellington bombers and then on to Lancasters. Bill had achieved his ambition, inspired by his brother Jimmy, and had become a pilot.

In 1945 the war ended and Bill had to decide on his post–war career. He went to Transport Command to fly Dakotas and there qualified for the equivalent of a civilian pilot's licence, which would have enabled him to fly on BEA or BOAC (the forerunners of British Airways). Bill, however, decided on a different flight-path and was posted to No. 1 Ferry Unit at Pershore.

It was during his tour of duties at Pershore that Bill was to once again 'meet' his brother. On 12 January 1947 Bill had to fly an Anson 19 twin-engine aircraft to Singapore. After stops in Paris and Italy, Bill was on the leg of the journey that would take him to Athens; being a small aircraft fuel was critical and it was important therefore to check prevailing weather conditions and so on.

According to the weather forecast the flight looked promising; unfortunately, after reaching the point of no return, the point at which you need the same amount of fuel to go on or to turn back, they ran into a severe thunderstorm. The storm forced the plane down to about 50 feet above sea level, to have flown any higher would have risked the plane being broken up from buffeting in the storm clouds. They were now flying low, in a sky darkened by storm clouds, and in very severe weather conditions.

In poor visibility they missed the islands in the Ionian Sea off the Greek coast when suddenly all three (Bill, his navigator and wireless operator), who were all up front in the plane, saw the coast approaching. Bill banked the plane to port and flew along the coastline. The coast was rocky and Bill decided that if no beach presented itself then he would have to ditch in the sea, an option which frankly carried a high probability of death or injury.

Suddenly the navigator announced, 'There's the Corinth Canal,' and instinctively Bill dived into the jaws of its opening. (Afterwards he admitted that he didn't know why he did it, and on reflection decided that the decision was 'suicidal', but he was following his instincts.) Inside the canal all the crew noticed the extraordinary peacefulness and silence that enveloped the plane. One of the crew said it was like being 'in a sort of cathedral'.

Bill says 'I knew – *absolutely and without a doubt* – that my brother was with me in the aircraft. It was as natural as I am talking to you now. There was nothing physical, but he was there.' This was a highly emotional moment; never before or after did Bill experience his brother's presence so intensely and of course there was the added emotion of the terrible danger they were in. Bill relaxed his hands, allowing his brother to 'take over' the controls rather in the manner of automatic writing received by sensitives and mediums.

They flew down the Corinth Canal for around four miles in the dark and came safely to the other end; then the 'presence' of Jimmy left. Even at this stage they noticed one strange thing; normally the aircraft could not fly *dead* straight in such violent storm conditions, it would be buffeted. However, during 'Jimmy's flight' the compass did not waver in the slightest, the plane was apparently flying absolutely straight.

Even after leaving the Corinth Canal the dangers were not over; fuel was extremely low, visibility was still non-existent and they still had no clues as to where to make for. On instinct (or with Jimmy's help?) Bill suddenly 'knew' when to turn, and did. Sure enough, ahead were the lights of Athens – and safety.

The plane touched down and the port engine ran out of fuel even as they were taxiing to a stop.

The following day the authorities made clear their opinion of the crew's story. 'You did *not* fly down the Corinth Canal,' they said. They were assuming that the crew had diverted to drop off smuggled coffee or some such item, which was in fact quite common practice just after the war. The reason that they 'knew' the plane could not have flown down the Corinth Canal was that its walls were only just wider than the wing-tips of the aircraft (a seventeen foot clearance) and even in good weather the flight would be all but impossible; in a storm there was really no practical possibility whatsoever. As Bill put it, 'At that moment I knew that I could not possibly have flown through the canal with only that [clearance] either side of the wing span.'

Of course Bill had not flown the canal. But Jimmy had!

The Ingro Tunnel
D: 1970s or 1980s
L: Nr. Keighley, West Yorkshire
S: W. Herbert

The Keighley and Worth Valley Railway Company have refurbished the private railway that runs near Keighley in West

Yorkshire. They are rebuilding Ingro Station and part of their work is at the Ingro Tunnel on that line.

On several occasions black smoke, from a steam locomotive, has been seen emanating from the tunnel at times when no steam locomotives were in the area. On one occasion D. Narey and Arnold Illingworth, investigating the phenomenon, reported that the smoke was blowing out of the tunnel although the breeze was blowing the other way.

The Lady in Black
D: 1970
L: Cheltenham, Gloucestershire
S: Andrew MacKenzie

In January 1970 Mrs Doreen Jackson was having a driving lesson in Cheltenham when she suddenly braked and changed gear, much to the surprise of the driving instructor. Mrs Jackson pointed out that she had had to do so to avoid a tall woman in black who was stepping into the path of the car, to which the instructor replied, 'I can see pink elephants too,' meaning he had seen nothing at all.

The woman in black had instantly disappeared. From the description given to Andrew McKenzie, the woman was dressed in old-fashioned clothes and held a hand up to her face. It is thought that the figure may be the ghost of Imogen Swinhoe who died in 1878. Other reports of her appearance indicate that she held a handkerchief up to her face and she was often described as a tall woman in black. Although Mrs Jackson did not see a handkerchief the apparition had the same general pose. There have been many reports of this particular apparition in the area.

An Old Man with his Lamp
D: 1980s
L: Upminster, Essex
S: W. Herbert

This report was made by a woman in the mid 1980s travelling between Barking and Upminster in Essex.

On a dark evening at around six o'clock the train slowed down and people were surprised to discover that standing next to the side of the tracks was a little old man, perhaps in his seventies, wearing an old-fashioned waistcoat and jacket and looking *very* anxiously at the train. As the train drew near he shone his green lantern from the small brick enclosure he was standing in as if to give an all-clear; the train went on its way.

The female passenger who made the report has tried to locate the old man, as she was surprised to discover someone of his age working in such an archaic way on that stretch of rail; she has been unable to do so. In fact even the wall and the arch he was standing in do not exist. The woman came to the conclusion that she had had the privilege of seeing a scene from the past and that the old man and his wall were part of an earlier railway system.

From her description of the old man, looking anxiously at the train, it seems he was just as put out by the apparition as she was. Exactly what was the nature of the experience? Is there some report somewhere, yet to be discovered, from an elderly Victorian railway worker of the night when an amazingly futuristic train 'haunted' his stretch of line?

The Orient Express
D: First half of the 20th century
L: Würzburg, Germany
S: Peter Underwood

The legend of the Orient Express has it that in 1923 a man committed suicide in one of the luxury train's compartments by shooting himself in the head. He had apparently been working for a diamond firm in Amsterdam and had stolen a package of diamonds. He boarded the Orient Express to escape to Brussels. At Würzburg he was said to have been warned by an unknown female that he had been found out and that he would soon be arrested. Shortly after the train left Würzburg Station he killed himself, his body being removed at the next stop.

Investigator Harry Price used the train, unaware of this story and of the fact that he was sleeping in the very same compartment. Near Würzburg he heard the sound of a pistol shot and felt that he was not alone. The train attendant admitted somewhat reluctantly that the compartment Price had been in had been the subject of 'complaints' before.

Recordings from an Airfield
D: 1972
L: Bircham Newton Airfield, Kings Lynn, Norfolk
S: Terence Whitaker

Bircham Newton Airfield was constructed in 1914 at the onset of World War I but left derelict until being recommissioned at the outset of World War II when personnel from the Royal Air Force, the Royal Australian Air Force and the Royal Canadian Air Force were stationed there.

After World War II, the site was taken over by a construction-industry training company and the officers' mess converted into a hotel. Another part of the building was used as a studio for making management-training films. Behind the hotel is a double squash court, one of the courts of which is reputed to be haunted. Two men playing squash were the first to see something out of the ordinary; one of the players looked up at the spectators' walkway overlooking the court and *saw a figure of a man dressed an RAF uniform looking down*. The player alerted his partner and together they watched as the airman walked along the walkway and disappeared at the doorway at the end. They became convinced that they had seen a ghost and decided to arrange for a tape recorder to be left in the squash court overnight. Their initial intention to remain there with the recorder all night was modified when they heard loud footsteps walking along the corridor!

Before leaving, the two men made certain that they locked the building with the only key. When they replayed the tape later what they heard was extraordinary. The tape had recorded all the sounds of an active airfield: voices both male and female, machinery, strange 'pinging' sounds, as well as *'strange unearthly groaning noises'*. Even more extraordinary was the sound of an aircraft apparently flying, although investigation indicated that there had been none in the vicinity during the period the recording was being made.

A BBC engineer analysed the recording and could find no fault with the recorder. The tape had not been previously used so there were no old recordings on it. There was some surprise at the suggestion that the sounds could have come from outside the squash court as it was felt unlikely they would have penetrated its nine-inch-thick walls.

The BBC television programme *Nationwide* conducted its own investigation into the haunting; a reporter spent the night inside the squash court with a tape recorder. She reported the sounds of doors banging, 'an intense feeling of cold', and indicated that the tape recorder had stopped at exactly 12.30 for no apparent reason. Cases of recording equipment failing during investigation into many areas of the paranormal are quite commonplace.

A medium entered the squash court and, in a trance, described an Anson aircraft which had crashed behind a nearby church killing its three crew, Dusty Miller, Pat Sullivan and Gerry Arnold. The medium said that the airmen were hanging around the airfield because they did not realise they had been killed!

Inquiries into the history of the area suggested that the airfield had been haunted in other ways. One student on a course there had had the bedclothes pulled off him and another had witnessed his curtains being torn and thrown around the room. An engineer working alone in the attic of what had been the officers' mess had been tapped on the shoulder and so scared out of his wits that he refused to work there again. There was also a report of a figure in RAF uniform walking through a solid brick wall – the wall had been built long after the war.

The Tay Bridge Disaster
D: 1880
L: Dundee, Scotland
S: W. Herbert

The Tay railway bridge, built by Sir Thomas Bouch, collapsed on 28 December 1879 during a violent storm, sending an engine and five coaches into the Firth of Tay with the loss of 90 passengers.

There is a strong local belief that on the anniversary of the accident a ghost train crosses the new bridge from the south towards Dundee, before plunging into the darkness as it did on its original ill-fated journey.

U-boat U-65
D: 1916
L: Seas around Europe
S: Daniel Cohen

The submarine boats used by the Germans during World War I were extremely successful, and as part of the fleet 24 such boats were commissioned to be built in the shipyards at Bruges in Belgium. One boat, U-65, was reputed to be haunted.

During its construction several workers were killed, though in major construction projects this is not overly rare. During the launching of U-65 in October 1916 one officer fell overboard and was drowned, and during its initial trial the U-boat could not surface for some twelve hours, causing the crew considerable fear. No explanation for the malfunction could be found.

The following day a torpedo exploded on deck killing six crew members, including a second lieutenant who was later to become the most popular candidate for subsequent hauntings.

A typical claim is this one, from a crewman who saw the dead lieutenant board the U-boat and walk towards the bow. The lieutenant stood at the bow staring at the crew, arms folded over his chest.

Some months later the ghost was seen again on U-65, now back in service, both by members of the crew and by the captain himself.

Seeking to stem the tide of stories about U-65, the head of U-boat Command, Admiral Schroeder, spent a night on the boat and announced in the morning that he had 'not been disturbed by any ghosts'.

The boat's former captain was killed during an Allied attack at Bruges; the ship next went out under the command of Lieutenant Commander Gustav Schelle, who had a unique cure for ghost reports, threatening to severely punish anyone who reported one!

It was a year later before anyone either saw the ghost or at least had the courage to report it: Master Gunner Erich Eberhardt claimed to have seen the ghost standing near a torpedo tube at the bow. The figure brushed past him and then disappeared. Shortly after this Eberhardt apparently stabbed himself to death.

Even the end of the U-boat was to prove enigmatic; it was found wallowing on its side by the crew of an American vessel. They thought it might be booby-trapped and were about to destroy it when it exploded; just beforehand the American crew reported seeing the figure of a man standing on the vessel, arms folded across his chest.

S.S. Watertown
  D: 1929
  L: At sea
  S: Various

In December 1929 two seamen from the crew of the *S.S. Watertown* died aboard ship and were given burial at sea. The next day their faces were seen imprinted in the waves. Their images were also reported on the following two voyages of the ship, always seen from the same position on the deck.

After those three voyages they were not reported again.

The White-Cloaked Lady
  D: 1987
  L: Samlesbury Hall, Lancashire
  S: Prof. Colin Gardner

Some 40 reports of a white-cloaked lady have been received from drivers, both driving alone and with passengers, and there have also been reports from others who have met her in slightly different circumstances. One such report concerns Alex Dunderdale and his wife, who were driving on the A677 near Samlesbury Hall on 16 November 1987.

As their car approached the entrance to the hall, Mr Dunderdale was horrified to see a woman in front of their car; although he braked he realised he would not be able to avoid hitting her. He did not and the car not only hit her but apparently ran right over her body before skidding to a halt. In a state of shock, Mr Dunderdale searched the road for her injured or dead body but could not find her. His wife had not seen the woman but had felt the car lurching as it had apparently run over her. Although Mr Dunderdale had seen her, dressed in white, he could find no sign of her on the road, under the car or off to the sides of the road where, injured, she might have crawled. He searched for over half an hour but returned to the car, no less frightened and shaken than when he had left it.

Other encounters with the White Lady have included people

seeing her standing by the side of the road who then discover she is not there when they stop to pick her up; and one or two people walking down the road after having missed the last bus have seen her appearing or disappearing in front of them.

11
Phantom Hitchhikers

Phantom hitchhikers are a special subdivision of ghosts; they hitchhike in the traditional way and are picked up by cars, seemingly to warn their drivers of danger before disappearing in an eerie and often frightening manner. In the phantom hitchhiker we can probably see more folklore and legend than in most varieties of ghost and haunting reports. As Hilary Evans (a prominent researcher into the paranormal) has pointed out, there is no obvious reason why the victims of this one particular type of incident should return to warn others when the victims of many other kinds of accidents apparently do not feel so motivated. Whatever the explanation, this section shows that the phantom hitchhiker is very much a worldwide phenomenon; examples in this compilation include stories from the United States of America, France, England and Africa.

The A38 Hitchhiker
D: 1958 and others
L: Nr. Taunton, Somerset
S: Michael Goss/Hilary Evans

A phantom hitchhiker, a man in a long grey overcoat, appears to be haunting a stretch of the A38 near Taunton in Somerset.

In August 1970 a woman from Taunton encountered the apparition standing in the centre of the road and was forced to veer to avoid him. Stopping to tell him what she thought of his choice of place to stand, she discovered that he had disappeared.

Local newspapers found a number of other people who had encountered the same apparition at the same place, including a motorcyclist who had crashed as a result. These local reports prompted lorry driver Harry Unsworth to tell how he had encountered the man several times in 1958. At the first meeting Unsworth gave the man a lift, having picked him up wet through from the rain at three o'clock in the morning. The man in the grey overcoat spent the journey of some four miles recounting tales of accidents that had occurred during the last few days and was not exactly bright company for the drive.

Mr Unsworth picked up the same passenger several times, usually in the pouring rain and wandering along with a torch in his hand.

In November 1958 a more mysterious event occurred. Having picked up the man in the grey overcoat, Mr Unsworth took him where he wanted to go but at his request waited so that the man could collect some luggage and then be driven further along the road. The man did not re-appear and Unsworth, irritated, drove off. Three miles up the road – some twenty minutes later – he encountered the figure again, though he was sure that no vehicle had come along the road and given him a lift. It was quite an achievement to have travelled so far in so short a time, though presumably not totally impossible. Unsworth tried to avoid the hitchhiker and drive past him, whereupon the man in the overcoat leapt in front of the lorry inviting an almost inevitable accident. Luckily there was no collision, but when Unsworth jumped out of the lorry cab he could see the man in the overcoat gesticulating wildly; he then turned and instantly vanished leaving Mr Unsworth extremely shaken.

Blue Bell Hill

D: 1974
L: Nr. Maidstone, Kent
S: Michael Goss/Hilary Evans

Maurice Goodenough was driving on Blue Bell Hill between Maidstone and Chatham just after midnight in the very early hours of Saturday, 13 July 1974. A girl, about ten years old, wearing a white blouse, socks and a skirt appeared from nowhere in Mr Goodenough's headlights. Despite braking as hard as possible and skidding, he felt the impact as the car hit the girl. When Mr Goodenough jumped out he found the young girl lying on the road, bruised and bleeding, though not to an excessive degree.

Afraid of what injuries she might have, Mr Goodenough carried the child to the side of the road, wrapped her in a blanket and left her while he drove to Rochester police station to seek help. The police joined him to return to the scene where they, found only the blanket and no trace of the girl.

A tracker dog was called in to assist in the investigation but was unable to find a scent to follow; no blood stains were found. Inquiries at local hospitals discovered no reports of anybody injured in the way described by Mr Goodenough and Mr Goodenough's car was undamaged.

If Mr Goodenough described the incident accurately, and there is no reason to doubt that he did, then a supernatural explanation is not quite the only one possible, though we are still left with a mystery. If the girl's injuries were not so serious she could have left the scene and gone home – it has even been speculated that she may have been on the run from the social services – but all of this is suspect in view of the fact that no one has been able to trace the girl in the time since.

Blue Bell Hill has a high incidence of ghost and phantom hitchhiker legends though the report to the police station probably makes Mr Goodenough's the most reliable report.

The search for the phantom hitchhiker's identity has thrown up a very specific if problematic candidate. On Friday 19 November 1965, around nine years before Mr Goodenough's encounter, a Ford Cortina was in collision with a Jaguar on Blue Bell Hill. The Cortina was occupied by four women, a 22-year-old girl who was to be married in Gillingham, Kent the following day and her three hen-party companions. The bride-to-be died five days after the collision at West Kent Hospital, one of her companions was killed in the accident and a second died on admission to hospital. The fourth was seriously injured. Both the Jaguar's occupants survived.

One of the three dead women is held to be the phantom hitchhiker, either the bride-to-be or, more often, one of her friends. Having been thwarted on the very eve of her wedding, perhaps the bride was not ready to die and is constantly trying to finish her journey.

It is obviously difficult to reconcile the figure of an adult woman with that of a ten-year-old girl; the bride-to-be may have been small, dressed in a young style, perhaps wearing white ankle socks, and in the panic of the crash, and in the darkness, may have been mistaken by the witness as being much younger than she was.

There are other, frustratingly uncorroborated, reports of sightings of the bride-to-be hitchhiker in the area on the anniversary of her crash.

Hitchhiker Causes an Accident
  D: 1977
  L: Nr. Frome, Somerset (B392)
  S: Michael Goss/Hilary Evans

There is no shortage of legends and paranormal reports from the Wiltshire, Avon and Somerset area in the south of England: UFOs and more recently corn-field circles in the hills around Warminster, Arthurian tales around Glastonbury and so on. The area also boasts its own phantom hitchhiker and a small country road from Frome to Nunney some ten miles west of Warminster has provided the location.

The witness (who prefers his name to be withheld) was driving on the Frome-Nunney road in August 1977 when he stopped to give a man a lift. The hitchhiker got into the back seat of the car and the witness locked the car doors. There was very little communication between the two, the most telling point being the hitchhiker's comment that it was cold. But when the witness asked his passenger a question he discovered that the reason he was receiving no response was because no one was in the car, yet he was certain the car door had not been opened during the drive. The witness reported the incident to Frome police station where, perhaps not unreasonably, he was breathalysed but found to be sober. Indeed he was described by the police as 'a highly distraught motorist' and they also accepted that, 'We have had people coming here in a state of virtual hysteria,' in connection with other reports of the phantom hitchhiker. The police, however, keep their feet firmly on the ground and point out that their own patrol cars travel these roads frequently but have not been involved in any phantom hitchhiker incidents.

The story takes a most unusual twist at this point. There are many 'repeater' phenomena in the paranormal and in particular people who see many ghosts or who experience many UFO events, but there are very few cases of people who experience more than one phantom hitchhiker event. Yet this witness was to provide a second report concerning the same stretch of road sometime after the first event.

The second encounter was quite unlike the first. In the second encounter the witness came across the hitchhiker standing in the middle of the road and skidded to avoid an accident, hitting either a lamp post, a telegraph pole or a hedge depending on the report. Needless to say, when the witness searched the area for the cause of the problem no trace of him could be found.

As a phantom hitchhiker account this does differ from the archetypal story in which the hitchhiker tends to be purely benevolent. Whereas many phantoms seem driven to get into cars and admonish the drivers for reckless driving, or save their lives by giving them a quick reminder of the Highway Code, the Frome-Nunney phantom seems to have graduated to actually trying to cause an accident that could have ended up with the witness and the phantom swapping insurance details on the 'other side'!

The story was to take a turn for the bizarre when building-society manager Ron Macey, who was organising the Queen's Silver Jubilee celebrations in the local area, decided to turn ghostbuster. Concerned that the local celebration should not be harmed by the phantom hitchhiker keeping people away, or possibly even with an eye to the potential benefits of publicity the ghost might bring, a series of ghost patrols were set up to investigate the events. It does not appear to have been a serious attempt at psychical research and adds very little to the overall understanding of this case. Unfortunately, as a result of the publicity, at least one driver encountered a floating white ghost with a huge grin – in this case flapping from the trees on strings (the product of very down to earth clowning about).

Candidates for the Frome-Nunney phantom have not been lacking; suggestions have included the victims of Judge Jeffrey's public hangings nearby, an American serviceman killed in a car crash and a husband wrongly hanged for his wife's murder.

In August 1991 we contacted Frome police station to find out whether or not they had had any recent reports; the policewoman on duty said that she had been there for two and a half years and although she had heard of the local legend she was certain that there had been no police reports filed on it during her time there.

Hitchhiker on a Motorbike

D: 1978

L: Uniondale, nr. Willowmore, South Africa

S: Cynthia Hind

South African Army Corporal Dawie Van Jaarsveld was motor-biking to Louterwater to see his girlfriend. It was the early months of 1978, and the early part of the evening on the Barrandas-Willowmore road near Uniondale.

The hitchhiker in this case was an attractive brunette in dark trousers and a blue top. Van Jaarsveld stopped to give her a lift, keeping one eye on the road around to ensure that she was not a decoy for a mugging. The girl indicated she wanted a lift and the corporal gave her a spare crash helmet and an earplug so that she could listen to the radio, as he was doing, which would keep her awake during the drive.

After a few miles the corporal was alerted by a bumping sensation and looked back to find his passenger gone. There was no trace of the girl and the spare helmet was strapped to the bike.

The investigator, Cynthia Hind, verified directly with the corporal that he had gone to a cafe in Uniondale and the proprietress there confirmed his distracted state of mind. Cynthia Hind then went to Louterwater Farm where one of the people on the farm also testified to the corporal's state of mind. According to another investigator, David Barritt, the witness identified the phantom hitchhiker from a photograph shown to him as Maria Charlotte Roux. She was a 22-year-old who had been killed in the early hours of the morning of 12 April 1968, ten years previously, in a car crash near Uniondale when a car driven by her fiancé veered off the road. This 'hitchhiker' is a much reported phenomenon of this area.

In May 1976 another witness, Anton Le Grange, had encountered what would appear to be the same hitchhiker, who had asked to be taken to an address that could not later be verified and who disappeared from the car during the drive. This disappearance seems to be unique amongst hitchhiker stories for Mr Le Grange heard a hideous scream from inside the car and saw the right rear door swing open as though somebody was opening it, although no one was visible. The car was travelling at speed at the time. Even more extraordinarily, the car was being followed by a Police Constable Potgieter and apparently he, too, saw the door opening.

This case offers, then, independent witnesses, independent incidents and some possibility of identifying the subject ghost. It also suggest physical manipulation of the car – rare in such cases.

The Lady Disappears

D: 1981
L: Quatrecanaux Bridge, Palavas, Montpelier, France
S: Hilary Evans

Sometime after 11 p.m. on the evening of 20 May 1981 two couples – the men in the front and the women in the back of a Renault 5 car – were driving back to Montpelier from a beach excursion.

The hitchhiker in this instance was a woman dressed in white and the driver of the car stopped for the hitchhiker on the basis that it was not safe for a woman to be alone on the road at that time of night. This apparently explains why the driver stopped when it was not normally in his character to do so and also why he did so even though it was hardly convenient since the car was already full; on the other hand the fullness of the car adds to the quality of the case.

On stopping, the driver told the hitchhiker they were heading for Montpelier and she nodded her head but said nothing. As in the Bagnères case (see p. 220) it was a two-door car and therefore the front passenger had to get out along with one of the girls from the back seat to allow the hitchhiker to get into the middle of the back seat, leaving her sandwiched between the two girls and effectively trapped.

Suddenly the hitchhiker shouted, 'Look out for the turns, look out for the turns! You're risking death.' The driver slowed down to negotiate the bend, his concentration no doubt disturbed by screams from the back seats where the two girls had just experienced the sudden vanishing of their recent companion.

The two couples checked the area to see whether she could have somehow got out of the car, although this was blatantly impossible in any normal circumstances, and they reported the event at Montpelier police station, to an Inspector Lopez.

Although Inspector Lopez warned the witnesses that he had little time for hoaxes and if that was what they were trying on they should stop before they dug themselves in too deeply, the reports were still made, apparently with sincerity, and Lopez stated, 'Their panic wasn't put on and we soon realised they were genuine. It worried us.'

Resurrection Mary

D: After 1930
L: Chicago, USA
S: Various

According to a much-told legend, Resurrection Mary is the phantom hitchhiking ghost of a Chicago woman who had a row with her boyfriend sometime in the 1930s, walked out on him and was knocked down by a car while hitching a lift to Archer Street in Chicago.

Prevented from ever resolving the argument with her boyfriend, she haunts the stretch of road, trying to complete the journey that she started over half a century ago.

Resurrection Mary gets her name from the cemetery in which the unfortunate young woman was buried.

The Silent Passenger

D: 1979
L: Stanbridge, Bedfordshire
S: Direct and various

On the night of 12 October 1979 Roy Fulton, a down-to-earth young carpet-fitter, was driving home from a darts match in Leighton Buzzard. He had had a couple of pints of lager but was far from drunk; indeed he would not risk drink-driving since he needed to be able to drive to earn his living. Later in the evening he was to report his encounter to the local police which would certainly have been unwise unless he was sure that he could not be prosecuted for drink-driving.

It was late in the evening and Mr Fulton was driving through Stanbridge. He was in Pedder's Lane and turned onto Station Road where the street lights end some hundred yards or so away from the T-junction. At that point Fulton saw a figure thumbing a lift and pulled up in front of him, looking at him in the headlights of his mini van. The figure had a dark jumper and trousers and an white open-collared shirt. He opened the door himself and sat in the car silently. Even when Fulton asked him where he was going he did not reply but merely pointed up the road; Fulton assumed he was going either to Dunstable or Totternhoe. After a few minutes, during which time the van had been travelling at no less than 40 miles an hour, Fulton turned round to offer the hitchhiker a cigarette and discovered he was not in the car. The interior light had not come on, indicating that the door had not been opened, and in any case it is highly unlikely that anybody could have jumped out of the moving car safely, particularly without alerting the driver.

Fulton put the brakes on and looked behind to see if he could see the hitchhiker but he couldn't. He also checked the rear of the mini van to ensure that the passenger had not somehow got into the back but this possibility was eliminated. As fearful reality dawned, he 'gripped the wheel and drove like hell' as he describes it in his interview with researcher Michael Goss. One analysis of the event holds that the area is very open and flat and would provide no opportunity for someone to hide but we believe that in an unlit area at the dead of night somebody could probably hide very effectively just by lying down in the grass at the side of the road providing car lights or torch lights did not actually pick him out. In any case our own examination of the area indicates that there are a number of possibilities for hiding. But what is most important is how the hitchhiker got out of the car in the first place.

Fulton reported his meeting to the Dunstable police who sent a car to the scene of the incident but did not require Fulton to accompany them. As is typical in such cases, there was very little the police could do, and since there was no apparent crime or breach of law and order requiring their attention, there was no reasonable action that they could have been expected to take.

As to the identity of the phantom hitchhiker, one suggestion made in a newspaper was that he was the ghost of a young Scots hitchhiker killed returning from a party, but no concrete evidence of such an event having taken place could be located by the newspaper's researchers.

A Warning from the Back Seat

D: 1976

L: Bagnères, France

S: Hilary Evans

In January 1976 a young woman hitchhiking near Bagnères in France turned out to be a phantom hitchhiker. On the road two young men from the town were putting a new car through its paces, in particular testing its performance at speed. Seeing the hitchhiker, they pulled over to give her a lift. It was a two-door car so the man in the passenger seat had to get out and push the front seat forward to allow the hitchhiker to get into the back of the car before getting back in himself. The door closed, the car pulled away again and they continued their performance test of the vehicle.

While sweeping round various bends in the road the hitchhiker apparently warned the men to be careful as there had been many accidents in that area. Accepting their passenger's reaction, the driver slowed the car down and the two reassured her. Later one of the men remarked over his shoulder to the hitchhiker, 'You see, Madame, other people may kill themselves here, but we got by all right.'

There was no reply; when the men looked back they found the backseat was empty, their phantom hitchhiker had gone. As is so often the case in these archetypal stories the impossibility of the hitchhiker being flesh and blood, if we accept the report at face value, is only underlined by the circumstances of the car itself. She could not get out of the doors without disturbing the front seats, to say nothing of the fact that the car was moving at speed throughout the journey.

The original source of this story is the magazine *Lumières dans la Nuit*, a copy of which was supplied to me by author Hilary Evans who refers to the case in his book *Visions, Apparitions and Alien Visitors*. I spoke to Hilary about the case recently and he told me that the road system where the event occurred had since been dramatically altered. Whether this will exorcise the hitchhiker is uncertain and only time will tell whether she is at last at peace.

12
Time Slips

This encyclopedia shows that it is unwise to think of ghosts as a single phenomenon but rather that they deserve to be classified as a range of disparate phenomena. Many ghosts are, on the face of it, apparitions of individuals out of their normal location or time. Perhaps at least some ghost reports of this nature can be explained as 'time slips'. This is the theory that occasionally 'windows' can open up between two times allowing some kind of vision through that window. Whether or not these are merely glimpses into other times, or whether some form of time travel takes place on the part of either the witness or the ghost, is still very much open to question.

This section includes a wide variety of these frequent claims including time slips between Wat Tyler's Peasant Revolt of the fourteenth century and 1942; several ghostly cottages appearing and disappearing at various times; a 70-year-old murder re-enacted with a new potential victim; rooms suddenly changing in their character and appearance; Vikings on the Isle of Wight in 1969; a bridge between 1484 and 1974; an argument in the spring of 1950 with a woman from before World War I; and what may have been a vision of a man from the future.

An Artist at Versailles
D: (No date)
L: Palace of Versailles, nr. Paris, France
S: (Not given)

Following the Second World War the Palace of Versailles was the subject of considerable renovation, to repair the damage from that tragedy. Many of the most beautifully sculptured and decorated rooms had been damaged and an artist was engaged to sketch and record the remaining decoration, and particularly the ceiling mouldings, so that the original designs could be reproduced throughout the renovated building.

The artist entered a state room which he described as most beautifully furnished and hung with tapestry. The windows were draped with silks and one of the chairs in the room was described as gilded.

It was not until he had left the room and was outside in the grounds that he realised he had been in that room every night for the past week and that it had always been totally bare, no tapestries, curtains or furniture.

The implication was that he had had a vision of the room's past, a past of great splendour which, we can speculate, was either the product of his own imagination, which was concentrating on the renovation at that time, or that his focusing on the splendour of Versailles had opened his mind to receiving an image from its past.

Beefeaters of Yesteryear

    D: 20th century

    L: Tower of London

    S: Joan Forman

An unnamed Yeoman warder was on duty in the Byward Tower, the main entrance to the Tower of London, when he looked up and was astonished to see four or five Beefeaters, apparently from a much earlier period in time, seated around the log fire smoking pipes. The whole room was quite altered in appearance, and it was only when the warder came back into the room after briefly going out that he found the scene had reverted to the normal situation and the present day.

Boldings Farm

    D: 1978

    L: Bridgnorth, Salop

    S: Andrew MacKenzie

On 21 September 1978 Kenneth Bull and his wife were coming to the end of their holiday at Bridgnorth. They took a bus to a nearby village to visit the local church and then decided to walk back down a small country lane. On the road they saw a sign saying 'Boldings Farm' and ahead of them a low wall of red bricks across the road. As they went further down the road Mr Bull saw that the wall ended at what seemed to be a tall ruined farmhouse made of the same bricks. They both looked away and when they looked back moments later found that the structures had disappeared completely. It appears that only Mr Bull saw the farmhouse although both saw the wall itself.

A study of ordnance survey maps of the area dating back as far as 1842 revealed no such structures. The time slip theory is, of course, only one possibility and – if correct – perhaps involved a 'spatial' slip as well. Or could it have been a vision of 'future' time?

Brickworks of Old
D: 1950s
L: Shoeburyness, Essex
S: Joan Forman

At some time in the mid-to-late 1950s Mrs E. Thomas of Shoeburyness, Essex was walking in the country near her home. As she approached her house she sensed the breathing of a horse nearby. She could apparently also hear the hooves of the horse on the gravel and it sounded as though it was panting as if it was pulling a heavy load. She could, however, see nothing.

Some time later she learned that the area had been a brick field, and horses had been used to pull the brick-laden carts along railway tracks at the very place where she had felt the horse's presence.

Brother and Sister
D: 1945
L: Stratford-upon-Avon, Warwickshire
S: Joan Forman

On a summer's afternoon in 1945 Mrs Hopkins of Stratford-upon-Avon was walking through the town and reached the street where the stationer's shop, in which her brother Billy had worked before the war, was to be found. Her brother had recently been killed in action and Mrs Hopkins said later that at the time her brother had been very much in her mind.

The streets were fairly deserted as it was half-day closing. Suddenly ahead of her she saw the figure of her brother and assumed, apparently without much surprise, that he was returning to work from his lunch break. The figure turned into the stationer's and disappeared. It was only at that point that Mrs Hopkins remembered her brother was dead and simply could not be there.

In her book *The Mask of Time* Joan Forman raises some important questions about this incident. At face value it is a straightforward ghost story and might easily be explained as such. However, the fact that Mrs Hopkins's brother was in her mind at the time increases the possibility of some sort of self-generated illusion; furthermore she described him as wearing his civilian clothes but, as Forman points out, it might have been reasonable for him to be dressed in khaki, the way Mrs Hopkins had seen him before his death. On the basis that the civilian clothes are the product of the civilian surroundings Joan Forman suggests that Mrs Hopkins experienced an event of the past superimposed on the present, fusing the two into one image.

A Chapel Out of Time

D: Late 19th or early 20th century

L: (Not given)

S: George Russell (*The Candle of Vision*)

The poet and painter George Russell was waiting for a friend inside the remains of a ruined chapel. Suddenly he seemed to have been transported back in time to when the chapel was in use, and he described a small crowd of people kneeling at the altar and an abbot or bishop standing nearby, holding a crosier. Behind the abbot was a boy carrying a vessel of some description.

Russell apparently saw the scene as if he were a part of it, but there is no indication that anyone noticed anything amiss about him. In his recollections he appears to have received not just impressions of the physical appearance of the figures he saw but also of their mental states (though of course that could be easily explainable by hallucination). He describes the emotional abandon of one member of the congregation at the altar, the vanity of the young assistants to the cleric and so on.

Had he 'time slipped' *into* the body of someone who was there at the time (in which case what did that person feel?) thereby causing no disturbance? Was he a ghost in their time? These questions of course remain unanswered.

Cottages from the Past

D: 1968

L: Wallington, Surrey

S: Joan Forman

In 1968 Mr P.J. Chase was waiting for a bus in Wallington, Surrey, and idly gazing up and down the road when he noticed two small cottages with thatched roofs and attractive gardens. One of the cottages had a sign on the wall showing the date 1837.

When he mentioned the cottages to another local man with whom he worked the man was adamant that there were no such cottages there but rather two brick houses. When Mr Chase went back to examine the cottages he found that his colleague was correct and the space was occupied by two brick houses rather than the cottages he thought he had seen.

When a number of local people who had lived there for some time were asked about the site, they confirmed that there *had* been two thatched cottages there earlier but that they had been demolished some years before.

The Fireplace Vanishes

D: 1918

L: London

S: Joan Forman

In 1918 Mrs R. Eadie, staying in London, was nursing a friend who had contracted the Spanish flu which had swept across Europe. Her friend lived in Addison Buildings, a large family house which had been converted into flats.

One night she was in the sitting room, facing the fireplace. As she looked up, 'the wall containing the fireplace vanished; the room had opened out into a large high-ceilinged reception room. The salon was filled with ladies and gentlemen; the latter wore knee-length, full-skirted coats of every variety and colour; white knee-breeches, white silk stockings with black buckled shoes. Their hair was worn in a queue and powdered.' Mrs Eadie describes in detail the dress of a former age: three-cornered hats, low-cut bodices, lace dresses and so on.

Suddenly the scene vanished and the room returned to normal. Whether or not Mrs Eadie had had a waking dream, perhaps relating to the book she was reading, is uncertain; what is clear is that she felt sufficiently moved by the experience to write about it many years later.

Galla Placidia's Tomb
D: 1933
L: Ravenna, Italy
S: C.G. Jung (*Memories, Dreams, Reflections*)

On his two visits to the tomb in Ravenna of the Empress Galla Placidia who died in AD 450, Swiss psychologist Carl Jung found his mood affected by the atmosphere of the place.

On his second visit, in 1933, Jung moved from the tomb to the Baptistry of the Orthodox. There he was immediately struck by the mild blue light filling the room from no apparent source. In place of the windows that Jung had seen on his first visit there now appeared four great blue mosaic designs of astonishing beauty. They seemed to be depicting maritime events, exactly fulfilling a promise made by the Empress that if she was safely carried across the sea she would build the Basilica of San Giovanni as thanks to the gods, adorning it with mosaics depicting the perils of the sea.

Jung attempted to buy photographs of the mosaics but could not find any. He asked a friend visiting Ravenna to purchase some for him and was told that he would not find any photos because the mosaics did not exist. Jung was astonished to hear this, and the lady who had been with him apparently refused to believe it as she too had seen them with her own eyes.

An analysis in the *Journal of the Society for Psychical Research* in 1963, by Professor Sir Cyril Burt, suggests that there are some fundamentally blue images in the Baptistry and that some of the specific themes described by Jung may have come to him from images he had seen in the Bible.

Such an explanation does not explain the woman's vision; perhaps Jung influenced her interpretation of the existing images – if not, then a 'psychic' explanation is still open.

The General Stationer's
D: 1973
L: Great Yarmouth, Norfolk
S: Joan Forman

At some time in 1973 – the exact time he could not recall – numismatist (coin collector) Mr Squirrel went to Great Yarmouth to buy envelopes in which to keep the individual coins of his collection. He was going to a general stationer's that he had not previously been to but which had been recommended to him. He believes that it was an old and established shop.

Outside the shop was a cobbled area, the shop front was newly and brightly painted, whilst inside the till was very old-fashioned and the floor covered with what he described as 'oil cloth'.

The shop assistant appeared. She looked to be in her early thirties and was wearing a long black skirt and a blouse with a cameo brooch at the neck. Her hair was piled in a bun. Although seemingly old-fashioned, such an outfit would not have been out of place in the early 1970s, when there was a great flux in the styles and fashions people were wearing. Mr Squirrel did not regard the scene as abnormal.

When he asked for the envelopes for his coins the assistant was able to supply him with these, explaining that they were sold to fishermen for keeping fish hooks in. He purchased 36 of the envelopes and returned home.

The one other fact which struck him, and which he particularly mentioned to a friend later, was that there was an extraordinary silence while he was in the shop – traffic noise was completely absent.

The following week he returned to the shop to purchase some more envelopes but was extremely surprised to find it looking completely different. The cobbles had disappeared and had been replaced by paving stones, the building itself looked rather dark and worn and many features of the inside of the shop were missing. The shop assistant was over fifty and quite obviously not the person who had previously served him, though she told him that she was the only assistant on the premises, that she had been there for many years and that there had never been a young lady working there. Nor did the shop sell the envelopes for his coins, and, as far as the assistant knew, it never had done.

Joan Forman, in *The Mask of Time*, suggests that the case has sufficient detail to indicate a possible time dislocation but points out, importantly, that there was the added and special fact of the handing over of the envelopes which would, if time dislocation *was* the explanation, mean that they had been handed from one time to another.

Since Mr Squirrel had retained some of the plastic envelopes, these were able to be dated by the manufacturers. Certainly they did not date from the early 1900s, which was the era suggested by the description of the stationer's shop. The manufacturers believed them to be just ten or fifteen years old when they examined them, which would place them in the late fifties, early sixties. They pointed out that cellulose film was used in the 1920s, although techniques of production were established even prior to 1914. Basically it did not seem that they were evidence of the time slip and indeed, as Joan Forman points out, 'seemed to eliminate such an explanation'.

One other theory put forward is 'family memory'; that the appearance of the shop was as it appeared to Mr Squirrel's coin-collecting grandfather and somehow 'came down' to the grandson.

There must be at least some room for the possibility that, despite the obvious sincerity of the witness, on his first visit he may have, erroneously, entered quite different premises which may have been rather old-fashioned but perhaps not so old as Mr Squirrel believed.

The absence of sound while Mr Squirrel was in the shop is interesting. A similar detail occurs in the case which took place in Cockeymore (see p. 229). Generally speaking, a stillness or quietness during sightings of ghosts and apparitions is fairly common. A very similar phenomenon is associated with UFO encounters, where a 'cone of silence' seems to envelop witnesses, particularly during close encounters. Precisely what this may mean is uncertain; in the case of these alleged time slips it is tempting to ascribe it to the fact that the past was simply quieter, with less traffic and so on, but that would probably be a simplistic answer. The cone of silence may be related to the apparition and its method of appearance, or it may, we would think more likely, relate to the witness and be a factor of the 'altered state of consciousness' which either creates the illusion in the witness's mind or enables the witness's mind to perceive realities that it otherwise would not perceive.

A Georgian House
D: 1926

L: Bradfield St George, nr. Bury St Edmunds, Suffolk

S: Sir Ernest Bennett (*Apparitions and Haunted Houses*)

In October 1926 Miss Ruth Wynne and fourteen-year-old Miss Allington walked from Rougham to look at the church in the nearby village of Bradfield St George. They walked through a farmyard and as they approached the road they could see on the other side an old brick wall surrounding a Georgian-style house with large trees in its garden.

In a letter dated 11 March 1934 (thus some seven and a half years after the event) Miss Wynne described the house as having a stucco front and Georgian-style windows.

Some four months after the October 1926 walk both Miss Wynne and Miss Allington revisited the site but found neither the wall nor the house; indeed they tried to locate it several times and never succeeded.

In correspondence in February 1937 Miss Allington was unable to remember any details of the house, which seems therefore not to have impressed itself on her memory as strongly as on Miss Wynne's.

The house has not been located; even in 1963 Tony Cornell of the Society of Psychical Research was in the area looking for the house but could find no building which matched the house reported by the two women.

Grandmother's Cottage
D: 1919 or 1920

L: Cockeymore, nr. Bury, Lancashire

S: Joan Forman

When Mrs Louisa W. Hand was eight or nine (and therefore the incident must have taken place around 1919 or 1920) she was playing in front of her grandmother's cottage in Cockeymore, Lancashire. As she ran back inside she suddenly saw that the furniture had changed; the witness believed it was older-looking. The door to the kitchen was no longer there; it was quiet, and darker than usual.

Thinking that she might have entered the wrong cottage, though this was unlikely since it was the first in the row, she ran out to check. Sure it was correct, she ran back in again and was confronted by exactly the same surroundings. Only on the third attempt, and after being outside with other children for a while, did she return to her granny's cottage to discover that it was back to normal.

Somehow the child had experienced what seems to have been a time slip twice before the scene reverted to normal.

The Guest House
D: 1933
L: Boscastle, Cornwall
S: *Journal of the SPR* (1942)

In June 1933 Mr and Mrs Pye were travelling by bus from Wadebridge to Boscastle, a town on the North Cornwall coast. As the bus approached Boscastle it stopped to allow one passenger to get off and while it was stationary Mr and Mrs Pye both looked out of the window at an attractive guesthouse just nearby. It had a terrace set out with tables and striped umbrellas. Mr Pye noted that although he didn't see a sign he was certain it was a guesthouse.

On arriving in Boscastle Mrs Pye walked back down the road to seek accommodation at the guesthouse but was unable to find it. Indeed both Mr and Mrs Pye searched for the guesthouse by bus and on foot but were never able to find it.

Intriguing as this case seems, there is, in fact, some evidence that a satisfactory explanation has been made. In 1962 a Miss Scott-Eliott closely examined the small coastal road from Tintagel to Boscastle along which the Pyes had travelled. She found a small private hotel on a steep hill which runs into Boscastle, surrounded by a twelve-foot wall and hedge hiding it from the road except at one small point. At the time of the Pyes' visit the building had been a private house though summer visitors often took tea on the drive in good weather. If they were doing so at the time the Pyes travelled past this may have been what created the impression in Mr Pye's mind that the building was a guesthouse despite the lack of signs. Miss Scott-Eliott also located a cafe at the foot of the hill in Boscastle which had striped umbrellas at the time of the Pyes' visit. It is therefore reasonable to suppose that the Pyes saw both buildings and superimposed their details. Of course, once on foot and able to take in the scenery more slowly, neither was able to locate the building which their minds had, in effect, created.

Mrs Hedges Takes Shelter

D: 1930s

L: Swindon, Wiltshire

S: R.J.M. Rickard and J. Michell (*Phenomena*)

During the 1930s Mrs Edna Hedges was cycling along the Roman road, Ermine Street, outside Swindon, during a storm. She was going to visit a friend. Looking for shelter, she saw a small thatched cottage just off the road down a small lane. It was apparently occupied as she could see smoke drifting from the chimneys. She went to the door which was opened by a tall, bearded, old man in a green waistcoat and when she asked for shelter she was invited in. The room was low-ceilinged, quiet (despite the storm) and there was a bright fire. Mrs Hedges claims that she never heard the man speak at all but suddenly just found herself back on the road continuing her journey. She could not remember leaving the cottage.

When she arrived at her friend's house some others were also there and were surprised to see that she was not wet despite having cycled through the storm. Mrs Hedges explained what had happened, but the others were adamant that there were no cottages on that stretch of road except for a derelict one which had been unoccupied for 50 years or more. Retracing her steps, she was able to confirm that the derelict cottage was indeed the one that she had been in; she could not explain it but insisted that her experience was real.

Miss Jourdain at St Hugh's College

D: Early 20th century

L: Oxford

S: Various

The Vice-Principal of St Hugh's College, Oxford in 1902 was Miss Eleanor Jourdain. She tells of having had several psychic visions of Oxford's past, including a pageant of people from medieval times which made its way down St Margaret's Road outside the college towards the gallows, transporting a hapless victim to his fate while the procession danced and cheered. Miss Jourdain went on to say that she had also had visions of the past in the college gardens.

Later in her life Miss Jourdain was to become well-known as one of the co-authors of the book *An Adventure* which tells the story of the ghosts of the Trianon (see pp. 237–41).

Leeds Castle
D: (No date)
L: Leeds, Kent
S: Alice Pollock (*Portrait of my Victorian Youth*)

Psychometrist Miss Alice Pollock was experimenting on one of the rooms at Leeds Castle in Kent known as Henry VIII's room, by touching objects in an attempt to experience events from another time. Miss Pollock was a relative of the family living at Leeds Castle; the relative chose this room as it was the one Alice Pollocks' own parents had used when they stayed there.

After a period of receiving no impressions whatsoever, the room suddenly changed, losing its comfortable modern appearance and becoming cold and bare and carpetless. Logs were burning in the fireplace which was now in a different position. A tall woman in a white dress, deep in concentration and greatly anguished, was walking up and down the room.

A history of the castle suggests that the room had been the prison of Queen Joan of Navarre, Henry V's stepmother, who had been accused of witchcraft by her husband.

The Lights in the Field
D: 1969
L: Isle of Wight
S: Joan Forman

On 4 January 1969 Dr White and his wife were driving across the Isle of Wight towards the village of Niton at the extreme southern tip of the island. It was the night of a bright full moon although there were several heavy dark cloud masses in the sky.

In a remote part of the island's centre, they were driving past fields in an area where the nearest farmhouse was some miles away. They realised that the fields ahead of them were covered with 'bobbing lights', what appeared to be torches held by many people moving around in the fields. As they got to the top of the hill they were climbing they could see that all the fields to their right were covered in these lights, looking almost like 'a great city'. At first they believed, reasonably enough, that they had probably seen shepherds in the fields. Then they decided that, in view of the great number of lights, they must be looking at some sort of agricultural exhibition, though they did think that a night in January was a rather odd time for one.

The mystery thickened as they approached what they thought was a cart track to a farm but which now appeared to be a very well-lit city street with buildings on either side. Yet when they actually reached the beginning of the farm track they discovered that it was exactly what they had expected it to be, a moonlit track with no buildings at all. They were beginning to be somewhat unnerved. At a crossroads south of Newport almost exactly at the very centre of the island, is the Hare and Hounds Inn, a familiar landmark on their journey. As they approached the inn they could see it was bathed in light. Figures carrying torches were running across the road ahead of the car. The fields beside them were also covered in lights. Ahead of them a very tall man ran in front of the car; they noticed he was wearing a leather jerkin and a broad belt. Dr White decided to stop and ask what was going on in order to relieve the tension.

A mere twenty yards from the inn, the lights and the figures disappeared, leaving the pub in darkness with just the usual lights shining from its windows. Now quite unnerved, the couple decided not to stop and drove on to Niton.

After their evening out they returned along the same route in the early hours of the morning but were not subjected to any further experiences.

The case is interesting for many reasons. Firstly, it appears that if some kind of apparition or time slip was taking place then the Whites were going in and out of it periodically rather than experiencing a single vision which then cleared. One suggestion that was made – that they might have been seeing a mirage of, say, Portsmouth 'bounced' off the clouds – seems unlikely given the close proximity of some of what they saw.

Mrs White herself suggested that perhaps they had seen a time slip of events at a different time in the same area. The principal suggestions are that they witnessed a Roman camp, or some sort of Viking encampment; the tall man seen outside the Hare and Hounds seemed more Viking than Roman in appearance.

The vision would seem to relate to the past rather than the future, since the lights seemed to be hand-held rather than fixed urban lights. The future would presumably be more likely to feature fixed lights in a built-up area unless we speculate about some sort of post-nuclear-holocaust world. Only the description of green, red and orange lights in the 'city street', where the farm track was, suggests something more modern, but a vision of the past is certainly not ruled out as an explanation for this extraordinary experience.

Man in a Dressing-Gown
D: 1990
L: South London
S: Direct

This story was related directly to us by the witness, 'Judy', a writer living in south London. She is still living in the same block of flats where she had the experience in 1990.

Judy started by saying, 'I really don't know if this is a ghost story or not.' She was at the point of waking up from sleep at around two or three a.m. and feels that she had had a dream. In the dream she was asleep in her own bed in her own room which is illuminated by an outside street light. In the dream an elderly man was standing at the end of the bed looking at her; she could see his head and face and she got the impression that he was wearing a dressing-gown. Perhaps the most interesting part of this tale is that as she looked at the man, he in turn looked *surprised*, looking at her. In a rather confusing sequence, Judy dreamt that she woke up and still saw the man and then *actually* woke up and discovered that he was in fact still standing there. This has all the hallmarks of hypnopompic imagery – images seen during the potentially hallucinatory state between sleeping and waking up. Nonetheless, to Judy it seemed very real and there was shortly to be a little corroboration from her pet cat.

'It gave me a terrific fright. I sat up in bed and he faded, he just faded and wasn't there anymore. There was no sense of anything evil, threatening or nasty at all. He wasn't frightening, it was just the fact that he had disappeared.'

Judy then went to get her pet cat to sleep with her. She put it on the bed, and after padding round and round as cats do before settling down, it suddenly turned round, sat bolt upright, ears pointing forward, and stared at exactly the spot where the man had been. As Judy put it: 'That gave me the giggles: I thought "serve you right for going and getting a cat for protection".'

When we discussed this incident Judy admitted that she considered the possibility that she had hallucinated and even that the cat's attention was possibly coincidental; perhaps it had seen a moth or insect that was invisible to Judy. Nonetheless the two incidents seemed just a little too alike for comfort and left a fairly indelible impression on Judy's mind.

Judy did some investigation of her own and became familiar with most of the people who had lived in the block since it was built. Her visitor did not match any of them, though the possibility of it having been a guest was not ruled out. Furthermore, the previous buildings on the site had been lower than the existing structure and there would have been no building at the level at which Judy lived. This would seem to rule out a 'recording'-type ghost from anything other than the existing block. Judy was sure that the figure was contemporary which further suggested something relating to the present time.

The interest of the case hinged on the surprised look on the figure's face. Perhaps some guest of a previous owner, going to bed one night, had suddenly seen the image of *Judy*, lying in the bed, and had then watched her fade away, leaving him with a ghost story of his own to tell!

A Mansion in a Wood
D: 1946
L: Hadleigh, Essex
S: *Journal of the SPR* (1961)

In 1946 brother and sister Grace and Bruce MacMahon were walking from Leigh-on-Sea in Essex to a creek near Hadleigh, passing a wood which they had seen many times and which was very familiar to them.

Both were shocked to discover a Georgian mansion standing near the wood that neither had seen before. They watched a young girl walk down the drive with a large dog, pass in front of them and disappear over a nearby hill.

The MacMahons were unable to locate the house in later searches in the area and could find no reference to it in local archives. No explanation has been forthcoming and subsequent researches failed to locate any house that would fit the description. Although it is tempting to speculate on a time slip, i.e. that the MacMahons were seeing either into the past or the future, this would seem to be ruled out by the fact that the young girl they saw was dressed in clothes appropriate to their own time.

A Murderer on Board
   D: (No date)
   L: Helvick Head, Ireland
   S: Ben Noakes

Playwright and schoolmaster Arthur Frewen was spending Easter at Helvick Head on the southeast coast of Ireland. One evening Frewen slept in the open and awoke, because of the cold, to find that the mist which had been around him had cleared. In total darkness he stumbled for some considerable time until he saw the light of what he thought was a cottage in the distance. On getting closer he discovered that the light was shining out of the open hatch of a boat.

Frewen looked down into the hatch and saw an old man working on a fishing net over a table. The old man looked up, saw Frewen and beckoned him to join him. The man gave Frewen a bowl of potato soup and took him to a cabin at the end of the boat where he could spend the night. Frewen hung his sister's red school scarf (which he had been carrying) on a peg behind the door. He heard the man walking down the passageway and some instinct made him close the bolt on the door preventing the man from getting in. Soon the man was shouting from outside, 'Open the door and let me in!' Filled with fear, Frewen smashed through the skylight and fled the boat.

When he had told his story to guards at the barracks where he was staying he eventually persuaded them to join him and go back to see the ship. When they got there all Frewen and the others could see was the shape of an old wreck which was quite clearly the ship he had been aboard. The timbers were slimy and old, rats moved under the old table. Frewen was filled with vivid recollections of what it had been like when he had been on board and it was without much surprise that he even discovered the red scarf hanging on the back of the door.

Frewen was told that the owner of the boat had been hanged in Dungarven some 70 years previously for the murder of an undergraduate. At the time of the encounter, Frewen, too, was an undergraduate.

Paris?
D: Pre 1969
L: Haiti, West Indies
S: R.J.M. Rickard and J. Michell (*Phenomena*)

Ivan T. Sanderson, a biologist and writer on the paranormal, told how he was once driving on the island of Haiti with his wife and an assistant when their car ran into mud and become absolutely stuck. The trio were therefore forced to walk for many hours until suddenly Sanderson saw houses lining the sides of the road in what appeared to be a medieval French street. He could even see shadows being cast by the moon at the correct angle in relation to the position of the buildings he was looking at. Sanderson claimed to know that this was a Parisian street scene.

Sanderson's wife also described exactly what Sanderson himself saw, suggesting that if it was a shared delusion it was an incredibly precise one. Otherwise they must both have seen something authentic in front of them.

The assistant, however, plodded right on through the scene, seeing nothing whatsoever. It was while they were lighting cigarettes offered by the assistant that they realised the image of the buildings had faded around them and they were back in their remote location.

The Petit Trianon
D: 1901
L: Versailles, nr. Paris, France
S: Charlotte Moberly and Eleanor Jourdain

Published in January 1911, Charlotte Moberly and Eleanor Jourdain's book, *An Adventure*, contains possibly the most famous of phantom-scenery cases. Written by the percipients of the events, it tells the story of their visits to the palace of the Petit Trianon at Versailles in the early 1900s, when they saw and apparently experienced visions of the 1700s.

Charlotte Moberly was the tenth of fifteen children of Winchester headmaster George Moberly, who went on to become Bishop of Salisbury. Devoted to her father, she became his secretary and never married. Like most women of the time, she received little formal education but her upstanding character and social background led to her being appointed (in 1886) Principal of St Hugh's Hall, at Oxford (later to become St Hugh's College). Miss Moberly was to live to the age of 90, dying in 1937.

Eleanor Jourdain, born in 1863, was the eldest of ten children of the Rev. Francis Jourdain, vicar of Ashbourne in Derbyshire. Miss Jourdain was educated at Oxford, reading Modern History, and went on to become a teacher first at Tottenham High School, then at a school in Clifton and later principal of her own school in Watford.

In 1901 the two ladies were introduced to each other to see whether they could work together at St Hugh's College. So they were not that well known to each other when, on 10 August 1901, they set out together from Miss Jourdain's Paris flat to visit the palace of Versailles. It was four o'clock in the afternoon when Miss Moberly suggested visiting the Petit Trianon, a small house and gardens within the estate at Versailles, presented to Queen Marie-Antoinette in 1774 by Louis XVI. There are two structures, some distance apart, known as the Grand Trianon and the Petit Trianon just northwest of the main palace of Versailles; and the ladies came first to the Grand Trianon. To have reached the Petit Trianon they ought to have turned down the Allée des Deux Trianons. However, they crossed this road and entered a small lane at right angles to it, not realising that by doing so they were passing the Petit Trianon on their right. Their route to the Petit Trianon was therefore fairly circuitous and took them around the gardener's cottage, the theatre and other pavilions.

Both ladies experienced feelings of depression and dreariness, a factor that occurs in many cases of people seeing phantom scenery (see also pp. 246 and 247).

As they passed what appeared to be the Temple de l'Amour, they saw a man of 'repulsive appearance' sitting on the balustrade surrounding the building. (Various suggestions have been made as to who this person might have been, including King Louis himself.) Another man directed them to the right and they came to the rear of the Petit Trianon. Miss Moberly saw a lady in summer clothes sitting on the lawn below the terrace, though it appears that Miss Jourdain did not. On reaching the terrace a young man directed them to the front of the house and walked around with them until they found the entrance of the Allée des Deux Trianons.

Inside the building they followed a group of visitors on a guided tour and then returned to their hotel for tea.

During the following week the two ladies discussed the possibility that the Petit Trianon was haunted as a result of the unnatural depression that they had suffered there, but made no other reference to their visit for some months. In November 1901, when the two ladies were talking about their visit, they considered it curious that only one of them had seen the lady in a summer dress sitting on the lawn outside the building. So they wrote independent accounts of their experiences to see how closely they matched.

Trying to discover whether or not the Petit Trianon was haunted, Miss Jourdain came across a story that Marie-Antoinette herself was often seen sitting outside the Petit Trianon on a certain day in August. Miss Jourdain even suggested that Miss Moberly had seen Marie-Antoinette.

Miss Jourdain revisited the scene on 2 January 1902, first examining the Temple de l'Amour, which she decided was not the building that they had first seen, although they had then believed it to be so; she then headed east towards the Hameau which they had not explored during the earlier visit. Miss Jourdain experienced the same depressing sensation as earlier and at one point observed two labourers loading a cart. She glanced up at the Hameau, glanced back and the cart and labourers were gone. Miss Jourdain came to a wood and walked through it, observing a man ahead. She became lost in the wood, and heard closer to hand the rustle of silk dresses and women's voices speaking French. She could also faintly hear the music of a band though she saw nothing.

Between 1902 and 1904 Miss Jourdain left her flat in Paris to revisit the Trianon many times; often her visits were in the company of her pupils. Miss Jourdain wrote to Miss Moberly telling her that the topography of the area was never the same as on that earlier visit they had made together.

On 4 July 1904 the two women visited the Petit Trianon again and Miss Moberly confirmed what Miss Jourdain's letters had told her, that the topography was different, distances seemed shorter, the grounds were less ornate and some features were not visible.

There have been many other sightings of apparitions at the Trianon, including a woman in a gold dress seen by a Mr and Mrs Wilkinson in October 1949, and a vision of a man and woman in antiquated peasant costume drawing a small cart behind them, seen in 1938 by Mrs Elizabeth Hatton. Indeed, in 1910, before *An Adventure* was even published, a Mr and Mrs Gregory described how, when they had entered the Petit Trianon, they had walked through a wood at the edge of which was a group of small houses; Mrs Gregory saw a woman shaking a cloth from the window of one these. When they read *An Adventure* after it was published, the couple returned to the Petit Trianon to find that no wood or houses could be found where they had seen them. Mrs Gregory also mentions seeing the same visions of gardeners and so on as those reported by Miss Moberly and Miss Jourdain in their book but claims she did not call them to her husband's attention as they seemed so perfectly ordinary.

The case has been the subject of considerable investigation and controversy. As Hilary Evans argues in his book, *Visions, Apparitions, Alien Visitors*, there is 'good reason to think that percipients were right in believing they had somehow shared a vision of the gardens as they had been in the eighteenth century, possibly at the outbreak of the French Revolution'. This would date their visitation to the 1780s.

There is always the possibility, of course, that the descriptions were either fantasy or hoax, but this seems to take no account of the background and character of the people concerned. If they did genuinely experience the 1780s, then the question Hilary Evans raises quite correctly is, 'Were they transported like time travellers back to that time or did they somehow become involved in a "replay" of events at the time which were brought forward to the 1901 and 1902 period where they were?'

It has been suggested that hauntings may be replays of 'recordings' stored in some unknown manner and it is tempting to consider that the extraordinary emotions stirred up by the French Revolution could have created such a recording. However, this would not allow for the apparent interaction between some of the subjects of the vision and the women themselves.

Michael Coleman, in his book *The Ghosts of the Trianon*, which also contains the complete accounts by the two ladies, concludes, after weighing the research both 'for' and 'against', that the women experienced nothing unusual. He suggests that the women may have been affected by a combination of drinking at lunchtime and the warmth of the day, resulting in their feeling rather ill. He believes that the women may have seen a present-day re-enactment of former events as part of the pageant, and in any case suggests that the women were seeking to confirm their beliefs rather than investigate their causes.

A Phantom Cottage

D: (No date)

L: Haytor, Devon

S: R.J.M. Rickard and J. Michell (*Phenomena*)

Ruth St Leger-Gordon, in her book *Witchcraft and Folklore of Dartmoor*, published in 1973, records that in a wood near Haytor in Devon there were several sightings of a phantom cottage, which would appear at certain times and be absent at others. A visitor to the district admired the cottage and commented on it to the owner of the wood who explained there was no cottage there; indeed when the visitor went back to prove it to herself she could not find the building.

At another time a new arrival to the area who had moved into a house on the other side of the wood saw the cottage but could not locate it after a thorough search; Ms St Leger-Gordon was able to establish that this second witness had not heard about the former sighting.

A surveyor working on the ordnance survey spotted the cottage and was surprised that he had missed it previously; he even reported smoke billowing from the chimney and clothes hanging out to dry. On closer inspection he could find no trace of the cottage but asked a passerby who confirmed that she too had once seen the cottage but couldn't find it either.

Ms St Leger Gordon took great pains to determine that all of these reports concerned the same cottage in the same place, but no search located even the remains or foundations of an old cottage. If it was a phantom it was possibly a phantom from the future rather than the past.

A Royal Tomb
D: 1974
L: Sheriff Hutton, North Yorkshire
S: Joan Forman

Sheriff Hutton is a small hamlet which lies north of the city of York and is the resting place of Prince Edward, Prince of Wales who died in 1484 at the age of ten, the only son of King Richard III. Edward was buried before his parents could return from Nottingham, where they were at the time, and there must have been a time of great sadness when King Richard and Queen Anne first visited their son's tomb.

In 1974 Joan Forman, a dramatist and writer of many books on ghosts and the paranormal, was researching a play on the life of King Richard and visited the tomb at Sheriff Hutton. She stresses that she was not trying to provoke a paranormal experience but was concentrating on the tomb in an attempt to understand intuitively the feelings of the parents as they themselves had presumably stood there many years before. As she placed her hands over the stone image of the Prince of Wales carved on his tomb she heard the church door open. Footsteps were apparently coming down the stairs into the church (which was irritating to Ms Forman as she hoped to have some time alone). When no one approached her she assumed that another visitor to the church was politely waiting for her to finish her studies.

Miss Forman believed that whoever was there was out of sight behind a large pillar and although she heard one or two mumbled words she couldn't make out any actual phrases. She felt riveted to the spot for a time but eventually felt that it was unfair to monopolise the most interesting part of the church. She left the tomb and walked up the aisle to apologise to whoever was there for keeping them waiting. In fact there was no one in the church

and no one around. The church door was closed rather than open
as she had expected from what she had heard. Ms Forman also
checked the clock mechanism to see if that could have caused the
noise she had heard but the clock was stopped. The only person
she could see was some 250 yards away, a gardener mowing the
lawn.

Ms Forman suggests that by touching the child's effigy she
might have caused a replay of an earlier incident, perhaps when
Queen Anne, the boy's mother, had first visited her child's grave.

Search for a Lake
D: 1952

L: New Forest, Hampshire

S: *Daily Mirror*

When Mr and Mrs Swain of Ilminster, Somerset and their sons
were on holiday near Beaulieu Abbey in the New Forest in
Hampshire in 1952 they came across a lake while driving through
a network of lanes. At the centre was a boulder and embedded
within it a sword extraordinarily reminiscent of Excalibur in the
legend of King Arthur. They have been unable to find the lake
again.

This has not been for want of trying. Approximately once every
three weeks in the years since their initial experience, the Swains
have tried to locate the lake without success. However they are
determined not to give up until they clear up the mystery. When
their story reached the the *Daily Mirror*, on 10 November 1969,
they had made approximately 250 visits over seventeen years
without success.

A Sighting under a Bridge
D: 1942

L: Abingdon, nr. Oxford

S: Joan Forman

In December 1942 Mrs B. McDougall was serving in the Wom-
en's Auxilliary Air Force and, together with two colleagues,
arrived at Abingdon Station on her way to the nearby RAF base.
They were walking, having missed their transport, and took a few
minutes to shelter under a bridge near the river. Mrs McDougall
believes that at that moment she found herself amongst Wat

Tyler's 'Peasants' Revolt' of the fourteenth century: she was pressed into a crowd of people hurrying under the bridge. Mrs McDougall felt hot, and could feel the heat and sweat of people pressing close to her. Their clothes were rough and course; her heart was beating hard from the fright. Coming out from under the bridge she suddenly found herself back in her own time, the dislocation being just a few seconds long.

The Skiing Party

D: 1950
L: Nr. Oslo, Oslo Fjord, Norway
S: Joan Forman

This case might be regarded as little more than a 'standard' apparition sighting, if there can be such a thing, were it not for the fact that the apparition seems to have acted in rather 'unghost-like' manner and was in fact witnessed by several people together.

In the spring of 1950 in a valley near the Oslo Fjord, several members of staff of both the British and American Embassies in Oslo, together with wives and friends, were out skiing. Amongst the party of eight was Brigadier K. Treseder of the British Embassy who described the event.

The skiing took place on land attached to a farmhouse at the bottom of the valley. The day's skiing was most successful due to the perfect weather and snow conditions. As the evening began to set in the party made its way back to their cars which were parked some 200 yards from the farm. A description of the terrain is important. The brigadier described the road being very straight and giving good vision for as at least half a kilometre in each direction. Snow covered everything and there was no cover on either side of the road where someone could be concealed. In addition the light was quite good enough for clear vision.

First to reach the cars were the brigadier and an American colleague; they were removing their ski equipment when they were challenged in English by a lady with a strong Scottish accent. She asked, if they had been skiing over her land.

The woman was tall, fairly old and dressed in an old-fashioned brown herringbone-tweed suit with a long skirt and a Norfolk jacket; she wore lace-up boots and a flat round cap. She seemed very irate, particularly when the brigadier admitted that they had indeed been skiing over the land behind them which she was suggesting was *her* land.

Having been joined by the brigadier's wife, the three of them were then given 'a thorough ticking off'. She regarded them as trespassers and ordered them to leave and never to return.

They were somewhat confused since they believed that in Norway in winter one was allowed to ski freely, but they apologised for trespassing and the lady turned away. Other members of the party, now approaching the cars, were asking what was going on, and the brigadier and his companions explained that the woman was objecting to their skiing on her property.

The reply from the other members of the party was, 'Which old lady?' In fact at this point no one, including the three who had previously seen her, could see the old woman at all. The road was empty, though no more than a few seconds had passed and the lady could not possibly have got out of sight from the position they were in. The whole party searched everywhere but could find nothing.

Then one of them actually suggested, that they might have been in conversation with a ghost. On the basis that the woman's clothes had gone out of fashion sometime before World War I. Their curiosity aroused, the party went to the farmhouse where a young couple and their two small children lived. There was no lady living there and they didn't know anyone who fitted her description. However, the farm had once been owned by the present farmer's great grandfather who had lived in it with his wife, a girl from Scotland whom he had married. Unfortunately there were no photographs of her. The farmer also confirmed that they were free to ski on the land if they wanted to.

It seems highly unlikely that three people could share an identical and somewhat bizarre hallucination. It also seems unlikely that the 'ghost' was of the 'recording' type since there seems to have been a very clear interaction between the apparition and the witnesses. Even in the unlikely event that the lady had challenged other skiers in her own time who happened to be standing in the very same spot as our witnesses, the explanation would hardly hold since the witnesses would have sensed the lack of genuine interaction. The interaction seems to have been genuine. But was the ghost a projection in to the skiers' time or were they a projection into hers and at what point did the bridge between times end?

Mr Spence

D: 1938
L: Man Sands, Devon
S: *Journal of the SPR* (1942)

During March 1938 Mr J.S. Spence took an outing to Man Sands, a cove on the Devonshire coast, on three successive days, a Tuesday, Wednesday and Thursday. It was the visit on the Wednesday which made Mr Spence believe something was amiss because the topography of the Sands had changed dramatically, but it reverted on the Thursday to what it had been on the Tuesday. Mr Spence believed that on the Tuesday and Thursday visits the cove appeared to him as it had been during an earlier period of time.

On the Tuesday Mr Spence had entered a cave which had opened up into a larger cavern. He had also found a dry-stone wall which appeared fresh, new and devoid of vegetation. He had felt heavy and depressed when suddenly a seagull broke the mood, his depression lifted and he found the scenery changed – he could no longer see the dry-stone wall but he located the gate that he had been looking for and had been unable to find earlier.

On the Wednesday, the tide was fuller than on the previous day, and therefore the cave inaccessible. He could not locate the dry-stone wall, at least not in the condition that he had originally found it, but he did locate a small damaged section of wall covered in ivy. He also saw the tree beside the gate that he had spotted after his mood had lifted the previous day but he could not see the small bent trees which he had seen previously and which he believed to be part of that earlier landscape.

On the Thursday Mr Spence did locate the cave but it was much smaller than he remembered and he was unable to get into it. Feeling the same depressing feeling as before, he walked around the scene and found the undamaged dry-stone wall, which he photographed. He was beginning to feel dizzy and rather ill at ease when suddenly his mood lifted and once again he was at the cliff edge next to the old broken ivy-covered wall. Yet again it seems to have been the noise of seagulls which either signalled his coming out of the mood or broke the tension, releasing his state of mind. He photographed the old damaged wall and returned home.

Subsequent analysis of the photographs revealed that the first one did not show the new wall as expected but nothing whatsoever. It has been suggested that the scene he was trying to photograph was his own hallucination. In the *Journal of the Society for Psychical Research* in 1947 J.T. Evans examines the case and concludes that it contains nothing that cannot be explained by misperception. It is suggested that access to the cave was governed by the exact time Mr Spence had arrived and whether or not the tide was high or low. Mr Evans also suggests that between the Tuesday and Thursday there was a rock fall which blocked part of the cave making it appear smaller and inaccessible to Mr Spence. Evans located the stunted windswept trees, but also the gate and the solitary tree. He believes that the dry-stone wall can be explained away because part of it appears to be ivy covered and the other part cleaner and not so 'aged' in appearance.

Three Figures from the Past
D: 1954
L: Wootton, Surrey
S: Andrew MacKenzie

Mary Barrington (a member of the Council of the Society for Psychical Research) related the story of a couple she referred to as Mr and Mrs Allan and their experience in the summer of 1954.

During a day out the couple visited a church in Wootton, Surrey. As they left the churchyard they climbed a hill to a bench to eat their lunchtime sandwiches.

As in so many cases of 'altered scenery', the Allans had both felt a depressing dark mood throughout the day and this persisted, making lunch no great pleasure for them.

Suddenly the air became silent, bird song stopped and Mrs Allan became aware of three figures behind her *although she never looked to see them*. Despite this, she maintained she could describe them as wearing black clerical clothes and that they were figures from the past. Quite unnerved, they left the area; further on they lay down on the grass and fell asleep. Their next clear recollection was of arriving at Dorking and taking the train home, though they have no memory of how they reached Dorking. This experience prayed on Mrs Allan for some years and later she and her husband made several attempts to locate the hill and the bench that they had been sitting on. Despite several visits to the church they could never match the lie of the land to the way it had been on their first visit. No locals could think of any nearby similar topography.

A suggestion as to the possible identity of the three men was given by an entry in the writings of seventeenth-century diarist John Evelyn who commented that on 15 March 1696 three would-be assassins of King William had been executed; this entry follows comments on a sermon delivered at Wootton Church. However, the three men were not at Wootton Church at the time of their execution – the only connection is in the mind of John Evelyn – and so this possible explanation is a complex one indeed.

Three Girls Find a Cottage
D: First half, 20th century
L: Buckfastleigh, Devon
S: R.J.M. Rickard and J. Michell (*Phenomena*)

A party of three girls were on a shooting expedition with their father on Dartmoor near Buckfastleigh. The girls became separated from their father and were lost in the darkness. Then they saw a light ahead, hurried towards it, and discovered a roadside cottage. As they approached the cottage they could see the warm friendly glow of firelight through the uncurtained windows. They looked through the windows and saw an old man and woman sitting by the fire.

Suddenly and without warning, the whole scene disappeared – the old man, the woman, the fire and the entire cottage itself. The girls found themselves in the dark again.

The Tramp in a Long Coat
D: 1966
L: Windmill Hill, Avebury, Wiltshire
S: Andrew MacKenzie

On a hot day in August 1966 Dr Martin Harris and his wife, Anne, were at Windmill Hill near Avebury, Wiltshire. (See also Edith Olivier's report of a ghost fair at Avebury, on pp. 250–1 below).

21. (Above) Ramsey Abbey, Northamptonshire: a deceased former abbot of this abbey contacted a seance at nearby Barnwell Castle (22), where Marie LeMoyne was walled up alive

23. St James's Palace: haunted by the ghost of valet Sellis – suicide or murder victim?

24. Woodfield, a house in Apsley Guise, Bedfordshire, said to be haunted by Dick Turpin, among others

25. Lord Lyttelton is warned by a ghost to prepare for his death in three days' time

26. (Below left) Jimmy Corfield, who 'flew' for his brother down the Corinth Canal (this photo was taken in 1940), and (27) Jimmy's brother, Bill Corfield (photo taken in 1947)

28. The two ghostly faces that 'followed' the *SS Watertown* after the accidental deaths of two men on board who were buried at sea

29. Peddars Lane, Stanbridge, Bedfordshire, where Roy Fulton picked up a phantom hitchhiker

30. Avebury, Wiltshire, where Edith Olivier saw a village fair 'out of time'

31. Heading for the church of Bradfield St George near Bury St Edmunds, Miss Ruth Wynne and her young friend Miss Allington saw a Georgian house 'out of time'

32. (Right) Miss Eleanor Jourdain who, with her colleague Miss Charlotte Moberly, experienced visions of the eighteenth century during a visit to the Petit Trianon at Versailles (33, below) in 1901

34. The Enfield Poltergeist: this photograph (taken from a sequence of shots) depicts the levitation and flight of 'Janet'

35. Maurice Grosse, one of the world's foremost authorities on poltergeist phenomena, who led the investigation into the Enfield poltergeist

36. 88 Newark Street,
Whitechapel, London:
poltergeist-like activity troubled
this house and (unusually)
remained to affect subsequent
occupants. The building is now
derelict

37. John Glynn surveys the
wreckage of his bedroom
caused by the poltergeist which
focused on him in his home in
Runcorn, Cheshire, in 1952

Dr and Mrs Harris were walking back from Windmill Hill after climbing to the top. They came over a slight rise and both saw a man walking slowly up the path beside the trees, a hundred yards in front of them. According to Mrs Harris, who wrote an account of the event to Andrew MacKenzie, she was relaxed and felt warm enough to take off her sweater.

The man they saw was heavy set, of medium height and somewhat stocky. He was dressed in a long, dark, heavy-looking overcoat and had a dark hat pulled down over his face. Mrs Harris believed he was in sight for 30–60 seconds, though they were not looking at him continually.

At least part of the mystery of this case hinges on the inappropriate clothing of the figure, given the warm weather conditions. It should, however, be borne in mind that as a general rule tramps 'on the road' in the English countryside will tend to wear all their belongings as the easiest way of carrying them, whatever the weather conditions.

Both Dr and Mrs Harris glanced away for a short time, a few seconds, and the figure was gone. MacKenzie suggests that by looking away the witnesses might have changed their state of consciousness. This may well be the explanation; nevertheless the apparition disappeared when it was passing a cluster of trees and the Harrises' first thought was that the figure had dived into the trees and might be laying ambush for them. This was not a particularly paranoid thought: a few weeks earlier their car had been broken into and the risk of a criminal attack was on their minds. Mrs Harris was genuinely concerned that the figure might jump out of the trees when they passed by. However, when they got to the trees she felt they were too small to have hidden the figure and they could see no one. She acknowledged that the figure could have been hiding by lying flat in the wheatfield but thought the explanation unlikely.

Two Suns

D: (No date)
L: Mount Merapi, Java, Indonesia
S: Joan Forman

During a student expedition to climb Mount Merapi in Java confusion and disorientation set in and the party broke up and scattered, the students finding their way back to base in twos and threes. Rescue services were sent out to locate those who were most delayed.

One of the students reported that when he looked up at the sun to get his bearings, he was astonished to discover that there were in fact two suns in the sky. Shortly afterwards he saw what looked like a palace, and two soldiers in uniforms of a previous age. There was no palace nor any guards at the location given or anywhere nearby; he had apparently suffered some sort of illusion. If so, it was a complex one: perhaps the palace and the guards had existed at some time in the past or indeed would exist at some point in the future and the student was seeing them through a time slip. However, that would not explain the extraordinary phenomenon of two suns. The chief explanations are either that a shining, sun-like body, something that would probably nowadays be described as a UFO, was in the sky, or that the 'ghost' landscape was superimposed on the existing one so it was possible for the boy to observe *simultaneously* the landscape of 'now' as well as the landscape of 'then'. If the sun was in a different position in the 'then' and the 'now', *both* might be visible. Any other explanation would most likely involve hallucination. But if this episode is evidence of anything other than hallucination, then it opens up fascinating possibilities if dual images of different moments in time can be seen simultaneously.

A Village Fair

D: 1916
L: Avebury, Wiltshire
S: Edith Olivier (*Without Knowing Mr Walkley*)

One day in October 1916 Edith Olivier was travelling from Devizes to Swindon and was approaching Avebury. She passed through a succession of huge stone megaliths and at the end of the avenue on which they were sited left her car to climb the earth mound which is the centrepiece of that ancient site. *As she did so she discovered that a fair was under way.* In her book *Without Knowing Mr Walkley*, Edith Olivier describes how the cottages and stone megaliths were obscured by failing light and falling rain, but that both were lit by the torches and flares from the fair's booths and shows. She describes coconut shies, swingboats, and the crowd of fair-goers. When the rain falling down the back of her neck had become uncomfortable she got into her car and drove away.

It was some years later when she discovered that the fair at Avebury, which had once been an annual event, had been abolished in 1850, over 60 years before she saw it; indeed her vision appears to have shown her an even earlier time than that, as the megaliths she had seen in the avenue approaching Avebury disappeared sometime before the turn of the nineteenth century.

13
Poltergeists

Most hauntings refer to haunted places; poltergeists have been described as haunted people. The extraordinary and often destructive action of poltergeists is usually attributed to one person around whom the phenomenon focusses. This has given rise to the theory that poltergeists are either internally generated by people in a state of stress or that external discarnate entities are able to latch on to one particular person through whom they then act. By its nature, poltergeist activity is probably the most frequently reported type of haunting and, as this section shows, it is a worldwide phenomenon with cases from the United States of America, Brazil, England, Germany, France, Scandinavia, Switzerland and Italy. This section includes some of the most famous poltergeist cases, such as the Enfield poltergeist of 1977, the Bell Witch case of 1817 and the Runcorn poltergeist of 1952. On pages 363–8, Maurice Grosse, probably the world's most experienced poltergeist researcher, describes how to investigate poltergeists.

The Ardachie Case
D: 1952
L: Loch Ness, Scotland
S: Colin Wilson

In 1952, Peter McEwan and his wife moved to Ardachie Lodge on Loch Ness in Scotland where they hoped to raise pigs. The couple hired a Mr and Mrs MacDonald as housekeepers to look after their small children.

On their first night the MacDonalds were disturbed in their beds by the sound of footsteps outside their room though no one seemed to be there. Later, in the bedroom, Mrs MacDonald saw an old woman gesturing towards her though neither Mr

MacDonald nor Mr McEwan could see her. To preserve their peace the MacDonalds moved to another room but shortly afterwards were again disturbed by noises and outside the door saw an old woman with a candle 'crawling along the corridor'.

They discovered that the house had been owned by a Mrs Brewin who had indeed had a habit of crawling along the floor on all fours at night holding a candle, an eccentric habit vouched for by several people who knew the house. Investigation by the Society for Psychical Research focused on a tree in the garden which was a favourite of Mrs Brewin's; they were aided in their investigation by Mrs MacDonald entering into a trance; she was presumably beginning to realise that, in spite of her protestations that she was *not* psychic, she may well have had some latent psychic ability that was coming to the fore.

Unable to come to terms with this phenomenon the McEwans and the MacDonalds left and the house was destroyed.

In his book *Poltergeist!*, Colin Wilson discusses an interesting theory about this case, put forward by researcher Stephen Jenkins. He believed that Ardachie Lodge was on the crossing point of four ley lines (very broadly, lines of earth energy along which there are held to be a higher incidence of paranormal experiences). The theory goes that the poltergeist spirits needed energy to manifest, that they were able to find *some* of the energy they needed in Mrs MacDonald's latent powers, but were finally able to activate them through the combination of her energy and that of the leys. This would explain why particular places are the site of frequent hauntings but also why there are certain peaks in activity at those places – presumably they are the result of particular people becoming the focus of energies there.

The Bell Witch

D: 1817
L: Robertson, Tennessee, USA
S: Various

The Bell Witch is one of the most unpleasant poltergeist cases on record. It eventually brought about the death of one of the percipients.

John and Lucy Bell lived with their nine children on a farm in Robertson, Tennesse. In 1817 one of the children, Elizabeth, seemed to be the focus of increasingly active poltergeist activity.

The phenomenon started with noises and scrapings, a common sign of the onset of poltergeist activity, and progressed to bedclothes being pulled off, and furniture and stones being thrown around. Both Elizabeth and her brother Richard had their hair pulled one night. Under investigation by the family and a neighbour, James Johnson, the poltergeist stepped up its activity, slapping Elizabeth around the face so that witnesses could see her cheek reddening. Elizabeth was sent to stay with a neighbour and the disturbances went with her, indicating that she was the close focus of the activity.

Elizabeth was always the focus and the activity went on for over two years or more (with repeats to follow). Later activity included strange lights outside the house, stones thrown at Elizabeth's brothers and sisters, and visitors to the house receiving similar slaps to Elizabeth.

Elizabeth's father, John, began to suffer from an illness attributed to the poltergeist. He was unable to eat, his tongue swelled and the poltergeist, which had now developed a voice, declared that he would be tormented for the rest of his life. Unfortunately this turned out to be true.

The voice had all the conventional characteristics of a poltergeist: it used violent bad language and was apparently identified as a combination of several individuals including a witch and a dead Indian.

It was reported that when Elizabeth was given an emetic to make her sick she threw up brass pins and needles and the poltergeist, which seems to have had a rather black sense of humour, suggested that if she did it again it would have enough to set up a shop.

Elizabeth became engaged to one Joshua Gardner who apparently did not meet the poltergeist's approval. It chose to reveal their most embarrassing personal secrets, eventually causing them to break off their engagement.

John Bell was reaching the end of his life. The poltergeist activity surrounding him increased – his clothes were pulled off him, his face distorted, and on 20 December 1820 he died while the poltergeist rejoiced, singing songs of triumph.

After Bell's death the poltergeist's activity diminished, and it finally disappeared with the words, 'I . . . will be gone for seven years.' Widow Lucy Bell and the two children who had remained with her at the farmhouse did hear manifestations seven years later but they did not last for very long and may indeed have been the product of their imaginations in the expectation of the original prophecy being fulfilled. Apparently the poltergeist made one more promise, to return in 1935, but failed to do so, or at least was not noticed by anybody.

The strange split of focus between Elizabeth and her father has led to some speculation as to exactly what the nature of the poltergeist's energy was. It has been suggested that there was some sort of incestuous relationship between the two which was resented by the girl and that she wrought this very peculiar form of revenge. Investigation has probably reached a dead end, given the time that has elapsed since the occurrences. Resolution could only come with greater understanding of the poltergeist phenomenon than we have at present.

Janine Bryant Bartell

D: (No date)
L: Greenwich Village, New York, USA
S: Philip Paul

In her book, *Spindrift*, Janine Bartell reported several experiences over a period of sixteen years.

Janine moved into a flat in Greenwich Village, New York with her husband. On her very first night there Janine awoke to see 'a monstrous shadow that loomed up from behind me'.

Soon she heard unexplained footsteps in the flat and experienced other poltergeist-like activity such as the sounds of breaking glass and crockery, although nothing was ever out of place.

A cleaning lady reported to Janine that she had seen a 'woman in white' in the apartment. A visitor to the flat asked her if the house was haunted after he had been there for only a few minutes.

A replacement cleaning lady reported a grey cat dashing into the bathroom though there was none in the house. And on another occasion Janine saw the black shape of a man move towards her, fly over her head and disappear through a window.

They moved out of the apartment and for three years lived

elsewhere, eventually moving back again to the apartment next door. Within a short period of time there were three suicides in the house, one tenant was fatally attacked and his wife later found dead and yet another tenant diagnosed as having terminal cancer. Other deaths took place after they moved out again.

Janine wrote her story, *Spindrift*, gave it to her publisher and died of a heart attack just a month later. The haunting stopped when Janine died, clearly suggesting, as is the case with most poltergeist activity, that she was its focus rather than merely the witness.

The Bull's Head

D: 1985
L: Swinton, nr. Manchester
S: *The Unexplained* magazine

In January 1985 Richard and Pamela Flammerty and their family took over and moved into the Bull's Head pub in Swinton, near Manchester. Just the following month they were to be assailed by poltergeist activity. Pamela's account is related first-hand in the Orbis publication, *The Unexplained*.

One night in February Pamela was alone in the accounts office, a thick-walled room off the cellar, checking the figures. She could hear a scraping sound from behind her. When she turned she saw a stool independently moving across the floor. It looked as if it was being pushed but no one was there to push it.

Then one afternoon, when the pub was closed, Pamela's youngest son ran upstairs to her and told her that there was a man in the pub. No one was found but her son and his brother were certain that a man in a blue jumper had been sitting in the pub. A former owner of the pub confirmed that he had had similar apparition sightings.

In an incident showing the overlap between areas of the paranormal – and one which will excite those researching electrical and mechanical interferences (and perhaps have some bearing on the fairly new work being carried out by Hilary Evans on street lamp interference, the claim by some that they can extinguish, or occasionally light, street lamps at will), Pamela and her husband were walking along the upstairs corridor late at night when one by one the light bulbs went out. There was no likelihood that this could have been caused by a fuse blowing, as they would all have been on the same circuit and would have gone out together. The couple were too frightened to investigate and locked their bedroom door that night. (Street light interference and other such interference may be the result of PK (psychokinesis) and this may give some clue as to the underlying cause of poltergeist activity – the two dominant theories are the exteriorisation from the witnesses or an external force which uses their energies.) In the morning every light in the building was on, including those that the couple clearly remembered turning off.

That same night they heard footsteps; but footsteps that sounded as if they were on a stone floor rather than on the wooden boards that were outside the room.

Late on Easter Sunday something of a cross between an experiment and a 'dare' ended up with a family friend and Pamela's stepfather being locked in the cellar for the night. Richard and Pamela were woken up by the friend, Steve McRey, screaming from the cellar. When they went down, he had a look of terror on his face. Pamela's stepfather lay unconscious at the foot of the steps, 'blood gushing from his head'. The two men had gone off to sleep but Pamela's stepfather had woken to the sound of Steve shouting. The lights had suddenly gone out and her stepfather had made a dash for the steps. 'An invisible hand suddenly gripped his left shoulder, and then a voice whispered harshly in his ear, "Derek".' He tripped over a beer barrel and struck his head, knocking himself unconscious.

A later event had elements which echo events in many paranormal areas, including UFO research. There had been trouble with the telephone line, so an engineer was called in and, while upstairs with the only people in the house, became certain that someone was downstairs using the telephone. When they went downstairs the telephone was off the hook although they were quite certain that it had been on the hook when they had previously inspected it.

The family eventually vacated the pub and Pamela Flammerty says, that in the time since, the hauntings have continued on a diminished scale, and in a more benign fashion.

This suggests that the phenomenon was more of a haunting than a poltergeist, which usually attaches itself to a particular person rather than to a place, but the episode is included in this section of the *Encyclopedia* because of its similarity to many poltergeist reports. It may even be that poltergeist activity around Pamela and her family 'overlaid' itself on a background of hauntings in the pub which remained after the family had left.

The Communicating Poltergeist
D: 1877
L: Derrygonnelly, nr. Enniskillen, Northern Ireland
S: Various

Society for Psychical Research investigator Rev. Maxwell Close and Sir William Barrett investigated poltergeist claims at Derrygonnelly near Enniskillen. The poltergeist consisted of rapping noises around the house even though everyone in the house was accounted for at the time.

Sir William Barrett attempted to communicate with the poltergeist silently, mentally asking it to knock a certain number of times. Sir William carried out the same experiment four times, sometimes indicating the number of raps requested by stretching the correct number of fingers while his hand was hidden in his pocket. On each occasion the correct number of raps was heard.

Of course, nothing in this experiment eliminates the possibility that Sir William was himself influencing the experiment in some way, albeit perhaps subconsciously or as a result of psychic abilities of his own.

Esther Cox's Haunting
D: 1878
L: Amherst, Nova Scotia
S: Various

In 1878 Daniel Teed was living in Amherst, Nova Scotia with his wife and two sons, as well as 22-year-old Jane Cox and eighteen-year-old Esther Cox (his wife's two sisters), his wife's brother William, and John, his own brother.

In August 1878 Esther Cox's boyfriend Bob MacNeal took her for a ride in a buggy and apparently made sexual advances to Esther of a less than subtle kind, taking her into the woods and ordering her to obey him at gunpoint. He was disturbed when someone else approached and he ran scared from Amherst, never to return. Despite MacNeal's behaviour, Esther was distraught and unhappy for several days at losing a man she cared for.

A few days later poltergeist activity began to be reported in Esther's bedroom. First of all she heard what sounded like a mouse, but none could be found; then a cardboard box apparently began moving independently.

The following night Esther began to be physically affected by something: her face reddened and her body swelled alarmingly. From outside the house there came a loud noise which was investigated by Teed, William and John, and on their return they found Esther had returned to normal appearance and was asleep.

A couple of days later Esther suffered all the bedclothes being ripped off her bed, and they flew off the bed again after having been replaced by Teed; Esther became ill and swollen again. During this episode the bedclothes flew at John Teed, Daniel's brother, and he left the house, never to return again.

While a doctor examined Esther, the pillow under her head expanded and contracted and noises were heard around the room. The bedclothes flew off again. Above Esther's bed writing appeared on the wall accompanied by a scratching noise: 'Esther, you are mine to kill.' Plaster flew off the wall and landed near the doctor and this spate of poltergeist activity continued unabated for some two hours.

The following day there were loud noises all around the house, in fact the disturbances continued for weeks. Eventually Esther revealed what her former boyfriend MacNeal had done, and Jane Cox suggested that he was somehow responsible for the phenomenon; loud noises around the house suggested that the spirit was agreeing with her.

During a period of convalescence to get over diphtheria Esther left the house and the phenomenon ceased. It returned when she did. The poltergeist turned really nasty shortly after this, attempting to set light to the house with lighted matches which fell around the room causing small fires. Alarmed neighbours strongly 'suggested' that Esther should be sent away. For a time Esther lived with a neighbour, John White, and the poltergeist phenomenon seemed to have abated although in fact it eventually started up during her stay at that house too. White invited Esther to work at the restaurant he owned but even there the poltergeist phenomenon manifested: the oven door removed itself from its hinges and metal objects attached themselves to Esther as if she carried a strong electromagnetic force. John White decided he could not continue in this way and asked Esther to return home. In fact she left Amherst for some time during which she was able to identify, by name, a spirit, Bob Nickle, as the one threatening her with harm (Bob Nickle and Bob MacNeal are perhaps significantly similar names).

In June of the following year, 1879, magician Walter Hubbell moved into the cottage in order to investigate the hauntings for a book. On Hubbell's arrival the poltergeist threw his umbrella up in the air, lobbed a carving knife towards him and tossed his bag away from him. It then went on to hit him with a chair from across the room and made a good few other chairs dance around. Hubbell tested the spirits by asking them questions such as the dates of coins in his pockets, and apparently they successfully communicated the correct answers by means of rapping noises!

Over the period of Hubbell's stay, when Esther was there the poltergeist activity accelerated, Esther had pins stuck in her hand and further fires broke out in the house.

Hubbell tried to capitalise on these events by putting on an entertainment for a paying audience. As the poltergeist did not enter into the spirit of the occasion all Hubbell got were demands to return the entrance fees. Hubbell left and wrote his book. In the meantime Esther had gone to stay with some friends and was working on Davidson's farm nearby. Her friends reported that objects were missing which were found in the Davidsons' barn and she was accused of theft; the case terminated abruptly when the barn caught fire and Esther was then accused of arson and sentenced to four months' imprisonment.

The poltergeist activity now stopped permanently.

In his books *Mysteries* and *Poltergeist!* investigator Colin Wilson suggests that the poltergeist was a manifestation of Esther's unconscious mind, the result of sexual frustration and regret at driving Bob MacNeal away. Perhaps the jail sentence was a sufficiently short sharp shock to 'bring her to her normal sense'. Such an explanation does not, however, as Wilson himself points out, explain the manifestations of writing on the bedroom wall and the knowledgeable rapping noises that answered Hubbell's questions. Most investigators at the time and since have dismissed the probability of outright fraud and suggest that there was some 'genuine' phenomenon occurring. A combination of these theories may lead us to believe that the poltergeist was the product of Esther's unconscious mind and the phenomenon of exteriorisation. It would also perhaps need to involve phenomena such as telepathy. There are too many unknowns, however, and at this distance in time it is unlikely that any further genuine investigation can now be undertaken.

The Dagg Case
D: 1889
L: Quebec, Canada
S: Colin Wilson

Poltergeist activity, which eventually manifested itself as a speaking entity, occurred in 1889 in Quebec, Canada on a farm owned by George Dagg.

It started with streaks of faeces or manure appearing on the floor of the house for which a young boy, Dean, was blamed. However, while the boy was out of the house the streaks continued to appear, proving that he was not the cause.

Poltergeist activity accelerated with crockery being displaced, windows smashed and fires spontaneously breaking out. The focus was identified as eleven-year-old Dinah McLean, an adopted child of the family.

In November 1889 an artist named Woodcock asked Dinah McLean to take him to the woodshed where she reported something connected to the haunting. Woodcock apparently heard both sides of Dinah's conversation with an entity – the entity's side of the conversation consisted mostly of obscenities. The entity identified itself as the devil and threatened to break Woodcock's neck. It calmed down when questioned by George Dagg and Woodcock together and admitted that it was only doing the hauntings 'for fun'.

A crowd soon heard about the phenomenon and gathered at the woodshed; apparently the entity performed for all and sundry. Indeed, Woodcock organised a statement signed by seventeen witnesses acknowledging that they had seen the spontaneous pyrotechnics, that they had witnessed stones flying and a mouth organ playing by itself.

Of particular interest, the entity made itself visible in a variety of guises to the two younger children of the house and to Dinah; as the devil, as a huge black dog and once as a man in white robes.

It seems that the entity then cleaned up its act quite significantly, abandoned its violent language and sang beautiful music, finally disappearing like an angel up into the air.

It has been speculated that this case shows the mischievous rather than the evil side of poltergeists.

Investigator Colin Wilson suggests that, having finally gained the attention it sought, the poltergeist calmed down and turned over a new leaf which is quite characteristic of the phenomenon. Poltergeists seem to act like humans, perhaps behaving badly either out of boredom or from a desire to impress. Once they achieve their goal they cease their disruptive behaviour.

Douglass Deen

D: 1949

L: Mount Rainier, Washington State, USA

S: Various

In 1949 thirteen-year-old adolescent Douglass Deen became the focus of poltergeist phenomena in his home in Mount Rainier, Washington State. At first there were scratching noises which were first thought to be vermin (however, a vermin-elimination company was unable to find any evidence of infestation). It progressed to movements of objects such as dishes and fruit flying through the air and pictures floating off the wall. Deen was disturbed in his bed which began to vibrate whenever he was in it, and the family eventually called in their local priest, Rev. Winston, to assist.

On 17 February 1949 the Rev. and Deen slept in a room together in twin beds. Deen's bed began to vibrate and the scratching noises recurred. When the Rev. asked Deen to sleep in an armchair, the chair began moving around and tilting and even a makeshift bed set up on the floor began sliding around as soon as Deen got in it.

Deen was taken away to hospital; in fact he was treated at both the Georgetown Hospital and at St Louis University, where he was given both medical and psychiatric help.

Since none of the treatments appeared to work, a Jesuit priest at the hospital eventually attempted exorcism. Even this was not successful until it had been attempted 30 times, after which the phenomenon stopped (although it has been pointed out that since poltergeist phenomena tend to be short-lived it may have simply gone away of its own accord, and not to have responded to the exorcism).

During the attempts to exorcise the spirit, Deen convulsed, shouted obscenities and even spoke in Latin, a language of which he knew nothing.

In 1971 author William Peter Blatty used this case as the basis of his fictional book *The Exorcist* which was later made into a highly successful film (in the book and film the protagonist's sex was changed to that of a young girl).

A Farmer's Poltergeist

D: 858 BC
L: Nr. Bingen, Germany
S: Legend

One of the earliest poltergeist reports occurs in the *Annales Fuldenses*, a chronicle which dates the event to 858 BC.

A farmer and his family living in a farmhouse near Bingen on the Rhine were apparently the focus of a poltergeist which threw stones, vibrated walls, caused fires, burnt crops and even audibly accused the farmer of a series of sins including having sexual relations with the daughter of one of his foremen. The poltergeist apparently followed the farmer wherever he went until other people refused to allow him anywhere near their homes.

Fred

D: 1966
L: Pontefract, W. Yorkshire
S: Colin Wilson

'Fred', or sometimes 'Mr Nobody', was the name given to a poltergeist which affected a family at East Drive in Pontefract between August 1966 and the summer of 1969. The poltergeist conjured up a massive catalogue of activity, the sheer diversity of which is fascinating. It included:

– Loud breathing noises at various times.

- Deafening drumming and other banging sounds.
- One of the witnesses dragged up a set of stairs, leaving marks on her throat as a result.
- Huge footprints left in the house.
- House keys showering down the chimney on to one of the witness's heads (one key has never been identified and is retained by the witness).
- The electrical system of a nearby car affected.
- A white mohair coat hidden in a pile of coal. When recovered, it was still completely clean.
- Inverted crosses stencilled on a wall.
- A cross stuck to a witness's back as if attached by a magnet.
- Drawers moving in and out in the furniture.
- Various substances from the kitchen, such as jam, smeared on doors and stairs.
- Eggs 'escaping' out of a locked basket that a witness was sitting on and materialising in thin air.
- A macabre 'haunting' involving a pair of one of the witness's gloves being made to 'peer' over and under doors (the witness eventually burnt the gloves, afraid to keep them).
- Furniture moving through the air.
- One particular witness who refused to believe in the poltergeist became the butt of its sense of humour when the poltergeist opened a fridge, slowly lifted a jug of milk above the witness's head and then poured it over her.
- A bite mark left in a sandwich.
- The plug removed from a tape recorder when one of the witnesses was trying to record the sounds (attempts to record paranormal phenomena are often affected in strange ways; even recorded interviews with witnesses sometimes fall foul of unexplained 'dead spots' on the tape at crucial moments).
- A grandmother clock thrown down the stairs and destroyed.
- A manifestation of a beautiful heavy perfume.
- Bedclothes thrown off the bed (very traditional!).
- A mattress thrown off the bed whilst the witness was still on it.

- A huge piece of furniture picked up and used to pin a witness down on the stairs, though no harm whatsoever was caused to the witness.
- A wooden pelmet detached and thrown out into the street.
- A long strip of wallpaper swaying like a cobra in front of one witness.
- A photograph of the witnesses slashed.
- The witnesses showered in a white chalky dust that appeared from nowhere.
- Spontaneously formed pools of water all over the floor.
- Green foam emitting from taps when turned on.
- A potato thrown across a room with such force as to shatter when it hit the wall.

There have been suggestions that the identity of the poltergeist might have been a monk who was hanged for a sex crime centuries ago, but there is no real corroboration for this theory. A hooded monk did appear in the house during the period of the hauntings but there was no direct or obvious connection between the two, and there does seem to be some qualitative difference between the mischievousness of the poltergeist and the quiet uncommunicative appearances of the hooded monk as reported.

The hauntings ended in a most curious fashion. A friend of one of the witnesses heard that spirits could be kept out by hanging cloves of garlic around the house; this they did and the hauntings stopped. It could of course have been that the natural end of the period of poltergeist activity had been reached.

One investigation was carried out by Colin Wilson who concluded that he believed the locality contained particular energy forces that enabled manifestations to form and that Philip, a fifteen-year-old living in the house, was the focus.

Wilson speculates that after a break of some two years following the first period of manifestations, during the second period the focus became Diane, a daughter of the family then fourteen years old.

The house became something of a local tourist attraction and in particular a magnet for ghost-hunters. On one occasion a bus driver announced to passengers as they passed, 'That's the haunted house,' and the bus apparently came to a standstill outside!

Several people who observed the house at night could see a strange glow around it. Whatever the source of this energy, it was not apparently coming from the national grid – the witnesses' electricity bills for the period were actually less than usual.

John Glynn's Poltergeist

D: 1952
L: Byron Street, Runcorn, Cheshire
S: Philip Paul

As a general rule poltergeist activity focuses on one person but in this 1952 case, although there is a clear focus on John Glynn, there is also a secondary focus on Glynn's grandfather, Samuel Jones.

The first signs of paranormal activity occurred at the farm where Jones was employed as a part-time worker. However, the events that took place a week or so later at Jones' home were what first attracted attention, in particular the attention of a diligent local paper, the *Runcorn Guardian.*

The family lived at 1 Byron Street, Runcorn and included Samuel Jones, a part-time farm worker aged 68, and his grandson sixteen-year-old John Glynn, the two of whom shared one large bed. There was also Jones' sister-in-law Lucy who shared a bed with John Glynn's eight-year-old sister Eileen. There were two other bedrooms in the house, which were used by non-family members.

The poltergeist activity began with noises in the bedroom John shared with his grandfather and others, apparently centred around a dressing-table which had been owned by Samuel Jones for 42 years, during which time nothing untoward had ever happened in connection with it. After the initial noises the dressing-table drawers would rattle and it would move, despite its very heavy weight.

During a seance organised by a medium, Philip France, and involving both Glynn and Jones, various objects including two Bibles were thrown around the room by the poltergeist. After the seance there was a pause of some ten days but the activity resumed when a clock was thrown five feet across the bedroom in the presence of a *Runcorn Guardian* reporter. The reporter, Jones and Glynn had been in the darkened room for only a short time when the reporter heard the dressing-table dragging across the floor, but when he examined it it seemed not to have moved.

After a pause of another week or so the activity again resumed and again reporters from the *Runcorn Guardian* were on the scene. As reported in the paper, 'in the presence of seven neutral observers', the poltergeist smashed furniture and threw books and drawers for some six hours. The newspaper also reported some minor activity at John Glynn's mother's home in Stenhills Crescent, Runcorn. At Glynn's own home the dressing-table moved about, a chair was thrown against the wall, a blanket chest began to 'dance', a clock crashed to the floor smashing its glass and a carpet moved from one side of the room to the other.

In an effort to introduce some sort of control, a *Guardian* reporter sat on the blanket-chest and seemed to be successfully suppressing the activity in it, although it was still going on elsewhere in the room; suddenly four books were hurled towards him, hitting him on the head and shoulder. Two drawers from a dressing-table smashed against the wall by his head.

Another observer, Mrs E. Dowd of Granville Street, Runcorn said that she did not believe it would throw anything at her when suddenly she was struck full in the face by a heavy book. Every time she entered the room something was thrown at her.

The bed, with three men sitting on it, was pulled away from the wall and the dressing-table created so much noise that speech became virtually impossible. When a torch was shone on the dressing-table it suddenly stopped its activity as if in response. Eventually, however, the dressing-table began to smash itself to pieces, first the mirror wings then the drawers and finally the joints of the main structure. On the bed, pillows were being moved around and the three men on it were being hauled about; bedclothes were pulled off the bed and thrown about the room. This burst of activity ended at around six o'clock in the morning.

The house was visited by the Rev. W.H. Stevens of the Wesleyan Church, Widnes and the Rev. Kinsey Lester of the Methodist Church, Widnes. Stevens and Lester, together with another investigator, stayed in the bedroom with John Glynn. A book struck the Rev. Stevens on the head and very shortly the dressing-table began to rock. Even though Stevens turned a torch on it, it continued to vibrate violently, and a heavy box turned over.

Rev. Stevens asked the poltergeist, to knock three times if it could hear him. As if in response, the dressing-table shook violently three times.

In an editorial in the *Runcorn Guardian*, it was pointed out that there was a great deal of evidence in favour of the case being genuine. There had been many independent witnesses, including their own reporters, two psychic researchers known for their scepticism, two police officers and three Methodist ministers, amongst others. All of the witnesses had seen phenomena occurring and fraud seemed unlikely in the circumstances.

Rev. Stevens, together with Rev. J.L. Stafford, conducted some rudimentary tests to investigate the possibility of fraud. John Glynn sat on a chair in the centre of the room away from the dressing-table and the Rev. Stafford held his shoulder. A Mr Thompson, a local man, held Glynn's right arm and hand. John Bury, another local witness, lay in the centre of the large double bed. Under these conditions there were virtually simultaneous movements of both the dressing-table and the chest which would have been impossible for any one of the people in the room to have contrived.

Rev. Stevens attempted to carry out a test 'behind the backs' of the other witnesses. A number of articles including a jigsaw puzzle were placed on the dressing-table; in the dark shortly afterwards, when no one was looking, the Rev. Stevens changed the position of the jigsaw. All the lights were out and the only person who could have reached the dressing-table was John Glynn himself and he was tucked up in bed with his hands under the covers. The Rev. Stevens had his torch to the ready and as soon as there was the beginning of a disturbance he switched on the torch and caught the jigsaw puzzle beginning its flight across the room; at the same time he could see John Glynn still with his arms beneath the bedclothes.

John Glynn was invited to the home of SPR researcher Clifford Davies, who was keen to see what would happen when Glynn was away from the house. Present were John Glynn, Clifford Davies and Glynn's friend John Bury. Clifford Davies' family were also present. During the meal Davies' wife Joan was pouring a drink of lemonade for John Glynn when the glass burst in her hand, cutting her finger and thumb. Davies immediately noticed that the glass had shattered and that the lemonade bottle was now empty although it had been virtually full at the time. John Glynn was soaking wet, the lemonade having exploded all over him. Davies tested the glasses later and failed to break one even by dropping it from a height of over eight feet.

Two nights later activity recommenced in the main centre of this poltergeist phenomenon, the bedroom at Byron Street. Parts of the now virtually destroyed dressing-table struck John Glynn, John Bury and another friend, Dennis Fallon, who were in the room at the time, and a pillow was ripped up. Other furniture moved simultaneously: a heavy, marble-topped washstand moved some three feet from the wall and the single bed Dennis Fallon had been lying on was overturned, tipping itself and the mattresses on top of him.

Police officers witnessed moving furniture and books being hurled and were completely baffled. The activity increased in violence and all three of the young men, Glynn, Bury and Fallon, suffered further blows from moving furniture.

The *Runcorn Guardian* tried to photograph the activity but the poltergeist remained shy of such publicity, never performing when a camera was present.

Up to this point the *Runcorn Guardian* had had a virtual monopoly on events with its reporters being invited to the bedroom to witness the poltergeist activity. Now, however, the *Runcorn Weekly News* seemed to be upset at not being invited and the *Weekly News* virtually accused Samuel Jones of fraud. It asked if he had 'something to hide'. Apparently their journalists had been ordered out of the house by Mr Jones for no apparent reason. The *Runcorn Guardian* came to Jones' defence and attacked the *Weekly News* for its comments, suggesting, that it was holding the views that it did because weekly news reporters had been ordered off the premises and that the newspaper was suffering from sour grapes.

To try to make the peace, Jones invited the *Weekly News* reporters to his home though the poltergeist apparently did not perform for them. Their reporter pointed out that, 'The fact that nothing happened strengthened the reliability of his evidence, for had there been any trickery the perpetrator of the tricks would almost certainly have arranged a performance for the benefit of the press.'

As is often the case with poltergeists, no resolution was ever found but the activity ceased after about three months and did not return.

It was not, however, the end of the story. The farmer on whose farm Samuel Jones worked had a story of his own to tell. About a week before the beginning of the outbreak of activity at Byron Street, one of the farmer's 53 pedigree pigs died. Jones was one of those employed to take care of the pigs. Within a few days several more died and no examination by veterinary surgeons could isolate the cause. The other animals were apparently 'nervous and frightened', including one pig that apparently tried to climb a wall as if in a bid for freedom. Within a fortnight, and therefore during the time that the activity was going on in Byron Street, all 53 pigs inexplicably died.

The farmer told a further extraordinary story: two days after the last pig died he saw what he described as a black cloud moving around in the yard. It was seven feet high and fairly shapeless but with two prongs sticking out of it. As he watched, it came close to him then entered the pigsties and seemed to search the now empty outhouse. His wife later told him that she had also seen the same thing on a different occasion. The same black cloud was seen in the farmhouse kitchen and when the farmer attempted to switch on the light he felt the two prongs brush against him, like solid blunt sticks. The farmhouse was also subjected to rattling drawers and other fairly minor poltergeist activity.

During the activity at Byron Street, the farmer visited the house at Jones' request and reported that in the so-called 'haunted bedroom' he had seen the same black 'horned' cloud on the large bed when John Glynn and John Bury were on it. The farmer himself had his coat thrown over his head several times from where he had left it.

Some months later the cloud was seen again at the farmhouse and this time it was 'attacked' by two dogs; it rose into the air and was not seen again. The farmer's wife claimed that she had once watched Samuel Jones leaving the farm and had seen the cloud apparently following him but had decided not to alert him since Jones seemed blissfully unaware of it.

Whether the black cloud and the other poltergeist activity were connected is not certain but for a while there seemed to be a fairly unusual 'dual focus' shared between both Samuel Jones and John Glynn. Maurice Grosse comments that 'it is unusual for poltergeists to cause real harm,' and feels that the death of the 53 pigs may have become part of the case only by association.

Guardian Spirit
D: 1928
L: Arakan, Burma
S: Maurice Collis (*Trials in Burma*)

In *Trials in Burma*, Maurice Collis describes seeing the ghost of an old Arakanese woman. He had been working late in the evening when he felt the building he was in shiver as if in an earthquake; his companion with him felt the movement also. He was suddenly confronted by a woman whom he saw standing on the steps. They did not communicate but looked at each other for a time and then she passed from sight, going down the veranda 'from which there was no exit except into the rooms'.

Collis was immediately certain that he had seen a ghost: 'There is no confusing a ghost with a mortal. It is not your eyes that tell you, but a sense that leaps up suddenly within.'

When he asked the locals about it the following day they confirmed that he had seen 'the female ghost bound to this spot by the old kings to guard their treasure'. Apparently a woman had been buried alive, to contain her spirit. Collis asked them why the house shook when the ghost appeared. He was told that it was because the ghost wished to attract Collis' attention. When he asked how she had done it they replied, 'It was not the house she shook, but Your Honour's mind.' (And presumably his companions mind as well.)

The Harpers' Poltergeist (The Enfield Poltergeist)
D: 1977
L: Enfield, Middlesex.
S: Guy Lyon Playfair, Maurice Grosse

The poltergeist which haunted a semi-detached house in Enfield, Middlesex between August 1977 and April 1979 was probably the most thoroughly investigated case of its kind in Britain and possibly in the Western world. Maurice Grosse, who headed the investigation into the Enfield poltergeist, was fortunately able to give his attention to the case full-time. He was not only extremely thorough in his work but, where necessary, called in an array of experts (some turned out to be helpful, some not) to examine the various aspects of the events there.

The other chief investigator on the case was Guy Lyon Playfair, who wrote up the story of the Enfield poltergeist in the book, *This House is Haunted*; no one wishing to understand this case and indeed poltergeist activity in general can afford not to read that book.

Maurice's involvement in the case may not itself have been pure happenstance: there are tentative suggestions, endorsed by Maurice, that his involvement was brought about by design. That may seem a radical claim yet the evidence has impressed many of those who have looked at the case.

In the afternoon of 5 August 1976 Maurice's daughter, Janet, then aged 22, died following a traffic accident. In *This House is Haunted* Playfair lists ten coincidences relating to Janet Grosse's death which, it is suggested, may have indicated the survival of her spirit and a wish to contact and direct her father. For example, Maurice 'found himself wondering whether Janet, if she had somehow survived her physical death, would send him a sign of some kind on the day of her funeral . . . It had not rained for several weeks, and Maurice thought to himself that a suitable sign would be a drop of rain.' At 8.15 a.m. the following morning, he looked out of the bathroom window and saw that the roof which extended from the window of Janet's room was soaking wet; there was no other sign of water or even dampness anywhere to be seen.

When I (J.S.) spoke to Maurice Grosse about the Enfield poltergeist case, during our meeting in November 1991, he also explained to me the coincidences that led to his being able to devote the appropriate amount of time to the case. Partly because of the possibility of the survival of his daughter's spirit, he had become actively interested in psychical research and had sent a report of the various coincidences surrounding his daughter's death to the Society for Psychical Research. It was them who, at his insistence, appointed him as the investigator on the Enfield poltergeist case. Maurice Grosse is an inventor with many worldwide patents for mechanical and electrical devices. Just before accepting the Enfield investigation he had sold a patent which would provide him with adequate funds to be able to devote himself full-time to the work.

During the investigation Maurice was talking about his daughter to Playfair and asked if she could be involved in the case. Maurice believed that the case had already shown too many meaningful coincidences; these included the case turning up at the SPR just when he had indicated he wanted to work on such a case. Maurice believed that his daughter was possibly directing him toward the case in order to help him understand the phenomena of poltergeists more fully.

Towards the end of the investigation a clairvoyant, Dono Gmelig-Meyling, was called on to the case for his opinions. Claiming to have made an 'out-of-body trip in the astral sphere', Dono indicated that he had located a 24-year-old girl connected with the case. Dono indicated that he saw a strong connection between Maurice and the case; at the time that this was going on in Enfield Janet Grosse, had she not died, would have been 24 years old. After a number of psychic perceptions including psychometry Maurice was told that his daughter was involved.

(Whether or not this case indicates a particular closeness between investigators and the case they are investigating – the very point that I had been investigating in respect of UFO investigations over the year or so prior to hearing Maurice tell me this – is debatable. Maurice found that possibility thought provoking even during the investigation.)

The case started with the sound of furniture moving in empty rooms although nothing was out of place and moved on to knocking noises that could not be explained. Then, in front of the mother of the family involved (who is referred to in Guy Lyon Playfair's book by the pseudonym 'Mrs Harper'), a very heavy chest of drawers started sliding along the floor unaided. Mrs Harper began to shake with fear.

Other members of the family, and neighbours, heard the knocking noises and tried, without success, to help identify the source. The police were called in and even during their first visit, at this very early stage of the haunting, WPC Carolyn Heeps was able to watch a chair moving apparently unaided towards the kitchen door; she believed it had probably moved some three or four feet and could not explain how. The police left, unable to offer any particular advice or help other than that they would 'keep an eye on the house'.

Within a short space of time objects such as marbles and Lego bricks began flying around in the house; bed sheets would be removed from beds; pillows would fly across the room; and Janet Harper, the girl believed to be the poltergeist's focus, was caught on camera in the act of levitating.

The list of activity in that house is almost endless. Apart from furniture moving or flipping through the air, the phenomena included doors and drawers opening and closing, toilets flushing, apports of small items such as coins appearing in mid-air (in one case a lace handkerchief that fell on to Maurice Grosse's head), wall-chimes swinging, spontaneous and mysterious failure of camera and video equipment, flash guns, tape-recording equipment and so on, books flying off the shelf (including one called *Fun and Games for Children*!), and footsteps. Various apparitions sighted included a grey-haired old lady, a young child, and an old man. Strangely shaped pools of water appeared spontaneously. There were what appeared to be attacks on Janet, including her feeling she was being choked or stifled, and interactive communication first by knocking and then by voice. Mysterious and occasionally obscene voices issued from both Janet and her brother Jimmy (apparently produced by the false vocal cords in a manner impossible for the children to have sustained normally); part of the house was destroyed including cemented pipe work being ripped out of the wall. An attack on Maurice Grosse happened when a cardboard box full of cushions 'shot off the floor beside the fireplace, flew over the bed, travelling about eight feet, [hitting] Maurice squarely on his forehead'. Something 'held' Janet by the leg, keeping her rigidly fixed on the staircase, crying, 'I can't move. Something is holding me!' There was automatic writing, writing which appeared spontaneously on walls, sometimes with the letters made from adhesive tape; bi-location (where Maurice Grosse was seen by one witness while he was also with another in a completely different part of the house); electronic voices recorded on tape; metal bending; appearance of excreta; what appeared to be objects moving through walls whilst Janet seems to have levitated from her bed *through* her bedclothes, which were left behind. Spontaneous combustion occurred, along with 'patterned piling' of furniture and objects, and Janet being physically hauled down the stairs, first while asleep and then when awake.

The total number of events will never be known but after just a few months the investigators had recorded over 1500; the poltergeist activity was seen by many witnesses apart from the family itself, including the investigators, the police and representatives of the media. It was also captured on tape, film and still photography.

For Maurice Grosse, the sheer volume of activity in circumstances where it simply could not have been faked was the most persuasive aspect of the case.

In the end the Enfield poltergeist went the way of most poltergeists: it simply faded away and was no more. Whatever the energies were that it had fed on or was created by – depending on your viewpoint – they had dissipated.

Jabuticabal

D: 1965
L: Nr. São Paulo, Brazil
S: Guy Lyon Playfair

In *The Indefinite Boundary* Guy Lyon Playfair relates the story of Maria José Ferreira who became a fatal victim of poltergeist activity in a manner reminiscent of the Bell Witch case (see pp. 254–6).

In December 1965 Maria became the focus of poltergeist activity in her house at Jabuticabal near São Paulo, Brazil. An attempt was made to exorcise the poltergeist but this failed and indeed exacerbated the activity. Stones and pieces of masonry from the house flew around and occasionally Maria was attacked, suffering bites and slaps. Maria's clothing caught fire spontaneously, endangering her life, and there was a suggestion that the poltergeist had attempted to suffocate Maria in her sleep by placing objects over her mouth and nose.

At the age of thirteen Maria drank insect repellent and was found dead, but it is not clear whether she drank the poison to commit suicide or whether the poltergeist 'attacked' her as it is held to have attacked John Bell in the Bell Witch case.

A Jammed Gun and a Haunted Car
D: 1960
L: Nr. Brasília, Brazil
S: Guy Lyon Playfair

On the night of 18/19 September 1960 a couple married that day, the bridegroom's parents, their driver and Dr Olavo Trindade, a distinguished Brazilian doctor, were driving along the main road to Belo Horizonte. They were only a few miles from Brasília, the country's federal capital. It was an empty landscape with no houses and few trees in sight.

The car began to show signs of overheating but when they stopped to investigate they found no cause. Whether or not this was a coincidence or the first onset of poltergeist activity is unclear.

Suddenly, while they were inspecting the car, stones began flying at them from the darkness all around, striking the witnesses and the car. The driver fired four shots from a gun, to no avail, and the party decided to drive to a nearby police post and ask for help.

At the station the police were shown two of the stones Dr Trindade had collected and offered to go back and examine the site of the encounter. Three of the party stayed behind and a policeman accompanied the remainder back to the original location where the stoning began again. This time when the driver tried to fire his gun he found it had jammed. Interference with mechanical and electrical apparatus is common enough in poltergeist activity and indeed in many other paranormal reports; whether or not the jammed gun could be attributed to a poltergeist or to more conventional reasons is, again, unclear.

Despite turning the car around to project the headlights on to the sparse landscape, they could see no sign of anyone. Eventually they returned to the police post, unable to take any effective action.

When the party set off again a further bombardment rained down on the car. Sand was blowing into the car although its windows were closed except for one small gap.

At this stage, the driver was sitting in the passenger seat and the bridegroom was driving. Suddenly the driver announced that somebody was trying to open the door and Dr Trindade leaned forward to try to keep it closed. He said, 'I could feel it gradually opening, by a terrible force . . . I gathered all the strength in my muscles together and finally managed to hold it shut, and I shouted at the driver to lock the handle. But the handle unlocked itself of its own accord and the door began to open again. This happened several times.'

The driver reported that he could see a vague form outside the window and tried to fire at it but his gun was still jammed.

Dr Trindade changed places with the groom's father so that he could try to keep the door closed since Dr Trindade's fingers were becoming sore. The father also felt the force and the whole party began praying for the 'affliction to return to the kingdom of Glory and leave everybody in peace'. It is not known when the force abated.

They reached their hotel destination at two o'clock in the morning; the driver immediately tested his gun and found it worked perfectly.

The groom's father had earlier noticed that the glass had come off his wristwatch and was wedged between his fingers and that the metal watchstrap was stretched out of its normal shape. The next morning, after leaving the damaged watch to one aside, the glass was back in its place and the wristband had returned to its normal shape. Furthermore, there wasn't a single scratch on the car.

The Joller Family Poltergeist

D: 1860

L: Stans, nr. Lake Lucerne, Switzerland

S: A. Gould & A.D. Cornell

The head of the family affected by poltergeist activity in this case during 1860–2 was a journalist and member of the National Council of Switzerland, Melchior Joller. His home was in Stans near Lake Lucerne and he recorded his experience in his diary which was then published in a pamphlet entitled *Narrative of Personally Experienced Strange Phenomena* published in 1863 and referred to in Alan Gould and A.D. Cornell's account of the case in their book, *Poltergeists*.

Joller was described as methodical and somewhat obstinate. After two years these characteristics were broken by the onslaught of the poltergeist activity.

Joller lived 'in moderate affluence' with his wife Caroline, their four sons Robert, Edward, Oscar and Alfred and three daughters Emaline, Melanie and Henricka, plus their house servants.

In the autumn of 1860 one of the maids complained that she could hear knocking noises on her bedstead; this was the beginning of all that was to follow.

Some weeks later Joller's wife and daughter (who had been sharing a bedroom) were woken up by knocking noises but Joller thought this of no importance at the time. In June 1861 Joller's son Oscar missed supper and was discovered unconscious in the wood store. He explained, on coming round, that he had heard knocking sounds and had gone in to investigate when suddenly the door had burst open and 'a whitish formless shape came in'.

The other children complained of hearing noises – footsteps and so on – and Henricka saw the apparition of a small child. In the autumn one of the maids complained of seeing 'grey shapes' and reported that on one occasion during the night someone had come up the stairs, which gave into the upstairs living room, and gone past her. The maid heard her name called many times. From the living room the maid heard 'profoundly disturbing sobs'. Joller dismissed that maid, believing her to be superstitious, and in October 1861 she was replaced by a girl of thirteen. All was quiet until the summer of 1862 when '*trouble began in earnest*'.

On 15 August 1862 Joller, his wife and son Robert went to Lucerne at seven o'clock in the morning. The rest of the family and the servant girl stayed at the house. Henricka heard rapping noises and told Melanie (then aged fourteen) and the servant girl. She then went into the corridor that the knocks seemed to be coming from, to investigate. Melanie called out, '*In God's name, if there is anything to it, let it come and rap.*' There seemed to be a reply in rapping noises. Oscar arrived and was told the story, called out the same challenge, but received no reply; Edward also repeated the formula.

They became frightened; there seems to be no particular reason for this beyond, probably, the contagion of fear that can spread between people. They fled the house.

While they were sitting on the stone steps outside, a fist-sized pebble fell between Melanie and Alfred (spontaneous falls of stone are quite common in poltergeist cases, see in particular 'The Jammed Gun' pp. 277–8). At lunchtime they went back into the house to prepare a meal and found every room- and cupboard-door wide open. These they closed, bolting them where possible, but soon they were all open again, including those which had been bolted. The children heard heavy footsteps coming down the stairs and ran out into the garden again.

The servant girl peered back into the kitchen and saw 'coming towards her a shape somewhat like a sheet hung up by one corner'. When she called to it the figure disappeared. Eventually the children hid in a barn where some labourers were at work and made occasional reconnoitres to see what was happening at the house.

Fairly traditional poltergeist activity seemed to be taking place: sounds, moving furniture and what appeared to be the sound of a deep and melancholy voice saying, 'Even if no one is around.' A spontaneously formed 'death's head' shape was seen on the floor (as if poured on) but it soon faded.

In the early evening a light was seen coming down the chimney. When the maid looked up to see what it was, she could see an object 'with innumerable little blue flames'. It apparently exploded inside the chimney, dowsing the fire with water.

Joller did not believe the stories he was being told. It was on Tuesday 19 August that he himself suffered the poltergeist activity and he recorded this in his diary. He heard rapping noises which seemed to reply to his own striking on the wall and promised the family that he would investigate it.

The following day Joller witnessed the door between the bedroom and the kitchen visibly bending as the banging sounds struck up again. He raised the catch and the door burst open. Immediately he could see a dark form but could not make out its shape. Suddenly it moved from the door to the side of the chimney but investigation of the chimney located nothing.

The following day Joller witnessed a force 'as powerful as a wooden mallet might make when swung with all the strength of a powerful arm'; doors slammed and opened with enormous force. The subject began to become the matter of discussion locally because other people could hear the sounds. In the kitchen Joller saw that the poltergeist had attacked bottles, glasses and other containers, leaving them as if they had been struck by a metal implement. Sounds arising from different parts of the house were so rapid in succession that it would have taken four or five people to have perpetrated them – one person simply would not have been able to move around fast enough.

On the night of 23 August in a first-floor bedroom Joller, his wife and a servant were all touched on the head 'as if by hand'. Both Joller and his wife grabbed at the hand and 'found it to be small and warm like a child's'.

On 16 September Joller witnessed an apple hopping around strangely. It jumped down the stairs, along the corridor and into the kitchen. After having been put on the kitchen table it again jumped off towards the corridor; the servant threw it out of the window but in an instant it flew back in again and landed on the kitchen table and then proceeded to bounce further around the house.

On 6 October a figure was seen on four different occasions by five different people; it was similar to a figure that had been reported on 10 September by Emaline. The figure was a melancholic woman with a bowed head.

Late in October 1862 Joller and his family fled to Zürich. What exactly happened to the family after that is uncertain but when contacted by Fanny Moser in the 1930s Emaline said that the phenomenon did not follow the family; neither did it continue in the house after the family's departure. Emaline did say that her father had had an experience one night after which he had said, '*Now I understand.*' It was never revealed what the experience was or what it was he had come to understand.

Joller died in 1865, the last three years of his life (following the poltergeist onslaught) a ruin compared to his former lifestyle. He had been ridiculed and attacked by family and friends and driven from his home. He died in poverty in Rome, an exile from his own country.

5 *Langmead Street*

D: 2nd half, 20th century
L: West Norwood, London
S: Philip Paul

Langmead Street is a tiny road off the High Street in West Norwood, just behind West Norwood Station. Like many south London streets it was damaged during the war and No.5 was taken over by the local council and repaired.

At the time of the incident the house was occupied by Mr and Mrs Greenfield (Senior), their sons Cecil and Dennis, Dennis' wife Gladys, Gladys' mother and two young children, Gordon aged eight and Patricia aged fourteen.

At first the family heard noises – scraping and tapping noises apparently from the loft – a fairly classical start to a poltergeist haunting. The noises could only be heard from the topmost of the three floors. As time progressed, the noises became louder until they could be heard from any part of the house and were described as sounding like furniture being dragged. Eventually they sounded more like 'something walking on the ceiling'.

After about four years of this not particularly intrusive but nonetheless disturbing activity, Cecil Greenfield awoke one summer night thinking he could hear someone moving around outside his first-floor bedroom. On opening the door he could see nothing outside. Thinking that someone might have been ill, and had gone downstairs to the kitchen, Cecil began to head towards the stairs when he realised that a grey-white, adult-sized figure was ascending the stairs towards him. He could not make out any details of a face but had the impression of arms folded at breast height. As the form approached, Cecil felt an icy coldness which gradually became more severe (though this may have been a reaction to the sighting); he also felt what he described as 'a sort of electric vibration'. As the form passed over a loose floorboard on the stairs, Cecil heard a creak that suggested it had mass or weight. Cecil screamed and the apparition instantly vanished. Cecil was found, 'white and shaking', by his parents, who had a bedroom on the same floor.

Just five days later Dennis and Gladys, arriving home from a party in the early hours of the morning, walked into the downstairs hallway and saw the same grey-white figure standing a little way up the stairs. Again, they could make out no features of a face, but this time they determined that it had its arms hanging by its sides. They ran to a neighbour's house and when they returned the figure had gone.

Fourteen-year-old Patricia also saw the same form, this time in the afternoon. She was hysterical for quite some time afterwards.

Becoming seriously concerned, Cecil Greenfield called the

police and Inspector Sidney Candler visited the house, having heard Cecil's description of crashes and bangs, moaning sounds as well as the weird lights that were now appearing. Candler and his colleagues found the inhabitants huddled together in the living room dressed in a curious mixture of night clothes with day clothes hastily thrown over them. The police searched the house from top to bottom but found nothing; yet the family persuaded them to stay until dawn when daylight seemed to ease their fears.

The next night the same disturbances happened again and Cecil again called the police. This time Candler arrived with eight constables. The household was once again gathered in the living room and one constable was posted on guard outside the door. Other officers were placed throughout the building, Candler roaming free around the house. During this police vigil, and with the family kept together in one place, there were 'raps, crashes and moans from the loft, the quilt was unaccountably snatched from a bed and a picture crashed from a wall, its cord unbroken and the hook undisturbed'. Candler said that he was sceptical when he first heard the story but agreed – after talking to the Greenfields – that something strange was happening to them.

Dennis described one very curious episode; he had entered Patricia's bedroom and seen her mattress 'lifting and curling up' as if being moved by invisible hands. Patricia was not in the house at the time. Even using all his strength, Dennis could not move the mattress which was now suspended in mid-air as if by an iron fist. Suddenly Dennis himself seemed to be seized from behind although there was no one else in the room. Thoroughly alarmed, he ended up with his shirt torn and soaked from perspiration. On another occasion young Gordon had apparently been flung down the stairs in some paranormal manner though he had not been injured.

Some claims were classic poltergeist events, including radios turning on spontaneously, flashes of light, and pictures moving of their own volition, but some were quite exceptional: Dennis once claimed he had seen a bottle of milk moving up the stairs one step at a time under its own power. Philip Paul believed that some of Dennis' claims were probably hallucinatory after the periods of strain he had been under, but rejected the idea that the events were being deliberately faked.

By the end of the summer new apparitions were appearing; Cecil saw a figure standing by his bed which disappeared after he had hidden beneath the bedclothes for a time. Shortly afterwards the heavy kitchen table moved when no one was in the room. There was evidence of wall writing on one of the first-floor bedrooms though it seemed to be quite meaningless – either 'MP S2 38' or 'MP SZ 38'.

Perhaps unfortunately, the events reached even the national press and inevitably became something of a local attraction. The investigator of this case, Philip Paul, considered the possibility that the family was faking the claims in order to be rehoused by the council – it would certainly not have been the first time that 'ghosts' had been used for this purpose. However, Paul rejected this idea after several investigations and interviews with the family. At one point he even gave them a way out by saying, 'Of course, if your ghost isn't real, you could stop all this discomfort very quickly. Simply give an interview to the press and say you invented it as a joke. Then you will only have to suffer for a day or two longer, after which it will all die away and soon be forgotten.' The family had been concerned by the local attention they were getting and this may well have seemed an attractive proposition if they had indeed been lying. Dennis replied that although the events and the crowds were causing stress, if they lied about the claim and pretended to have invented the stories they would be in a difficult position if they had to call in the police again.

No resolution was ever found and, as is typical of poltergeist hauntings, the effects gradually faded and disappeared altogether.

Two years later the Hewitt family replaced the Greenfields and, although they were well aware of the history of the house, they claim to have had no experiences during their time there. They seem to have had a fairly healthy attitude to the history of the house, referring to the apparition as 'Horace', but any conversation with him was entirely one sided – Horace never joined in.

Some years later, the now retired Inspector Candler summed up his feelings to Philip Paul, confirming that he believed the family had undergone some strange experience. He admitted that he was still baffled by the case.

Emma Lindroos

D: 1885
L: Ylöjärvi, Tammerfors, Finland
S: A. Gould & A.D. Cornell

In 1885 poltergeist activity flared up in the village of Ylöjärvi, approximately 15 kilometres from Tammerfors (now Tampere) in Finland. 71-year-old Efraim Martin, his 77-year-old wife Eva and their 13-year-old servant girl Emma Lindroos lived in a small three-room cottage there. It was assumed that the poltergeist activity was centred around the young girl.

For approximately two weeks during January 1885 the household suffered such poltergeist activity as doors rapidly opening and closing, spontaneous damage to walls and furniture, objects inexplicably flying through the air, and even a sheep found in the cow stall with all its legs tied together. There were also unknown voices. The phenomena occurred at all times of the day and night, and many sightseers were drawn to the location because of them.

At the end of January, Emma Lindroos was taken away from the family as she was suffering from tuberculosis; she died a few months afterwards. On her departure from the house the poltergeist activity stopped, not to return.

The extraordinary twist to this story followed in March 1885, when the Martins and Emma Lindroos were prosecuted, on the grounds that they caused the poltergeist, in league with the pavers of darkness, to help sell brandy. An analysis of witness statements was published in *Psychische Studien* in 1922 and reported by Alan Gould and A.D. Cornell in their book *Poltergeists*.

The statements included the following:

Gerhard Grönfors saw a pair of shoes moving on the floor, one shoe after the other. The witness believed the phenomenon was being caused by an unknown force. The following day Grönfors saw thin pine boards hopping and dancing around each other and two bread sticks dancing and striking each other. Another witness saw this too.

Sexton Lindell witnessed a stool thrown upside down, a basket of pinewood thrown at him and plates on a dining table smashed against each other.

Amanda Lindell, the sexton's wife, confirmed her husband's

claims and saw shoes flying from the corner of the room, and plaster falling from the walls.

Karl Lindholm saw a candle holder flung against the door and believed this was caused by an invisible force because of the way it moved through the air.

Helene Punala confirmed Lindholm's sighting; she was sitting beside the table where the candle holder had taken off and knew that no one had thrown it.

The prosecution failed and the accused were acquitted. The authors' own analysis of the trial was that possibly 'this trial was to some extent at least a put up job, instigated so that the Martins, who seemed to have been much respected locally, could clear themselves from malicious gossip'.

88 Newark Street

D: 1952
L: Whitechapel, London
S: Philip Paul

Newark Street is in the heart of London's East End. In 1952 No. 88 Newark Street was occupied by Harry Conway and his family. They had a seven-year-old son who slept in a bedroom on the second floor of the four-storey building. Frequently the child, in terror, would tell stories of icy fingers that had pulled the bedclothes off his bed. Finding it difficult to believe that the child was not just having nightmares, the family watched their son deteriorate into a nervous wreck, finally requiring hospitalisation. *This was when the family decided to move.*

Noises were heard around the house, and the lock on their son's bedroom door had to be changed several times as it was either found inexplicably locked or unlocked when it should not have been. An aunt staying in the house experienced the same problems with her bedclothes as her nephew.

The poltergeist hauntings of 88 Newark Street were not confined to the Conway family but carried over to the next occupants of the property, something of a deviation from the poltergeist 'norm'. In June 1954 Harry and Brenda Cox moved into the house both to live and to set up their dress-manufacturing business. The cutting tables and machinery were fitted into work rooms on the top floor, Harry and Brenda took a living room and kitchen on the first floor and a bedroom on the second and shortly afterwards Alec and Vera Bessell moved into the ground floor. Alec Bessell was employed by Cox.

It was not long before the staff working on the top floor claimed that they had heard footsteps outside their rooms, but no matter how hard they tried they had never been able to see anyone. Cox thought they were imagining things.

A few days later Cox and his wife both heard footsteps outside their room when no one should have been there. Believing it to be a burglar, Cox took a poker and went to investigate. He found nothing; the entrance door was secure.

One evening Alec and Vera Bessell arrived home at around eleven o'clock, believing the Coxes to be in their rooms or in bed. They could hear heavy thumping noises and something that sounded like a sweeping sound from the Coxes' rooms above them and thought it was rather inconsiderate time for them to be doing the housework. It was twelve-thirty when they heard the Coxes arrive home late. Unnerved, the Bessells told them about the noises but when they checked their rooms they found nothing had been disturbed.

In the early hours of the morning Harry and Brenda Cox woke up feeling an icy chill – the bedclothes were being slowly pulled off the bed; this happened four more times and began to cause the family considerable psychological strain. Cox claimed in an interview with investigator Philip Paul that his hair had stood on end and he had become motionless. He could not move his limbs. Eventually he was able to release himself from the sensation and get downstairs. He described the event as the most horrifying experience he had had.

If Alec Bessell was away on business the Coxes would sleep in Vera's rooms to keep her company; from there they could often hear sounds in their own unoccupied rooms above. Once, at midnight, they heard 'heavy measured thumps descend the 48 stairs from the top to the bottom of the house'. They found nothing.

Cox made sure that the Yale lock on the room they were in was locked; the following morning no one had been near it and it was found unlocked. One first-floor door for which there was no key was found locked and Cox had to break in.

Some friends, Michael Winter and his family, came to stay with the Coxes and, for lack of space Michael Winter and Harry Cox slept in the living room together. During the night Winter saw coat-hangers, on rails in the room, spinning round. He also felt movements on the bed though Cox was adamant that he (Cox) had not woken up at all during the night.

Brenda and Vera, together in the downstairs kitchen, watched an artificial flower fly across the room which heralded the onset of a period of similar activity: jugs and tumblers moved from the sideboard to the chairs, cups and medals scattered over the floor and – it was evidently a poltergeist with a distinctly human attitude towards the Inland Revenue – a vase of water poured over completed income-tax forms!

During a visit by Harry Cox's parents, his father suddenly heard a sound 'like a cat in pain' coming from a glass-fronted cabinet in the room. They could find nothing to account for the noise.

A medium who visited the house believed the haunting was being caused by the ghost of a man with a wooden leg. In the end the effects faded away, as poltergeist phenomena tend to do.

Kenzo Okamoto

D: c. 1973
L: Ponta Pora, Matto Grosso, Paraguay
S: Guy Lyon Playfair

Poltergeists are usually extremely reluctant to be obliging and often frustrate researchers by their unwillingness to perform for 'sceptics'. Not so the one which afflicted emigré Kenzo Okamoto and his family in their remote farm twelve miles from Ponta Pora in Paraguay.

To begin with, the poltergeist did not seem to have focused exclusively on the Okamoto family. For example, some neighbours of the Okamotos were terrified when their bed was lifted up into the air and they were pushed around by an invisible force. Everyone evacuated the farmhouse, except for one 'stout old lady' of 76 who worked on Okamoto's tomato patch. She found herself being bombarded with tomatoes and threatened Okamoto that she would call the police; he assured her he had 'nothing to do with it'. His own children were later to be pelted by tomatoes.

The poltergeist apparently now moved in on the Okamoto family. Stones rained down inside the house.

A reporter, Kazunari Akaki, visited the farm, spending five days there investigating the poltergeist. He was highly sceptical and unconvinced by many of the occurrences. For example, an upstairs room was full of objects that had apparently been mysteriously transported there from the ground floor. Akaki helped to move them all back, only to discover that they had all moved back upstairs again when he came back from a trip into town. He began to believe it was simply Okamoto playing tricks.

During dinner he was unimpressed by the falling stones and when he was getting ready for bed he was similarly unconvinced by chocolates falling on the floor of his bedroom which he thought 'could . . . have been thrown over the partition'.

The following afternoon his scepticism was dramatically demolished. As Guy Lyon Playfair relates in his book *The Flying Cow*, when Akaki returned to the house after driving Okamoto's Toyota jeep (which weighed 2.12 tons), he parked it outside the front door. He had no sooner got into the house when he heard a noise, went back outside and saw that the jeep was now 40 yards away with no tyre marks in the soft mud between the spot it was now in and the place where it had been parked. And the position it was now in was uphill from where it had previously been.

Akaki noticed that the poltergeist activity seemed to be more in evidence when the engine of the jeep was running and also that it peaked at twilight. Combining these factors, he asked Okamoto to bring the jeep back to the front door, with the engine running, at twilight. Back in the house Akaki discovered torch batteries flung against the wall and an iron railing lying on his bed. It had not been there when he had been in the bedroom only a few minutes prior to that.

The poltergeist went on to cause spontaneous combustion, which is a rare occurence in poltergeist cases but not unheard of (see, for example, the Enfield (Harpers') poltergeist, pp. 272–6). One of the objects to catch fire was a damp shirt hanging on the back of a chair, apparently burned as a result of contact with 'a fireball' that suddenly appeared and equally suddenly vanished though leaving an inch-wide mark on the family's dog. When this happened the dog had been asleep, and he had not been disturbed enough to even wake up.

Burn marks also appeared on wooden partitioning in the house and on a thatched roof. It was astonishing that the thatch did not catch fire, being highly inflammable.

One potentially sinister, but in the end harmless, event occurred in May 1973 when Okamoto's ten-month-old baby disappeared, complete with pram. The child and pram were found outside the house under a tree after a period of searching. The child was unharmed and dry although it had been raining throughout the time the baby was missing.

No focus for the phenomena could ever be determined, and the poltergeist eventually quietened down.

Old Jeffrey

    D: 1716
    L: Epworth Rectory, Lincolnshire
    S: Various

It was after the famous founder of Methodism, John Wesley, had already left home that his parents, the Rev. Samuel Wesley and Susanna Wesley, reported a series of poltergeist hauntings at Epworth Rectory in Lincolnshire. Samuel Wesley wrote 'An Account of noises and disturbances in my house at Epworth, Lincolnshire in December and January 1716'.

'One night when the noise was great in the kitchen, and on a deal partition, and on the door in the yard, the latch whereof was often lifted up, my daughter Amelia went and held it fast on the inside, but it was still lifted up, and the door pushed violently against her, though nothing was to be seen on the outside.' The sounds included breaking glass, groaning and cackling.

Mrs Wesley wrote to one of her children: 'One night it made such a noise in the room over our head as if several people were walking; then . . . running up and down stairs, and was so outrageous that we thought the children would be frightened so your father and I rose and went down in the dark to light a candle. Just as we came to the bedroom at the bottom of the broad stairs, having hold of each other, on my side there seemed as if somebody had emptied a bag of money at my feet, and on his as if all the bottles under the stairs (which were many) had been dashed in a thousand pieces. We passed through the hall into the kitchen, and got a candle and went to see the children. The next night your father got Mr Hole to lie at our house and we all sat together till one or two o'clock in the morning and heard the knocking as usual. Sometimes it would make a noise like the winding up of a jack, at other times like the night Mr Hole was with us, like a carpenter planing deals, but most commonly knocked thrice and stopped and then thrice again, and so many hours together.'

The Wesley children were not frightened by the poltergeist but seemed to treat it almost as a friend; they named it 'Old Jeffrey'.

Like most poltergeists, the events simply faded away after a few months.

François Perrault's Poltergeist
D: 1612
L: Mâcon, France
S: Colin Wilson

This case is particularly interesting as it illustrates two common characteristics of poltergeists most clearly: they often bring messages and they are notorious liars.

In September 1612 François Perrault returned home after a short absence to find that both his wife and her housekeeper had been subjected to poltergeist activity. It had begun with curtains drawing themselves in the middle of the night and bedclothes being ripped off the bed. There had been terrible disturbances in parts of the house, loud noises heard and crockery thrown around the kitchen.

The poltergeist became audible, starting with a simple five-note tune and moving on to bring messages to Monsieur Perrault. The poltergeist claimed that M. Perrault's father had been murdered; it also named the perpetrator of this and other crimes and then went on to tell various unpleasant stories about local people, none of which turned out to be true. M. Perrault did not believe that his father had been murdered either.

Two months later the poltergeist activity suddenly stopped.

The Phantom Drummer
D: 1661
L: Tedworth (or Tidworth), nr. Ludgershall, Wiltshire
S: Various

Most modern theories about poltergeists suggests that they are either some form of exteriorisation from children, usually around the age of puberty, or that they are the manifestation of non-human spirits or, more rarely, spirits of known dead persons. In the case of the phantom drummer of Tedworth, if we are to believe William Drury, he was himself the cause of the poltergeist activity while he was still very much alive.

In March 1661 magistrate John Mompesson (who also later wrote about the case) was visiting Ludgershall in Wiltshire, one of the areas of England most rich in paranormal activity. William Drury, a vagrant who had recently arrived in the town, had been annoying the townspeople by playing a drum in the streets and the magistrate ordered it confiscated. Drury escaped from confinement before coming to trial.

Some weeks later Mompesson returned to his house in Tedworth (where, for some reason, the Ludgershall bailiff had sent the drum) to find that the house had been disturbed for some nights running by unexplained knocking and banging. Mompesson himself chased the sounds through the house one night, armed with a pistol, but was unable to locate their source. In bed, however, he began to make out the sound of drumming amongst the other noises. . .

The hauntings went on for two years, focusing on Mompesson's children who had to endure the noise of drumming around their rooms. The poltergeist had quite a sense of humour: one of the servants apparently asked the poltergeist to hand him a plank of wood and ended up in a tug of war with the poltergeist for some twenty minutes until Mompesson broke up the fight!

The activity intensified over time with anomalous lights being seen, doors slamming and spontaneous fires breaking out. There is one report of Mompesson's horse being found with its back legs wedged firmly in its mouth. It died shortly afterwards.

The extraordinary facts behind the case were yet to become clear. William Drury was arrested in Gloucester in 1663 for theft and apparently asked his captors if they knew anything about what was happening in Wiltshire, asking if they had heard about the drumming in the Tedworth house. Drury said Mompesson, was plaguing him and would continue to punish him for taking away his drum. Alas for Drury, he was then condemned as a witch and transported. During Drury's absence from England

Mompesson was left in peace but when Drury escaped transportation and came back to England the haunting immediately resumed.

How such a haunting could take place is uncertain, though it is interesting that Drury claimed to have learnt magic while he was a soldier in Oliver Cromwell's army.

The case was investigated by a local preacher, Joseph Glanvil, who wrote about the case two years after it occurred, and published a report on it some twenty years after the event.

The Rev. E. Phelps' Seance
D: 1850
L: Stratford, Connecticut, USA
S: Colin Wilson

The Rev. Phelps was fascinated by paranormal activity. In March 1850 he held a seance to attract the attention of spirits and succeeded beyond his expectation, possibly due to the fact that there were two good foci in his house.

Shortly after the seance the Phelps family returned from church to discover that their house had been disturbed by poltergeist activity. The family went to church again the same afternoon, but the Rev. stayed back to watch over the house. He reported no disturbances though he admitted he may have dazed off for a while, but when the family returned the same activity had taken place except this time a distinct sense of humour was at play.

Furniture had shifted and clothes had been laid out as if to suggest they were being worn and the poltergeist had used cushions and pillows to create a display of human-sized dummies. The poltergeist put on several such displays, which were extraordinarily lifelike and executed far more quickly than would normally be possible – one such tableau was formed within minutes when it would have taken several people several hours to create it, according to one observer.

More conventional poltergeist activity also took place, with various objects thrown around and loud noises heard.

It was decided that the two foci were the Rev. Phelps' son, Harry, aged twelve, and his daughter Anna, sixteen, both near the age of puberty. The poltergeist activity accelerated and Harry was attacked by flying stones and his trousers damaged in front of a visiting colleague of his father's. There was spontaneous combustion, smashing of various objects, and physical attacks on Anna.

At last the poltergeist activity ceased spontaneously whilst the mother and her children were away from the house.

The Riberio Poltergeist

D: 1972

L: Sorocaba, West of São Paulo City, Brazil

S: Guy Lyon Playfair

Brazil has been described (by Guy Lyon Playfair) as 'the world's most psychic country,' and this is true in almost every area of the paranormal, to varying degrees. In *The Flying Cow* Playfair examines, among others, extraordinary accounts of mediumship, psychic surgery and reincarnation. Researchers in the modern, technological paranormal, including those phenomena embraced by the term 'UFO research', are well aware of the strangeness of South America, and Brazil in particular, not only in terms of the high number of cases reported but also because of their unique qualities. Furthermore, the areas of São Paulo and Minas Gerais around the town of Sorocaba have provided some of the world's most extraordinary UFO abduction stories, including the first ever reported alien abduction, that of farm worker Antonio Villas Boas in 1957. Playfair recorded the following poltergeist story which brings out two important points about the phenomenon.

On 18 July 1972 the home of Mr Fernando and Mrs Alda Riberio and their six children in Sorocaba, west of São Paulo City, became the initial focus of poltergeist activity.

Characteristically, the first indications of the poltergeist were knocking noises and household objects flying around and occasionally breaking. During the course of the activity 'almost every single piece of furniture in the house [was] overturned, some of them more than once'. Playfair describes in *The Flying Cow*, how on one occasion a large motor tyre outside the house rose three feet into the air and hovered there, frightening Mr Fernando.

An investigation was undertaken by the Brazilian Institute for Psycho-Biophysical Research (IBPB) led by Hernani Guymeraes Andrade. Sounds were recorded on tape; in particular the investigating team had been in the house – and every one of the household was under observation – when there was an enormous crash from the kitchen. On investigation a heavy wooden shelf – far too heavy for the family dog to have knocked over – had crashed to the floor injuring the dog's paw.

When the family moved out of the house to stay with relatives, the poltergeist activity went with them and a neighbour commented, 'It looked as if a tractor had driven through the place.' Probably to the relief of the relatives, when the family moved back to their own house the trouble went back with them.

There were signs that this poltergeist was physically dangerous; despite the potential danger of poltergeists this is actually a very rare occurrence. Alda Riberio was hit on the head by a flying brick and one of her daughters was scalded by water from a kettle which was torn out of her hands when she was making coffee.

One of the important points about the case was brought out by Playfair: it normally took three men to lift the concrete water tank that the poltergeist had overturned; on that basis poltergeists could presumably be a lot more destructive than they are.

Twelve-year-old Yara was suspected of being the focus, having been present on all occasions of activity, but the case was never solved as the family fled the area, not to be heard of again.

Playfair made the important observation that the poltergeist apparently did not like to perform at night when there were lights switched on but was content to do so during daylight hours; the lights may have indicated to the poltergeist that it was under scrutiny.

Rivail Investigates
D: 1860
L: Rue des Noyers, Paris, France
S: Colin Wilson

Leon Dénizarth Hippolyte Rivail, a Parisian intellectual of the mid-nineteenth century, took a particular interest in paranormal phenomena and, amongst others, investigated a poltergeist in the Rue des Noyers.

It was an extremely malevolent poltergeist, smashing windows and objects all over the house, and ultimately it drove the occupants away. Rivail used a medium whose contact, a spirit known as 'St Louis', was able to get in touch with the poltergeist. The poltergeist was apparently a bad-tempered creature who instantly threatened to throw stones at those who had disturbed him. Rivail asked the poltergeist, 'Was there anyone in the Rue des Noyers who helped you play tricks on the occupants?' The poltergeist said that it had operated through a maid servant who had been extremely frightened by what had been happening. (This is further evidence that there needs to be some sort of focus for poltergeist activity, though in this case the personification of the poltergeist conflicts with many modern investigations which suggest that poltergeists are 'forces' rather than individual spirits. The matter becomes even more complicated if one takes into account cases of mischievous spirits that have been known to tell lies to mediums and in effect 'pose' as poltergeists.)

The 'poltergeist' in this case identified himself as a rag-and-bone man who had died at the turn of that century and who was taking revenge for the fact that he had been mocked for drinking too heavily when he was alive.

The Serving Girl
   D: 1867
   L: Massachusetts, USA
   S: A.Gould & A.D.Cornell

In 1868 *Atlantic Monthly* reported a poltergeist case centred on an Irish servant girl, Mary Carrick, who worked for a family in Massachusetts.

On 3 July 1867, shortly after Mary had joined the family, all the service bells in the house began to ring even after they had been disconnected. They were mounted near the ceiling, about eleven feet up, and would ring even when she was in the room and others were watching her closely, presumably all but eliminating the possibility of a deliberate hoax.

On one occasion the girl was placing a tea tray on to a heavy stone slab weighing some 50 lbs. when it suddenly leapt up, struck the tray and knocked the crockery off. Later the same slab jumped up in the air and fell with such force that it broke in two, without the girl having any contact with it at all.

It was too much for Mary, who became hysterical, raved in her sleep and had nervous attacks. On 18 September she was committed to an asylum, where, having apparently recovered, she eventually became employed as a housemaid. Whether her hysterical nature 'created' the poltergeist or whether it 'latched on to' her because of her nature is an unresolved question in this and similar cases.

'Wee Hughie'
D: 1961
L: Sauchie, Scotland
S: A.R.G. Owen

In 1964, Dr A.R.G. Owen, a Fellow of Trinity College, Cambridge and a director of the Horizons Research Foundation, Toronto, published *Can We Explain the Poltergeist?* In this he referred to a poltergeist in Sauchie, Scotland, which was well documented and well witnessed. Dr Owen's analysis and comments are most pertinent to an understanding of the poltergeist phenomenon.

Sauchie is just north of Alloa on the river Forth. In 1961 Dr Owen was able to stay in the area and interview several people whom he regarded as 'responsible' and who had witnessed the phenomenon and 'observed it critically'. These were the Rev. T. Lund, MA, BD, a minister of the Church of Scotland, Dr W.H. Nisbet, MB, ChB, a physician, Dr W. Logan, MB, ChB, also a physician and who shared a practice with Dr Nisbet, Dr Logan's wife (herself a physician) Dr S. Logan, MB, ChB, DPH, and Miss M. Stewart, a teacher at Sauchie Primary School.

The focus – or what Maurice Grosse refers to as 'the epicentre' – of the case was Virginia Campbell, then eleven years old and the youngest child of the family. She attended the Sauchie Primary School.

Virginia was described as 'extremely shy' and her teacher, Miss Stewart, found communication with her difficult. Miss Stewart noted, however, that Virginia made friendships easily, was above average intelligence, creative and artistic and fond of dancing. Generally she was regarded as mature and responsible.

Virginia was maturing rapidly during the period of time when the poltergeist activity was under way. She had not yet gone through puberty but this was approaching. During the poltergeist activity Virginia seemed to be upset and emotional but in the circumstances this could hardly be regarded as evidence of ill health, as Dr Owen himself pointed out.

Dr Owen visited the family during the period of poltergeist activity and believed them to be normal and happy, with a good family relationship. Virginia had even christened the poltergeist 'Wee Hughie' and was interested in, and perhaps even proud of, him.

During the course of the poltergeist's activity there were several events, particularly between November 1960 to January 1961, which were witnessed by responsible people and these are listed in Dr Owen's account and summarised below:

At teatime on 23 November the family were in the living room when they saw a sideboard move out from the wall a distance of some five inches and move back again, apparently unaided. That night knocking noises were heard all around the house and the Rev. T. Lund came to the house at midnight and heard these sounds. He seems to have narrowed the source down to Virginia's bedhead under conditions that proved it was not being hit by Virginia or any other person. Lund felt the bedhead vibrating whilst the knocking sounds were heard. He watched a large linen-chest rocking and lifting, travelling some eighteen inches over the floor and sliding back again.

The Rev. Lund also watched Virginia's pillow rotating through 60 degrees although her head was on it – 'it seemed quite impossible that she could do this herself'. The Rev. again saw the linen-chest moving and heard knocking noises. On this same day, Thursday 24 November, Dr Nisbet also heard sounds and saw a strange movement on the surface of Virginia's pillow which he again believed was an effect Virginia could not have created herself.

On Friday 25 November Virginia was in school in the afternoon and Miss Stewart saw her apparently trying to hold down the lid of her desk which was raising itself. The teacher saw that Virginia was not raising it herself. The desk immediately behind Virginia, temporarily unoccupied, was also seen by the teacher to rise about an inch off the floor and then settle gently down to its original position. Miss Stewart immediately examined it for 'strings, levers or anything else' and found nothing. At school again on Monday, 28 November, Virginia was standing next to

Miss Stewart's desk, away from the table. Her hands were behind her back. A blackboard pointer lying on the desk vibrated, moved and then fell off the desk. Miss Stewart could feel the vibration and could see the desk was moving; the right hand end was swinging around.

On Thursday 29 November Drs W. and S. Logan visited Virginia at a relative's house where she was staying. They heard many rapping noises centred around Virginia. Although previously sceptical about the poltergeist claims Mrs Logan came to believe that the sounds from Virginia's room were not being caused by anyone in it. Dr Logan, later that night, witnessed Virginia in a trance, giving strangely uninhibited replies to unheard questions.

In many poltergeist hauntings (see, in particular, the Enfield (Harpers') poltergeist 'case and the Bell Witch case) the focus will have periods of extreme profanity and abusiveness, which seem to be hinted at here.

After November the poltergeist activity lessened considerably with one attested occurrence in January when a bowl of bulbs in Miss Stewart's classroom moved across the top of her desk as the pointer had previously done. Other minor phenomena continued until around March after which they ceased.

Dr Owen commented that the case had five witnesses who were convinced by the strange claims being made. While it would be possible for one person to be the victim of fraud or even of a genuine mistake, it seemed unlikely that all five should be so. Apparently the Rev. Lund believed that the poltergeist originated from within Virginia rather than from an outside entity; Dr Logan and Miss Stewart also suggested this interpretation.

Wine Shop Disturbances
   D: 1900
   L: Via Bava, Turin, Italy
   S: Prof. Lombroso (*After Death – What?*)
At the turn of the century, Professor Cesare Lombroso investigated the case of a poltergeist which was causing havoc in a wine shop and bar in Turin. Bottles were exploding or being smashed, tables and chairs were being lifted and moved around and cutlery was being disturbed.

The proprietor, Signor Fumero, welcomed Professor Lombroso's investigation since the local police had warned him that the disturbances would have to stop or he would be in trouble – the average policeman tends not to be terribly receptive to the idea of poltergeists.

Down in the wine cellars Professor Lombroso was immediately greeted by smashing glass as he entered; he witnessed bottles spinning on the floor and shattering with no apparent cause. His investigation immediately ruled out the more obvious trickery such as thin wires to make the bottles spin and so on. Lombroso also witnessed bottles rising from the shelves and exploding. In other parts of the house furniture and cutlery were being thrown around and one piece of equipment was so violently smashed to the floor that it was bent out of shape.

Despite the destructive power of the poltergeist Professor Lombroso noted that no one was actually being injured. In the first instance the Professor believed that the focus of the poltergeist was Signora Fumero who appeared to be a rather highly strung individual. Professor Lombroso asked Signora Fumero to take a few days' holiday, during which time the poltergeist was absent from the shop, and it seemed that the correct solution had been found. However, when Signora Fumero returned the poltergeist returned too. To ensure that he had located the correct focus the Professor asked Signora Fumero to go away again, for a few more days. Apparently she was extremely annoyed to be treated like this because of a few errant spirits and she heaped violent curses on them for causing such disruption to her life. But this time the poltergeist did *not* stop its activities when the signora was away – and from that point on, all the poltergeist activity focused solely on items associated with the signora. Her shoes levitated from an upstairs bedroom and came down the stairs and into the wine bar, landing at the feet of one of the customers; plates and bottles that the signora had handled were smashed but nothing touched by others was harmed.

So although Signora Fumero appeared to be something of a focus she was evidently not the direct cause of the poltergeist since it had continued in her absence. Eventually a young man at the awkward (and highly significant) age of puberty, who was working as a waiter in the wine bar, was suspected of being the focus and was dismissed. The wine bar haunting ceased, never to recur.

Elenora Zugun
   D: 1925
   L: Talpa, nr. Dorohoi, Northern Romania
   S: A. Gould & A.D. Cornell/C. Wilson

In February 1925 a Romanian girl aged 12, (born 24 May 1913) Elenora Zugun, began to be affected by poltergeist activity; stones fell on her house, objects levitated and windows were broken. The onset of the poltergeist followed an event the previous day when Elenora had found some money which she had used to buy sweets. Her grandmother, thought to be a witch in the locality, warned her that she would be possessed by the devil who had left the money to entice her.

Elenora returned home from her grandmother's to her own house at Talpa: in Northern Romania, the poltergeist followed her there, indicating that she was the focus. As a result of the poltergeist's activities Elenora was sent to a monastery and then the sanatorium.

Psychical researcher Countess Wassilko-Serecki was interested by the case and brought Elenora to live with her. The poltergeist changed its characteristics, attacking Elenora and leaving scratches and bitemarks on her body. Even in front of witnesses teeth marks would appear on her body causing her great pain. Saliva was found in some of the marks and was sent for chemical analysis: the saliva was not Elenora's.

Elenora attracted wide attention from many researchers, the first to investigate the case in Romania were Kubi Klein and Fritz Grunewald who recorded many instances of poltergeist activity, principally moving objects. In 1926 British researcher Harry Price visited Countess Wassilko-Serecki and Elenora and he observed scratch and bitemarks and the movement of several objects. Following his visit, he invited the Countess and Elenora to come to London and the National Laboratory of Psychical Research. The two were in London with Harry Price from 30 September to 14 October 1926. Two researchers at the National Laboratory, W. Hardwick and Robert Blar, reported seeing marks appear on her body while Elenora was under close observation and it is not thought she could have 'cheated'. Between November 1926 and January 1927 Elenora was examined by Dr Walter Kröner and colleagues who saw the same manifestations as the other researchers.

At the onset of Elenora's menstruation in 1927 the poltergeist stopped, allowing Elenora to get on with her life.

14
Doubles, Bi-locations, Doppelgängers and Vardogers

There are many occasions when what appears to be a ghost is reported but the ghost is in fact that of a person known to be or discovered to be still alive. Occasionally the double is actually mistaken for the real person.

Doubles arise where one person is reported by different people to be in two different places at the same time, with each of the so-called 'doubles' apparently acting quite normally.

Bi-location refers to that peculiar experience where one person apparently 'divides himself' into two and is witnessed by the *same* group of people. Often the two forms seem weakened by the division. The most startling example of this is the case of a school teacher seen by many of her pupils both in her chair and outside the window at the same time.

Doppelgängers are a particular type of double where the two versions of the same person are seen in close proximity, both acting out exactly the same motions. Doppelgängers are reputed by some to be forewarnings of death.

Vardogers are those peculiar experiences of doubles where the 'double' appears to precede the real person. In these cases the real person may go to a location they have never been to before, only to be greeted as if they are the long lost friend of several of the people there (who have apparently been speaking to and interacting with his vardoger).

A wide variety of these extraordinary phenomena are included in this section. Whether they are ghosts and hauntings in the true sense is debatable; there is, however, no doubt that the nature of these experiences is at the very least a close cousin of hauntings and there must be many occasions when there is considerable confusion as to whether the witness is seeing a double or a ghost, and reporting appropriately.

The Anaesthetised Cat
D: 1966
L: Devon
S: T.C. Lethbridge

On Friday 28 October 1966 author T.C. Lethbridge was contacted by a lady who wanted to speak to him and an interview was fixed for 11 a.m. on Monday 31 October. On the Saturday after the telephone call Lethbridge's eighteen-year-old cat was discovered to have broken a tooth and developed a mouth infection. An appointment was therefore made with the vet at Axminster for 11.30 a.m. on Monday, almost the same time as the appointment with the lady.

On the Monday morning, at five to eleven Lethbridge's wife took the car up the hill, carrying the cat in a travelling basket. At the top of the hill she met her husband's visitor coming down the lane by car; her car arrived at Lethbridge's house at exactly eleven o'clock.

Lethbridge greeted the visitor, and her sister who had driven her, and they went into the hall of Lethbridge's Tudor house. Shortly after their arrival (Lethbridge estimated it to have been seven minutes past eleven), the lady looked up and said, 'Is this the cat you write about in your books?' Lethbridge saw that the cat was standing on the firestool apparently smelling the visitor's hand which was very close to his nose. Lethbridge confirmed that it was the cat and thought no more about it. He remembered the cat jumping down and going over to the corner of the room where his drinking bowl was but paid no real attention to the matter.

The visitors left and shortly afterwards Lethbridge's wife returned, having left the cat with the vet to have its tooth out under anaesthetic. Sadly the cat never recovered from the anaesthetic and the infection and ten days later was dead. It was after the cat's death that Lethbridge realised that the same cat had been in two locations – both at the vet's and also on the firestool smelling his visitor's hand. Lethbridge checked with the visitor but while she confirmed that the conversation had indeed taken place, neither she nor her sister had actually *seen* the cat.

Lethbridge himself declared, 'How the conversation could have taken place unless she had seen it, I do not know!'

Lethbridge speculates that the cat, in preference to being shut up in a basket travelling down the road, had projected itself back to its more comfortable home. Lethbridge believed that the cat did this on several other occasions too: it was known as a 'keyhole cat' because of its ability to get to the far side of shut doors.

Mr Birkbeck and Mr Hill
D: 1907
L: Bloomfield Terrace, London
S: Lord Halifax

In 1907 Mr H.W. Hill wrote to his close friend Mr W.H. Birkbeck in Norwich.

The following day Mr Hill was at home in London and at 3.45 p.m. saw his friend coming towards his door. He described his friend as being of striking appearance and not easily mistakable.

After a while it became obvious to Mr Hill that his friend was not in fact going to call. He wrote again to Mr Birkbeck asking what he had been doing that afternoon at 3.45.

Mr Birkbeck wrote back saying he had been out shooting but at 3.45 had thought of his friend, Mr Hill, and had remarked to his companions that he must get a letter off to him, in reply to the first letter.

Victoria Branden
D: 20th century
L: Canada (?)
S: Victoria Branden

In her book, *Understanding Ghosts*, Victoria Branden relates the story of her own doppelgänger experience. It is particularly interesting to note the similarities between this case and cases of phantom highwaymen, phantom hitchhikers and UFO encounters. In particular, the encounter occurred as Ms Branden drove around a curve in the road and there seems to have been a suspension of consciousness or a feeling of strange isolation and quiet, both of which are common in these other types of experiences.

She was driving along when she suddenly saw a huge truck

heading towards her on the wrong side on a collision course. Reality seemed to be suspended and suddenly she was aware that beside her in the passenger seat was another version of herself. The doppelgänger was dressed in exactly the same clothes and was sitting passively, hands folded in its lap and head dropped forward.

Miss Branden could not see the expression on the figure's face but believed that it probably concealed an evil smile; she felt a hideously malign and threatening feeling from the entity.

Mrs Butler

D: 1890s
L: Ireland and Hampshire
S: Augustus Hare (*The Story of My Life*)

The story of Mrs Butler's projection or bi-location was related to Augustus Hare by a Miss Broke in November 1894. Insufficient details of the case are given to allow any follow-up research. Nonetheless it is not at odds with many other cases of bi-location and astral projection.

Mrs Butler was a lady living in Ireland who one morning described to her husband a beautiful house with a lovely conservatory and an enchanting garden. She had apparently 'visited it' in her dreams the previous night. Indeed she thought it so perfect she could hardly believe it could really exist. She dreamt of visiting the same property many times and often described the house to her husband; sitting in the library, walking on the terrace, looking in the bedrooms and so on.

It became something of a joke amongst her friends and family who would ask her whether she had visited 'her house' in the night.

Some years later the Butlers decided to move from Ireland to England. They went to view a house in Hampshire and as they approached Mrs Butler said, 'Do you know, this is the lodge of my house.' She insisted that it was indeed 'her house', and there was no doubt in anyone's mind which house she meant.

Although the housekeeper offered to show them around, Mrs Butler asked whether it would be all right if *she* did the showing and she was able to do so very successfully. Only in an upstairs passage was Mrs Butler puzzled. 'That door is not in my house,' she said and the housekeeper, understandably puzzled, simply commented, 'I don't understand about your house, Mam, but that door has only been there six weeks.'

The Butlers decided to buy the house and got it for an extraordinarily low price although no one would explain the reason why. After they had signed the deeds they went to the estate agents and asked whether, since they were no longer in a position to back out, they would please tell them why the price was so low.

The agent had apparently been quite distressed to see Mrs Butler but had now recovered; he said to her: 'Yes . . . there can be no harm in telling now. The fact is that the house has had a great reputation for being haunted: but you, Madam, need be under no apprehensions for you are yourself the ghost!'

The implication would seem to be that Mrs Butler had been haunting the house while she believed herself to be dreaming of it. With no research or scientific evidence to support it, this story seems too perfect to be true. Indeed, it has all the qualities of good drama and is far too neatly tied up, although, of course, it could have a core of truth.

Colin

D: (No date)

L: New Zealand

S: Ngaio Marsh (*Black Beech and Honeydew*)

The writer Ngaio Marsh was teaching Colin, the son of a New Zealand doctor, and had become very attached to the boy. He lived in a cottage nearby and often visited Marsh during the morning, bringing flowers. One day, Ngaio's mother said that Colin was coming up the garden path with a bunch of geraniums. He was wearing a smart new jacket. Her mother shouted to Ngaio to go and meet him but when she walked down the path Colin was nowhere to be seen; she concluded that perhaps he had gone home again.

It was the next morning when he arrived, saying that he had intended to come the previous day but had been forbidden by his nanny as he had been naughty. He said, 'And I'd got my new coat on and I picked you a bunch of ginraneums' (sic).

Mrs Dansie

D: 1936

L: Middlesex Hospital

S: Dr Margaret Murray (*My First Hundred Years*)

Mrs Marion Dansie was a patient in the Middlesex Hospital in May 1936. At 5 a.m. one morning the door to the room she was in was apparently pushed open from the outside and a nurse walked in, smiling to Mrs Dansie. She came around the side of the bed and Mrs Dansie said, 'Good morning. How nice to see you, but why are you on duty now?' Mrs Dansie recognised the nurse as one of the day staff. By way of response, the figure vanished completely!

When the day staff came on duty the nurse whom Mrs Dansie had seen earlier was not amongst them as she had been taken ill during the night.

This was certainly not a death apparition as both Mrs Dansie and the nurse recovered from their illnesses; some sort of projection or bi-location was almost certainly in operation.

Faces with a Message

D: Late 19th or early 20th century

L: London and Cornwall

S: W. Hudson (*A Hind in Richmond Park*)

In *A Hind in Richmond Park* W. Hudson describes seeing faces appearing in the air in front of him which he believed to be telepathic messages. His interpretation of this was rather questionable: he believed that the telepathy worked best if the wind was in the right direction; blowing to him from the subject. Hudson believed that the wind had a powerful effect on the mind, and that it was possible for the winds to make the mind more receptive to telepathic messages. Nonetheless his story is an intriguing one.

Walking down a London street, he suddenly saw the face of a girl appear in front of him. The face was the only thing that appeared and the image seemed to be reacting with the strong wind blowing at the time. It was fluttering and waving to and fro, vanishing and re-appearing rather like a 'flag or some filmy substance agitated by the wind'.

It was the face of a girl who he knew very well and who was very dear to him. She lived some 80 miles away with her family.

Hudson was amazed and wrote to the girl's mother to ask if all was well. He wasn't satisfied with her assurance that it was and became convinced that something was troubling the girl of which the mother was unaware. He went to visit the family. On the second day of the visit the mother announced that there was something she felt she should tell him. The young girl whose face Hudson had seen had apparently argued with her family at around the time he had seen her face, more or less rejecting their deeply held religious beliefs. This had caused very great tension and she had decided to leave the family and find Hudson, even if she had to walk the whole way and live on charity.

Johann Goethe
D: 18th century
L: (Not given)
S: Various

Walking home one day after a heavy fall of rain the eighteenth-century poet and dramatist Johann Goethe saw his friend Friederich walking in front of him and in fact wearing his own (Goethe's) dressing-gown. When Goethe arrived home he found Friederich standing in front of the fire wearing the dressing-gown. Apparently Friederich had been on his way to see Goethe when he had been caught in the rain and the housekeeper had lent him the dressing-gown while his overcoat dried out. Some bi-location seems to have taken place whereby Friederich projected an image of himself to Goethe.

On another occasion Goethe was riding away from his love, Frederica, feeling very gloomy when he suddenly saw his own double riding in the opposite direction dressed in a grey suit with gold embroidery. It was eight years later when he was riding along the same road in the opposite direction that he realised he was now wearing a grey and gold suit and that, in the earlier episode, he had somehow seen himself eight years in the future.

Erikson Gorique
D: 1955
L: Norway
S: Colin Wilson

In 1955 New York importer Erikson Gorique made his first ever visit to Norway. When he arrived at his hotel he was greeted by the clerk as if he was an old friend. He then met another dealer who recognised Gorique as someone he had met two months previously. It appeared that Gorique's double had preceded him.

Such doubles are known as 'vardogers' or 'forerunners': in other words a double which appears ahead of the reality.

Harold
D: 1958
L: Chicago, USA
S: Hilary Evans

Edward Podlasky, related the story of Harold of Chicago in *Fate* magazine. One day in 1958 Harold was suffering from an attack of migraine when he sat down to dinner. Sitting opposite him was an exact replica of himself copying every movement. After the meal the replica vanished. Harold reported several doppelgänger experiences when he had migraine.

This is typical of many such reports with no apparent purpose or explanation. A similar case is that of a man who moved his lawn while his doppelgänger walked alongside him in exactly the same posture, even pushing the handles of an invisible lawn-mower, up and down the lawn until the job was finished, when it promptly disappeared.

These cases are surprisingly common.

Pauline Parker
D: (No date)
L: Hereford
S: Joan Forman

When Mrs Pauline Parker was shopping in Hereford she met an old friend, 'Captain Daintry' (pseudonym). It was 10.15 a.m., and they talked briefly before Mrs Parker invited him to join her and her husband for coffee, which he accepted. She was concerned because it was cold outside and the captain, nearly 80 years old, was not very well.

Mr and Mrs Parker waited for some time but the captain did not join them. Later they sent a note to the captain apologising for leaving before he had arrived (in case he had arrived after they had left though in fact he had never done so) and inviting him to join them at a later date.

The captain wrote back, somewhat puzzled and saying that he *had not been in Hereford on the day in question* but – perhaps importantly – he did recall meeting Mrs Parker somewhere but couldn't remember where.

Mrs Parker and her husband thought that perhaps his memory was failing him because of his age and wrote again to him to jog his memory. However, the captain replied that he was quite certain that at that time he had been in bed, recovering from tiredness after a dinner party the previous evening; this was corroborated by his housekeeper who had brought him breakfast in bed. According to Mrs Parker, she had met him at 10.15 a.m. and according to the captain and his housekeeper he had not come down from bed until 10.45.

Various possibilities were considered by both Mrs Parker and the captain, but they were dismissed; it was unlikely to be a double, in the sense of someone of similar appearance to the captain, since it was he who had greeted Mrs Parker in the first place. It also seems unlikely that it was an out-of-body experience on the part of the captain, since Mrs Parker recalled that 'he took my arm', which would seem to imply a very physical contact. This physical contact is of course difficult to explain even in cases of bi-location, where in many cases there is no certainty of physical presence but rather only of appearance. There does, however, seem to be some corroboration from the captain in his admitting that he had a vague recollection of seeing Mrs Parker somewhere – suggesting that there *was* some sort of interaction, the nature of which was never solved.

Elizabeth and Hefin Pritchard
D: 20th century
L: Bangor, Wales
S: Rev. J. Aelwyn Roberts

There is often a great similarity between the self-described claims of a person projecting what seems to be a physical double and out-of-body experiences projecting an astral body. Often the only distinction is in other people's perception (where witnesses are available) or, more rarely, in the manipulation of matter. An example of this was reported by J. Aelwyn Roberts in his book *The Holy Ghostbuster*.

William Pritchard and his wife ran a general store and post office in Bangor in Wales. They had a son, Hefin, who was working with the RAF in Canada.

One November night Elizabeth Pritchard woke up extremely agitated and woke her husband. She described what her husband took to be a terrible dream. However, Elizabeth described it very much as if she was there at the time. She was in a blizzard and could hardly see her hand in front of her face. She could hear the sound the old bomber planes made (these were the type that Hefin flew as an instructor). Suddenly through the snow she saw one of these planes flying very low in the blizzard. Then it crashed into the mountain. The nose of the plane was buried in the snow and Mrs Pritchard waited to see if her son or anyone else would emerge from it. She could see smoke coming from underneath the left wing. Since there was no activity Mrs Pritchard went to the door of the plane and opened it.

Despite protestations about the unlikeliness of this detail from her husband, she continued that she had opened the door and gone inside the plane. Three men were in the front but all were dead, another was in the back of the plane and he had been virtually cut in half and was also dead. Lying on the floor of the plane, face down, was Hefin. He had hit his head and had lost a lot of blood; his leg was twisted round and she believed he might be dead.

Elizabeth's husband still maintained that she must have been dreaming.

Although letters usually came regularly from Hefin, for some reason they now stopped, causing concern. It was three weeks before a letter did arrive. The letter seemed to indicate that in fact Elizabeth's fright was nothing more than a dream. Her son was fine; he'd been moved to another base in Canada and he had been taken off flying duties for a bit. Because of the move his leave would be postponed and it would be some six months before he could come home. All was well and the months passed until eventually the day came when they could pick up their son from Bangor Station.

The train door opened and Hefin came down on to the

platform leaning heavily on one crutch and waving to them. Once home Mr Pritchard pointed at his evident wounds and asked Hefin to explain. Hefin said that he had been on a training trip over Alaska, with five men in the plane, and they had flown into a terrible blizzard. They had been flying very low to get a bearing when suddenly the plane had crashed into a mountain. Luckily another plane had been close behind them; its pilot had been able to give accurate position readings when it got back to base and rescue planes had got to them very soon. Four of the crew had been killed on impact and he himself was unconscious when they had found him, bleeding profusely from a head wound and with his leg shattered.

Hefin explained why he had written the letters. He had not wanted to worry his parents and had told them that he had been posted away as a cover story. He needed to delay his return home as the doctors had prevented him travelling for some months. Mr Pritchard asked his son when the crash had happened but it was Elizabeth who interjected with the accurate information that it was at one o'clock in the morning of Thursday, 17 November in the previous year.

Unless we speculate that Hefin himself had an out-of-body experience, examined the details of the plane crash and then transmitted them to his mother, there is some evidence here of Elizabeth having somehow made the trip to Alaska to get all the details she had, because Hefin himself was unconscious when Elizabeth 'examined' him. Hefin didn't see the plane hitting the mountain from the perspective that his mother had, although she accurately described what happened. Hefin was unconscious at the moment of impact and did not see the bodies of his four comrades, indeed he only found out about their death days later. Hefin did not see the wisps of smoke coming from under the wing. If only he had been conscious; how would he have reacted to his mother's presence and what exactly would he have seen when that door opened?

This particular case is one where it cannot easily be determined whether or not it was a physical double being projected or merely an astral body; most of the evidence would indicate that this is very much a case of astral projection but for one particular detail, the opening of the door. That alone suggests a physical presence and the fact that the other person involved was unconscious and therefore not able to distinguish either way brings us to include this particular case in this category, inappropriate though we admit it may turn out to be.

The Rev. Pritchard and the Rev. Nairne

D: c. 1850

L: Clapham, London

S: Lord Halifax

When the Rev. Spencer Nairne was seventeen he was walking through Clapham arm in arm with a schoolfellow when he passed his headmaster, the Rev. C. Pritchard, walking rapidly in the opposite direction. Both boys touched their hats to him, as was the tradition, and he returned their salute without looking directly at them, passing on behind them.

After two or three minutes exactly the very same thing happened again and both boys were quite certain that the headmaster could not have played a trick by somehow running around to repeat the performance nor was it likely that he would be inclined to do so. Both Spencer Nairne and his friend, Henry Stone, were certain of the events as related though they never mentioned it to their headmaster. Nor did he ever mention it to them, though presumably he must have encountered *them* twice within three minutes too.

(Also see 'The Rev. Spencer Nairne and Miss Wallis' on pp. 321–2).

Mrs Florence Punter

D: 1967

L: Epping, Essex

S: Andrew MacKenzie

In 1967 or thereabouts Mrs Punter had one of her daughters' boyfriends to stay as a guest in her home in Epping, Essex. One morning he asked Mrs Punter if she had gone into his room during the night as he thought he had seen her standing by the dressing-table dressed in a white nightdress. Mrs Punter replied that she did not have a white nightdress.

Two years later, towards the end of 1969, Marian Punter, an

older and at that time married daughter, was staying with her husband at the house and was in the upstairs' sitting room watching a programme on television. Her mother was in the downstairs' lounge watching television with her father and doing some knitting.

At around eleven o'clock in the evening Marian Punter looked out of the sitting-room door towards the bathroom and saw what appeared to be her mother coming out to go downstairs. She was wearing what looked like a white nightdress. Marian thought it was rather strange that her mother had not said good night and in any case she usually used her own bathroom on the first floor. However, it was not a major incident and was dismissed by the couple. Twenty minutes later Mrs Florence Punter, fully dressed, came into the sitting room and said good night to her daughter and son-in-law. Marian was surprised, wondering why she had not spoken to her when she was upstairs earlier. She also wondered why she had got dressed again, just before going to bed. Florence Punter was adamant that she had been downstairs with her husband all evening and also confirmed for the second time that she did not own a white nightdress.

It is possible to speculate that the figure was an apparition of an unidentified woman in white but it seems highly likely that a daughter would recognise her own mother even if not seeing her full face; in any case the earlier sighting also seemed to suggest recognition of Mrs Florence Punter. It would seem that on two occasions she has been seen as an apparition, while alive – a bi-location or doppelgänger event. The fact that Mrs Punter does not own a white nightdress adds a certain mystery to the report which has not been resolved.

Other paranormal events – poltergeist activity – were reported by the family. Marian Punter recalled that in August 1974 when she was staying at the house she had awoken in the morning and was about to smoke a cigarette when her bed moved away from the wall and then back again, while, in January 1972, a young man staying at the house had felt himself being lifted from the bed, and felt the bed shake. In the morning he was ashen-faced and shaking; he thought he had been given a message. He could no longer stay in that room.

The Projection of Mrs N.
D: 1940s or 1950s
L: Devon
S: T.C. Lethbridge

When T. C. Lethbridge moved to Branston in Devon in 1947 he was soon visited by the daughter of the former owner of his home. She told Lethbridge's mother-in-law that the house had a ghost although she had never seen it herself. Apparently her mother had often seen it 40 years ago and it was a little old woman with white hair and a red coat.

Lethbridge heard that many local people had seen the same figure. However, during the time that Lethbridge lived at the house he never saw the apparition nor could he find anybody else who had done so. However, he was sure that he could identify it.

Lethbridge and his family had already got to know 'Mrs N.', who was very 'psychic' and who frequently dropped into the house for tea and a chat. In cold weather she wore a long cherry-red coat and no hat, displaying a shock of curly white hair. Lethbridge writes: 'I have not doubt that Mrs N. was the ghost.' Lethbridge speculates that since it is unlikely that Mrs N. would have projected a vision of herself 40 years older than she was at the time of the sighting, then the projection must have come from some other source and indeed possibly from himself or his wife (projecting backwards through time presumably). Alternatively, this may be an example of multiple time slips on Mrs N.'s part.

Whatever the answer this seems to have been some kind of projection of Mrs N. who was alive at the time and indeed did not die until August 1960.

Mrs N. featured in another 'haunting' episode with the Lethbridge family. One night Lethbridge had been experimenting by mentally drawing pentagrams around his bed. On a night two weeks later his wife woke with a feeling that there was somebody else in the room; although she could not see anyone she saw a faint glow near the foot of the bed. When that faded she felt they were then alone again.

When Mrs N. dropped in for tea the next evening she told Lethbridge that she had visited his house the previous night but could not get near the bed because of triangles of fire around it. She asked if someone had been putting protection on Lethbridge.

Lethbridge explained the situation and told her that although he didn't mind her visit he would be grateful if she wouldn't repeat it as they had felt her presence and were uncomfortable with it. The Lethbridges were certain that Mrs N. could have not known about the pentagrams without discovering them for herself in some way; she could not have entered the house conventionally as the doors were locked.

Beynham Pyne
D: (No date)
L: New Zealand(?)
S: Ngaio Marsh (*Black Beech and Honeydew*)

In Ngaio Marsh's autobiography, *Black Beech and Honeydew*, she refers to a story her mother told her. Her mother had been reading a book one afternoon and had looked up to see the apparition of a bed with a small boy in it. The light was strong around him and he turned his head and smiled.

Some weeks later the family received a message to say that a cousin, Beynham Pyne, was to have his tonsils out. When Ngaio Marsh's mother arrived at the sick room she immediately believed that what she would see inside would be exactly the scene she had seen those weeks before; but in fact she was wrong. The bed was in the wrong place, Beynham did not turn his head and the light was coming from the wrong direction. They left the room for the operation to take place and returned to see how the patient was getting on.

When they re-entered the room the bed had been moved to provide better lighting. As they entered Beynham turned his head and smiled.

Queen Elizabeth I
D: 1603
L: Richmond Palace, London
S: Joan Forman

Neither the Virgin Queen nor her palace at Richmond, where she died, are strangers to hauntings and paranormal stories. These include the story of a crisis apparition or possible bi-location shortly before her death.

In the winter of 1603, when she was 60, Queen Elizabeth

caught pneumonia and was forced to take to her bed. Slowly dying, she lay, apparently asleep. One of her ladies in waiting (in one account, Lady Guilford), believing the Queen to be at least asleep or possibly unconscious, left the chambers to return briefly to her own apartment. As she was walking down the corridor she saw the figure of Queen Elizabeth striding purposefully towards her. She looked away quickly and then back – there was no sign of the Queen or indeed anyone else. Calling off her mission, she returned to the royal bedchamber to find the Queen exactly as she had been – still either asleep or unconscious.

Mark Roberts

D: 20th century
L: Llandegai, Wales
S: Rev. J. Aelwyn Roberts

The 'Holy Ghostbuster', Rev. J. Aelwyn Roberts, reported several paranormal encounters. One affected his own son Mark and daughter Felicity. Mark was a trainee reporter working in Manchester and was at home in Llandegai for a few days. He had been into Bangor and arrived home, walking in through the front door.

Felicity, his sister, was astonished to see him, commenting that she had just passed him in the dining room and that he could hardly have been to Bangor. She also added that he was wearing different clothes in the dining room, in particular the embroided yellow waistcoat that had been Mark's Christmas present from his mother. Mark insisted the waistcoat was at his lodgings in Manchester.

This appears to be an example of bi-location or projection. The Rev. was slightly concerned that the waistcoat might be an omen and was glad to see the back of it when it had been given to charity. In fact no significance appears to have attached to the event, a fairly simple example of bi-location.

Ruth

D: 1960s or 1970s
L: London
S: Lynn Picknett/Hilary Evans

Investigated by psychiatrist Dr Morten Schatzman, Ruth (the only name by which she was known publicly, even in a television adaptation of her story) had the extraordinary experience of being able to produce apparently solid images of living people.

The principal image she produced was her father. He appeared to her, apparently solidly, and, according to her, casting shadows, but causing her a repugnance as he had sexually abused her when she was young. She could apparently see, smell and even hear him although he was living on the other side of the Atlantic at the time. One laboratory experiment proved that Ruth was able to focus on this 'solid' body in front of her although no one else could see anything. Schatzman taught Ruth to control the apparition, to refuse to fear it and even to manipulate it and force it to disappear when she wanted it to.

Ruth could also create images of other people but had no control over the creation though she could dismiss them at will. She could also touch them, describing them as cold, exactly as ghosts in close proximity are often described. Ruth's apparitions were perfectly normal in appearance, acted perfectly normally with respect to furniture and other articles in the room, appeared to Ruth to interact with other people in the room at the time and so on. It is thought that she may have created images which were seen not just by herself but others. An apparition of her husband was seen not only by herself but by her father who could identify it as such, and on another occasion Ruth's husband spoke to an apparition of Ruth for some time before realising that it was not the 'real' her. Whether or not Ruth was the person creating these images or whether other people around her had similar abilities is of course unclear. Precisely what Ruth was creating, or the mechanism with which she created it, is still unknown but Schatzman remained convinced of the genuineness of the phenomenon and it may go some way towards explaining doubles and bi-locations.

Amelie Saegée

D: 1846

L: Livonia, Latvia

S: Hilary Evans

In 1860, fourteen years after the experience, one of Amelie Saegée's pupils related a story about her then teacher, Saegée, and her doppelgänger.

Aged 32 at the time, Amelie Saegée was a teacher in Livonia, Latvia. She apparently had a predisposition for being seen in two places at once, sometimes with both forms in close proximity – such as both standing at the blackboard in the same classroom where the double exactly duplicated the actions of the real person – and sometimes separated by a greater distance. On one occasion the teacher was outside in the garden while her double sat on a chair in the classroom. If the reports are to be believed then thirteen pupils witnessed the incident at the blackboard and all the pupils in the school witnessed her both in the garden and while also sitting indoors.

Amelie said that while she was in the garden it occurred to her that, with the headmistress absent, the classroom was probably unattended and that *she* ought to be giving the class. Perhaps a feeling of reluctance meant that her projection was not, as it were, entirely willing and may explain why her double seemed rather insubstantial (indeed one pupil walking closely by is said to have passed through a portion of the double, suggesting a ghostlike quality to it) and the real Amelie in the garden was apparently looking very drowsy and exhausted. This seems to have been a characteristic of her bi-location: her strength had to be divided between the two forms.

The story has a rather sad ending in that news got around about the bi-location and Amelie was asked to leave the school. At that point she admitted that this was the nineteenth time she had been asked to leave her job because of this same problem.

Sister Mary and the Jumano Indians
D: 1600s
L: Agreda, Spain and New Mexico
S: R.J.M. Rickard and J. Michell (*Phenomena*)

This extraordinary story from the 1600s is often cited as an example of teleportation and indeed perhaps it is so. However, it is equally possible that it is a case of bi-location since there is no evidence that Sister Mary was ever found missing from her convent. Sister Mary was born in 1602 and it is estimated that between 1620 and 1631, she made over 500 trips to America by some paranormal means, probably never leaving the Spanish convent in Agreda which was her home. In America she converted the Jumano Indians of New Mexico to Christianity. The Catholic authorities tried to dissuade her from making these claims but the testimony of missionaries to the Mexican Indians eventually forced them to authenticate her experiences.

In 1622 Father Alonzo de Benavides of the Isolita Mission in New Mexico asked both the King of Spain and the Pope who had gone on ahead of him doing missionary work with the Jumano Indians. The Indians themselves said they had been taught about Christianity by 'a lady in blue', a nun who had given them objects such as crosses, rosaries and a chalice. Indeed the chalice did come from the Spanish convent. In 1630 Father Benavides was back in Spain and heard of Sister Mary's claims. It appears that the American and Spanish details coincided perfectly.

The Rev. Spencer Nairne and Miss Wallis
D: 1859
L: Aberdeen, Scotland
S: Lord Halifax

In 1859 the Rev. Spencer Nairne was to visit Norway together with a party of friends and relatives. Before the trip, they were walking up the main street of Aberdeen; the light was good even though it was eight-thirty in the evening. Nairne was walking with John Chalmers, one of the party, and recognised a lady named Miss Wallis approaching from the opposite direction. Nairne had known Miss Wallis for some twenty years or more (he was 26 at the time) though she was not a close acquaintance. She had been a governess in other branches of his family. He had great respect for her and comments that he would never have met her without going out of the way to speak to her. They passed close enough to touch one another and certainly to recognise each other. Miss Wallis was walking arm in arm with a man and talking to him and quite plainly she saw and recognised Nairne.

As he began to address her she suddenly vanished and he looked up and down the road trying to find her in vain. He even searched many of the shops in order to satisfy himself that she had not turned into any of them.

It was some three weeks after the cruise to Norway, that the Rev. Nairne encountered Miss Wallis, in London, where she was with his mother and his cousin. Before he could begin to ask her the obvious question, she said to him, 'Now I have a quarrel to settle with you, Mr Nairne. You cut me in Aberdeen a little while ago.' Nairne explained that he had seen her, that he was sure she had seen him and that he had gone to speak to her when she had disappeared. Miss Wallis explained that that was exactly what had happened to her; she had turned round to talk to him but he had disappeared. Apparently the man she had been walking with was her brother, and she confirmed Nairne's description of the two of them walking together. She had said to her brother, 'Why, there is Mr Nairne. I must speak to him.' When they could not find him, Miss Wallis's brother had said, 'I am so sorry. I have often heard of Capt. Nairne and I should have been glad to meet him.' Miss Wallis then explained that it was not the captain but his son, the Rev. Spencer Nairne, to whom she referred.

Much later the question of dates came up. It was established that Nairne had been Aberdeen on 31 May. Miss Wallis explained that she had *not* been there at that time but that she and her brother had been there at the end of July, several weeks later. At that time Nairne had been in Norway.

Both had apparently seen projections of each other at the same spot, but out of time.

(See also entry for 'The Rev. Pritchard and the Rev. Nairne', p. 314.)

Two Visions at Once

D: (No date)

L: (Not given)

S: T.C. Lethbridge

T.C. Lethbridge describes an extraordinary experience when he and his wife were both in the presence of a friend of theirs, but not, it seems, in the *same* presence.

Lethbridge starts by explaining that his wife had trained him to notice what might be thought of as trivial details; the two of them would make a point of noticing trivial social things that interested them. Lethbridge's wife would often test him by asking what kind of clothes a person he had met had been wearing, which encouraged him to look out for these sort of details.

On one occasion Lethbridge and his wife were together with two friends whom they referred to as Mr and Mrs X. The two women sat side by side opposite the two men. Lethbridge points out that he was within just a foot or two of the woman and noticed no change in her appearance at any time.

It was only when Lethbridge and his wife were in the car on their way home that his wife described the Mrs X she had seen. Her description was of a woman looking older than expected, with white hair. Mrs Lethbridge also pointed out that wearing a white jumper had not helped her appearance. She went on to describe a silver Celtic brooch that Mrs X had been wearing.

Lethbridge had seen the same woman, but his description was very different. He believed that the woman he had seen was wearing a light chocolate-coloured dress and a gold brooch with a yellow stone. Her face had appeared smooth and unlined and her hair 'only slightly salted'.

Lethbridge did not believe that either he or his wife had made a mistake in their observations; he believed that some sort of time slip had taken place and that one of the two of them was seeing Mrs X in a different time, either as she had been or was one day going to be.

Lethbridge points out, interestingly, that had there been only one witness to the meeting the disparity would never have come to light and that there may be a great many other similar instances which simply never come to light.

15
Ghostly Balls of Light and Ghosts of Marshes and Moors

'Classic' ghosts include the black monk and white lady sightings reported all over the United Kingdom. Many of these can in fact be traced back to the shapeless forms seen in marshes and on open land as whirling white or formless black shapes. It is speculated that these are natural phenomena but which, through legend and folklore, have given rise to this particular type of ghost report.

Add to this the belief that the soul which detaches from the physical body temporarily or permanently at death can occasionally be seen as a glowing ball of light. Recent studies of 'earthlights' (the natural light emissions of rocks under stress) and UFOs (which involve a great many reports of balls of light) suggest that there are many possible explanations for these phenomena. Nonetheless ghostly balls of light, white ladies and black monks continue to be amongst the most frequently reported sightings of what people believe to be ghosts. This section, probably more than any other, is likely to contain no genuine ghosts whatsoever but, that said, it certainly contains some of the most powerful folklore and mythology concerning ghosts and hauntings in existence.

A Cameron Funeral
D: c. 1935
L: Nr. Killin, Loch Tay, Scotland
S: Alasdair McGregor

There are many reports of ghostlights in the area of Loch Tay and Loch Rannoch in Perthshire, Scotland.

In 1935 two young sons of the Cameron family living on a farm at Morenish on Loch Tay died of fever while the eldest son was abroad serving with the army. The two young boys were buried at Kenmore at the eastern end of the loch: When the eldest son returned home he wanted them to be buried at Killin at the *western* end of the loch and arranged for their re-burial.

On the night before the re-interment two bright balls of fire were seen speeding along the surface of Loch Tay. The following day the boat carrying the coffins followed that exact course.

H.J.P.'s Fireball

D: (No date)
L: Homestead, Miami, Florida
S: BOLIDE

Mr 'H.J.P.' (name withheld) gave this report of a light phenomenon which entered his house when he was living in Homestead in Florida. The description is similar to many ghostlight and ball-lightning reports, but the interpretation is rather more unusual.

The ball of light entered by a window and moved towards the witness, forcing him to draw his knees in where he sat. It made a 90-degree turn into the hall and then another 90-degree turn to go out of the hall window. Although both windows were screened, there was no damage to either. The witness's wife had also seen small balls of fire six to eight inches in diameter moving through the window but until that moment her husband had not been able to understand her claims. He declared: 'This fireball was definitely controlled by some outside sources, judging from the entry and the pathway it has taken.'

The Ghost of an Irish Pedlar

D: 1922 and others
L: Bearnn Eile, Isle of Lewis
S: Alasdair McGregor

The ghost of Bearnn Eile inhabits the island of Lewis in the Outer Hebrides.

Legend has it that in the eighteenth century an Irish pedlar was touring Lewis selling his wares when he called at a house in Doune Mor to ask for directions. One of the members of the household offered to walk with the pedlar on his way and, having reached an isolated place, murdered him with a hammer. According to the story, the murderer carried the corpse 200 yards in order to bury it in soft peat. The money he had stolen from the pedlar he hid in a nearby well.

The ghost of Bearnn Eile is a light which has been seen by many people and which is reputed to travel from the spot where the body lay to where the old well concealed his money.

In 1922 three witnesses saw the light and supposedly dug up the ground around the well to discover a small sealskin purse containing a number of Irish pennies from the mid-1700s. The lights have not been seen since this event.

Ghost Lights Near the Coast
D: 1930 and others
L: Gruinard Bay, Scotland
S: Alasdair McGregor

Gruinard Bay is in the far north of Scotland. There have been several accounts of 'ghost lights' around that coastal area and they are associated, at least in the minds of the local people, with local tragedies. The lights have been seen on a number of occasions just off the coast near Little Gruinard and up towards the hamlets of First Coast and Second Coast. One such report came from local man Hector MacLeod, who noted the peculiar quality of the light in that it gave off no rays. MacLeod's cousin John Gunn, Sir Alexander Gibb's ploughman at Gruinard, confirmed the sighting. He cycled regularly between his home and Gruinard House, along the other side of the bay from the road up to First and Second Coast and on several occasions he saw the light pass close by him, making a strange noise in his ears.

In 1930 Sir Alexander Gibb was having repair work done at Gruinard House when Lady Gibb's maid committed suicide. One of the workmen at the house said that he had seen the light regularly for some days and had twice passed a phantom funeral on the road. Locally, the Gruinard Bay light became associated with the maid's suicide.

Jenny Burntail
D: 1923
L: Burton Dassett, Warwickshire
S: Various

Jenny Burntail is the local name for a light seen around All Saints

Church in Burton Dassett and the surrounding area including Edgehill, in Warwickshire. Edgehill was the scene of a Civil War battle in 1642 which has since become famous as a site of 'phantom army' apparitions (see page 122). The area has many ghost traditions as well as modern paranormal events. It is also crossed by a major ley line.

The Jenny Burntail lights were particularly in evidence in 1923 and 1924 during which time the area was struck by a severe earth tremor. 'Earthlights' or 'spooklights' are therefore thought to be the most likely explanation.

Mr George White, one of the witnesses in February 1923, gave the following account: 'It was about seven p.m. and we had been there a short time . . . We turned around and about two hundred yards away was a strong and dazzling light like that of a motor headlamp. It was a perfectly lovely sight, and held us fascinated. It flitted about and passed through bushes and over fences at high speed; then it passed over us and disappeared with a flash into the ground. We could feel it hover around, and it appeared to be looking for something, for the lights swept the ground. The light . . . was so bright, and yet there was a ghastly red blue patch on the top. Later when we saw it around Burton Dassett Church, there was a tinge of orange colour. There was nothing whatever to be afraid of . . . I was a sceptic before, but I swear I have never seen anything like it.'

The media at the time seemed to be intent on producing a ghost out of this fairly innocuous light phenomenon. The *London Daily Mail* of Tuesday 13 February 1923 wrote: 'Two south Warwickshire villages, Fenny Compton and North End, have acquired a ghost. Just which village it belongs to does not seem to have been decided, nor is there any evidence of burning desire on the part of either villages to lay claim to sole possession. Several people in each village, would, as a matter of fact, be quite pleased to give it to the other. The first person to see the spirit was a shepherd. He declared that he had seen a figure of spectral light wandering down the valley. Various unkind remarks were made, and he was given to understand that in all events in this respect the truth was not in him. He had his revenge four nights later. A number of men were out in the hills together and the apparition manifested itself once more as a light that swayed and hovered around them.

The shepherd received apologies. The ghost appears to be very indefinite in shape but all reports agree that it is clothed in light – "a dull bluish flame rising off into the air" by one account. It is an active sort of spook, often appearing in a dozen different places in the same evening. It seems to delight in scaring women for it is said to go and dance around any woman who is so rash as to walk across a meadow alone after dark. There are of course the sceptics who declare that it is not a ghost at all, that it is nothing but marsh gas, that faintly luminous exhalation of carburetted hydrogen which sometimes rises from damp places, and gave rise to all the legends of the will-o'-the-wisp.'

Mary Kingsley's Sighting
D: 1895
L: Lake Ncovi, West Africa
S: Mary Kingsley (*Travels in West Africa*)
The explorer Mary Kingsley was bathing alone from her canoe on Lake Ncovi during an expedition to the area between the Ogowe and Rembwe Rivers in the Gabon, West Africa.

She saw coming through the forest on the lake shore a violet ball the size of a small orange which hovered over the beach. It was joined by another similar ball and the two appeared to circle around each other over the beach. Mary pursued the balls, but they escaped her, one going off into the bushes and the other into the lake itself. She was even able to watch this second ball glowing as it sank down deep into the lake.

Local natives explained that the light was an *aku*, a devil's spirit.

Light in the House
D: 1979
L: Fleetwood, Lancashire
S: BOLIDE
During the early evening of 3 December 1979 a family in Fleetwood, Lancashire, described a ghostlight, possibly ball-lightning, which appeared in their living room. The room was lit by a 60-watt table lamp and the television was turned off although plugged in. A spherical light about six inches in diameter floated down the chimney, which was sealed, and into the room. It

looked something like a soap bubble but was dull purple in colour and seemed to be covered in a furry or spiky surface. It was transparent and appeared smooth inside with the spikes radiating outwards. There was no sound. The bubble drifted towards the television screen and at approximately eight inches from it disappeared with a loud crack, leaving behind the smell of an electrical discharge.

Lights and White Ladies
D: 1913
L: Linley, nr. Ironbridge, Shropshire
S: BOLIDE

Linley is a remote hamlet due south of Ironbridge in Shropshire. Poltergeist phenomena have been recorded there including furniture, crockery and clothing moving unaided. There is also a tradition of a ghostly 'white lady' associated with the area.

In 1913 a ball of light was seen moving, with apparent intelligence, around the few cottages that make up the hamlet; similar balls of light were also seen inside Linley Hall and the adjacent St Leonard's Church.

Spirals of light 'vapour' have been seen moving around in the area which may well have given rise to the reports of ghostly white nuns and black monks seen in the area.

While such moving lights may account for ghost reports in earlier times, current 'earthlight' theories hold that in this area they are being caused by two faults which run past the hamlet of Linley to the west and the east. Such faults are thought to create light phenomena during periods of geological stress, the energies of the underground strains being emitted as self-illuminated lights – possibly a form of plasma energy.

Lights on a Mountain
D: 1982
L: Mount Senohara, Japan
S: BOLIDE

At approximately seven-thirty in the evening of 31 July 1982 a light was seen at the top of Mount Senohara by housewife Yoko Yarimizu from outside her house. She told other members of the family what she had seen and they joined her outside. They could see an orange luminous body at the crest of the mountain although the 'ghostlight' itself had disappeared. The luminous body also disappeared just a few seconds later, then reappeared and disappeared several times. Shortly afterwards *two* luminous bodies, one orange and one blue, appeared side by side then also came and went several times.

By eight o'clock the media were on the scene, having been alerted by the family but nothing happened until 9.30 when a blue light appeared. Cameraman Nobuyu Kikobayashi attempted to photograph the light but it disappeared immediately.

The Marfa Lights

D: 1883
L: Mitchell Flats, Texas, USA
S: Various

The Marfa Lights are globes of light that dance and hover around the Mitchell Flats area in Texas. They were first reported by Robert Ellison, a rancher, in 1883. The lights originally had a place in the folklore of the local native Indians, the Mescalero Apache, and were said to be the spirit of a heartbroken brave wandering in search of his lost squaw.

The lights are described as approximately the size of a basketball dancing and hovering a little above the ground. They have been frequently, if irregularly, reported. Pat Ryan, editor of the *Marfa Independent*, has searched for the lights many times but has not yet seen them. On the other hand Joe Skelton, who runs the petrol station next door to the newspaper offices, claims seven sightings. He described one occasion when he was driving and his wife was asleep in the car beside him. He thought he could see in his rear-view mirror an 'eighteen-wheeler too close for comfort'. When he looked over his shoulder it was gone.

On another occasion he was driving to a ranch near the McDonald Observatory with a friend following in a pickup; both vehicles were equipped with Citizen's Band radio. Both saw the lights in the hills but, more curiously, there seemed to be an interaction between the lights and the people themselves. Every time Skelton radioed his friend the lights would go out. As he said, 'We drove on a couple of miles and the exact same thing happened again. As soon as we had started talking about it, it would go out.' Skelton also added, perhaps with tongue somewhat in cheek, 'Those lights have made good Christians out of a lot of people who weren't before.'

Frank Talbert, a Dallas newspaper columnist, since deceased, also reported that when he tried to inspect the lights they would go out. Whatever the origins of the lights, this interactive quality is one that should be further studied – UFO researcher Harley Rutledge and the teams investigating the lights in the Hessdalen Valley in Norway in the mid-1980s all reported times when the lights they were investigating seemed to be responding either to their wishes or their actions.

Since the original sighting of 1883 there have been many other reports: in 1900 Roy Stillwell watched the lights around what is now the Big Bend National Park; several reports were made by cowboys in 1919; and Ferdinand Weber saw them in 1927 in south eastern Presidio County where he was told they were the ghosts of the Chisos Apaches. In the 1930s Salomon Ramos, a cowboy working near Paisano Peak, watched them on the horizon.

Hallie Stillwell has lived in the Big Bend area for 60 years or more and has seen the lights many times. They were also investigated by author Elton Miles, who also managed to see them during one visit to the area.

Interestingly, the Marfa Lights have chimed in with local folklore on many occasions. As well as the association with the spirits of the Indian tribes, in 1943 there were rumours that the lights were artificial and being used to guide in German supply planes – the story went that the Germans were putting together a massive camp in the desert from which to invade the United States. This rumour inspired Mrs Eva Kerr Jones to recall a tale from 1918, during World War I, when it was also believed that the lights were the preparation for an attack on the United States. Specific and highly unreliable 'identities' have been put forward for the lights: Pancho Villa in 1914 and the ghost of Adolf Hitler following World War II are perhaps the most extraordinary. It shows the ease with which a phenomenon which probably has a natural cause can create all manner of folklore; and since English history going back much further in terms of documented reports it is highly likely that similar lights are the source of at least some 'white lady' and 'black monk' legends.

The Marfa Lights have even given rise to legends within legends. Rumour, quite unsubstantiated, has it that during World War II pilots were killed chasing the lights into the mountains, and that on one occasion a jeep chasing the lights went missing and when it was located, nothing was found of its passengers but one sock! Alternatively the jeep had scientists aboard who were either melted, never found or found in a state of hysteria. At least the source of these stories has in all probability been tracked down: C.W. Davis of McCamey told this story to Charles Nichols in 1972: 'One of the people involved was a personal friend of mine. He told me that him and two of his buddies were sort of drunk and decided to look for the lights. They stole a jeep, which they wrecked. They were afraid of getting caught, so they set fire to the jeep and sneaked back to the air base.'

Legends which are more akin to ghost stories include this one, told by Mrs W.T. Giddens: 'I've seen the ghostlights all my life and can't remember their causing any harm other than fright. They like to follow you out in the pasture at night, seem to be drawn to people and stock, and animals don't seem to fear them at all.' Mrs Giddens explained that her father had once been lost in a blizzard and that the lights had somehow communicated to him that he was off his trail and heading in the wrong direction; they led him to safety in a small cave where he sheltered for the night with the largest of the lights staying close beside him. The lights were able to communicate that they were spirits from long ago. In the morning he woke up to find that their description of his error was exactly correct and that he had survived both the blizzard and being lost and was able to get home very easily from where the lights had led him. There are similar stories of the lights leading cowboys to safety in Presidio County.

Another legend has it that the lights are the ghost of a rancher who once owned the area and that they shine on his birthday, though in fact they do not have that degree of regularity.

Many ghost-related explanations of the lights are linked to the native Indians of the area. One version holds that a group of Indians were ambushed and killed and only their scout escaped; the lights are supposed to represent the scout who is still trying to find his people. Another legend has it that the lights are the ghost of Chisos Apache chief Alsate. He and his tribe were betrayed in

Mexico and enslaved, after which he managed to escape. After his death he continued to protect his tribe by guiding them with his lighted spirit.

When the pioneers 'opened up the west' *they* in turn became the source for the legends of the lights. One story, told by Beau White of Marfa, was related to him by his grandfather: in the Davis Mountains in the 1850s Mexican bandits destroyed the home of a rancher, raped his wife and daughter and left the whole family to die, running off into the Mitchell Flats to hide their loot. The rancher returned home to discover the devastation wreaked on his family and chased the bandits, cornering them in a cave where he shot them and burned them alive. The Marfa Lights are said to be either the Mexicans coming back to look for their hidden spoils or the rancher looking for his money with his lantern swinging in his hand.

Similarly, the lights are said to be the camp fires of a ghostly wagon train that was wiped out by Indians during settlement days whilst a far less likely-sounding legend has it that a Texas woodcutter chopped down a tree that fell on him and killed him, smashing off his arms and legs. The Marfa Lights are his limbs trying to find his body!

The Miller's House
  D: 1840
  L: Willington, Tyne and Wear
  S: A. Gould & A.D. Cornell
In 1840 ghostlight phenomena were reported in a miller's house, owned by a Quaker, Mr Joseph Proctor, at Willington, near Newcastle-upon-Tyne. One particular room in the house was said to be haunted by disembodied human sounds and strange blue lights, which would 'render it impossible to be occupied as a sleeping apartment'. Various animal hauntings were reported; we have included these in section 16, 'Ghostly Animals' (see p. 347).

In order to test the phenomenon Dr Edward Drury visited the mill with a friend on 3 July 1840. The house was securely locked up and examined and Dr Drury sat on the third-storey landing waiting for the phenomenon to manifest itself. At around ten minutes to midnight there was a noise which sounded like the pattering of bare feet on the floor. They could hear what sounded like coughing in the haunted room although it was empty and they heard a rustling sound coming up the stairs.

At a quarter to one Dr Drury saw the figure of a woman dressed in grey clothing. Her head was slightly bowed and one hand was pressed on her chest as if she was in pain. The right hand pointed towards the floor, the index finger pointing downward. The apparition approached Dr Drury cautiously and pointed towards his friend who was sleeping nearby. Drury then rushed towards the apparition, giving 'a most awful yell' but found nothing of substance and ended up collapsing on his friend; for the next three hours he could recall nothing. During this period he was carried down the stairs in a state of fear and terror. Dr Drury later said that he was surprised how unaffected he had been. The only lasting effect was a 'dullness' in his hearing.

The Min Min Light
D: 1912 and others

L: Western Queensland, Australia

S: BOLIDE

For hundreds of years a light phenomenon has plagued the Winton-Boulia area of Queensland, Australia. It appears as an oval fluorescent light, sometimes stationary but often hovering or bouncing and rolling in the air. It has been chased by people both on horseback and in motor vehicles but has never been caught and on one or two occasions *it* has done the chasing. It appears to have many similarities to the Marfa Lights of Texas (see pp. 331–4).

There is no regular times or seasons when the light is guaranteed to appear; it is seen in different months and during different phases of the moon. There have been periods of several years when no sightings have been reported. So convincing is it that there have been reports of people seeing the light approaching and believing it to be a nearby car; in expectation of the imminent arrivals, they have put a pot of coffee on the camp fire to welcome them, only to discover that there is no one around.

One sighting in 1912 was recorded by the manager of Warenda Station on whose property the Min Min Hotel is built. Mr Henry G. Lamond reported seeing the light one night in the middle of winter, either June or July. He was on horseback, having left Warenda Station to ride 27 miles to Slashers Creek for lamb marking the following day. At around two o'clock in the morning, with a cold wind in the air, Lamond was singing to himself to break the monotony. The Min Min Light appeared on the road ahead coming from the direction of Winton. When he first saw it the light appeared to be approximately half a mile away and too high above the road for it to have been a vehicle. The light was green in colour, floating and casting a glow all around. Lamond's horse was not disturbed in any way by the sight. Lamond pointed out that had it been a car approaching she would have been nervous. The light eventually came so close that by its illumination Lamond could see the hairs on his forearm. Suddenly the light went out. Although the horse had remained passive throughout the encounter when Lamond struck a match to light a cigarette the horse reacted violently.

Another report of the light came from a stockman riding to the local police station after the old Min Min Hotel had been burnt down sometime between 1916 and 1918. It was approximately ten o'clock in the evening when the stockman was riding to Boulia, passing close by the Min Min graveyard. In the middle of the cemetery the witness saw a strange glow which increased in size and hovered over the graveyard. The stockman became afraid and spurred his horse to gallop as fast as possible to Boulia but the light seemed to follow him. Only just outside Boulia did the light disappear. The report was substantiated by two other people who had also seen the light; they had attempted to follow it only to discover that it was now attempting to follow *them* after they had turned off the track and given up the chase. It disappeared before making any contact.

A station hand made a further report just a few nights later. He too had apparently seen the light rising out of the graveyard – confirmation of the earlier sighting.

In 1981 Queensland Commissioner for Police, N.W. Bouer, received what he described as 'perhaps the best authenticated recording of this remarkable phenomenon' from Det. Sgt. Lyall Bowth of the police Stock Investigation Squad at Cloncurry. Bowth said that he had seen the Min Min Light near Boulia when he had been with members of the Long Reach Stock Squad. They were approximately 60 kilometres east of Boulia on the road to Winton. On 27 April 1981 they were at a paddock at Bulla

Bulla and had set up camp. On 2 May they decamped and that afternoon only Bowth and the camp cook, a 40-year-old part-aboriginal woman, were left. Bowth went to bed around 8 p.m. on the night of Saturday, 2 May and read for about an hour before going to sleep. He had not been drinking that day. At approximately eleven o'clock he woke up and saw a light that he first took to be a car headlight some 1,500 to 2,000 metres northeast of his position. The light was away from the main road, near the Hamilton River channel and somewhat below tree-top level. It may not have been moving but gave the impression of movement by fluctuating in intensity. Bowth watched it for about half an hour, realising it was probably the Min Min Light. He went to sleep again but woke up at one o'clock in the morning. He saw that the light was now where the cook was camped, which meant it had moved approximately 1.000 metres from where he had seen it before. Its bright white intensity had now dimmed to a yellow colour. It illuminated the ground below but was too far away from Bowth for him to identify details. Bowth watched the light for five or six minutes when it suddenly dived towards the ground and extinguished itself. He did not see it again. The following morning Bowth checked with the cook but she had not seen anything, having slept through the night. She confirmed that no one had visited the camp.

Det. Sgt. Bowth investigated the phenomenon the following morning and concluded that it had not been a camp fire, no mirages were likely and there were no vehicle tracks anywhere that could have accounted for the light.

A 'Moped' in a Field
D: 1976
L: Warminster, Wiltshire
S: Direct

On Friday 8 October 1976 four members of the Dagenham Paranormal Research Group – Andy Collins, Barry and Stephen King, and Alan Denham – were a few miles north of Warminster, to the east of the hamlet of Upton Scudamore, at just after 3 a.m. when they saw a so-called 'spooklight'. The party were driving slowly along a country road when directly to the right of the car they saw a bright light approximately 100 yards away and some four to five feet off the ground. It seemed to be approximately eight inches wide, round in shape, brilliant white and dancing up and down. It was a very foggy night and the light came out of the fog and illuminated both the ground and the air.

The light appeared to be approaching the party.

They thought it might be the headlamp of a farmer on a moped coming to turn them off his land. As Andy Collins wrote in a letter to the authors in November 1991, 'Of importance to the story was the sense of disinterest among all witnesses at the time of the sighting, almost as if it could wait. Sort of, "Oh, look, there's a strange light. Must be the farmer come to throw us off his farm."'

They kept the light in sight and it continued to act as if it were the headlight of a moped driving over a ploughed field. They eventually lost sight of the light when it was blocked by a row of trees.

In the morning they inspected the area but could find no moped tracks.

Andy and his colleagues are familiar with modern interpretations of such phenomena and in his letter he makes the point that the light was seen in an area associated with 'crop circle' formations (which often have associated light phenomena) and also points out that Barry King is 'a powerful psychic with a history of UFO events'. The reporters believed that it was a similar phenomenon to the 'phantom motorcyclist' seen in the same area and reported in Arthur Shuttlewood's book *The Flying Saucerers*.

The Mother of Gold

D: Since 1830, including 1980
L: Various places in Brazil
S: BOLIDE

The Mother of Gold, or *Mae de Ouro*, is a ghostlight that has been reported for over 150 years in various areas of Brazil. It is described as a slow-moving, yellow-orange glowing ball about the size of a human head. According to the legend, if you follow the Mother of Gold and look in the first body of water it crosses, you will discover your fortune in gold.

Cynthia Luce reported a sighting of the Mother of Gold in June 1980, early one evening. She lives in a remote mountain village on 66 acres of land which she bought very cheaply, apparently because the land was haunted; indeed the locals laughed behind her back for purchasing haunted land at any price!

On the evening in question Luce was with her daughter, two maids and a gardener. The yellow-orange ball passed from east to west, wavering like a butterfly some five feet off the ground, and around thirty feet away from them. The gardener attempted to touch it at which point the ball faded away, reappearing some fifteen feet ahead of him. Convinced this indicated intelligence, he became unnerved and did not try again.

Although Luce never saw the light again, she noted that several of her servants also saw it and she received many reports from local villagers who had heard that she was collecting the reports. She explained to them that such light phenomena were regarded as natural and not paranormal. Whether they were convinced is another question!

The Penanggal
D: 1895
L: Changkat Asah, Malaya
S: Sir George Maxwell (*In Malay Forests*)

In Malaya there is a belief that when a woman dies in childbirth she sometimes becomes a particularly hideous spirit known as a *penanggal* (which means literally 'that which is detached'). According to tradition, during the night her head and a small part of her entrails break free from the grave and fly flame-coloured through the countryside, the open mouth sucking the blood and life from any man falling within its powers. This apparition can only exist at night and must return to the grave before daybreak. Should it become lost or delayed it is destroyed. Legend has it that the destroyed remains of a *penanggal* are found, perhaps caught in thorn bushes, in the materialised form of the head of the woman it once was.

This would appear to be a legend similar to earthlights or spooklights in England and America and those will-o'-the-wisp lights that may be responsible for 'white nun' and 'black monk' apparitions.

One report of the *penanggal* lights was made in 1895 by Sir George Maxwell. He was quartered approximately a mile away from a hill called Changkat Asah, which was the object of a great deal of superstition among the Malay people. The hill was reputed to be the abode of spirits; it was held that no one could survive on its slopes after dark. 'Every *jin* and *efrit* known to the Eastern mind: the malignant demons that change their form at will; the familiar spirits of sorcerers; heads of women that roam the forest to suck the blood of men; the voice-folk whom all can hear and none may see – every kind of spirit lived on Changkat Asah. The mass of stone that forms its highest point was said to be a *bilek ahntu*, "a spirit room". The Malays believed that this formless mass took shape at night; and men have told me that the lights in this meeting room of the spirits might occasionally be seen from the plain below.'

Maxwell recounts the story of the unfortunate Beginda Sutan, who undertook night work on the hill against the warnings of the local people. Unable to persuade them to join him, he decided to shame them into doing so by staying on the hill alone. When the men returned the next morning they found him raving mad. Maxwell met Beginda Sutan once and confirmed that he was deranged as a result of his experiences. Even to that time he had never been able to describe what had happened on the hill.

Maxwell himself 'staked out' the hill one night, although on this occasion he was not looking for spirits but for a tiger which had terrorised an officer. Suddenly Maxwell saw two lights far up in the Bernam Valley, moving towards the village. Suddenly the lights rushed towards him as if aimed directly at him and sped by within 50 feet. The tiny lights turned to firey globes the size of a human head and moved at terrific speed. Maxwell wrote that he could see the lights were a natural phenomenon (either chemical gases or electric fluids) – either something akin to will-o'-the-wisp or St Elmo's fire.

During the night he saw several more such lights moving down the valley and at one point over a hundred could be seen dancing around, floating lazily or whizzing rapidly, depending on the currents of air that were moving them. Whatever Maxwell's belief about the phenomenon, he was sure that this must have been what had sent Beginda Sutan mad. As Maxwell pointed out, given

Sutan's cultural conditioning, he had interpreted the lights – which were quite beautiful – as evil spirits and must have thought he would spend his remaining life lost amongst the ghosts.

When Maxwell told an important government official of his sightings he was told that he was lucky to have survived. The *penanggal* had indeed originated from the old graveyards.

The Phantom Hummer
    D: c. 1986 and others
    L: Dylife, mid Wales
    S: BOLIDE

Dylife is a small hamlet in the Cambrian Mountains of mid-Wales which was once a famous mining village. The mine shafts and horizontals are still there.

As reported in the *Cambrian News* on 14 November 1986, a man, known only as 'Jeff', was investigating the old mine workings. He had some experience of old workings and was not afraid to be down there. While he was walking through a horizontal, shining a flashlight before him, he heard a humming noise ahead of him which he described as being like somebody's voice. Assuming that there was somebody else in the tunnel, he called out but got no response. The humming appeared to be coming from the other side of a pool of water and he shone the torch in that direction. Ahead of him was only blank rock though the noise still seemed to be coming from there. He turned off the lamp, reasoning logically that if anyone else was in the tunnel they would have to have a lamp too and that he would be able to see them.

Ahead of him he saw 'a white or a pale blue shape about the size of a small man. It gave off a sort of glow, but not like a torch.' Jeff, quite reasonably, beat a hasty retreat out of the mine. Jeff heard later that lights had occasionally been seen emerging from the mine at night and moving off slowly into the sky.

Spooklights
    D: Many sightings, investigated 1970
    L: Whittington, New Jersey, USA
    S: Various

Near Whittington in New Jersey, America, there is a disused

railway track (since taken up). According to local legend, the track is haunted by the ghost of a railway employee who can be seen walking along it swinging his lantern.

While there have been few reputable reports of the apparition of the man, sightings of 'the lantern' have been quite frequent. The light is described as approximately eighteen inches across, globular and with an inner, deeper glowing core.

It has been suggested that the legend grew up from the appearance of the lights and that they are due to a geological fault running parallel to the old railroad track which, when under strain, creates the light phenomenon known as 'earthlights' (or 'spooklights' in the USA).

A UFO Sighted

D: 1931
L: Alton, Hampshire
S: T.C. Lethbridge

In *The Essential T.C. Lethbridge* part of a chapter is devoted to the subject of UFOs, unidentified flying objects. Having had a sighting of *something* at Alton in Hampshire while driving from Fareham to his mother's house at Bracknell in the summer of 1931, Lethbridge seemed very unclear as to what category to put it into. This underlines the problem of the artificial barriers which researchers have put up around certain aspects of the paranormal. What Lethbridge described was a ball of light, but he seems unsure as to whether it ought to be regarded as a UFO on the grounds that, '*The only experience I have ever had was not of a kind to inspire belief in visitors from another planet or anything of that nature.*' Of course serious UFO researchers do not expect every single UFO to contain aliens, but UFOs remain a valid phenomenon for study nonetheless. Many researchers, however, regard ball-of-light phenomena as ghost phenomena and there have certainly been close correlations between the two when balls of light have been seen in churchyards and even in buildings, sometimes in conjunction with apparitions. Equally, they are said to represent souls or astral bodies, so it is not surprising that there should be a difficulty in classification.

Lethbridge's sighting is a fairly basic one and one that recurs many times in this section. Whether it does represent anything to do with ghost phenomena is arguable; nonetheless since such sightings will have been the stimulus for at least some ghost reports it is important that this category be examined.

As Lethbridge was approaching Alton he turned a bend and looked down a lane to his left. Approximately twelve feet above the middle of the lane he could see a shining disc or globe. It looked bigger than the moon (as we normally see it) and was much the same colour. It was slowly descending towards the lane. Lethbridge did not see it hit the ground as he was passing by very quickly and it was only later that he wondered whether he ought to have stopped to see what had happened and whether it had left any traces.

Lethbridge had various theories about the sighting: one person at Cambridge suggested it was ball-lightning; he himself believed it might be an incandescent ball of gas but he said, clearly with the extraterrestrial hypothesis in mind, that he didn't think this was a UFO or flying saucer. It very likely wasn't a flying saucer but it certainly was a UFO as it was unidentified, appears to have been flying and if not an object certainly appeared to have been flying and if not an object certainly appeared to have objective reality. But there are those who, with a different frame of mind at the time, might have seen the same thing and believed it to be the soul of one departed or whatever. No one is yet qualified to make definite comments either way.

A White Lady

D: 1920
L: Wadsley Common, Sheffield, S. Yorkshire
S: Various

Wadsley is in the northwest of Sheffield in South Yorkshire and in 1920 became momentarily famous for its white-lady ghost. She was seen in Worrall, Wadsley and Loxley but thought to originate on Wadsley Common. She glided silently around, raising her arms in lament. According to the legend, the lady walks, if 'walks' be the word, between nine and eleven at night.

As reported in the *Sheffield Daily Independent* of 5 February 1920, Clarence Swain was out walking with his sister when they saw the figure. Both he and his sister were alarmed by the sight and Swain commented, 'Me nervous! I was never feared before of man or spirits but if that wasn't a spirit I am beat.'

A miner, John Grayson, also saw the ghost on the same spot, again with its arms waving in the air as if in despair. Many others also claimed to have seen the ghost.

Despite the very human-like description of this 'white lady', local researchers are convinced that this particular report belongs in the category of 'white nun' apparitions which can be explained as leaks of natural energy from the earth. Almost certainly the apparition of Wadsley Common consists either of emissions of earthlights or, more likely in this case, will-o'-the-wisps caused by the release of underground gasses. These swirling elongated shapes can appear very human-like and to someone alone in a desolate area late at night it is all too easy to begin to see faces and movements of limbs.

Mary Helena Williams

D: 1884
L: Eston-in-Cleveland
S: *Journal of the SPR* (1894)

On 23 September 1889 Mary Helena Williams, known to her family as 'Lily', reported a ghostlight. The report is corroborated by her sister Isabella.

This is Miss Williams's own account as told to the Society for Psychical Research. 'I was living at home with my parents at Eston-in-Cleveland. There was a working man called Long living in the village, not far from our house, whose wife was taken ill. Dr Fulton, who at that time was staying with us, came in one night between nine and ten o'clock and said Mrs Long was dying. After that we sat talking over the fire for a good while, and then my sister Isabella and I went off to bed. We slept in a back bedroom, and after we got to this bedroom I said, "Oh, I've forgotten something in the large bedroom." To this latter I proceeded by myself, and, as I approached the door, something seemed to say to me, "You'll see something of Mrs Long, living or dead." But I thought no more of this, and entered the bedroom, which I had to cross to the opposite end for what I wanted. When I had got the things in my hand I noticed a lovely light hanging over my head. It was a round light – perfectly round. I had taken no light with me, but went for the things I wanted in the dark. I looked to see if there was any light coming in from the windows, but there was none – in that direction there was total darkness. I grasped one hand with the other and stood looking at the strange light to be sure that I was not deceived and was not imagining it. I walked across the room to the door and all the way the light was hanging between my head and the ceiling. It was a palish blue. It emitted no rays, so that all the rest of the room was in darkness. It was wider in circumference than my head, so that as I walked I could see it above me without raising my head. As I left the room it remained, and when I looked again was gone. It was in a corner, where the darkness of the room was deepest and the least chance for illumination from the windows on the right and left and I first saw it above my head. I had no fear, but a kind of sacred awe. The light was unlike any other that I ever saw, and I should say brighter than any other, or, at least, purer. Looking at it did not affect the eyes. It was akin to the electric light: something of a cloud, though every part of it was beaming and running over with the light. It left me at the bedroom door. On first seeing it a strange impression seized me, and after it left me I was so impressed that I could not speak of it to anyone for a day or two. I wondered at the time whether it had anything to do with Mrs Long, and on inquiry I found that she died just about the time when I saw the light. If there was any difference, I judged it would be a little before, but there would not be much in it. This was about 11 p.m. and about four years ago. It left an impression on my mind which I have never forgotten, and shall never forget. Mrs Long was not ill many days – about two or three – she died rather suddenly. I was rather interested in her. I did not see her during her illness, but had often seen her and talked to her before. I was perfectly well at the time and was in no trouble or anxiety. My age at the time was twenty-three. I have had no experience of the kind before or since. I saw no figure, only a lovely light. Before telling my sister, I made her promise she would not ridicule me nor call me superstitious.'

Isabella added: 'I recollect my sister Lily seeing the bright light. When she came back to the room where I was she was quite pale, and sat down on the floor. She was so awestruck that she did not tell us what she had seen until the next day. I remember that a woman who lived near us died about the time my sister saw the light, and that we connected the two circumstances together.'

16
Ghostly Animals

Whether or not ghosts are the spirits of the dead, recordings of actions from the past, visions of other times or any of the other possible explanations offered by the cases in this encyclopedia, not all ghosts are perceived to be human. There are many reports of ghostly animals and this section contains reports of ghostly tigers, birds, cats, snakes, bears, and even a butterfly. Most common of all are the black dogs which form perhaps the most frequently reported body of animal-ghost legends across the UK (with even the occasional headless black dog to turn legend into pure horror!). In truth, it is difficult to be certain with such claims where reality stops and legend takes over.

The Animal Companions of Rosemary Brown

D: 20th century
L: Balham, London
S: Rosemary Brown

In her book, *Look Beyond Today*, Rosemary Brown, an extraordinary medium who claims a great many contacts with artists of various varieties, devotes a small chapter to her involvement with animal spirits. She writes, 'One of my earliest memories is of seeing a cheetah.' Apparently he was with her all the time and she treated him as a pet. As Ms Brown got older so the cheetah's visits became less frequent, but later he was replaced by another big cat.

Ms Brown was sitting up one night comforting her husband who could not sleep because of chronic asthma when she suddenly became aware of a heavy weight lying on her legs. She could sense purring and could smell the smell of a tiger. Indeed she then saw a huge tiger lying across her lap. Her husband asked her to describe the tiger, which he apparently could not see.

When she described its markings her husband identified it as Sabrina, a tiger cub owned by his family while they were abroad. Her husband's family had been in Egypt and had cared for Sabrina, sharing their home with her.

Sabrina's ghost apparently made several visits to the family and, according to Rosemary Brown, would appear at times when the house was empty, as if to guard it.

Rosemary Brown also reports two experiences of seeing snakes in spirit form: on one occasion she saw a hooded cobra that her husband and his father had cared for in the past, whilst a vision of several snakes would appear when Rosemary Brown was with a particular second cousin. Apparently one of the cousin's boyfriends had worked with a snake act in the circus.

In Switzerland, Rosemary had seen a vision of a brown bear – very friendly – standing in her bedroom doorway. Following the teachings of animal trainer Barbara Woodhouse, she apparently blew in the animal's face and the creature cheerfully ambled away and disappeared!

Black Dogs

D: Many sightings
L: Various
S: Various

Black dogs are the most frequently reported ghostly animals. In fact they are treated as something of a phenomenon in their own right. There are so many reports that only a sample are included here and occasionally only a mention of the local name in order to show the widespread nature of this subject.

Sax Rohmer spent a night in Peel Castle on the Isle of Man where a legendary phantom dog haunts the underground passages near the guardrooms. Reports of the dog were so frequent that it almost became a normal part of the guardsmen's lives, although they insisted on giving it a wide berth. One guardsman, entering the guardroom alone, ran back to his colleagues obviously very frightened but was never able to speak about what he had seen in the short life remaining to him.

Rohmer heard doglike howls coming from inside the blocked-up passageway where the guardroom had been.

Rohmer believed that the dog dated from early pagan rituals.

Daniel Cohen's *Encyclopedia of Ghosts* tells of the black dog which haunts the Vaughan family, its appearances heralding the death of one of them. One of the Vaughan children contracted smallpox. At dinner his mother said she would go upstairs to look after him. She came down saying the child was asleep but asking her husband to go up and drive off a large black dog that was lying on the bed. She had not been told of the family legend, to avoid worrying her, but her husband feared the worst; he went upstairs and could find no dog. The child was already dead.

In Budleigh Hill, Somerset a black dog was seen in 1907, with 'great big fiery eyes as big as saucers'. A very similar description is given of Barguest, the black dog of Trollers Gill in Yorkshire.

A farmer on Dartmoor heard an animal behind him which turned out to be a large black dog. He tried to stroke it but the creature had substance and ran off; 'a stream of sulphurous vapour issued from its throat'. When the farmer chased it it exploded in a blinding flash!

This phenomenon of bursting into flames seems to have close links with fireballs, balls of light and ball-lightning. Contact with such energies may well cause combustion and harm to the recipient. They may, however, represent nothing paranormal but rather something that we do not yet understand.

In Somerset a black dog haunts the road from St Audries to Perry Farm and appears to people just before their deaths.

Black Shuck is a Norfolk black dog with just a single eye that burns like a lantern; where he has been there is burning and the smell of brimstone.

In Aylesbury, Buckinghamshire, a farmer struck out in the dark at the glowing eyes of a black dog; it instantly vanished.

In Hatfield Peverell in Essex the driver of a wagon on a country lane struck a large black dog which exploded, setting both him and his wagon alight.

Old Shock is the Suffolk variety of black dog, described by a local writer as, 'A mischievous goblin in the shape of a great dog, or of a calf, haunting highways and footpaths in the dark. Those who are so foolhardy as to encounter him are thought to be at least thrown down and severely bruised, and it is well if they do not get their ankle sprained or broken; of which instances are recorded and believed.'

One dog is known as the Padfoot of Northern England and has huge saucer eyes and backward pointing feet.

A ghost dog named Shriker, also known as Trach, of Burnley, often presaged death to those who saw it. It was a large shaggy animal with broad feet that made a splashing sound as it walked. It could disappear instantaneously.

One or two of these cases can be told in a little more detail.

The British composer Lionel Monckton died in 1924. A group of Monckton's friends had been sitting in their club when one of them, Donald Calthrop, said to the others that he thought something might have happened to Monckton. They dismissed this idea. Suddenly Calthrop saw a dog in the corner of the room which he believed was Monckton's dog (the animal was often brought into the club). No one else could see the dog and they all thought that Calthrop was joking. However, some hours later the news came of Monckton's unexpected death which had occurred at about the same time that Calthrop had seen his spirit dog.

The most horrific black dog encounter took place in Bungay in Suffolk. On the morning of Sunday 4 August 1577, there was a violent thunderstorm while many of the townsfolk were in church. Inside the church a black dog appeared, illuminated by the lightning flashes and seen by the whole congregation. It ran down the central aisle and through the people, reportedly striking dead two people who had been praying. It is also said to have run into a third person who shrivelled up *like a drawn purse* but remained alive, as well as breaking the church clock and scratching the stone and metal-work of the doorway. The event is recorded on the market weathervane which shows a hideous and demonic black dog, wide-eyed and slavering.

Even more remarkably a similar black dog is said to have run through a church at Blythburgh, only seven miles away, killing three people and seriously affecting others. Marks on the Blythburgh church door were clearly visible. The Surrey puma and the Pooka of Ireland are 'black dogs' too.

Almost inevitably, this ghost phenomenon has its own subsection – *headless* black dogs.

In 1825 a headless dog haunted the streets of Manchester and appeared outside an old church, terrifying a tradesman named Drabble by putting its paws on his shoulders and running him back to his house at fierce speed.

The humpbacked bridge at Ivelet in Swaledale is haunted by a headless black dog which apparently foretells tragedy. It glides on to the bridge and disappears over the edge. The bridge lies on the Corpse Way, the path used for bringing the dead down to the church, and this may have some bearing on the story.

The Black Frog of John of Clanranald
D: Late 17th century
L: Moidart, Scottish Highlands
S: Ben Noakes

In 1679 John of Clanranald became the twelfth chief of his clan based at Tioram in Moidart on the west coast of the Scottish Highlands. He was not a particularly pleasant person; once shooting two clansmen to demonstrate his abilities with a rifle.

As a result of committing some evil act, he apparently became obsessed with the idea that he was being haunted by a huge black frog. In an effort to escape this supernatural creature he sailed to the Outer Hebrides, where he owned land, but found the frog waiting for him when he landed. According to one of his descendants, the present captain of Clanranald (who happily has no such creature threatening him!), John of Clanranald even locked the frog up in a cell, apparently without much effect.

In the end, it seems the frog turned out to be useful: during a storm off Iagg, the nearest major island to Moidart, John was apparently persuaded by his crew to take the frog on board and the storm died away, saving everyone from drowning.

Bolingbroke Castle
D: (No date)
L: Lincolnshire
S: Christina Hole

Bolingbroke Castle in Lincolnshire is reputedly haunted by the spirit of a witch who was imprisoned there and who takes the form of a hare. The ancient source of the story, the *Harleian MS* says: 'One thing is not to be passed by, affirmed as a certain truth by many of ye inhabitants of ye Towne upon their owne knowledge, which is that ye Castle is Haunted by a certain spirit in ye likeness of a Hare which, at ye meetings of ye Auditors doeth usually run between their legs, and sometymes overthrows them, and so passes away. They have pursued it downe into ye Castle yard and seene it take in at a grate into a low Cellar, and have followed it thither with a light, where, not withstanding that they did most narrowly observe it (and that there was noe other passage out, but by ye doore or windowe, ye room being all above framed of stones within, not having ye least chink or crevice) yet they could never find it.'

It was also claimed that dogs chased the spectral hare, only to become absolutely terrified when it disappeared in front of them.

Cherry
D: 1974
L: Tapiola, nr. Helsinki, Finland
S: Andrew MacKenzie

Cherry was a boxer dog owned by Mrs Pia Virtakallio of Finland. At the time of this incident Mrs Virtakallio was living in Tapiola near Helsinki. Sensing somebody looking at her, she turned her head and saw in the hallway her boxer dog Cherry, to whom she had always been very attached. However, Cherry had died two years earlier and as she realised this the dog vanished. Mrs Virtakallio said that although Cherry had died aged eleven, she believed that when she saw her the apparition had the appearance of a two-year-old dog. Mrs Virtakallio did not have a pet at the time of the sighting so could not have mistaken some other dog for Cherry.

William Courtney
D: 1953
L: Sarina, W. Australia
S: Daniel Cohen

In 1953 William Courtney was living in Sarina in northern Australia. He had just had to have his greyhound, Lady, of whom he had been very fond, destroyed.

On the night that the dog had been put down Courtney heard footsteps pattering along the passageway from his front door. He heard the footsteps enter the room and could hear what sounded like a heavy mass dropping on to the floor next to his bed. Courtney expected to see Lady stretched out on the floor next to him but on turning on the light discovered the room was empty.

Courtney had heard the noise at the time when Lady usually came in for the night.

Whether or not this was just wishful thinking or auditory hallucination caused by grief is of course open to question but in many similar cases there is really no doubt in the minds of the percipients. Occasionally there is even some corroboration as in the case of 'Red' (see pp. 357–8).

The Dower House
D: 1968
L: Killackee, S. Ireland
S: Daniel Cohen

The Dower House in Killackee, Ireland was used as an art centre by artist and poet Margaret O'Brien and her husband Nicholas. They bought it in 1968. Workmen renovating the building after a period of disuse were troubled by the appearance of a large black cat.

Mrs O'Brien dismissed their claims as 'nonsense', the result of 'country people alone in an empty house in a lonely location, at night telling each other stories, thereby frightening themselves'.

She apparently changed her mind when she saw the creature for herself. It was a black cat about as big as a medium-sized dog and it was squatting in the hallway. All the doors of the house had been locked prior to its appearance and remained so on inspection afterwards.

One of the workmen, Tom McAssey, was working with two other men when he suddenly felt the previously warm room become icy cold; the locked door now stood open. A shadowy figure stood in the darkness outside and when McAssey shouted, 'Come in, I see you,' to it, thinking it was someone playing a joke, there was a deep guttural growling noise causing all three workmen to run in panic. They slammed the door shut but it instantly opened again and a monstrous black cat with red and orange eyes was seen crouching outside. McAssey also reported seeing another shadowy figure which said, '*You cannot see me. You don't even know who I am,*' in a deep voice.

Mrs O'Brien had an exorcism ceremony performed in the house in 1968 and all was quiet for around a year. Unfortunately actors staying at the centre in 1969 held a seance which seems to

have 'opened the door' to other disturbance though the black cat
is not reported to have reappeared.

Drayton Church
D: 1749

L: Uxbridge, London

S: Christina Hole

During the eighteenth and nineteenth centuries Drayton Church
near Uxbridge was reported to be haunted by a large black bird.
In 1749 noises were heard in the vaults under the church and a
raven was seen in the church itself. Some of the bell-ringers
cornered it in the roof where it behaved just like any frightened
bird. However, when two of the men reached out to grab it, it
disappeared in front of their eyes. They were quite adamant that
it had not escaped, it had simply vanished into thin air.

There was also a report made to the parish clerk by three men
who said that they had seen a bird sitting on a coffin in one of the
vaults and pecking at the wood; the parish clerk had also seen it.
However there is no evidence in this particular report of anything
spectral other than, possibly, by association.

In 1869 ladies arranging flowers on the altar saw the large black
bird perching in one of the pews.

In 1883 Mrs De Burgh, many members of whose family lay in
the vault below, heard the sound of a large bird fluttering in the
chancel though she did not see it.

The most common explanation of the bird was that it was the
spirit of a murderer who had committed suicide. There have been
no reports of it for many years.

A Horse on the Stairs
D: 1940

L: (Not given)

S: Peter Underwood

Peter Underwood, President of the Ghost Club, outlined this case in
his autobiography having discovered it when he was in the army.

A large country house had been taken over for army officers.
Apparently a former owner had ridden his horse into the house and
along the hall and then attempted to get it to climb the staircase. The
horse had missed its footing and crashed into the hall below,

crushing two guests and breaking the necks of both horse and rider.

Tradition had it that the ghostly figure mounted on a white charger had been seen in the upper rooms of the house, suggesting that the rider and his horse persisted in their attempts to reach the top landing *postmortem*. It has even been suggested that the apparition of the ghostly horse was what caused the other horse to miss its footing. Whatever the nature of the apparition, various officers heard the sound of the horse moving along the hall, and up the stairs, the sounds always ceasing before reaching the top.

Underwood himself 'staked out' the house but heard nothing, though apparently the sounds came back just a few evenings later; witnesses heard the horse coming up the drive, they stood in the open doorway and must have been surprised to hear the sounds actually pass them and go into the house. One officer even claimed that he could see the horse and rider 'in a shadowy kind of way'. Suddenly there was a crack and the landing rail gaped open as if something had fallen through; then there was a dull thud from the hallway below.

Underwood examined the broken landing rail, which seemed to have been damaged by great force; he was left wondering to just what extent the 'supernormal' can affect the physical.

Madame Butterfly
D: 1948
L: Theatre Royal, Bath, Avon
S: Keith Poole

A number of notable ghosts haunt the Theatre Royal in Bath. Theatregoers and actors alike have seen many apparitions of the Grey Lady (indeed Dame Anna Neagle reported seeing her two or three times).

The most extraordinary ghost report from the theatre, though almost certainly an association of the events described below rather than a true paranormal event, is that of a phantom butterfly. In 1948 the theatre hosted a Christmas pantomime which included a butterfly ballet where the dancers were dressed up as tortoiseshell butterflies. A live tortoiseshell butterfly was then seen flying about, which at least had coincidence value, but legend now has it that at every Christmas pantomime since, the butterfly ghost reappears.

The Monkey of Drumlanrig Castle

D: 1700s
L: Dumfriesshire, Scotland
S: Joan Forman

Drumlanrig Castle, owned by the Duke of Buccleuch and dating
from the seventeenth century, has a history of hauntings by some
kind of monkey or ape. In documents dated 1700 there is a room
known as the 'haunted' room or 'yellow monkey' room.

During World War I the castle was commissioned for use as a
hospital and staffed with a matron and nurses. One morning the
matron asked to see the hospital organiser, the wife of the duke's
agent. The matron announced that she would be leaving immediately but would not give a reason. When pressed, she said that she
had '*seen something awful in the night*'. She did not elaborate further
on her reasons for leaving and suggested rather enigmatically that
the resident family would not appreciate her doing so anyway. The
room she had been using was the 'yellow monkey', or 'haunted', room.

The young Lady Alice Montagu-Douglas-Scott, later Princess
Alice, the Dowager Duchess of Gloucester, stayed in the castle as
a child as it was the home of her grandparents. Her mother told
the story of being in the castle with her sister (Princess Alice's
aunt) as a young girl and walking along a long passageway
holding a candle. They saw a furry creature moving towards them
down the corridor and then became alarmed when their candle
blew out leaving them in total darkness. They bolted for their
bedroom and hid inside.

On another occasion Princess Alice's mother was found standing in the hall shaken and white; she claimed that she had just
seen a huge monkey sitting in one of the chairs.

There is no precise explanation for these ghost stories, although it
is known that in those days many animals from far off foreign lands
were kept by the aristocracy as symbols of prestige and curiosity, or
as trophies of foreign conquests and there may have been a time
when a living monkey roamed the castle corridors.

The Old Chapel Lane Cat

D: Early 20th century
L: Ropley, Hampshire
S: Christina Hole

In *The Annals of Old Ropley* Miss Hagen tells of a cottage in Old Chapel Lane which was haunted by a cat. A woman who lived there met the animal several times, either on the stairs or sitting by the fireside; it behaved quite normally, but would then disappear quite suddenly. For a reason not made terribly clear, the lady believed it was her mother's ghost, and was convinced that it walked exactly like her dead mother!

The Phantom Bear
D: 1816
L: Tower of London
S: Christina Hole

In January 1816 (1815 in some accounts) a sentry guarding the Jewel House (now the Martin Tower) in the Tower of London saw a dark form coming towards him up a flight of steps. Incredibly, it was the form of a large bear and when he thrust at it with his bayonet the weapon sliced harmlessly through the body, jamming into the door behind. Unperturbed, the bear simply kept on coming, and the sentry collapsed in a fit. The keeper of the Crown Jewels at the time, Mr Edmund Lenthal Swifte, said: 'His fellow sentinel was with him and testified to having seen him at his post, just before the alarm, awake and alert, and to having spoken to him. Moreover, I then heard the man tell his own story. I saw him once again on the following day, but changed beyond recognition: in another day or two the brave and steady soldier, who could have mounted a breach and led a forlorn hope with unshaken nerves, died, the victim of a shadow.'

It is worth pointing out, however, that at this time the Royal Menagerie was kept at the Tower and contained elephants, lions and bears.

Red
D: 1965
L: (Not given)
S: Raymond Bayliss

Many tales concerning the reappearance of family pets were collected by researcher Raymond Bayliss in his book *Animal Ghosts*. A classic story in the book is that of Mrs Joy Baterski whose Irish setter, Red, died in August 1965. The dog had been in the family for fourteen years and there was much grief at its passing. On the night of the animal's death and burial in the family's yard they heard the very distinctive barking of their pet which they were certain could not have been any other dog. Both Mr and Mrs Baterski heard it and a neighbour confirmed that, Red had a most unusual bark unlikely to be mistaken for another dog. After hearing the dog for over thirteen years the owners would surely have recognised the bark, they thought.

So alarmed was Mrs Baterski that at one point she even asked her husband to dig up the dog's remains in case he was somehow alive and trapped in the ground, but her husband assured her that he must be dead. Over a period of some four weeks they were awakened at least five times.

The barking continued until a new pet was brought into the house, whereupon it stopped.

Rex
  D: 1916 (?)
  L: America (?)
  S: Daniel Cohen

Rex was one of many dogs owned by Albert Terhune, a noted American writer of dog stories. Rex died in 1916. Sometime after the death a friend of the family, the Rev. Appleton Grannis, was staying with the Terhunes. They had not been in touch for some time and the Rev. knew nothing of Rex. While Albert Terhune and the Rev. were talking, the Rev. suddenly saw a dog looking in the window which disappeared by the time Terhune turned to look at it. The Rev. claimed that it was nothing like the dogs he had seen around the house. When he described it, it very clearly matched Rex, including an easily identifiable scar on his face.

It seems that Rex also made another appearance to another friend of the family, Henry Healy. Albert Terhune also noted that other dogs continued to avoid Rex's 'favourite spot'.

The White Birds
  D: 1885
  L: Salisbury Plain, Wiltshire
  S: Christina Hole & various

There is a tradition in Salisbury that whenever the Bishop of
Salisbury dies white birds like albatrosses are seen on Salisbury
Plain. They are believed to be spectral as they apparently glide
through the air without moving their wings.

In 1885 the daughter of the then bishop, a Miss Moberley saw
them rising from the palace garden. Her father died shortly
afterwards.

On 16 August 1911 Miss Edith Olivier saw two large white
birds and noticed that their wings were not moving. She alerted
some boys that were with her in a wagonette, only one of whom
saw them. The wagonette passed under some trees and the birds
had disappeared when they emerged. Miss Olivier was apparently
unaware of the legend of the white birds of Salisbury Plain and
was certainly unaware of the bishop's impending death; indeed
the bishop's own family were not concerned for his health and
were going about their business normally when he died suddenly.
It was on hearing of the legend that she made the connection
between what she had seen and what had happened.

The White Dog
D: No date
L: Walberswick, nr. Southwold, Suffolk
S: Penelope Fitzgerald

Walberswick near Southwold on the Suffolk coast is the location
of a frequently reported white dog thought to have been waiting
for its owner for the past century or so.

One such report comes from the author Penelope Fitzgerald
who was taking a pony across Walberswick Common when it
reacted badly to a white apparition in the bracken which resembled four large milk containers. On closer inspection it appeared
to be a large white dog, 'like a very large pointer', and it was only
afterwards that the witness realised how strange it was that the
dog had managed to get away through the dry bracken without
making a sound.

The witness herself stated that many people do not recognise
ghosts even when they encounter them; it is later that they reflect
on some strange aspect of the encounter. While this is certainly
true it is also true that even at the time people often have some
almost subliminal sense of 'something not quite right' which stays

in their mind. However, it can often take a long time for the realisation of what was 'wrong' to surface.

Willington Mill

D: 1834

L: Nr. Wallsend, Tyne and Wear

S: Daniel Cohen

During the last century Thomas Davidson was courting a girl who lived at Willington Mill near Newcastle (*see also 'The Miller's House'* on pp. 334–5) when he saw a white cat coming towards him. Rather unkindly, he tried to kick it and discovered that his boot went straight through the animal, which promptly disappeared. It reappeared shortly afterwards, this time hopping like a rabbit which must have greatly added to its eerie appearance. Apparently having not yet learnt his lesson, he took another swing at it and went straight through it again. The third time the animal appeared, it seemed determined to frighten Davidson off as it was luminous and the size of a sheep. Davidson's son recalled that his father had been paralysed by the encounter and that his hair had stood on end.

In the furnace room of Willington Mill a Mr Wedgwood reported seeing a spirit tabby cat which also seemed determined to impress the percipient with its eeriness by wriggling like a snake and passing through a solid stone wall.

Over the years, donkeys, dogs, cats and monkeys have all been heard or seen at the mill.

THE PRACTICE OF INVESTIGATING GHOSTS

17

How to Investigate Poltergeists
by Maurice Grosse

Maurice Grosse was the principal investigator in the 'Enfield (Harpers') Poltergeist case'. He is recognised throughout the world as an authority on poltergeist investigation. The following is from an interview given by Maurice exclusively for this book, for which the authors and publishers are grateful. The authors would also like to add a personal note of thanks to Maurice for his help and advice given in respect of cases we have been involved in.

'I use the words 'poltergeist-type' investigation because, let's face it, nobody really knows what a poltergeist is. There are two main theories on poltergeists. The first is the theory popular with run-of-the-mill scientists, if they are interested at all, that poltergeists are the exteriorisation of part of the human personality. This is normally someone in a situation of high stress.

The second theory, and the one that I favour, is a combination of the exteriorisation of personality together with exterior forces at work.

If you were a spiritualist, you would interpret that exterior force as the spirit of somebody who lived and had died; if you incline towards other beliefs, you might say it's some sort of entity that doesn't belong to anything that we understand or know.

The essence of investigating a poltergeist case is first of all to find out whether it's a genuine case or whether it's an aberration of the people involved. In the latter case they may *believe* it's a poltergeist but it's not; it's something that they are doing, something they are manifesting themselves – not paranormally, but normally – yet they don't even know they're doing it.

You can make mistakes very easily in poltergeist cases but they are mistakes that can't be sustained. If there is repetition of events by the poltergeist you can make a mistake once (in the sense that you can be tricked), you can even make a mistake twice but in lots of poltergeist-type cases you get a repetition, not of exactly the same things, but a repetition of something similar from time to time. Then you know it's not a mistake, it's something that's real.

The first thing I do is ask a few questions: if the answers are too pat I start getting a bit worried. If, when they are telling me the story, and I look at them and they appear to be very puzzled by what's happening, then I'm on the road to believing that theirs could be a real case. Those people who come to you and say, 'This and that is happening and it's a spirit of so and so' are often very fixed in their minds. I have this problem very often with spiritualists who may be having very genuine paranormal things happening, but their interpretation is such that they may be misleading not only themselves, but misleading the investigation in part.

Once you are satisfied within your own mind that you have a genuine case on your hands – and your experience is your only real guide – then you have to decide how to investigate it.

First you have to establish a few things. It is my experience that in the majority of poltergeist cases there is always a high-stress factor in the background. I can't think of a case where there has been genuine paranormal activity where there hasn't been some sort of stress factor in the background, even if the witnesses deny it. The chances are, even if they deny it at the beginning, as you go on you will see that a high-stress factor will be somewhere in the background. And this is what I believe appears to cause poltergeist phenomena. I have no explanation as to how or why, I just believe they are caused by a high-stress situation.

I find there is only one direct route to understanding the case, if you can do it. That is to get the people to whom the things are happening involved in their own investigation of their case. In other words, instead of you going in and saying, 'I'm the expert, I've come to sort it out,' you say, 'I've come to help you. And we will try and sort it out together.'

Don't try and give explanations from the word go because it's fatal; the chances are that your explanations right at the start will be rejected if the witnesses are of a different frame of mind. As you go on, you can explain what you *think* a poltergeist is, but never be adamant about it, because there are no certainties. This is where spiritualists make mistakes when they investigate poltergeists. They will say, 'Oh yes, it's the spirit of Aunt Maisie, she's coming back and she is interfering . . . and so forth. I will exorcise her.' Well, it doesn't work like that.

One of the questions that I'm very often asked is, 'Are you psychic?' Whether I am a 'sensitive' or not, I don't know but, in any case, I don't think that has got very much to do with poltergeist cases. Often when I go to a case people say, 'Do you feel something?' I say, 'I'm sorry, I don't feel anything.' I am waiting to see what the situation is and what will happen. Mediums or spiritualists will say, 'Yes, there's so and so here and I can feel it,' and so on. As a scientific investigator, that is fatal. You must never do that.

Once you're sure that you've got a genuine case, the next step is to win the confidence of the people involved. To start with you listen to them, it's that simple. You don't talk to them, you listen to them. A lot of investigators make the mistake of talking *at* the witnesses. They don't want to be talked at, they want to talk to you. So you've got to be a good listener. As you listen you will pick up the story. If they exaggerate you will soon find out.

I must point out that I never use the word 'victim' although it's generally used. I don't think it right because the witnesses aren't victims at all, though they might feel like it for a time. I think most poltergeist cases involve people who are very special and who are having a very special experience.

Once you are involved in a case you've got to have time; there is no question of walking in, walking out and that's the end of that. You've got to go back. Then you hope that you will experience some of the things that they have said that they experienced. With persistence, the chances are quite good that you will.

When that 'something' happens you must determine in your own mind whether it's real or whether you've been caught up in what they have imagined has happened to them.

If you are involved in a case you may get some exaggerated claims thrown at you. You must be ready for that, but be cautious not to dismiss the case just on those grounds.

You don't really get rigged tricks because unless you are an expert conjurer it's very difficult to rig many of the things that happen. This is where I come up against the views of the sceptics and I would say to them that it's very difficult to rig up anything to fool the investigator over a long period of study.

Perhaps when the same thing happens again and again you should start getting suspicious, because very rarely in poltergeist cases do the same things keep on happening. They differ. You may get things flying through the air but they're different things, not the same things. You may get a stone, you may get a coin. You may get a toy aeroplane suddenly flying across, anything. Anything can happen in poltergeist cases. But when they happen they are not quite the same. Rigged-up tricks happen the same all the time. And if anybody is rigging tricks you will catch them out in no time. When the kids played around in the Enfield case (see pp. 272–6), as they occasionally would, kids being what they are, I always knew. After all, you are usually with them for months.

When you are dealing with children you must remember that children always imitate. And once they are used to the real phenomenon, the chances of them having a game with you are pretty high. But you've got to make a judgement then. Because you see something that is faked by a child doesn't mean to say that it's not based on something that's genuine. Kids imitate, we all know that. What you've got to be careful of is if adults do the same thing. Then you have to start rethinking. That said, I qualify this by saying that sometimes when the real stuff *is* happening, and then when you come along nothing happens, sometimes somebody is tempted to do something to impress you; that does happen. But then you have to make a judgement; in other words is what they are exaggerating in front of you based on the truth?

A good comparison is like taking your car to the garage for electrical faults; they never seem to happen when the mechanic is looking at them and you feel tempted to somehow fake it just to show him what's wrong.

When you know the case is genuine and things are happening you have to decide what course of action to take for yourself and the family involved. Are you there to see the phenomena happening, are you there to investigate the case, are you there to make it go away or are you there to look after the family? In some cases welfare comes first because the people are so upset and so frightened; you might then decide to get rid of what's happening there and the only way to get rid of it is, I believe, to reduce the stress. Try and bring out from the background of the family what is worrying them, what's causing their problems. It's not always easy but it's essential. If you don't deal with it the poltergeist activity will go on and on. Sometimes it suddenly disappears, but normally whilst a stress situation is there the thing will go on.

The starting point is to find out who the epicentre is. Sometimes it's not one person, sometimes it's a combination of several. When I find who the focus is I usually suggest to them, can I give them some relaxation hypnotherapy? All you do is put them into a hypnotic trance and calm them down and suggest to them that things are not as bad as they think they are. In the majority of cases this works quite well, especially with children; with adults it's a little bit more difficult.

If that doesn't work you have to get together with the family and say, 'Look, we've got a bit of a problem here. It doesn't seem to be responding. Let's investigate it together. When I am not here you write down everything that happens and then we will try to get rid of it together.' Very often they get so involved in their own case that it starts to disappear; once they start focusing on what's happening and not on their own problems the whole thing becomes an interest to them. The stress levels have been reduced.

The only situation where that doesn't work is when you've got highly superstitious people who are fairly convinced they are being attacked by spirits, witchcraft, black magic, or whatever. When you get into those situations it is very, very tricky indeed. If the witnesses are absolutely set in their own minds as to what is going on then it's very difficult to reduce their stress.

This brings us to exorcism. I've always been in two minds about exorcism. Exorcism is a religious practice and I've never been sure in my own mind just how much religion has got to do with poltergeist activity. If poltergeist activity is a product of the people involved and it's their psychological situation that's causing it, whatever the mechanism, then why bring religion into it at all?

Sometimes exorcism might ease their stress, but sometimes exorcism makes it worse. I have been in situations where an exorcist has been called in and the whole thing has got completely out of hand. On the other hand I've been in cases where exorcism has been used and the happenings have gone away because the people have been satisfied.

There is the question of why poltergeists generally seem to damage property but not seriously hurt people. I think that if the people themselves are – unconsciously or subconsciously – controlling the situation, the poltergeist is not likely to do damage to people, but to damage property is a bit more understandable: frustrated people pick up things and throw them, they don't usually throw something at somebody else. They throw them at the walls or on the floors, in the fireplace. Some people do get hurt, there may be a certain amount of masochism; in some poltergeist cases people are pinched and they come out in bruises. Perhaps they are punishing themselves; you've got deep-rooted complexities at work.

Remember we are dealing with a phenomenon which has, to our knowledge, no explanation as yet. Anybody who says that they *know* what poltergeists are is deluding himself. I have opinions, of course. I think that we are living in a multi-dimensional universe. A great deal of this universe we are not normally able to perceive. If you accept that then many things become possible. We normally explain things in terms of Newtonian physics, but we can assume that outside the realms of our five senses and our instruments are other forces at work which may be either within us, may surround us or may be separate from us. The forces are there, but we cannot detect them. Perhaps these forces are normally dormant, but if a high-stress situation comes along and we cannot satisfy our inner feelings with our own five senses, frustration creeps in; perhaps that frustration releases energies which interact with those forces, affecting physical things. Now, if this stress situation is utilising these outside forces, then they might 'pick up' something else that can actually interfere, in effect saying, 'That's a jolly good game. We'll play that one as well.' In lots of poltergeist cases these poltergeists seem to have gone to the same school. They all seem to play the same tricks.

All this might begin to explain what is happening, but I must make clear again that I am not trying to say I have got a certain explanation.'

18
The Ghost-hunter's
Toolbox

The ghost-hunter's toolbox may consist of a small holdall containing half a dozen items or a car boot full of high-tech equipment, depending on the circumstances of the report and the personal preferences and facilities available to the ghost-hunter. There is no definitive list of items that should be carried; indeed it is better that there should not be as every ghost-hunter should be using his or her own creative flair to find newer and perhaps more advantageous ways of doing the job. Nonetheless, the following list of items is recommended for at least some circumstances:

Notepaper and pens or pencils. There are many occasions when jotting down a note as a reminder is important. There will also be times when the ghost-hunter is interviewing a witness who may feel uncomfortable being tape-recorded (see also below). Even when tape-recording, it does not hurt to jot down important points on paper as the investigation of paranormal activities is plagued by a history of tape-recorders apparently malfunctioning, whether by design or accident.

Tape-recorder and or dictaphone. These may be used to interview witnesses, but there is the danger that the psychological impact of setting up a tape-recorder in front of a witness can either inhibit him or, on the contrary, encourage his imagination to run riot, as if he was 'performing for the media'. Therefore before using a tape-recorder, unless the witness is obviously at ease with it, consider note-taking and follow it up with tape-recorded sessions only after you have built up a certain rapport with him.

The second use for audio recording equipment is, of course, to record the activities of the haunting itself. To this end, you should also have a virtually endless supply of cassettes suitable for the machine in question and make sure that recording is continuous; ghosts are rather like policemen – they are never around when you want one and pop up when you least expect them! In fact, if possible, have two tape-recorders to hand, partly so that one is recording during the change over of tapes in the other, and partly to act as a back-up should something go wrong with one of them. (On the other hand if both malfunction at the same time that in itself may constitute evidence!)

Batteries. ENSURE THAT YOU HAVE ADEQUATE SUPPLIES OF BATTERIES FOR ALL ELECTRICAL EQUIPMENT, EVEN WHERE YOU ARE PROPOSING TO USE A MAINS SUPPLY. IN THE EVENT OF A SUPPLY FAILURE YOU WILL THEN HAVE BACK-UP. YOU WILL ALSO HAVE POWER SHOULD BATTERY-RUN EQUIPMENT NEED REPLACEMENT BATTERIES. This applies not only to tape-recorders but also to video cameras, torches and any other electrical instrumentation.

Video camera. This may, of course, be beyond the resources of some ghost-hunters but if one can be bought or borrowed, it can be extremely useful, particularly where some visual apparition is expected. The best cameras are those that can operate in low levels of light and have a variety of wide-scanning or directional microphone capabilities. It may also be useful to have a TV monitor to hand if the camera is to be placed away from the ghost-hunter. This will mean the ghost-hunter can see events at the time on TV rather than waiting to see the tape-recording. The main consideration here is not just the cost or inconvenience of transporting such equipment but the effect it is going to have on the witness. He or she may take exception to a high-tech invasion of their haunted living room!

Obviously adequate supplies of video tapes are vital too. It is highly recommended that recorded tapes are retained where possible. Do not keep recording over the same tape. It may be necessary to review the tapes later.

There are few instances of reliable phenomena being recorded on video but it *has* happened and the more times this is achieved in research conditions the better.

Stills camera. Whether or not video equipment is available, it is always useful to have a camera, partly because you may be able to record some event happening but also because it is the easiest way to record the physical parameters of a building or other location. Make it as simple or complex a camera as you prefer, but make sure that you are able to use it adequately so that when the ghost does put in an appearance you don't spend the entire time fumbling with the lenses!

Make sure that you have plenty of film and back-up batteries for cameras that require them. Take flash equipment too for use when necessary (there is the old joke about trying to photograph a cooperative ghost and finding the flash batteries have run down – 'the spirit was willing but the flash was weak!').

Torches. Many ghost-hunts will take place at night or in darkness and it is advisable to have a torch to hand (plus, as always, back-up batteries and so on. Spare bulbs are also advised). You should be aware that one or two fraudulent poltergeist cases have happened where the witness insists on conditions of darkness. The witness will of course give permission for you to switch a light on when they cry out so that you can see the 'manifestation' occurring; if fraud is suspected it is a good idea to have a torch which the witness *sees* you leaving somewhere out of your immediate reach while you secrete a *second* torch in your pocket, without the witness's knowledge. When you hear a sound which perhaps you have come to suspect indicates the witness getting ready to throw an object, or whatever, you can then surprise him or her by switching on the hidden torch and catching them in the act. (In the case of the Runcorn poltergeist just this technique was used but in this case – according to the investigator – a book was seen lifting itself up of its own accord from a dressing-table, actually strengthening the evidence for the case.)

Markers. For a whole variety of reasons you may need to make marks on walls or furniture. If, say, a ghost should appear and then disappear through a wall, it would be useful to mark the exact position where it went through as this may later be identified as the site of a former door, or whatever. The markers may include Post-it Notes as used in offices which can be affixed to walls and removed without damage. Chalk and charcoal are also possible choices. The only golden rule is don't use an indelible marking pen and ruin your witness's decor.

Measuring tape, adhesive tapes, string, wool, and wax. This

paraphernalia is used to seal doors or windows and then check if
the seal is broken. There is no definitive list but ghost-hunters
should familiarise themselves with the area they will be studying
and prepare the appropriate materials.

Candles. When the electricity has failed candles are the last
resort. They can also be used for testing draughts – though be
extremely careful if you even *suspect* a gas leak to be the cause of
the 'haunting' and do not use a naked flame. If the candle keeps
blowing out have a jam jar to hand which you can put the candle
in to protect it from draughts. (If it keeps blowing out inside the
jam jar. . .)

Thermometer (or preferably three or four). Many hauntings
are proceeded, or accompanied by significant changes in temperature and it is useful to have accurate recordings of these changes.

Compass. This is useful for recording the direction of movements of sightings but also because apparitions or hauntings may
be accompanied by what seem to be changes in the magnetic
field, the compass going haywire. If this should occur it may
constitute evidence and even give warning of an impending event
should the same phenomenon be noticed on a later vigil.

Containers. If ectoplasm, apports, or some other paranormal
object should manifest, it is important to get it into a sealed
container as quickly as possible. This will prevent contamination
and the object can then be studied in laboratory conditions later.
(But should the object then disappear from its sealed container . . .)
You should also have something to pick any such material up with to
reduce the risk of contamination: tongs, spoons, and so on.

Ghost-hunters need to familiarise themselves as much as
possible with the location they are to study. Ordnance survey
maps of the area, plans of buildings, if possible even historical
plans of former buildings on the same site are all potentially
revealing. Geological maps of the area may also be useful.

The list goes on: magnetometers, walkie-talkies, movement-
sensitive alarms, even radar, all these may be useful though it is
highly likely that the average ghost-hunter will not have this
equipment or certainly not take it to every event. In circumstances where there is overwhelming evidence of extraordinary
phenomena equipment such as this may be borrowed from a
sympathetic laboratory, ideally with a skilled operator in tow. Of

course, you should always obtain prior permission from the owners of the property and the witness for this level of equipment to be installed.

At the other end of the scale, there is no definitive list of simple equipment; thimbles, adhesives, plumb-lines, screwdrivers, hammers and so on can all come in useful. The golden rule is be prepared. In other words, consider what you are about to investigate, discuss it with the witness, plan your approach and put together the equipment you consider most appropriate for it.

In addition to equipment, there are other essentials that the ghost-hunter should take: appropriate clothing is important – warm and waterproof for outside ghost-watching in particular. Food and drink is essential too: you may be provided with sandwiches and coffee by the owners of the houses under watch but it is hardly fair to expect to be fed three square meals a day. In any case most ghost-hunts take place at the dead of night when the family would not want to be disturbed, or in deserted buildings or even ruins. Take enough supplies to see you through the vigil, and remember that, wherever you are, you are someone's guest; take your rubbish home with you.

Consider the physical demands of the vigil; if it is to take place in the middle of a field or in the deserted ruin of a monastery, for example, take a small folding garden chair. Otherwise, at some point during the night you will inevitably lie back to rest your back 'for just a few minutes' and more than likely wake up with the dawn. If half a dozen ghosts had walked right over you you would probably be none the wiser!

Obviously the ghost-hunter should be attentive and vigilant at all times; the evidence seems to suggest that, more important even than the equipment, the best recording equipment is *you*. However, *too much* vigilance will create tension and in extreme cases even hallucination. Remember that you are likely to be in darkness and silence, conditions which can cause sensory deprivation and even moderately altered states of consciousness. To combat this we recommend the following:

Never undertake a ghost-hunt alone; you will then have 'back-up'. Also, if you are alone, if you *do* see something you will spend the rest of your life trying to convince people it was not your imagination.

Relaxation will help; this may mean one of you periodically taking time out to play a quiet game of Patience, Solitaire or whatever while the other maintains a more vigilant watch. Be selective about how you relax; however; do not take handheld video games that involve flashing lights and noise – for rather obvious reasons!

There may be occasions when you try to create the appropriate conditions for a sighting – usually because the witness wants to go down that particular route of investigation. Use your judgement. An amusing but true point: it has been discovered that certain paranormal activity (in particular ESP and psychokinesis) may be enhanced when the subjects under scrutiny have been exposed to pornographic material!

Vigils

It may be useful to outline what actually happens at a ghost-hunt or vigil. They are, of course, all unique. Nonetheless, however varied the conditions, there are certain common elements.

The start of a vigil is usually characterised by a mood of suppressed excitement and tension, and the expectancy that *this* time may be 'the one'. As a result of conversations with the witness or possibly because this is the first visit to a location which has, up to this point, only been described to the investigator, there will be high expectations.

In the early stages of the vigil, there is a tendency to be highly critical in interpreting 'happenings' – sounds in particular – which is the right attitude. However, at three or four in the morning (when the biorhythms are at their lowest ebb, apparently) there is a tendency to start interpreting all manner of sounds or shadows as paranormal. It is at this time, particularly, that all the members of the investigation team should be vigilant to ensure the maximum chance of correctly interpreting sightings or sounds.

Some people, during night vigils, report feeling desperately tired. They will also tend to feel coldness and it is wise to check the thermometers to find out whether the coldness is internal or external; usually it is internal and the result of a need for sleep. On vigils where results *are* being logged, most particularly poltergeist vigils, then the activity is usually sufficient to keep attention levels high, but even in these conditions, and particularly if the vigils are extended over several days, tiredness is inevitable.

If more than one location is to be investigated simultaneously then arrange for changes of 'watch' to break the monotony and tension and to break up the period of the vigil.

19
Philip
– The 'Manufactured' Ghost

This book is a compilation of ghost phenomena from around the world; in the main it addresses ghosts as spontaneous phenomena and classifies them according to type. Such classification is not rigid, and there are many areas of overlap.

Throughout the *Encyclopedia* there are many references to ghosts at seances, particularly where seances have been used as a form of investigation. There is, however, no specific classification relating to ghosts at seances; famous 'ghosts' such as Katie King and her like really belong in a different compilation. It must be remembered that ghosts at seances are not so much a classification of ghosts as a theory to explain them, i.e. that they represent the spirits of people who have died. This is the theory embraced by Spiritualism, and although it is probably the best known theory of ghosts is far from being the only one, or even the likeliest.

A compilation of seance-related spirits would also have to encompass automatic writing, mediums, spirit guides, electronic voice phenomena, healing, ectoplasm, even telepathy and a host of other paranormal areas that are outside the boundaries we have chosen. Most of these phenomena make an appearance in this compilation, but only where they relate to specific incidents.

That said, there is one 'ghost', more properly a spirit, who demands a classification of his own. 'Philip' 'came through' in a series of seances, but under extraordinary circumstances. Understanding 'Philip' may lead to an understanding of all ghost phenomena.

A Toronto-based research group, under the leadership of Dr A.R.G. Owen, undertook an exceptional experiment in 1972. They decided to see if it was possible to manufacture a ghost.

They decided that before he could be 'brought into being' every member of the experiment would have to 'believe' in him. Consequently they created his totally fictitious background with great care and detail: a romantic story set in England in the seventeenth century. One member of the society even drew his portrait.

He would be an English aristocrat, married but having a romantic liaison with a gypsy girl. This girl would be burned at the stake as a witch, and Philip would fail to intervene to save her life, giving him reason to communicate, perhaps to look for forgiveness or understanding. Periodically his ghost would be seen on the battlements of his country estate, pacing in anguish.

After re-inforcing their own 'belief' in the existence of Philip, the group of eight tried to 'manifest' Philip. Their first, very serious, attempts produced no results and it was not until the summer of 1973 that they began to be successful, *when a relaxed and happy atmosphere had been brought to the research* (a lesson for all researchers into the paranormal, perhaps?).

The method of communicating with Philip was through rapping noises, first heard while singing; he was responsive to certain songs and to 'his' name. Questions were asked of Philip, and the answers were generally in accordance with the constructed personality the team had devised for him.

Philip graduated to moving a table on which the researchers lightly placed their hands; occasionally it would shoot across the room at considerable speed.

Astonishingly, Philip was not at all camera-shy but was quite happy to perform in front of the television cameras when he was taken to Toronto City Television in 1974 in the form of the table through which he communicated. In the studio the table apparently moved independently and responded to questions by 'rapping happily'.

An extraordinary twist in the tale was yet to follow. One member of the group broke ranks and claimed to Philip, 'We only made you up, you know.' The rapping stopped; denied belief, Philip ceased to exist. He was 're-born' later, only after a period when the researchers had 're-learnt' to believe in him.

20

What are Ghostbusters
Actually Doing?

What ghostbusters are doing may seem obvious – we are hunting ghosts. But what is the actual purpose of this?

Let us take the situation where a sceptical ghost-hunter is invited by a witness to examine phenomena which the witness is convinced are paranormal in origin. For the sake of argument we will assume that the ghost-hunter does not feel that this is likely to be the case. Indeed, at the outset of an investigation it is wise for the ghost-hunter to maintain that level of healthy scepticism while at the same time keeping an open mind. Supposing that our sceptical ghost-hunter investigates the phenomenon and accepts that it does indeed have a paranormal origin and constitutes proof of the existence of ghosts (whatever we take that phrase to mean). This does not contribute very much towards the work of convincing the world of the authenticity of ghost phenomena. We might therefore go further and say that what we are searching for is evidence that can be convincingly presented to others.

Consider another scenario, then, where our witness invites us to a ghost-hunt and where, as a result, we come away with sixteen hours of continuous videotape of the ghost walking through walls and across the ceiling, or whatever, visually and audio-recorded conversation between the witness, the ghost-hunter and the ghost, information from the ghost which can be verified in archives and museums all over the world, plus still photographs of the ghost. We can accompany this with magnetometer readings showing massive increases in magnetic-field disturbances at the times when the ghost appears, positive readings on portable radar, appropriate film of thermometer fluctuations and, just for good measure, a few apports of coins materialised by the ghost at the investigator's request directly into sealed jam jars. What then? It sounds like the sort of evidence that any ghost-hunter would give his third eye for and thanks to which he would be credited with finally solving one of the world's great mysteries.

But what actually will happen when he presents this evidence to the world? Firstly he will come up against the jealously and in-fighting which goes on endlessly amongst all researchers in both the conventional sciences and the para-sciences; his method will be questioned and his honesty brought into doubt. Even if he is part of a ten-man team, all of whom are in total agreement about the evidence, this is how it will be. In fact in all likelihood the first bickering will take place amongst those ten. The genuinely committed researchers will feel a grudging admiration but will probably still take every opportunity to pick apart the evidence if they can find the tiniest flaw in it. And once the material is presented to the world at large the ghost-hunter can look forward to literally spending the rest of his life defending himself against allegations of fraud, mainly from the scientific establishment – whose institutions have a massive interest in not accepting challenges to science – and partly from the media, which seems to have a natural tendency to say 'black' the minute anybody says 'white'.

One thing we must certainly do as ghost-hunters is to attend to the needs of the witness. In the case of those afflicted by poltergeist activity, they are seeking respite from their anguish and the ghost-hunter's job in these circumstances is to either bring them that respite or facilitate it by bringing in other professionals as necessary. However real poltergeist activity is, whether it is psycho-kinesis, an external entity or whatever, there is every evidence that it manifests in conditions of stress and stress is best dealt with by medically trained professionals. No serious researcher should ever lose sight of the importance of attending to the needs of the witness.

All ghost-hunters not only want to be sure in their own mind as to exactly what ghosts are but they want to share that belief with others fairly unanimously. Total unanimity will never be possible; there are people even today convinced that the earth is flat and other people who probably could never even be convinced that the Pope is Catholic, but between these extremes there *are* those who are open to the right sort of evidence. The ghost-hunter is looking for this evidence. It seems that recorded data of an event is *not* the right sort of evidence. To be convinced of the reality of a phenomenon, science demands that it can be predicted and then reproduced in experimental conditions. Because that is not the case with spontaneous paranormal phenomena, including ghosts and apparitions, science rejects them. This is a blinkered approach which fails to recognise that there are many aspects of the world around us which once could *not* be understood, predicted and reproduced, but which now *can* be – science has found the appropriate measuring instruments, and from that has gone on to predict and create the necessary conditions for proof. In rejecting the paranormal and refusing to even look for the necessary measuring instruments, science is closing itself off from the full richness of the world. What it should be doing is acknowledging that spontaneous phenomena may well be authentic because they are attested to by such enormous numbers of people; it should be assisting researchers into the paranormal to find the measuring instruments that they presently do not have. Then we might be getting a little closer to the ghost-hunter's goal.

In the meantime ghost-hunters should be collecting the evidence not only of *what* happened *but the conditions under which it happened* and should be correlating it with as much other evidence of similar events as possible.

Let us create a third scenario. Let us suppose that a recording-type ghost is reported by many people over a long period of time, all of whom know nothing of each other's reports. It always manifests at a particular location, and always does the same thing. For the sake of argument, let us suggest that the recording is being 'replayed' because the atmospheric humidity is z, the degree of copper and zinc in the surrounding rocks is y, the temperature is x, there are geological stresses underground creating a strain of w, each of the witnesses has just undergone the tragedy of bereavement with whatever effects that may have on brain chemistry and emotions, plus a host of other factors. In these circumstances it would be hardly surprising if the exact combination of factors only occurred on rare occasions. Nonetheless, there *would be* such occasions. The ghost-hunter should therefore be accumulating as much, even trivial, data about each ghost appearance as possible in order to be able to recognise the clues to the 'playback button'.

Assuming that a ghost-hunter could correctly pinpoint *all* of the necessary factors then it would be possible either to predict with a reasonable degree of accuracy when those factors could come together (and an appropriate watch maintained) or, perhaps, to recreate them experimentally. Then we would begin to see the acceptance of paranormal phenomena by conventional science.

Conventional science, however, may nonetheless have to make some compromises. One of the 'laws' of science is that any experiment, if it is truly dependent only on the experimental factors, should be capable of being replicated by anybody with the same equipment under the same conditions. Studies of the paranormal seem to indicate that the state of mind of the researcher and the witness are a genuine factor in manifesting certain spontaneous phenomena. This claim may be a red herring and science may be right to condemn it. On the other hand it *may* be correct and science has a duty to put it to the test. If (as has been suggested by such people as Professor of Physics John Hasted) the results of phenomena such as psycho-kinesis are improved when the percipient genuinely feels that he is working in a supportive partnership with the investigator, then science has a duty to accept that as part of the test conditions. Until we know what *all* of the factors involved in creating certain phenomena are we must remain open-minded.

As in every area of research there will be different standards of research and researchers. It may be a controversial opinion, but we believe that until we know what the subject is truly all about we cannot define with certainty the criteria that constitute a good or bad researcher. Obviously we have opinions about the various sources from which we have drawn for this compilation. But we have deliberately included some stories that might be regarded as rather dubious as well as better documented cases because the clues to the ultimate answers may lie in *any* of these reports. Apart from totally fabricated reports, which we trust we have weeded out, we are quite happy to include reports from people who may not have been very methodical in their research if in fact something they have recorded points to a valuable clue. There is a fine line between recklessness and radical thinking and all we can say is that we have done what we think is right and hope that it adds something to the overall picture. It is a view that we have always held and we certainly cannot say that it has met with universal agreement, but our counter-argument has always been that those who believe our instincts to be wrong have themselves produced nothing more concrete.

Cross-reference to Sections of Common Interest

The main body of the encyclopedia is divided into sixteen broad classifications of ghost phenomena. There are, of course, occasions when a particular case crosses more than one classification (i.e. animals associated with poltergeist cases could, depending on the circumstances, be classified either under ghostly animals or poltergeists). For this reason the following is a guide to the principal cases where readers may wish to follow up occurrences of particular phenomena.

1 Ghosts and Visions Associated with Particular Places
See also:

Bibliography and Recommended Reading

After Death – What?, Prof. Cesare Lombroso, Small, Maynard & Co., 1909

The Airman Who Would Not Die, John G. Fuller, Souvenir Press, 1979

Apparitions and Haunted Houses, Sir Ernest Bennett, Faber and Faber, 1939

Black Beech and Honeydew, Ngaio Marsh, Collins, 1966

Bluebird and the Dead Lake, John Pearson, Fontana, 1965

Britain's Haunted Heritage, Keith Poole, Robert Hale, 1988

British Goblins, Wirt Sikes, 1880

Bugles and a Tiger, John Masters, Michael Joseph, 1956

Burke's Guide to the British Monarchy, edited by Hugh Montgomery-Massingberd, Burke's Peerage Ltd, 1977

The Candle of Vision, George Russell, Macmillan & Co., 1918

The Collected Works of W.H. Hudson (A Hind in Richmond Park)

Det Ockulta Problemet, Dr John Björkhem, Uppsala, 1951

Early Reminiscences, Rev. Sabine Baring-Gould, John Lane, 1923

Encyclopedia of Ghosts, Daniel Cohen, Fraser Stewart, 1984

England's Ghostly Heritage, Terence Whitaker, Robert Hale, 1989

The Evidence for Phantom Hitch-Hikers, Michael Goss (editor Hilary Evans), Aquarian Press, 1984

Flights of Fancy, Lynn Picknett, Ward Lock, 1987

The Flying Cow, Guy Lyon Playfair, Souvenir Press, 1975

The Ghost Book, Alasdair Alpin McGregor, Robert Hale, 1955

The Ghost of Flight 401, John G. Fuller, Souvenir Press, 1978

Ghost and Ghoul, T.C. Lethbridge, Routledge & Kegan Paul, 1961

Ghost Watch, Prof. Colin Gardner, Foulsham, 1989

The Ghosthunter's Guide, Peter Underwood, Javelin Books, 1988

The Ghosts of the Trianon, C.A.E. Moberly and E.F. Jourdain, Aquarian Press, 1988

Gods, Spirits, Cosmic Guardians, Hilary Evans, Aquarian Press, 1987

Haunted England, Christina Hole, Fitzhouse Books, 1940

Haunted Royal Homes, Joan Forman, Harrap, 1987

The Holy Ghostbuster, J. Aelwyn Roberts, Robert Hale, 1990

I Saw a Ghost, Ben Noakes, Weidenfeld and Nicolson, 1986

In Malay Forests, Sir George Maxwell

The Infinite Boundary, Guy Lyon Playfair

Journey from Obscurity, Harold Owen

Look Beyond Today, Rosemary Brown, Phantom Press

Lord Halifax's Ghost Book, Lord Halifax, Geoffrey Bles, 1936

The Mask of Time, Joan Forman, Macdonald and Jane's, 1978

Memories, Dreams, Reflections, C.G. Jung, Collins, 1967

My First Hundred Years, Dr Margaret Murray, William Kimber, 1963

No Common Task, Peter Underwood, Harrap, 1983

Phantasms of the Living, Edmund Gurney, M.A., F.W.H. Myers, M.A., F. Podmore, M.A., Society for Psychical Research, 1886

Phantoms of the Railways, W.B. Herbert, David and Charles, 1988

Phenomena, R.J.M. Rickard and J. Michell, Thames and Hudson, 1977

Poltergeist, Colin Wilson, New English Library, 1981

Poltergeists, Alan Gould and A.D. Cornell, Routledge & Kegan Paul, 1979

Portrait of My Victorian Youth, Alice Pollock, Johnson, 1971

The Seen and the Unseen, Andrew MacKenzie, Weidenfeld and Nicolson

Some Unseen Power, Philip Paul, Robert Hale, 1985

The Story of My Life, Augustus Hare, George Allen, 1896

This House is Haunted, Guy Lyon Playfair, Souvenir Press, 1980

Travels in West Africa, Mary Kingsley, Virago Press, 1982

Trials in Burma, Maurice Collis, Faber and Faber, 1938
Understanding Ghosts, Victoria Branden, Victor Gollancz, 1980
Visions, Apparitions, Alien Visitors, Hilary Evans, Aquarian Press, 1984
Without Knowing Mr Walkley (Personal Memories), Edith Olivier, Faber and Faber, 1938

Journals and Magazines
The journals of the Society for Psychical Research, and in particular: Volumes 6, 22, 27, 34, 41, 42 and 53

Birmingham Gazette, 1923
Birmingham Mail, 1923
Cambrian News, 1986
Daily Mail, 1923
Daily Mirror (for 'Search for a Lake')
Evening Despatch (Birmingham), 1923
Royal Lymington Spa Courier and Warwickshire Standard, 1923
The Unexplained
Weekend Magazine (for Otterburn case)

The authors are particularly grateful for access to the research material of BOLIDE – The Ball of Light International Data Exchange. This research programme was instigated and maintained for many years by Hilary Evans and is now a project of the research department of the British UFO Research Association (BUFORA), in conjunction with the International Committee for UFO Research (ICUR).

Many other publications have been used as background reading. The reader is therefore encouraged to seek out as wide a variety of sources as possible in order to understand the full complexity of ghost phenomena. However, because of their long-term involvement in the subject, we would strongly recommend the reader to any books written by Andrew MacKenzie, Peter Underwood, Harry Price, Guy Lyon Playfair, Joan Forman and Colin Wilson.

Index of Headings, Sub-headings and Cases

Index of Names

Index of Places